WRITING AMERICA

WRITING AMERICA

Literary Landmarks
from Walden Pond to
Wounded Knee

A READER'S COMPANION

Shelley Fisher Fishkin

RUTGERS UNIVERSITY PRESS
NEW BRUNSWICK, NEW JERSEY, AND LONDON

LIBRARY OF CONGRESS CATALOGING-INPUBLICATION DATA

Fishkin, Shelley Fisher

Writing America : literary landmarks from Walden Pond to Wounded Knee, a reader's companion / Shelley
Fisher Fishkin

pages cm

Includes bibliographical references and indexes

ISBN 978-0-8135-7597-1 (hardcover : alk. paper)

ISBN 978-0-8135-7599-5 (epub)

ISBN 978-0-8135-7600-8 (web pdf)

1. Literary landmarks—United States. 2. Authors, American—Homes and haunts—United States.
3. American literature—19th century—History and criticism. 4. American literature—20th century—History
and criticism. 5. American literature—Mintority authors— History and criticism. I. Title.

PS141.F57 2015

810.9—dc23

2015002728

A British Cataloging-in-Publication record for this book is available from the British Library.

For permissions to reprint previously published material, please see the section beginning on page 369.

Visit our website: http://rutgerspress.rutgers.edu

Manufactured in the United States of America

CONTENTS

ILLUSTRATIONS

WRITING AMERICA

The Welshman's House, built in Hannibal, Missouri, by slaves around 1839, is mentioned by Mark Twain in *Tom Sawyer*. It was saved from demolition, restored, and moved to North Third Street by the Marion County Historical Society, where it now houses Hannibal's newest museum, Jim's Journey: The Huck Finn Freedom Center, at 509 North Third Street. The museum opened in September 2013.

PHOTO CREDIT: PHOTO BY TERRELL DEMPSEY.

Introduction

THE LITERARY LANDSCAPE

I have frequently seen a poet withdraw, having enjoyed the most
valuable part of a farm, while the crusty farmer supposed that he had
got a few wild apples only.
—Henry David Thoreau, *Walden*

Literature, the novelist E. L. Doctorow once observed, "endows places with meaning" by connecting "the visible and the invisible" and finding "the hidden life in the observable life." And if literature endows places with meaning, places can help us better understand how works of literature came to be what they are. *Writing America* examines intersections between public history and literary history, exploring the physical places that shaped the lives and the art of authors who had a major impact on American literary history as we recognize the field today—sites that their art continues to imbue with meaning.

The physical landscape of American cities and countryside is constantly changing. Buildings deteriorate and decay or are torn down to make way for something new, while open space and places of natural beauty are similarly vulnerable to dramatic transformation over time. The fact that a site is on the National Register of Historic Places does not guarantee that a structure will remain in that location (Mark Twain's study in Elmira, New York was moved, as was Edgar Allan Poe's cottage in New York City) or that it will not burn down (the fate of Kate Chopin's house in Cloutierville, Louisiana). Indeed, some of the sites described in this book may be moved, destroyed, or significantly altered by the time you read this introduction. Being listed on the National Register protects a site only from threats to it that involve the federal government. Nonetheless, there is a slightly higher likelihood that sites listed on the National Register will be preserved in a form that will at least be recognizable to future generations. For this reason, nearly all of the places featured in this book are officially designated National Historic Landmarks,

National Historic Sites, National Historic Monuments, National Historic Districts, National Historic Battlefields, National Historic Trails, or National Parks (the handful that are not are officially designated state or city historic landmarks).

Sites appear on the National Register for a range of reasons. They must strike individuals or communities as having sufficient cultural, architectural, or historical significance to warrant preservation; they must retain much their original character in key physical ways; people who care about them must mobilize to craft proposals to get them listed; and owners must be willing to forgo some of their freedom to make structural changes. Sometimes the links between American literature and National Register sites are clear: houses belonging to Harriet Beecher Stowe and Paul Laurence Dunbar, for example, are on the register because of their connections to these authors. But the dynamics of placing sites on the National Register do not always coincide neatly with the dynamics of producing memorable American literature. What about the literature produced by writers too poor or too transient to have permanent homes capable of being preserved—such as early-twentieth-century writers who were impoverished workers from China or Russia, for example, or late-twentieth-century migrant farm workers in the Southwest? Relegated to the margins of American literature for much of the twentieth century, writers like these—now recognized as important creators of American literature—may still have no sites on the National Register directly connected to them, a fact that made this book especially challenging if I wanted it to reflect the richness and diversity of American literature as we recognize it today.

As Dolores Hayden observed in 1997 in *The Power of Place: Urban Landscapes as Public History*, in New York and across the country, "centuries of neglect of ethnic history have generated a tide of protest—where are the Native American, African American, Latino, and Asian American landmarks?" The neglect of landmarks associated with working people rather than elites is also a cause for concern, as Hayden reminds us: "The power of place—the power of ordinary urban landscapes to nurture citizens' public memory . . . remains untapped for most working people's neighborhoods in most American cities, and for most ethnic history and most women's history." She adds that "even bitter experiences and fights communities have lost need to be remembered—so as not to diminish their importance." Although there has been change in the right direction since Hayden wrote these words, across the country there are still relatively few landmarks associated with people who were not rich, not white, or not male, despite the fact that such people, at any given time in America's past, together made up the majority of Americans. As of this writing, there are still no homes on the National Register associated with Chicano, Asian American, or Jewish American authors. Rather than limit the scope of this book to landmarks with obvious literary roots and the writers linked to them, I have pressed into the service of literature sites that are on the National Register for historical, architectural, military, engineering, technological, or religious reasons. In many cases, this book explores their connection to American literature for the first time.

Writing America does not aspire to be comprehensive. Only a multivolume work many times its size could do justice to the complexity of the literary heritage of the United States, the physical places that shaped it, and the places that it helps us interpret and understand. Rather than trying to be exhaustive, this book is unabashedly eclectic—a small sampling of people and places that make the literary landscape of the United States so intriguing. I selected the landmarks that anchor each chapter based on their association with writers whose work continues to draw me into its orbit after many readings, or whose work has had a seminal impact on society. I've included a number of selections from the poems, stories, plays, essays, and novels that these writers wrote in order to make the power of their words more immediate. If what you read prompts you to head to the library or the Internet in search of more, that's all to the good; but I saw no need to make you wait until you could get there, preferring to share a sampling of the works right here. I've tried to give a sense of the reach these writers have had, as well—the authors whom they empowered, angered, or inspired—not just in the United States but around the world.

Writing America focuses on a wide range of historic sites that have been preserved in enough of their original form to warrant being listed on the register. There are some authors' homes here—but there are also streets, theaters, chapels, schools, docks, plantations, and battlefields; a statue, a body of water, a bicycle shop, a ship, a YMCA, a factory, a hotel, graveyards, internment camps, a lighthouse, and an irrigation pumping station. There are sites in the Northeast, the South, the Midwest, the Northwest, the Southwest, and the West, all of which helped to inspire or serve as the setting of some of the most engaging poetry, fiction, drama, and nonfiction American writers have produced. More than a hundred sites are included—but there might have been many more. No site made it into the book if it did not serve as a lens through which a significant chapter of literary history might be viewed. Each site had to provide an opportunity to recall, rethink, or revisit literature that mattered to me. In that respect, my choices are, ultimately, quite personal ones.

My motives for writing this book are personal, as well, reflecting the fact that my own first encounter with several of the places discussed here changed my mental map in dramatic ways. My mother's decision to take me to Mark Twain's house in Hartford, Connecticut, when I was a child ignited a lifelong fascination with Twain that led me to write two books and fifty-three articles, essays, columns, book chapters, and reviews; edit thirty-three books; coedit two special issues of academic journals; deliver lectures on four continents; and bring a play he wrote to the Broadway stage. My visit to the Mark Twain Historic District in Hannibal, Missouri, in 1995 prompted me to think long and hard about the ways in which the town's erasure of its slave past—of the role of African Americans in shaping Twain's life and work, and of Mark Twain's biting critiques of American racism after he left Hannibal—echoed America's efforts to bury rather than engage its troubled history of race relations. I became intrigued, as a result, with the broader issues of public memory and public history that this book explores. That memorable first trip to Hannibal also planted the seeds of new courses I developed at Stanford with titles like "Race and Reunion: Slavery and the Civil War in American Memory," and "Reimagining America: Cultural Memory and Identity since the Civil War."

A trip I took to Paul Laurence Dunbar's home in Dayton, Ohio, in 1999 persuaded me that a reevaluation of Dunbar's place in American letters was long overdue; it kindled an interest in the writer and his work that led me not only to write several articles about him, but also to propose the international conference that took place at Stanford during the year that marked the hundredth anniversary of his death, and to coedit both a new anthology of his writings and a special issue of *African American Review* devoted to reappraising his achievement.

My visit in 2002 to the Angel Island Immigration Station in the San Francisco Bay sparked an interest in the place of Chinese Americans in the national imaginary that has infused my teaching and writing ever since. When I moved to Stanford in 2003, memories of what I saw at Angel Island and what I learned there about the Chinese Exclusion Act impelled me to think about the relative invisibility of the twelve thousand nineteenth-century Chinese laborers whose work on the first transcontinental railroad was key to creating the fortune with which Leland Stanford founded my university. Although their lives have been imagined in fiction, memoir, and drama by many canonical Asian American writers, their voices have been lost, and we know relatively little about their experience. They are now at center of the research project I codirect with my colleague Gordon Chang: the Chinese Railroad Workers in North America Project at Stanford University, which involves more than a hundred collaborators across North America and Asia in fields including American studies, history, literature, archaeology, anthropology, architecture, digital humanities, and the arts.

The incontrovertible evidence that I have of the ways in which physical places and objects have refocused my own interest in chapters of American literature and of the nation's past, and my recognition of ways in which my understanding of so many poems, stories, novels, essays, and plays has been enriched by an awareness of the places that shaped them compelled me to write this book.

Although different factors shape historic preservation and canon formation, some parallel dynamics come into play. Historic preservation involves decisions about what to preserve or restore, guided by assumptions about why a particular act of preservation or restoration is desirable; these decisions are not unlike those that are always being made about which writers merit inclusion in the literary canon. The stories we tell about the physical structures, material culture, and natural spaces we have preserved or restored fall under the rubric of the public history. The stories we tell about what literature is worth saving and why fall under the rubric of literary history. Both public history and literary history are shaped by the values of the communities that create them. A community's sense of identity, its aspirations, and its insecurities, all help determine what neighborhoods, buildings, and spaces get targeted for preservation. Similar factors shape not only which writers achieve canonical status at any point in time, but which of their works become canonical, as well.

The town of Hannibal, Missouri, for example, is into historic preservation in a big way. Virtually the entire economy of the town runs on Twain tourism. But when I first went there in 1995, the only evidence I could find in the Mark Twain Historic District that Hannibal had been a slaveholding town were two tiny ads for runaway slaves on a page from the *St. Louis Republican* from 1849 that "reached Hannibal when Sam Clemens was 14 years old," on display at Mark Twain's Boyhood Home. At a show presented at the Mark Twain Outdoor Theatre at Clemens Landing that promised to bring to life "in a very special way" episodes from *Tom Sawyer, Huckleberry Finn,* and *Life on the Mississippi,* there was no Jim, no black actor in the cast, and no reference to the fact that slavery had been a prominent institution in both Hannibal and the fictionalized version of it in Twain's novels.

Hannibal, of course, was certainly not alone in its willful neglect of its slave past. As Jennifer Eichstedt and Stephen Small note in *Representations of Slavery: Race and Ideology in Southern Plantation Museums,* the "absence of discussions of the system of slavery or those who had been enslaved" may well be the norm, rather than the exception, at sites that owe their very existence to the slave culture that sustained them. They were unsettled by the degree to which southern plantation museums engaged in what Iwona Irwin-Zarecka, in *Frames of Remembrance,* called "social forgetting." The kind of slavery known in Hannibal was not "the brutal plantation article," as Twain once put it. But it was slavery nonetheless, with its own combination of rapacity, disrespect, disempowerment, and degradation.

Since the powers-that-be in Hannibal did not consider the story of Hannibal's slave past and Twain's reflections on that past to be the kind of feel-good story that encourages tourism, they presented instead a version of nineteenth-century childhood drawn less from the life that young Sam Clemens led when he lived there than from the saccharine fantasies spun by the master-storyteller who grew up down the road in Marceline, Missouri, in the decades after Twain's death: Walt Disney. While the Mark Twain Historic District erased the black presence in Twain's life and works, the town also erased all signs of the bustling of black-owned businesses that had thrived in segregated Hannibal during the decades after Twain's death. Not surprisingly, the self-appointed guardians of Twain's legacy in Hannibal valued the Twain who wrote *Tom Sawyer* more than the Twain who penned searing critiques of his hometown after he left. They had no use for the Twain who came to see clearly the outrageousness of people who thought of themselves as religious, upstanding citizens buying and selling other human beings; they saw no value in honoring the memory of the Twain whose merciless satires skewered the hypocrisy of a democracy founded by slaveholders on principles of individual liberty.

In Hannibal, as in many places in the country, slavery and segregation may be gone, but the persistence of the racism that allowed both to flourish still makes presenting these chapters of the past challenging and difficult. It strikes many as simpler—and safer—just to forget the whole thing. Hannibal is far from alone in sidestepping painful parts of its past. Michael Kammen notes in *Mystic Chords of Memory* the appeal of nostalgia in sites of public memory across the nation and the "pattern of highly selective memory" that goes with it: "Recall the good but repress the unpleasant." Hannibal may have been keen about historic preservation, but the history it preferred to preserve, as the director of the Visitors and Convention bureau told me in 1995, involved little boys who "played marbles." Definitely not little boys sold away from their mothers at the corner of Third and Center Streets. I made Hannibal's willingness to exploit its connection to Twain while burying both his writings and the world in which he had lived under a barrage of kitsch nostalgic fantasies central to my 1997 book, *Lighting Out for the Territory: Reflections on Mark Twain and American Culture.*

A progressive local attorney named Terrell Dempsey, prompted, in part, by reading my book, decided to find out what he could about the history of slavery in Hannibal himself. The groundbreaking volume he published in 2003, *Searching for Jim: Slavery in Sam Clemens's World*, a book rich with recovered archival materials, offered the powers-that-be a host of new opportunities to tell Hannibal's story in fresh ways. But neither the town nor the Mark Twain Boyhood Home and Museum was quite ready to seize those opportunities. The same year that Dempsey's book came out, African American residents of Hannibal erected a granite monument commemorating a significant chapter of Hannibal's past that no longer existed: the twenty-three once-thriving black-owned businesses that had been located on the Broadway side of Wedge between 1920 and 1984. The handsome memorial adjacent to the Save-a-Lot parking lot on North Broadway features the names of long-gone barber shops, beauty shops, taverns, taxi companies, social clubs, fraternal organizations, funeral homes, nightclubs, a grocery store, a doctor's office, and a printing company—testimony to the existence of a community with roots in slavery that had survived and thrived despite a history of discrimination and exclusion. But as soon as the monument was in place, some white Hannibal residents waged a protest: what about the white businesses in the area that were no longer there? They erected their own counter-monument across the street, a curiously cryptic little marker "Dedicated to the memory of the businesses of the Wedge and the Market Street Area, 2003."

Signs of change, however, were in the air. As Regina Faden, a former executive director of the Boyhood Home and Museum notes (in "Presenting Mark Twain"), in response to my criticisms of Hannibal in *Lighting Out for the Territory*, which were increasingly echoed by visitors as well as other scholars, the museum's board and began "to reevaluate the stories the museum was telling." But late as 2003–2004, as Faden notes in "Museums and the Story of Slavery," some board members loudly complained that the Boyhood Home "should not be tainted by the story of slavery." Faden, who became executive director of the institution in 2004, tells us that in 2005, the complaining board members were overruled, and "several text panels addressing Twain's experience with slavery in Hannibal" appeared for the first time in the home's Interpretive Center. That decision "cost the museum the goodwill of its largest donor." Cindy Lovell, who became executive director in 2008, continued the museum's efforts to deal with slavery and race more responsibly, giving a talk at a local black church on slavery in Hannibal, for example, and sponsoring workshops to help high school teachers deal with issues of race in Twain's work. In 2010, a rough pallet—a handmade rug on which Sandy, a young slave who lived with the Clemens family, would have slept—was placed on the kitchen floor in the Boyhood Home.

In 2011, community historian Faye Dant began collecting photographs, newspaper clippings, directories, furniture, clothing, and other artifacts depicting African American life in Hannibal from slavery through the 1950s for an exhibit on "Hannibal African American Life and History" that she curated at the Hannibal History Museum in downtown Hannibal. Over the next two years she tirelessly gathered additional materials from the town's black residents. She also worked to gain support from the Marion County Historical Society, the Missouri Humanities Council, the Hannibal City Council, and Hannibal's mayor. Her efforts culminated on September 21, 2013, with the grand opening of a new museum in town—Jim's

Journey: The Huck Finn Freedom Center. It is now the first building that visitors encounter when they turn off the highway en route to the Mark Twain Historic District. The museum is housed in the old Welshman's House, a one-room stone structure thought to have been built by slaves about 1839, a building that Twain mentions in *Tom Sawyer*. The Marion County Historical Society saved it from demolition and moved it from its original location a few blocks away to its current address at 509 North Third Street.

Dant, the museum's founder and executive director, claims to have been inspired by my books: by my condemnation (in *Lighting Out for the Territory*) of Hannibal's failure to acknowledge its slave past and the town's erasure of those slaves' descendants—hard-working people who raised close-knit families, started businesses, and managed to thrive despite segregation and discrimination—and by my analysis (in *Was Huck Black? Mark Twain and African-American Voices*) of the key roles African Americans had played in shaping Twain's work, and of Twain's efforts to oppose racism through his writing and through his actions. Dant was determined that the new museum rescue and preserve for future generations the history that the town had ignored, along with neglected aspects of Mark Twain's involvement with African Americans and his efforts to undermine racism.

The museum's grand opening featured a lecture by Larry McCarty, a direct descendent of Daniel Quarles, the slave whose storytelling at the farm where Sam Clemens spent his summers filled young Sam with awe and admiration, and upon whom the character of Jim in *Huck Finn* was partially based. It was presided over by Board President Donald L. Scott, brigadier general (ret.) U.S. Army, a product of Hannibal's once-segregated schools who has served his country in many prominent roles, including that of founding director of AmeriCorps National Civilian Community Corps and deputy librarian and chief operating officer of the Library of Congress.

During the Civil War, the old Welshman's House had been used by Union troops to store munitions. The new museum contained materials that were pretty combustible in their own right: stark emblems of a past that the town had tried to bury, such the signs by which the nation had tried to separate whites from blacks and ensure that the canvas on which its black residents could paint their lives was as constricted as possible: Jim Crow–era signs like "Colored Waiting Room" nestle against the medals and citations testifying to what the town's black residents had achieved despite the obstacles thrown in their way. Outside, a very different sign towers over the small stone building that houses the museum—a huge billboard erected by the Hannibal Visitors Bureau located next door at 505 North Third Street that reads, "Welcome to Historic Hannibal. Write Your Own Story." Writing their own story is exactly what the black Hannibal residents who donated family photos and letters and mementos to the new museum are trying to do. But will those stories change the stories the town tells about its past?

As of the fall of 2014, the local Twain establishment continued to ignore the new museum. Despite the fact that it is fewer than four blocks from the Boyhood Home, staff there failed to mention it when teachers from across the country arrived for a workshop on teaching *Huck Finn*. The official website of the Hannibal Visitors' Bureau did not include it on its map of attractions. And despite numerous pleas, the sightseeing tours of historic Hannibal that the Hannibal Trolley Company offers visitors every day during the tourist season drive right past the museum but fail to mention it.

While the story the new museum tells is a story in which slavery figures prominently, it does not end with slavery: it is also the story of the racism that persisted long after slavery ended, and persists still—a story that became increasingly important to Mark Twain himself. *Huckleberry Finn* may be a book set during slavery, but it was written decades after slavery had ended: it is a book about racism, a fact that helps account for its continuing relevance to a nation—and world—that still has trouble coming to terms with issues of race. But that story is one that Hannibal still prefers to bury or ignore. "America's Home Town" is still mainly ruled by Tom Sawyer and kept gleaming with gallons of whitewash.

If questions of local identity and pride make white Hannibal residents "recall the good but repress the unpleasant" (to borrow words Michael Kammen used in another context), national identity and pride may well have had a similar impact on American literary critics' sense of what they should value in Mark Twain's work. As Maxwell Geismar put it in *Scanlan's* in 1970, "During the Cold War era of our culture, mainly in the 1950s although extending back into the '40s and forward far into the '60s, Mark Twain was both revived and castrated. The entire arena of Twain's radical social criticism of the United States—its racism, imperialism, and finance capitalism—has been repressed or conveniently avoided by the so-called Twain scholars precisely because it is so bold, so brilliant, so satirical. And so prophetic." But while most Americans in the twentieth century had been encountering a "castrated," tame Twain, to borrow Geismar's word, readers in China and the Soviet Union were encountering a Twain unafraid to launch salvos at the hypocrisy and failings of the country that he loved.

I have only relatively recently begun to understand the extent to which Mark Twain's achievement as a writer, and his role as a social and cultural critic, may have been distorted by imperatives of the Cold War. Perhaps in part *because* Chinese and Soviet writers and critics lauded the Twain who was a searing satirist and social critic, American writers and critics may have largely dismissed *that* Twain as a figment of the communist propaganda machine and valorized *America's* Twain as a writer to be celebrated primarily as a humorist. The propaganda functions to which Twain's writings were put are obvious; but Americans threw out the baby with the bathwater when they downplayed the validity of Twain's criticisms of his country—which were also criticisms of *their* country. With a few exceptions—most notably work by Philip Foner and Maxwell Geismar—Twain's trenchant critiques of the country he loved tended to be as ignored in the United States at midcentury as they were celebrated in China and the USSR. Only in the 1990s would American scholars generally decide that this aspect of Twain deserved their attention.

The larger point I'm making is that neither historic preservation nor canon formation takes place in a vacuum. The pride—and the prejudices—of the communities doing the preserving shape what places remain for future generations to encounter and what history about those places gets remembered. And the pride—and the prejudices—of the communities constructing the canon shape what literature gets valued and taught. But some fresh perspectives and insights can surface when public history and literary history are thoughtfully brought together.

As we will see, sites that have been preserved for their significance in architectural or religious history or the history of technology can illuminate chapters of literary history in ways that may have never occurred to members of the historic preservation community who worked to get them on the National Register. And by the same token, literary figures never associated with a site—even authors born years after a historic site was restored or preserved and put on the National Register—can shape the narrative of what happened there and how we understand it today in new ways. Teasing out some unexpected links between public history and literary history can allow us to gain fresh perspectives on familiar places and writers; it can also help us appreciate the stories about America that places and writers we may never have met before have to tell.

This book takes an uncomplicated view of physical landmarks by counting as a "landmark" a site that appears on the National Register. But what are "literary landmarks"? The historic preservation community would probably define the term as physical landmarks directly associated with authors or their books, while literary scholars would lean toward a definition involving works of literature that had particular importance in literary history—generally works already widely accepted as having earned a place in the canon. *Writing America* is infused by a much more capacious definition of "literary landmark." Authors discussed in this book include some canonical figures who might have been included in a book about "literary landmarks" half a century ago—Whitman, Thoreau, Melville, Stowe, and Twain, for example. But it also features many who might not have been there, because their work was not valued then as it is now, at least in part because of the writer's race, ethnicity, or gender. Writers discussed here whose works were absent from earlier generations' rosters of "landmark" authors include Gloria Anzaldúa, Nicholas Black Elk, Abraham Cahan, S. Alice Callahan, Frederick Douglass, Paul Laurence Dunbar, Allen Ginsberg, Jovita González, Langston Hughes, Zora Neale Hurston, James Weldon Johnson, Emma Lazarus, John Okada, Américo Paredes, John P. Parker, Tomás Rivera, Morris Rosenfeld, Yoshiko Uchida, Richard Wright, Hisaye Yamamoto, Anzia Yezierska, and many others—as well as contemporary writers who have already left their mark on American letters such as David Bradley, Elizabeth Cook-Lynn, Rolando Hinojosa, Lawson Fusao Inada, Maxine Hong Kingston, Irena Klepfisz, Genny Lim, N. Scott Momaday, Simon Ortiz, Wendy Rose, and Tino Villanueva. The writers in this book all figure in the new canons of American literature that are emerging in the twenty-first century, their work increasingly anthologized, read (in the college classroom and beyond), and explored by scholars. This book also recognizes the importance of American literature in languages other than English, including, for example, discussions of poetry and fiction originally written in Spanish, Yiddish, or Chinese. The sometimes quirky and occasionally opinionated interpretations of these writers' work that I present here do not, however, aspire to being "canonical": they are simply my own.

Reading the work of the writers examined in this book can help illuminate the complexities of the physical, social, and cultural landscape that shaped their writing—and encountering that landscape, in turn, can help us gain insight into the nuances and complexities of their art. Each chapter explores what the writers experienced at a particular site, how those experiences shaped their art, what the visitor may see there today, and how the tensions and energies surrounding the site today resonate with aspects of what these writers experienced and evoked. To convey some of the broader traditions and trajectories of American literature emanating from these places, each chapter radiates beyond the writers associated with the main anchor site to later writers influenced by them, as well, suggesting how the writers' legacies continue to have an impact on American letters. Although it is the product of years of research, *Writing America* wears its scholarship lightly. The selected readings at the end of each chapter will point readers to the voluminous scholarship on which this book builds, and without which it would not have been possible—scholarship in American literature and American history, in material culture studies, architectural history, and museum studies.

Sometimes the physical place and the literature are so intimately connected as to be inseparable. The Chinese poems carved on the walls of the Angel Island

Immigration Station in the San Francisco Bay, for example, or the poem by Emma Lazarus, "The New Colossus," engraved on a plaque inside the base of the Statue of Liberty in the New York Harbor are two such cases (although in Lazarus's case, the association began twenty years after the poem was written). At other times, the link is less direct. The historic irrigation pumping station in Hidalgo, Texas, propelled the water into the fields that poet-essayist Gloria Anzaldúa worked in as a child and later wrote about in searing, powerful essays and poems; the Tenement Museum in New York City was not unlike the nearby tenement in which novelist Anzia Yezierska grew up, and which played such a key role in her fiction.

Sometimes a place owes its very existence to literature: the houses I discuss that belonged to Harriet Beecher Stowe and Paul Laurence Dunbar, for example, were literally built with what these successful authors earned from the sales of their books. Sometimes a place owes its preservation to the literature that helped teach us to value it: naturalist John Muir, for example, who did so much to ensure that future generations would be able to see what he saw at Yosemite and other sites of natural beauty, and whose work laid the foundation for the creation of the National Park Service, drew much of his inspiration from early readings of Henry David Thoreau's *Walden* and the essays of Ralph Waldo Emerson. Nearly a century later, Thoreau's book inspired a group of prominent musicians, authors, actors, and activists to work to ensure that the woods surrounding Walden Pond itself were saved from development.

If literature has played a role in teaching us to value parts of the physical world, the physical world has also played a role in helping us understand aspects of literature. I was unprepared for some of the lessons that architecture and artifact taught me about the literary past as I researched this book. I was surprised by the resonances between the humble materials and careful carpentry of Walt Whitman's birthplace home and the poems the poet would go on to write. I was struck by the ways in which the exotic architecture along Hollywood Boulevard that cavalierly made all the cultures of the world its own reflected the tendency of so many films made there to turn ethnic and racial "others" into stereotyped creatures of the imagination as far from real people as Grauman's Chinese Theatre was from China— a tendency that inspired writers from some of those ethnic and racial groups to set the record straight with poetry and fiction of their own. I hadn't expected to find the mélange of Spanish, Mexican, Anglo, and German architectural elements in buildings in the Lower Rio Grande Valley to be such an apt metaphor for the cultural hybridity that is such a central theme in the poetry and fiction produced there. Nor had I imagined that a sugar bowl in Sinclair Lewis's Minnesota boyhood home would evoke the significance of the history that helped make Lewis who he was—or that a bathroom in a Lower East Side tenement building would shed the light it did on Anzia Yezierska's first reaction to Hollywood. And I certainly hadn't expected to gain new insight into the racial politics of Paul Laurence Dunbar's poetry from a distinctive piece of furniture his mother kept in the home he purchased for the two of them in Dayton, Ohio.

Places, like works of literature, are open to multiple interpretations. The "meanings" of places and of literature are sometimes hotly contested. The significance of Sauk Centre, Minnesota, for example, to the people who live there may have little to do with the town's significance in the national imagination as a result of Sinclair Lewis's writings; and people still argue over what word to use to describe an event that happened at Wounded Knee, South Dakota, more than a century ago. While this book uses historical sites as windows on literary history, it also uses literature as way of framing, interpreting, and understanding the social, political, and cultural meanings of physical places.

In the chapters that follow, we will see the New Bedford Historic Whaling District through the work of two nineteenth-century writers for whom it was a temporary home, Herman Melville and Frederick Douglass, and we will explore Hannibal, Missouri, through the writings of Mark Twain. We will view the Hollywood Boulevard Historic District that Nathanael West, F. Scott Fitzgerald, and Raymond Chandler encountered. We will watch what transpired at the Angel Island Immigration Station through Genny Lim's drama that takes place there. We will view the Schomburg Library in Harlem through the eyes of Langston Hughes and Nella Larsen, and we will see historic districts of the Lower Rio Grande Valley through the eyes of writers born and raised there—Américo Paredes, Tomás Rivera, Gloria Anzaldúa, Jovita González, Jovita Idár, and Rolando Hinojosa-Smith. We will hear what happened in 1890 at Wounded Knee from Black Elk, who was there and saw it himself; from S. Alice Callahan, who tried to make sense of it in a novel she published a year later; from Vine Deloria, who was taken there as a child; from Mary Crow Dog, who helped seize and occupy the site in 1973; and from poets N. Scott Momaday, who was moved by a hundred-year-old photograph of the dead, and Wendy Rose, who saw artifacts connected with the massacre in an auction catalog.

When we go to these sites today, we can still encounter some of the tensions reflected in what these writers wrote about them. The racism exposed and condemned by Mark Twain, Paul Laurence Dunbar, and Gloria Anzaldúa has still not been eradicated. One can grasp more fully the roots of these writers' frustration and despair in visits to the locales that shaped their art—in Hannibal, Missouri, which still largely erases the place of slavery in its past, and downplays Mark Twain's role as an antiracist writer; in Dayton, Ohio, which instead of celebrating the interracial adolescent friendship of Paul Laurence Dunbar and the Wright brothers, ignores it almost entirely; and in the Rio Grande Valley, where the disregard for Mexican farm workers' health and well-being that cut short the life of Anzaldúa's father continues to curtail the life expectancies of the people who pick the fruit and vegetables that appear on our dinner tables.

Visits to these sites can help us think about questions that are as unresolved today as they were when these writers wrote about them. A trip to the Angel Island Immigration Station, or the Statue of Liberty, or Wounded Knee, or the Original Main Street or the Roma Historic District, or Angel Island, or Manzanar can help us think about questions like: Who is an American? What is an American? What unites us? What divides us? Who and what are still left out of the nation's narratives of who and what we are, and where we came from? What counternarratives are erased and suppressed in public spaces? Who gets to tell our public stories? Whose voices get silenced? Who gets heard? I hope this book will stimulate you to think about these questions, as it leads you to physical places and imaginative terrains that reflect and refract each other in ways that cast unexpected lights and shadows on the alchemy by which American writers have transformed the world around them into art, changing their world and ours in the process.

FOR FURTHER READING

Benson, Susan Porter, Stephen Brier, and Roy Rosenzweig, eds. *Presenting the Past: Essays in History and the Public.* Philadelphia: Temple University Press, 1986.

Chinese Railroad Workers in North America Project at Stanford University. http://web.stanford. edu/group/chineserailroad/cgi-bin/wordpress.

Csicsila, Joseph. *Canons by Consensus: Critical Trends and American Literature Anthologies.* Tuscaloosa: University of Alabama Press, 2004.

Dempsey, Terrell. *Searching for Jim: Slavery in Sam Clemens's World.* Columbia: University of Missouri Press, 2003.

Dupré, Judith. *Monuments: America's History in Art and Memory.* New York: Random House, 2007.

Eichstedt, Jennifer L., and Stephen Small. *Representations of Slavery: Race and Ideology in Southern Plantation Museums.* Washington, DC: Smithsonian Institution Press, 2001.

Faden, Regina. "Museums and the Story of Slavery: The Challenge of Language." In *Politics of Memory: Making Slavery Visible in the Public Space,* edited by Ana Lucia Araujo. New York: Routledge, 2012.

———. "Presenting Mark Twain: Keeping the Edge Sharp." *Mark Twain Annual* (2008).

Fishkin, Shelley Fisher. "American Literature in Transnational Perspective: The Case of Mark Twain." In *Blackwell Companion to American Literary Studies,* edited by Caroline F. Levander and Robert S. Levine. Hoboken, NJ: Wiley-Blackwell, 2011.

———. *Lighting Out for the Territory: Reflections on Mark Twain and American Culture.* New York: Oxford University Press, 1997.

———, ed. *The Mark Twain Anthology: Great Writers on His Life and Work.* New York: Library of America, 2010.

———. *Was Huck Black? Mark Twain and African American Voices.* New York: Oxford University Press, 1993.

Foner, Philip S. *Mark Twain: Social Critic.* New York: International Publishers, 1958.

Foote, Kenneth E. *Shadowed Ground: American Landscapes of Violence and Tragedy.* Austin: University of Texas Press, 1997.

Frisch, Michael. *A Shared Authority: Essays on the Craft and Meaning of Oral and Public History.* Albany: State University of New York Press, 1990.

Geismar, Maxwell. "Mark Twain and the Robber Barons." *Scanlan's Monthly,* March 1970, 33–39.

Gillis, John R. *Commemorations: The Politics of National Identity.* Princeton, NJ: Princeton University Press, 1994.

Glassberg, David. *Sense of History: The Place of the Past in American Life.* Amherst: University of Massachusetts Press, 2001.

Hayden, Dolores. *The Power of Place: Urban Landscapes as Public History.* Cambridge, MA: MIT Press, 1997.

Horton, James Oliver, and Lois E. Horton, eds. *Slavery and Public History: The Tough Stuff of American Memory.* Chapel Hill: University of North Carolina Press, 2008.

Irwin-Zarecka, Iwona. *Frames of Remembrance: The Dynamics of Collective Memory.* Piscataway, NJ: Transaction Publishers, 2007.

Kammen, Michael. *Mystic Chords of Memory: The Transformation of American Culture.* New York: Vintage, 1993.

Kaufman, Ned. *Place, Race, and Story: Essays on the Past and Future of Historic Preservation.* New York: Routledge, 2009.

Lauter, Paul. *Canons and Contexts.* New York: Oxford University Press, 1991.

Levinson, Sanford. *Written in Stone: Public Monuments in Changing Societies.* Durham, NC: Duke University Press, 1998.

Loewen, James W. *Lies across America: What Our Historic Sites Get Wrong.* New York: The New Press, 1999.

Lubar, Steven, and W. David Kingery. *History from Things: Essays on Material Culture.* Washington, DC: Smithsonian Institution Press, 1993.

Olick, Jeffrey K., Vered Vinitzky-Seroussi, and Daniel Levy, eds. *The Collective Memory Reader.* New York: Oxford University Press, 2011.

Rosenzweig, Roy, and David Thelen. *The Presence of the Past: Popular Uses of History in America Life.* New York: Columbia University Press, 1998.

Shackel, Paul A. *Myth, Memory, and the Making of the American Landscape.* Gainesville: University Press of Florida, 2001.

Sollors, Werner, ed. *Multilingual America: Transnationalism, Ethnicity, and the Languages of American Literature.* New York: New York University Press, 1998.

Troillot, Michel-Rolph. *Silencing the Past: Power and the Production of History.* Boston: Beacon Press, 1997.

West, Patricia. *Domesticating History: The Political Origins of America's House Museums.* Washington, DC: Smithsonian Institution Press, 1999.

Walt Whitman Birthplace, Huntington Station, New York, where the future poet caught his first glimpse of the ordinary plant that would inspire his most extraordinary book: grass.

PHOTO CREDIT: WALT WHITMAN BIRTHPLACE PHOTO COURTESY OF GEORGE MALLIS, PHOTOGRAPHER.

1

Celebrating the Many in One

WALT WHITMAN BIRTHPLACE
246 OLD WALT WHITMAN ROAD,
HUNTINGTON STATION, NEW YORK

Humble local materials—wood and stone—were what a Long Island carpenter used to build this simple house for his growing family in the second decade of the 1800s. Some large rocks provided the foundation. Roughly cut whole tree trunks bound together by wooden pegs sat atop the boulders forming the base. The walls, too, were made from hand-hewn logs attached to each other with wooden pegs. It was all covered by a roof of cedar shingles.

The child who was born in this house in 1819 would learn carpentry from his father, Walter Whitman, the man who built it. But young Walt, as he would come to be known, would not be remembered as a builder of houses. Instead, he would serve his readers by becoming a builder (as he put it in the preface to his most famous book) of paths "between reality and their souls." He would be remembered for teaching Americans how humble local materials—the lives of ordinary people and the world that surrounds them—could be the stuff from which great poetry could be wrought: distinctive, compelling poetry in the American grain that would change his countrymen's ideas of what American poems (and poets) could be.

The second child of Walter Whitman and Louisa Van Velsor entered the world in the first-floor "borning room." His father liked the radical political philosophy of Tom Paine, while his mother was attracted to the mystical, democratic ideas of Quaker preacher Elias Hicks. They named several of their other children after presidents—George Washington, Thomas Jefferson, Andrew Jackson—but it was the child who bore his father's name who would take his parents' passion for democracy to new heights.

Walt Whitman lived in this pleasing, airy country farmhouse until he was four years old, when the family moved to Brooklyn. The unusually large windows his

17

father built throughout the house drenched it in more sunlight and fresh air than was customary for houses of its kind in the area. It was through those windows that Walt caught his first glimpse of the world beyond the bedroom in which he was born. It was the world just outside those windows that he would immortalize in poetry some thirty-five years later when he would write, in a poem that would be known as "There Was a Child Went Forth,"

> There was a child went forth every day,
> And the first object he looked upon and received with wonder or pity or love or
>   dread, that object he became,
> And that object became part of him for the day or a certain part of the day . . .
>   or for many years or stretching cycles of years.
> The early lilacs became part of this child,
> And grass, and white and red morninglories, and white and red clover, and the
>   song of the phoebe-bird,
> And the March-born lambs, and the sow's pink-faint litter, and the mare's foal,
>   and the cow's calf, and the noisy brood of the barnyard or by the mire of
>   the pond-side . . . and the fish suspending themselves so curiously below
>   there . . . and the beautiful curious liquid . . . and the water-plants with their
>   graceful flat heads . . . all became a part of him.
> And the field-sprouts of April and May became part of him . . . wintergrain
>   sprouts, and those of the light-yellow corn, and of the esculent roots of the
>   garden,
> And the appletrees covered with blossoms, and the fruit afterward . . . and
>   woodberries . . . and the commonest weeds by the road; . . .

The lilacs and morning glories that the child saw, the apple trees and wood berries are no more. Only one acre and a barn remain from the sprawling farms and orchards worked by his ancestors in this area since the mid-1700s. But this one acre is enough to remind us of that part of the natural world that inspired Whitman's most compelling poetic vision—for it is covered in grass from the same soil that nurtured the grass that the poet tumbled in as he was learning to walk, the grass that the child saw when he "went forth" and the grass that he "became" in the poem that would come to be known as "Song of Myself" in the stunning book he published in 1855, titled *Leaves of Grass*:

> A child said, What is the grass? Fetching it to me with full hands;
> How could I answer the child? . . . I do not know what it is any more than he.

I guess it must be the flag of my disposition, out of hopeful green stuff woven.

Or I guess it is the handkerchief of the Lord,
A scented gift and remembrancer designedly dropped,
Bearing the owner's name someway in the corners, that we may see and remark,
   and say Whose?

Or I guess the grass is itself a child ... the produced babe of the vegetation.

Or I guess it is a uniform hieroglyphic,
And it means, Sprouting alike in broad zones and narrow zones,
Growing among black folks as among white,
Kanuck, Tuckahoe, Congressman, Cuff, I give them the same, I receive them
   the same.

And now it seems to me the beautiful uncut hair of graves.
Tenderly will I use you curling grass,

Walt Whitman used that grass not only as the title of his book, but also as an object lesson in how the poetic imagination works. By showing the reader the ways in which the poet's imagination can transfigure something as common as leaves of grass, Whitman makes good on his promise to share with his reader "the origin of all poems." This is how you do it, the poet seems to say: look at the grass; *really* look at the grass; see it and see all that it connects with, all that it resonates with, all that it suggests, all that it sparks in your imagination. And somewhere along that path between the concrete physical world and the world of the spirit, Whitman seems to say, a poem will be born. For the poet, Whitman teaches us, "a leaf of grass is no less than the journey work of the stars."

Until he wrote *Leaves of Grass*, Whitman thought poetry came from somewhere else entirely. His earliest poems feature the saccharine, sodden, abstract, and sentimental musings standard in popular graveyard verse, featuring lines such as "But where, O Nature, where shall be the soul's abiding place?" They were rhymed and trite and eminently forgettable, filled with exotic subjects (a descendent of the royal family of Castile, a young Inca girl), archaic and stilted language ("'tis said," "o'er,"), and pompous diction ("dark oblivion's tide").

But at the same time that he was writing hackneyed poetry, he was writing journalism that was often quite innovative for a series of New York newspapers. For example, the "city walks" to which Whitman treated readers of the New York *Aurora*, the city's fourth-largest daily paper, were as fresh and vivid as his attempts at poetry were stale and pale. While an article titled "New York Market" published in the *Tribune* was typically filled with the prices of cotton and flour, the "Market" piece that appeared in the *Aurora* was dense with vivid concrete detail. In the Grand Street market he enters, Whitman waxes rhapsodic about the "array of rich, red sirloins, luscious steaks, delicate and tender joints, muttons, livers, and all the long list of various flesh stuffs" that "burst upon our eyes!" And he observes the people— a "journeyman mason . . . and his wife," "a white faced thin bodied, sickly looking middle aged man," a "fat, jolly featured" woman who is "keeper of a boarding house for mechanics." "A heterogeneous mass, indeed, are they who compose the bustling crowd that fills up the passage way. Widows with sons, . . . careful housewives . . . men with the look of a foreign clime; all sorts of sizes, kinds and ages, and descriptions, all wending, and pricing, and examining and purchasing."

Whitman's great breakthrough as an artist came when he realized that the same subjects, styles, stances, and strategies that he had explored as a journalist could be central to his project as a poet, as well. The wonder of the "heterogeneous mass" (a variant on the "many in one" theme that would always be so important to him) would be central to all of his greatest poems, reflecting not only the diversity of people who made up the human community, but also the diverse states that joined together to form the United States of America (and whose union was embodied in the nation's motto, "e pluribus unum").

In "Song of Myself," the dazzling autobiographical language experiment Whitman published in 1855, the theme of the "many in one" comes together for him in powerful ways. He celebrates his vision of the "many in one" not only in relation to the human community and the nation, but also in relation to himself. The child who "went forth" from the farmhouse in South Huntington had learned to appreciate the connections between himself and all that was outside him, and had learned to look with awe on the essential puzzle of identity (of oneself, of one's country, of the universe)—the many in one.

In his preface to the 1855 *Leaves of Grass*, Whitman provided a job description for the poet he aspired to be:

> His spirit responds to his country's spirit. . . . To him enter the essences of the real things and past and present events—of the enormous diversity of temperature and agriculture and mines—the tribes of red aborigines—the weather-beaten vessels entering new ports or making landings on rocky coasts . . . the union always surrounded by blatherers and always calm and impregnable—the perpetual coming of immigrants—the wharfhem'd cities and

superior marine—the unsurveyed interior—the log-houses and clearings . . . the fisheries and whaling and gold-digging . . . the noble character of the young mechanics and of all free American workmen and workwomen . . . the perfect equality of the female with the male . . . the factories and mercantile life and laborsaving machinery—the Yankee swap . . . the southern plantation life—the character of the northeast and of the northwest and southwest—slavery and the tremendous spreading of hands to protect it, and the stern opposition to it which shall never cease till it ceases. . . . For such the expression of the American poet is to be transcendent and new. . . . Let the age and wars of other nations be chanted and their eras and characters be illustrated and that finish the verse. Not so the great psalm of the republic. Here the theme is creative and has vista. . . .

Whitman was urging outright rejection of the very sorts of exotic subjects he himself had once aspired to making poetry out of. "Away with novels, plots and plays of foreign courts," he would later exhort in "Song of the Exposition": "I raise a voice for far superber themes for poets and for art, / To exalt the present and the real." The image of Whitman that stares out at the reader from the volume's frontispiece conveys a sense of the author as an unpretentious workingman concerned not with the foreign, exotic, or affected, but with "the present and the real" of his own time and place.

Whitman's call for a poet very much like himself was not as original as the book of poems he produced; indeed, it distinctly echoed a plea that Ralph Waldo Emerson had made in 1842 in a lecture on poetry that Whitman covered as a New York journalist (Emerson later published the gist of this lecture in his essay "The Poet"). But if this vision of the poet was not without precedent, the poetry Whitman presented to the world certainly was. Upon receiving a copy of *Leaves of Grass*, Emerson sent Whitman one of the best-known letters in literary

Walt Whitman (1819–1892) as he chose to present himself on the frontispiece of the first edition of *Leaves of Grass* in 1855.
PHOTO CREDIT: COURTESY OF THE LIBRARY OF CONGRESS, PRINTS AND PHOTOGRAPHS DIVISION, WASHINGTON, DC.

history: "I find it the most extraordinary piece of wit and wisdom that America has yet contributed. . . . I give you joy of your free and brave thought. . . . I find incomparable things said incomparably well, as they must be. I find the courage of treatment which so delights us, and which large perception only can inspire," Emerson wrote. "I greet you at the beginning of a great career. . . ." (Whitman, who would also pen and publish anonymous glowing reviews of his own work, used Emerson's letter—without his permission—to promote later editions of the poems.)

Not all readers shared Emerson's admiration for *Leaves of Grass*. Some readers were confused or outraged by the book's defiantly free verse, uncorseted in rhyme or meter, by its sensuous embrace of all things human, including the body and its voracious lusty appetites—both heterosexual and homosexual. "Through me forbidden voices," Whitman intoned, "Voices of sexes and lusts, voices veil'd and I remove the veil." One New York journalist called the book "a mass of stupid filth." Whitman later told a friend that Emerson once suggested that he take out some of the more offensive parts, but Whitman refused. "If I had cut sex out I might just as well have cut everything out," he told Horace Traubel years later. Whitman would lose his job as a clerk in the Department of Interior when his boss found out that he was the author of that "vulgar" book. (It was the third edition of *Leaves of Grass* that Secretary James Harlan found, containing the forty-five "Calamus" poems about Whitman's love for a man.)

Carl Sandburg called *Leaves of Grass* the "most highly praised and most deeply damned book that ever came from an American printing press as the work of an American writer; no other book can compete with it in the number of bouquets handed it by distinguished bystanders on one side of the street and in the number of hostile and nasty brickbats flung by equally distinguished bystanders on the other side of the street."

Leaves of Grass embraced both the scorned and the celebrated. Whitman wrote, in "Song of Myself,"

> The prostitute draggles her shawl, her bonnet bobs on her tipsy and pimpled
>   neck,
> The crowd laugh at her blackguard oaths, the men jeer and wink to each other,
> (Miserable! I do not laugh at your oath nor jeer you;),
> The President holds a cabinet council, he is surrounded by the great secretaries, . . .

The poet sings songs for the farmer and the factory worker, the citizen and the slave. Whitman's openness, his celebration of the miracle of the human body and of sexuality, his intoxication with everyday life, his sense of the value of the most ordinary of experiences, and his belief that every person could be a poet in his or her own right—may have infuriated bureaucrats, Puritans, and narrow-minded journalists, but these qualities helped inspire virtually every American poet who came after him, and many fiction writers, as well. Some writers welcomed the challenge Whitman held out to them, viewing him as a kindly, energizing kindred spirit; others rebelled, chafing at the thought that the poetry they might write was related in any way to poems that Whitman himself proudly characterized as a "barbaric yawp." Either way, Whitman required—demanded—their attention.

Whitman himself sought that impact. In his first book of poems, the 1855 *Leaves of Grass*, he exhorted the reader to "no longer take things at second or third hand . . . nor look through the eyes of the dead . . . nor feed on the spectres in books, / You shall not look through my eyes either, nor take things from me, / You shall listen to all sides and filter them from yourself."

> Long enough have you dreamed contemptible dreams,
> Now I wash the gum from your eyes,
> You must habit yourself to the dazzle of the light and of every moment of your
>   life

> Long have you timidly waded, holding a plank by the shore,
> Now I will you to be a bold swimmer, . . .

And in "Poets to Come," he made his charge more precise:

> Poets to come! orators, singers, musicians to come!
> Not to-day is to justify me and answer what I am for,
> But you, a new brood, native, athletic, continental, greater than before known,
> Arouse! for you must justify me.

> I myself but write one or two indicative words for the future,
> I but advance a moment only to wheel and hurry back in the darkness.

> I am a man who, sauntering along without fully stopping, turns a casual look
>   upon you and then averts his face,
> Leaving it to you to prove and define it,
> Expecting the main things from you.

"I make a pact with you, Walt Whitman— / I have detested you long enough,"

Ezra Pound wrote in his 1913 poem, "A Pact." Pound hated the rawness and rough-
ness of Whitman's poetry but recognized its importance nonetheless. "His crudity
is an exceeding great stench," Pound wrote, "but it *is* America." Whitman came
along "before the nation was self-conscious or introspective or subjective," Pound
tells us, but his poems were "a start in the right direction." The new wood Whitman
broke was now ready to be carved and polished. Pound wrote, "Mentally I am a
Walt Whitman who has learned to wear a collar and a dress shirt (although at times
inimical to both)."

   Writing in 1955, the centennial of the first edition of *Leaves of Grass*, Allen Ginsberg follows Whitman to a mid-twentieth-century version of the markets that so
fascinated Whitman in his days as a New York journalist. In "A Supermarket in
California," Ginsberg writes,

> What thoughts I have of you tonight, Walt Whitman. . . .
> In my hungry fatigue, and shopping for images, I went into the neon
> fruit supermarket, dreaming of your enumerations!
>
> What peaches and what penumbras! Whole families shopping at
> night! Aisles full of husbands! Wives in the avocados, babies in the tomatoes!
> —and you, García Lorca, what were you doing down by the watermelons?
>
> I saw you, Walt Whitman, childless, lonely old grubber, poking
> among the meats in the refrigerator and eyeing the grocery boys.
> I heard you asking questions of each: Who killed the pork chops?
> What price bananas? Are you my Angel?
> I wandered in and out of the brilliant stacks of cans following you,
> and followed in my imagination by the store detective.
>
> We strode down the open corridors together in our solitary fancy
> tasting artichokes, possessing every frozen delicacy, and never passing the
> cashier . . .

The exuberance of Ginsberg's celebration of Whitman's embrace of life in all its
concreteness is matched by that of San Francisco poet laureate Lawrence Ferlinghetti's celebration of the power with which Whitman liberated poetry from the
artificiality and effeteness that had long constrained it (and that, in Ferlinghetti's
view, often continues to constrain it). "Poets, come out of your closets," Ferlinghetti
wrote, in "Populist Manifesto." "Open your windows, open your doors, / You have

been holed-up too long / in your closed worlds." Much as Whitman urged the poet to leave the library and strike out for to the Open Road, Ferlinghetti urged poets to abandon little literary games and boring poetry readings and "descend / to the street of the world once more," claiming their birthright as "Whitman's wild children."

Whitman's inclusiveness, honesty, and respect for the poet in each of us have helped empower as poets individuals marginalized in society at large because of their race, ethnicity, or sexual orientation, or for their politics. He served this role for African American poets Langston Hughes, June Jordan, and Yusef Komunyakaa; for writers on the left, including Mike Gold, Emma Goldman, Meridel Le Sueur, and Tillie Olsen; for Native American poet Joseph Bruchac; for Asian American writer Maxine Hong Kingston; and for gay and lesbian poets including Allen Ginsberg, Thom Gunn, and Mary Oliver. (He also spoke to Stephen Vincent Benét, John Berryman, Richard Eberhart, Edwin Honig, David Ignatow, Erica Jong, Jack Kerouac, Galway Kinnell, Denise Levertov, Edgar Lee Masters, Judith Moffett, Charles Olson, Kenneth Patchen, Theodore Roethke, Muriel Rukeyser, Carl Sandburg, Louis Simpson, Gary Snyder, Wallace Stevens, Diane Wakoski, William Carlos Williams, James Wright, and many, many more.)

Langston Hughes viewed a 1927 invitation from the Walt Whitman Foundation to give a talk at Whitman's final residence in Camden, New Jersey, as "a great honor." Speaking in front of Whitman's house on Mickle Street, Hughes noted Whitman's humane portrayal of African Americans and claimed him as an important forebear. He also embraced Whitman's approach to poetry as his own, stating, "I believe that poetry should be direct, comprehensible, and the epitome of simplicity." He called Whitman "America's greatest poet," and believed that *Leaves of Grass* was "the greatest expression of the real meaning of democracy." For the centennial of *Leaves of Grass*, Hughes wrote a poem about Whitman titled "Old Walt." In his poem "I, Too," Hughes answered the call of Whitman's "Song of Myself" and "I Hear America Singing" with his own response: "I, too, sing America. . . ." Hughes went on to edit three anthologies of Whitman's poems. He frequently urged black writers to read the poet whom Louis Untermeyer had called "the Lincoln of our literature."

Poet Yusef Komunyakaa lauds Whitman for his radical empathy, noting his ability to identify with the slave on the auction block in the poem "I Sing the Body Electric." Komunyakaa, who first read Whitman in high school, recalls having been completely entranced by the music of Whitman's verse, the breadth of his imagination, the reach of his compassion, and the intensity of his belief in democracy: "I had never heard anyone speak so passionately about democracy," Komunyakaa has said, "except perhaps James Baldwin." He goes on to say that the "idea of being empathetic is also embedded in the idea of democracy. For Whitman this is not an abstraction. His seems really intense empathy. I think what he basically believed is that one is not fully human until he possesses the capacity of empathy through the imagination." Komunyakaa writes that "one has to imagine another person free before he or she can even see that person, feel that person in a moment of shared freedom." He includes allusions to Whitman in his poems "Kosmos," "The Poetics of Paperwood," and "Praise Be." In her essay "For the Sake of a People's Poetry: Walt Whitman and the Rest of Us," poet and essayist June Jordan credits Walt Whitman with encouraging her to believe that the life of a woman of color could be the stuff out of which poetry could be made. Maxine Hong Kingston looked to Whitman for inspiration and support when she wrote her ebullient novel of Chinese America, *Tripmaster Monkey: His Fake Book*. (The book's hero is a word-drunk poet, playwright, and talker named Wittman Ah Sing whose ideas about the creation of self and community and democracy—and whose wildly ambitious project as an artist—echo those of his namesake.) And Native American poet Joseph Bruchac finds resonances between Whitman's celebration of the earth and nature and Native American traditions Bruchac is exploring in his own work as a poet. (In his poem "Canticle," written in the 1980s, Bruchac acknowledges some of the debt he owes to "the old gray poet.")

The "old gray poet," or "the good gray poet," as he was often known, was also a good gay poet—and that fact has helped inspire fellow gay poets for more than a century. In "What Think You I Take My Pen in Hand to Record?" in the sequence of poems he called "Calamus," Whitman playfully asks his readers why they think he wrote a particular poem:

> What think you I take my pen in hand to record?
> The battle-ship, perfect-model'd, majestic, that I saw pass the offing to-day
>   under full sail?
> The splendors of the past day? Or the splendor of the night that envelops me?
> Or the vaunted glory and growth of the great city spread around me?—no;
> But merely of two simple men I saw to-day on the pier in the midst of the
>   crowd, parting the parting of dear friends,
> The one to remain hung on the other's neck and passionately kiss'd him,
> While the one to depart tightly prest the one to remain in his arms.

His songs of "manly affection," as he sometimes called them, as well as his embrace of the body in all its physicality, would help embolden Allen Ginsberg, in poems like "Love Comes," to write with openness and honesty about the joy male lovers feel exploring each other's bodies; and it would inspire poet and photographer Duane

Michals to publish *Salute, Walt Whitman*, a montage of photos and text that claims Whitman as a gay ancestor.

While Americans often think of Whitman as the closest thing we've ever had to a national bard, some of his most fervent followers can be found outside the United States. Nicaragua's Rubén Darío, Chile's Pablo Neruda, Argentina's Jorge Luis Borges, the Dominican Republic's Pedro Mir, and Spain's Federico García Lorca carried on intense imagined conversations with Whitman in their poems, and twentieth-century Portuguese poet Fernando Pessoa (writing, on this occasion, under the name Alvaro de Campos) went so far as to claim that he had become Whitman—and that Whitman approved. In his impassioned "Saudação a Walt Whitman" (Salutation to Walt Whitman), he wrote, "Look at me: you know that I, Alvaro de Campos, engineer, / Sensationist poet / Am not your disciple, am not your friend, am not your singer, / You know that I am You, and you are happy about it!"

In 1972, in a speech titled "We Live in a Whitmanesque Age," Pablo Neruda said that "what really counts is that Walt Whitman was not afraid to teach—which means to learn at the hands of life and undertake the responsibility of passing on the lesson! . . . There are many kinds of greatness, but let me say (though I be a poet of the Spanish tongue) that Walt Whitman has taught me more than Spain's Cervantes: in Walt Whitman's work one never finds the ignorant being humbled, nor is the human condition ever found offended. . . . Walt Whitman was the protagonist of a truly geographical personality: the first man in history to speak with a truly continental American voice, to bear a truly American name."

Whitman, that most American of American poets, was also the poet of a radical internationalism, projecting a cosmic brotherhood that linked the many nations of the world into one humanity—yet another manifestation of "the many in one." In poems like "Salut au Monde!" with its focus on rivers and oceans and mountains more permanent than any political boundaries drawn on a map, he envisions a world liberated from institutions that divide people, a world united in common democratic purpose, in which all men and women embrace each other as equals. It is not surprising that his liberatory rhetoric helped make him an icon for leftist and internationalist thinkers. "I hear it was charged against me that I sought to destroy institutions," Whitman wrote, "But really I am neither for nor against institutions." What he wanted to "establish . . . in every city of these States inland and seaboard, / And in the fields and woods, and above every keel little or large that dents the water, / Without edifices or rules or trustees or any argument" was "the institution of the dear love of comrades." In 1915, Floyd Dell, coeditor of the socialist monthly, *The Masses*, noted that "Walt Whitman seems to have been accepted by Socialists as peculiarly their poet." And in 1932, John Dos Passos remarked that "Walt Whitman's a hell of a lot more revolutionary than any Russian poet I've ever heard of." Whitman inspired writers on the Left, including journalist/novelists Mike Gold, Meridel Le Sueur, and Tillie Olsen, and playwright Clifford Odets (who named his son after Whitman). The Walt Whitman Fellowship International, organized by Whitman's friend Horace Traubel, attracted Emma Goldman and Eugene V. Debs in the United States, as well as prominent leftist intellectuals in Europe, Asia, and Latin America, many of whom translated Whitman into their native languages.

As they read him in their own tongues, writers around the world remade Whitman to fit their own cultural needs, using him to help them define themselves and their countries, explore universal themes, and shape their sense of the United States. Ngugi wa T'hiongo of Kenya mined Whitman's poems for epigraphs to the chapters in one of his novels. The Malayali poet Balachandran Chullikkad from the South Indian city of Cochin told critic Stephen Greenblatt that "Whitman is a Malayali poet." Whitman makes an appearance in James Joyce's *Finnegan's Wake*. He shaped the imagination of D. H. Lawrence, impressed E. M. Forster, and delighted Thomas Mann. He became a cult figure in Germany and a Symbolist hero in France. His democratic message held special appeal for Communist leader Antonio Gramsci in Italy and helped encourage Croatian patriots with dreams of freedom. In Russia, his work spoke to Ivan Turgenev, Leo Tolstoy, and Vladimir Mayakovsky. In Israel, philosopher Gershom Scholem was attracted to him, while in China he was a key inspiration for the modern poet and dramatist Guo Muruo. No poet is more influential worldwide, and no poet has garnered as many responses from other writers as Whitman has.

Whitman may be claimed by the world, but it was the rolling lilac-scented hills of his childhood and the beaches of the nearby Long Island shore that gave his soul sustenance, and to which he frequently returned throughout his life. His father had moved the family to Brooklyn when his son was four, hoping to take advantage of a building boom there. But his plans didn't work out, and he soon moved the family back to Long Island—or "fish-shape Paumanok"—as the Indians called it. Whitman joined his family there during his teens, working as a schoolteacher in several surrounding towns and founding and editing a local weekly still in existence today, the Huntington *Long Islander*. As he recalled in *Specimen Days*, he bought a white mare named Nina, and "every week went round the country serving my papers, devoting one day and night to it. I never had happier jaunts—going over to south side, to Babylon, down the south road, across to Smithtown and Comac, and back home. The experiences of those jaunts, the dear old-fashion'd farmers and their wives, the stops by the hay-fields, the hospitality, nice dinners, occasional evenings, the girls, the rides through the brush, come up in my memory to this day."

The Long Island shore drew Whitman throughout his life, inspiring some of his most memorable poems—such as "As I Ebb'd with the Ocean of Life." "As I ebb'd with the ocean of life, / As I wended the shores I know, / As I walk'd where the ripples continually wash you Paumanok . . . ," Whitman tells us, he cast his eyes on nature's debris—"Chaff, straw, splinters of wood, weeds, and the sea-gluten, . . . / Scum, scales from shining rocks, leaves of salt-lettuce, left by the tide." Walking with ". . . the sound of breaking waves the other side of me," he writes, "As I inhale the impalpable breezes that set in upon me, / As the ocean so mysterious rolls toward me closer and closer, / I too but signify at the utmost a little wash'd-up drift, / A few sands and dead leaves to gather, / Gather, and merge myself as part of the sands and drift."

As he watched the tide ebb and flow, leaving on shore bits of the sea and carrying back to sea bits of the shore, Whitman felt himself connected to the back-and-forth ebbing and flowing of his life breath itself, and of the life breath of his poetry— "my respiration and inspiration," as he put it in "Song of Myself." He would recite verses of Greek and Latin epic poetry as he walked along the beach. Later in life he would recall that the only reason he wasn't intimidated by Homer and Virgil was that he read them "in the full presence of Nature . . . with the sea rolling in." Nature humbled him. The depth of its simplest mysteries made the poet's song shallow by comparison.

He returned to his birthplace for the last time during the summer of 1881. His affection for the landscape of his childhood is clear from "A Week at West Hills," a letter he wrote to the New York *Tribune* about his trip that August:

Sir: I have been for the last two weeks jaunting around Long Island, and now devote this letter to West Hills (Suffolk County, 30 miles from New York), and the main purpose of a journey thither, to resume and identify my birth-spot, and that of my parents and their parents, and to explore the picturesque regions comprised in the townships of Huntington and Cold Spring Harbor. I shall just give my notes verbatim as I pencilled them.

Went down nearly a mile further to the house where I was born (May 31, 1819) in the fertile meadow land. As I paused and looked around I felt that any good farmer would have gloated over the scene. Rich corn in tassel, many fields; they had cradled their wheat and rye, and were cutting their oats. Everything had changed so much, and it looked so fine. . . . Seems to me I have had the memorable though brief and quiet jaunt of my life. Every day a point attained; every day something refreshing, Nature's medicine. All about here, an area of many miles, Huntington, Cold Spring Harbor, East and West and Lloyd's Neck (to say nothing of the water view), the hundreds of tree-lined roads and lanes, with their turns and gentle slopes, the rows and groves of locusts, after the main objects of my jaunt, made the most attraction, as I rode around. I didn't know there was so much in mere lanes and trees. I believe they have done me more good than all the swell scenery I could find.

Most of the lanes and trees surrounding the his birthplace have given way, by now, to residential houses and commercial enterprises—pizza parlors and Chinese restaurants that are reminders of "the perpetual coming of immigrants" to which Whitman alluded with such welcoming energy and joy in "Song of Myself." But the neat, well-crafted farmhouse that remains and the grass that surrounds it are reminders of the "transcendent and new" art that can be made out of the ordinary, the near, the common, and the familiar.

WALT WHITMAN'S CIVIL WAR

THE FREDERICKSBURG AND SPOTSYLVANIA
COUNTY MEMORIAL NATIONAL MILITARY PARK
Visitor center: 1013 Lafayette Boulevard, Fredericksburg, Virginia

ANTIETAM NATIONAL BATTLEFIELD
Visitor center: 5831 Dunker Church Road, Sharpsburg, Maryland

MANASSAS NATIONAL BATTLEFIELD PARK
Visitor center: 6511 Sudley Road, Manassas, Virginia

ANDERSONVILLE NATIONAL HISTORIC SITE
AND NATIONAL PRISONER OF WAR MUSEUM
Main entrance: 760 POW Road, Andersonville, Georgia

For Whitman, the ultimate embodiment of the theme of the "many in one" was the United States of America itself, a singular political body composed of many states with varied climates, terrain, inhabitants, economies, and sensibilities. During the years leading up to the Civil War, he was an outspoken Free Soil democrat, opposing the extension of slavery into newly acquired territories. When the Civil War threatened to tear the country apart, he was terrified at the prospect of seeing the many-in-one disintegrate.

Whitman's brother George joined the Union forces in 1861 and during the next four years would serve in twenty-one engagements or sieges. In December 1862, Walt Whitman learned that George had been wounded at Fredericksburg and immediately went to find him at his regiment's encampment in Falmouth. George's wound turned out not to be serious, but Whitman's encounter with the soldiers changed his life. He returned to Washington, DC, as a volunteer nurse, or "wound-dresser," and served in that role throughout the rest of the war.

There were some forty hospitals in Washington at the time, crowded with wounded and dying soldiers far from home. Whitman made some six hundred hospital visits during the next three years, and his notebooks are filled with his responses to the more than eighty thousand soldiers he saw. He helped dress their wounds. He brought them ice cream, candy, fruit, stationery, stamps, books, and tobacco. He wrote letters for them, read to them, hugged them, listened to their stories with compassion, and recorded what he saw and heard. He would go on to call the Civil War "the very center, circumference, umbilicus of my whole career." In poetry and prose, he would try to come to terms with the overwhelming human cost of preserving his country.

Whitman tells us that he "kept little notebooks for impromptu jottings in pencil to refresh my memory of names and circumstances, and what was specially wanted, &c. In these I brief'd cases, persons, sights, occurrences in camp, by the bedside, and not seldom by the corpses of the dead." He drew on his forty-some notebooks—"blotch'd here and there with more than one blood-stain"—when he published the nonfiction *Memoranda during the War* and *Specimen Days*, as well as the volume of poetry titled *Drum-Taps*.

The four major battles fought between 1862 and 1864 in the vicinity of Fredericksburg, Virginia, where George Whitman was wounded, make it the bloodiest ground in North America. Approximately 110,000 soldiers lost their lives in the Battles of Fredericksburg (December 11–13, 1862), Chancellorsville (May 1–4, 1863), Wilderness (May 5–6, 1864), and Spotsylvania Court House (May 8–21, 1864). The Fredericksburg and Spotsylvania County Memorial National Military Park commemorates the sacrifice they made for their country, preserving the scene of the four battles as well as historic buildings associated with them.

Many of the thousands of soldiers Whitman comforted in Washington hospitals during his years as a volunteer nurse were wounded, he tells us, during the battles of Second Bull Run (August 30, 1862) and Antietam (September 17, 1862). At Antietam, twenty-three thousand men were killed or wounded during just twelve hours of fighting, making it the bloodiest one-day battle in American history. At the Second Bull Run (or Manassas), 1,747 Union soldiers and 1,553 Confederate soldiers lost their lives, while more than 20,600 more were wounded, captured, or missing. Antietam National Battlefield and Manassas National Battlefield Park memorialize the soldiers who gave their lives during these bloody battles.

The moving poems Whitman published in *Drum-Taps* evoke the experiences of many of the young men wounded and killed on the Civil War's battlefields. "A March in the Ranks Hard-Prest, and the Road Unknown" and "A Sight in Camp in the Daybreak Gray and Dim" paint images of the grim field hospitals that sprung up near Civil War battlefields. "The Wound-Dresser" evokes Whitman's experiences tending the needs of the many wounded and dying soldiers he tried to assist and comfort.

A March in the Ranks Hard-Prest, and the Road Unknown

A march in the ranks hard-prest, and the road unknown,
A route through a heavy wood with muffled steps in the darkness,
Our army foil'd with loss severe, and the sullen remnant retreating,
Till after midnight glimmer upon us the lights of a dim-lighted building,
We come to an open space in the woods, and halt by the dim-lighted building,
'Tis a large old church at the crossing roads, now an impromptu hospital,
Entering but for a minute I see a sight beyond all the pictures and poems ever
    made,
Shadows of deepest, deepest black, just lit by moving candles and lamps,
And by one great pitchy torch stationary with wild red flame and clouds of
    smoke,
By these, crowds, groups of forms vaguely I see on the floor, some in the pews
    laid down,
At my feet more distinctly a soldier, a mere lad, in danger of bleeding to death,
    (he is shot in the abdomen,)
I stanch the blood temporarily, (the youngster's face is white as a lily,)
Then before I depart I sweep my eyes o'er the scene fain to absorb it all,
Faces, varieties, postures beyond description, most in obscurity, some of them
    dead,
Surgeons operating, attendants holding lights, the smell of ether, the odor of
    blood,
The crowd, O the crowd of the bloody forms, the yard outside also fill'd,
Some on the bare ground, some on planks or stretchers, some in the death-
    spasm sweating,
An occasional scream or cry, the doctor's shouted orders or calls,
The glisten of the little steel instruments catching the glint of the torches,
These I resume as I chant, I see again the forms, I smell the odor,
Then hear outside the orders given, *Fall in, my men, fall in;*
But first I bend to the dying lad, his eyes open, a half-smile gives he me,
Then the eyes close, calmly close, and I speed forth to the darkness,
Resuming, marching, ever in darkness marching, on in the ranks,
The unknown road still marching.

from **The Wound-Dresser**

I

An old man bending I come among new faces,
Years looking backward resuming in answer to children,
Come tell us old man, as from young men and maidens that love me,
(Arous'd and angry, I'd thought to beat the alarum, and urge relentless war,
But soon my fingers fail'd me, my face droop'd and I resign'd myself,
To sit by the wounded and soothe them, or silently watch the dead;)
Years hence of these scenes, of these furious passions, these chances,
Of unsurpass'd heroes, (was one side so brave? the other was equally brave;)
Now be witness again, paint the mightiest armies of earth,
Of those armies so rapid so wondrous what saw you to tell us?
What stays with you latest and deepest? of curious panics,
Of hard-fought engagements or sieges tremendous what deepest remains?

. . . .

Bearing the bandages, water and sponge,
Straight and swift to my wounded I go,
Where they lie on the ground after the battle brought in,
Where their priceless blood reddens the grass the ground,
Or to the rows of the hospital tent, or under the roof'd hospital,
To the long rows of cots up and down each side I return,
To each and all one after another I draw near, not one do I miss,
An attendant follows holding a tray, he carries a refuse pail,
Soon to be fill'd with clotted rags and blood, emptied, and fill'd again.

I onward go, I stop,
With hinged knees and steady hand to dress wounds,
I am firm with each, the pangs are sharp yet unavoidable,
One turns to me his appealing eyes—poor boy! I never knew you,
Yet I think I could not refuse this moment to die for you, if that would save
    you.

. . . .

Thus in silence in dreams' projections,
Returning, resuming, I thread my way through the hospitals,
The hurt and wounded I pacify with soothing hand,
I sit by the restless all the dark night, some are so young,
Some suffer so much, I recall the experience sweet and sad,
(Many a soldier's loving arms about this neck have cross'd and rested,
Many a soldier's kiss dwells on these bearded lips.)

In a section titled "Releas'd Union Prisoners from the South" from *Specimen Days*, Whitman describes the men he sees who were released from southern prison camps like Andersonville. Andersonville National Historic Site, a park consisting of a national cemetery as well as the site of the largest of many Confederate prisons, held more than forty-five thousand Union soldiers during the fourteen months of its existence. Almost thirteen thousand died from malnutrition, disease, overcrowding, poor sanitary conditions, and exposure to the elements. The park was created by Congress both to "to provide an understanding of the overall prisoner of war story of the Civil War" and "to interpret the role of prisoner of war camps in history, to commemorate the sacrifice of Americans who lost their lives in such camps," a mission particularly addressed in the park's National Prisoner of War Museum.

Releas'd Union Prisoners from the South

The releas'd prisoners of war are now coming up from the southern prisons. I have seen a number of them. The sight is worse than any sight of battle-fields, or any collection of wounded, even the bloodiest. There was, (as a sample,) one large boat load of several hundreds, brought about the 25th, to Annapolis; and out of the whole number only three individuals were able to walk from the boat. The rest were carried ashore and laid down in one place or another. Can those be *men*—those little livid brown, ash-streak'd, monkey-looking dwarfs?— are they really not mummied, dwindled corpses? They lay there, most of them, quite still, but with a horrible look in their eyes and skinny lips (often with not enough flesh on the lips to cover their teeth.) Probably no more appalling sight was ever seen on this earth. (There are deeds, crimes, that may be forgiven; but this is not among them. It steeps its perpetrators in blackest, escapeless, endless damnation. Over 50,000 have been compell'd to die the death of starvation—reader, did you ever try to realize what *starvation* actually is?—in those prisons—and in a land of plenty.) An indescribable meanness, tyranny, aggravating course of insults, almost incredible—was evidently the rule of treatment through all the southern military prisons. The dead there are not to be pitied as much as some of the living that come from there—if they can be call'd living—many of them are mentally imbecile, and will never recuperate.

RELATED SITES

• Walt Whitman House
330 Mickle Street, Camden, New Jersey

As the United States grew between 1855 and the year of Whitman's death in 1892, so did *Leaves of Grass*, which would appear in nine successive editions. The reissue of the 1881 seventh edition in 1884 sold more copies than any previous edition, enabling Whitman to buy a small, two-story, gray frame house with a tin-covered roof—a "shanty" as he called it—on Mickle Street in a workingman's neighborhood near the railroad tracks in Camden, New Jersey, for $1,750. It was the only house he ever owned. Whitman had come to Camden in 1873 from Washington, DC, when he was recovering from a paralytic stroke, to be with his critically ill mother at the home of his brother George. His mother died later that year. Whitman, too ill to return to Washington, stayed in his brother's house in Camden for the next eleven years. When his brother's business was moved to Burlington, New Jersey, Whitman chose to stay in Camden and buy the house at 328 Mickle Street (since renumbered 330). Unable to care for himself, he invited a neighbor, a widow named Mary O. Davis, to move into the house rent free in exchange for housekeeping and cooking services. He issued a new edition of *Leaves of Grass* while living here, and two collections containing new poems.

Impoverished, and debilitated by a series of strokes, Whitman spent much of the time here painfully bedridden—although he looked forward to outings in the horse and buggy that his friends had presented to him as a gift. As a steady stream of nurses helped him cope with his deteriorating health, many friends and admirers came to call, including Oscar Wilde. The most attentive of his many admirers and his most regular companion was Horace Traubel, a young aspiring writer from Camden who recorded for posterity comments Whitman made during his closing years. On September 5, 1891, some six months before his death, Whitman called

Traubel's attention to a patch of grass growing near his home. "More and more as I grow old," he told him, "do I love the grass: it seems to supply me something—some dear, dear something—much my need, yes, greatly needed."

Visitors to 330 Mickle Street can see, in addition to personal artifacts and facsimile manuscripts of his work, Whitman's bath tub, his rocking chair, and the knapsack he used to peddle his books.

Walt Whitman in his home on Mickle Street in Camden, New Jersey, 1891. Platinum print made by sculptor Samuel Murray.
PHOTO CREDIT: COURTESY OF THE HIRSHHORN MUSEUM AND SCULPTURE GARDEN, SMITHSONIAN INSTITUTION, WASHINGTON, DC.

❧ Fulton Ferry Historic District
Fulton Ferry, Brooklyn, New York (roughly bounded by the East River and Washington, Water, Front, and Doughty Streets)

Whitman loved to ride the ferry between Brooklyn and Manhattan. Ferry service had existed here for two hundred years before Whitman immortalized it in his famous 1856 poem, "Crossing Brooklyn Ferry," where he spoke across time to others who, more than "a hundred years hence," would see what he saw from this spot:

> Others will enter the gates of the ferry, and cross from shore to shore;
> Others will watch the run of the flood-tide
> Others will see the shipping of Manhattan north and west, and the heights of
>   Brooklyn to the south and east;
> Others will see the islands large and small;
> Fifty years hence, others will see them as they cross, the sun half an hour high;
> A hundred years hence, or ever so many hundred years hence, others will see
>   them,
> Will enjoy the sunset, the pouring in of the flood-tide, the falling back to the
>   sea of the ebb-tide.

"Just as you feel when you look on the river and sky, so I felt," Whitman writes. "Just as any of you is one of a living crowd, I was one of a crowd; / Just as you are refresh'd by the gladness of the river and the bright flow, I was refresh'd."

❧ Seaport Museum
South Street Seaport Historic District: 21, 23, 25 Fulton Street, New York City

Walt Whitman worked as a journalist in this lower Manhattan neighborhood in the 1840s, editing publications including the New York *Aurora* at 162 Nassau Street, where he published the densely concrete "city walks" that prefigured *Leaves of Grass*. The South Street Seaport Museum (which occupies buildings built in the mid-1840s to house various commercial enterprises) contains a room-size replica of a mid-nineteenth-century printing shop that resembles those in which Whitman worked.

❧ Langston Hughes House

20 East 127th Street, New York City

Langston Hughes was living in this Harlem townhouse with his adopted uncle and aunt, Emerson and Ethel (Toy) Harper, in 1954 when he wrote a poem about Walt Whitman, "Old Walt." When Hughes left for Africa as a crew member on the freighter *West Hesseltine* in 1923, Arnold Rampersad tells us, he took a box of books on board—"mostly the detritus of his year at Columbia and the mark of his devotion from childhood to the lonely world of the written word." But, as Hughes later recalled, seeing in them emblems of "every thing unpleasant and miserable" in his life—including "the stupidities of color prejudice, black in a white world" and "the fear of not finding a job," he decided to throw them away. He threw each book overboard, feeling unburdened and relieved. All but one: Rampersad writes, "He had flung overboard the symbols of his hurt. But he had also kept the symbol of his best self, and of what he hoped to be. He saved his copy of Walt Whitman's *Leaves of Grass*: 'I had no intention of throwing that one away.'" In a 1946 essay titled "The Ceaseless Rings of Walt Whitman," Hughes had written that Whitman "wrote without the frills, furbelows, and decorations of conventional poetry, usually without rhyme or measured prettiness. Perhaps because of his simplicity, timid poetry lovers over the years have been frightened away from his *Leaves of Grass*, poems as firmly rooted and as brightly growing as the grass itself." Responding to Whitman's line "(I am large, I contain multitudes)," Hughes writes, "Certainly his poems contain us all. The reader cannot help but see his own better self therein."

FOR FURTHER READING

The Writers: Works and Words

Bruchac, Joseph. "To Love the Earth: Some Thoughts on Walt Whitman." In Perlman et al., *Walt Whitman: The Measure of His Song*.

Dell, Floyd. "Whitman, Anti-Socialist." *New Review* 3 (15 June 1915): 85–86.

Dos Passos, John. "Whither the American Writer." *Modern Quarterly* 6 (Summer 1932): 11–12, 26.

Ferlinghetti, Lawrence. "Populist Manifesto." In Perlman et al., *Walt Whitman: The Measure of His Song*.

Ginsberg, Allen. "A Supermarket in California." In Perlman et al., *Walt Whitman: The Measure of His Song*.

Hughes, Langston. "The Ceaseless Rings of Walt Whitman." In Perlman et al., *Walt Whitman: The Measure of His Song.*

———. *Collected Poems of Langston Hughes.* Edited by Arnold Rampersad and David Roessel. New York: Alfred A. Knopf, 1994.

———. "Walt Whitman and the Negro." In *Essays on Art, Race, Politics and World Affairs.* Vol. 9 of *The Collected Works of Langston Hughes.* Edited by R. Baxter Miller. Introduction by Arnold Rampersad. Columbia: University of Missouri Press, 2002.

Jordan, June. "For the Sake of a People's Poetry: Walt Whitman and the Rest of Us." In Perlman et al., *Walt Whitman: The Measure of His Song.*

Kingston, Maxine Hong. *Tripmaster Monkey: His Fake Book.* New York: Vintage, 1990.

Neruda, Pablo. "We Live in a Whitmanesque Age." In Perlman et al., *Walt Whitman: The Measure of His Song.*

Perlman, Jim, Ed Folsom, and Dan Campion, eds. *Walt Whitman: The Measure of His Song.* Minneapolis: Holy Cow! Press, 1981.

Pessoa, Fernando (Alvaro de Campos). "Salutation to Walt Whitman." In Perlman et al., *Walt Whitman: The Measure of His Song.*

Pound, Ezra. "A Pact." In Perlman et al., *Walt Whitman: The Measure of His Song.*

Whitman, Walt. *Complete Poetry and Collected Prose.* Edited by Justin Kaplan. New York: Library of America, 1982.

Wilkenfeld, Jacob. "Celebration and Confrontation: Yusef Komunyakaa in Conversation about Walt Whitman." *Walt Whitman Quarterly Review* 30, no. 3 (2013): 150–160.

Backgrounds and Contexts

Allen, Gay Wilson, and Ed Folsom, eds. *Walt Whitman and the World.* Iowa City: University of Iowa Press, 1995.

Buinicki, Martin T. *Walt Whitman's Reconstruction: Poetry and Publishing between Memory and History.* Iowa City: University of Iowa Press, 2011.

Erkkila, Betsy, and Jay Grossman, eds. *Breaking Bounds: Whitman and American Cultural Studies.* New York: Oxford University Press, 1996.

Fishkin, Shelley Fisher. "Walt Whitman." In *From Fact to Fiction: Journalism and Imaginative Writing in America,* by Shelley Fisher Fishkin. New York: Oxford University Press, 1988.

Greenblatt, Stephen. "Racial Memory and Literary History." In special issue, "Globalizing Literary Studies," *PMLA* 116, no. 1 (January 2001): 48–63.

Huang, Guiyou. *Whitmanism, Imagism, and Modernism in China and America.* Selinsgrove, PA: Susquehanna University Press, 1997.

Kaplan, Justin. *Walt Whitman: A Life.* New York: Simon and Schuster, 1980.

LeMaster, J. R., and Donald D. Kummings. *Walt Whitman: An Encyclopedia.* London: Routledge, 1998.

Rampersad, Arnold. *The Life of Langston Hughes.* Vol. 1, *1902–1941, I, Too, Sing America.* New York: Oxford University Press, 1986.

————. *The Life of Langston Hughes*. Vol. 2, *1941–1967, I Dream a World*. New York: Oxford University Press, 1988.

Reynolds, David, ed. *A Historical Guide to Walt Whitman*. New York: Oxford University Press, 2000.

Traubel, Horace. *With Walt Whitman in Camden*. Vol. 8, *11 February 1891–30 September 1891*. Edited by Jeanne Chapman and Robert MacIsaac. Oregon House, CA: Bentley, 1996.

Thoreau's Cove, Lake Walden, Concord, Massachusetts. Thoreau often gazed at Walden Pond from this vantage point during the years when he lived in a cabin on its shores between 1845 and 1847.

PHOTO CREDIT: DETROIT PUBLISHING COMPANY; COURTESY OF THE LIBRARY OF CONGRESS, PRINTS AND PHOTOGRAPHS DIVISION, WASHINGTON, DC.

2

Living in Harmony with Nature

WALDEN POND STATE RESERVATION
ROUTE 126 (WALDEN STREET AND CONCORD ROAD),
CONCORD AND LINCOLN, MASSACHUSETTS

Near the end of March 1845, twenty-eight-year-old Henry David Thoreau, a sometime "teacher, surveyor, pencil-maker, handyman, and natural historian" as he once put it, "borrowed an axe and went down to the woods by Walden Pond nearest to where I intended to build my house, and began to cut down some tall arrowy white pines, still in their youth, for timber. . . . It was a pleasant hillside where I worked, covered with pine woods, through which I looked out on the pond, and a small open field in the woods, where pines and hickories were springing up." On July 4—appropriately enough, Independence Day (although Thoreau claimed it was merely a coincidence)—he moved into the one-room cabin he had constructed to begin a sojourn of about twenty-six-months in the woods. The plan was simplicity itself: "I went to the woods because I wished to live deliberately, to front only the essential facts of life, and see if I could not learn what it had to teach, and not, when I came to die, discover that I had not lived." Indeed, simplicity itself is one of Thoreau's favorite topics in *Walden*, the book he published about his experience: "Every morning was a cheerful invitation to make my life of equal simplicity, and I may say innocence, with Nature herself," he wrote. "Simplicity, simplicity, simplicity!" he preached. "Simplify, simplify," he exhorted his readers.

But like the limpid surface of Walden Pond, the apparently simple narrative of those twenty-six months covered hidden depths that readers still find challenging to probe. *Walden* was an exhilarating and infuriating book—a sermon on simplicity that was far from simple; a celebration of honesty that hid or masked as much as it revealed; a book that sometimes pretended to be what it was not and at other times turned out to be exactly what it claimed to be; a book that was supremely humble and supremely arrogant at the same time.

Understanding Thoreau turns out to have been no easier for his closest friends than it is for posterity. If anyone might have been expected to understand what Thoreau was up to, it would probably have been Ralph Waldo Emerson, who wrote philosophical essays that had inspired Thoreau when he was a student at Harvard, who took Thoreau into his home after graduation (employing him as editor, gardener, and handyman), who gave him permission to build his cabin in Walden Woods (rent-free on land that Emerson owned), and who delivered the eulogy at Thoreau's funeral. But the Sage of Concord remarked, at Thoreau's death, "I cannot help counting it a fault in him that he had no ambition."

No ambition? Too much ambition might be more accurate. Evidently, Emerson could not imagine that over the next century, seeds that Thoreau had planted as a writer would sprout into a vast body of American nature writing, literary journalism, and protest literature that would help inspire mass social movements on several continents, help spark the development of the field of ecology, and help set in motion the train of events that would lead to the creation of our national parks. "If one advances confidently in the direction of his dreams, and endeavors to live the life which he has imagined, he will meet with a success unexpected in common hours," Thoreau wrote in *Walden*. The millions of visitors who have made the pilgrimage to Walden Pond to see where it all began are further testimony to the unexpected success enjoyed by the writer who came here "to live deep and suck out all the marrow of life."

What Thoreau described as "a small pond, about a mile and a half south of the village of Concord and somewhat higher than it, in the midst of an extensive wood between that town and Lincoln, and about two miles south" of the field where the Battle of Concord was fought, began to be formed ten thousand to twelve thousand years ago as the glacier that covered New England began to melt. Walden Pond is the deepest lake in a state that boasts more than a thousand other lakes. As Barksdale Maynard notes in *Walden Pond: A History*, "With an average depth of forty feet, a 102-foot, seven-story office building could be fully dunked in the middle of the pond." The 61.5-acre lake, Maynard writes, "is as big as forty-seven football fields."

Thoreau was born in Concord in 1817 and lived there most of his life. His family had moved to nearby Chelmsford and Boston for a few years, where his father, John, a shopkeeper, had followed business opportunities. They returned to Concord in 1823, when John set up what would eventually be a highly successful pencil factory, and where his mother, Cynthia, took in boarders. He would never, in fact, stray very far from this area, finding in it world enough to satisfy his curiosity and interest. Indeed, Thoreau recalled a trip to the area around Walden Pond as a young child in 1822 as the experience that first kindled his love of nature. During his sophomore year at college, he read Emerson's essay "Nature" (1836) and found in it a philosophical justification for his growing attraction to the world beyond the library, parlor, and classroom. Emerson's affirmation of the presence of God in all living things (the ever-present "Over-soul"), and his stress on self-reliance held great appeal to a Thoreau increasingly intrigued by the possibilities of living self-sufficiently in nature. "The lover of nature" Emerson wrote, finds a "wild delight" running through him when he is in nature's presence, even if he is carrying the burden of "real sorrows" at the time. "Not the sun or the summer alone," he wrote, "but every hour and season yields its tribute of delight; for every hour and change corresponds to and authorizes a different state of mind, from breathless noon to grimmest midnight." But it was these comments that must have particularly attracted Thoreau's attention: "In the woods . . . ," Emerson wrote, "a man casts off his years, as the snake his slough, and at what period soever of life, is always a child. In the woods, is perpetual youth. Within these plantations of God, a decorum and sanctity reign, a perennial festival is dressed, and the guest sees not how he should tire of them in a thousand years."

When Thoreau moved to this heavily farmed part of Massachusetts, the land around Walden Pond was one of the few areas that remained wooded. The pine-oak woods around the pond were a convenient source of firewood for the land's owners, who didn't clear them because the sandy soil was too dry for farming. But fourteen years after Thoreau built his cabin there, civilization had so encroached on the woodlands that many of the trees he had studied were gone, leading him to propose in an 1859 journal entry that each town should have "a park, or rather a primitive forest, of five hundred or a thousand acres, where a stick never should be cut for fuel, a common possession forever, for instruction and recreation." His vision of public ownership as a means to guarantee the preservation of wilderness for future generations was prescient, indeed. ("In wildness," he wrote, "is the preservation of the world.") Naturalist John Muir, whose heavily annotated copies of Thoreau's work show that he read it with great care, would be instrumental in advocating the preservation of wild spaces on a national level, helping to provide a rationale for the creation of the National Park Service. It would all come full circle in 1965, when the secretary of the interior, Stewart Udall, designated Walden Pond a National Historic Landmark. And when Walden Woods was threatened by developers in the 1980s, Thoreau's inspiring and empowering words helped environmentalists raise the funds to ensure that the site would remain undeveloped, owned by a public trust inspired by the philosophy of the man who dreamed that "all Walden wood" might be "preserved for our park forever, with Walden in its midst." The area around the pond today is actually more wooded than it was when Thoreau built his cabin.

It is part of the Walden Pond State Reservation, hundreds of acres of open space protected by the Massachusetts Forests and Parks System.

Just as Thoreau had built his cabin with recycled boards and nails from a shanty he bought from a man named James Collins, Concord residents built other structures around town with recycled parts of Thoreau's cabin, which had been moved from its original location to the other side of Concord by some farmers in 1849 to store grain; in 1868, the roof of the deteriorating cabin was used to cover a local pig pen. But in 1872, ten years after Thoreau's death, visitors began leaving rocks and flowers and twigs on a cairn near where the cabin used to be as tributes to the man who helped them see these woods with new eyes. And in 1945, one hundred years after Thoreau moved to Walden, a Thoreau admirer and amateur historian named Roland Wells Robbins established the precise location of the original cabin when he uncovered and excavated the foundation of the chimney. Two years later, the Thoreau Society dedicated the inscribed fieldstone that still marks the site of the cabin's hearth.

Thoreau built his simple cabin on this site in Walden Woods, Concord, Massachusetts, in 1845.
PHOTO CREDIT: DETROIT PUBLISHING COMPANY; COURTESY OF THE LIBRARY OF CONGRESS, PRINTS AND PHOTOGRAPHS DIVISION, WASHINGTON, DC.

During most of the nineteenth century, Emerson was the figure who most drew visitors with literary interests to Concord. But by the 1890s, Thoreau was beginning to attract such interest that Franklin Benjamin Sanborn, the last surviving member of the group of antebellum Concord Transcendentalists that had included Emerson, Thoreau, Bronson Alcott, and others, predicted that "Thoreau will continue to grow, while Emerson will become more and more of a back number." One visitor who made the pilgrimage to Walden was John Muir, who came in 1893. Muir described Walden Pond as "a beautiful lake about half a mile long, fairly embosomed like a bright dark eye in wooded hills of smooth moraine gravel and sand, and with a rich leafy undergrowth of huckleberry, willow, and young oak bushes, etc. and grass and flowers in rich variety." "No wonder," Muir thought, "Thoreau lived here two years. I could have enjoyed living here two hundred years or two thousand." During his visit, the pond was a popular bathing and picnic spot, and a busy railroad ran past its west end. But if the sounds of civilization distracted Muir from the peacefulness of the place, he didn't mention it. Even today, despite Walden's continuing popularity for picnics and hikes, it is possible to walk the trails around its shores in solitude—at least on dank and drizzly afternoons unappealing to picnickers. Visitors still leave stones on the cairn near the site where Thoreau lived. A replica of the ten-foot-by-fifteen-foot cabin stands in the parking lot, constructed principally of local hand-hewn pine.

"I know of no more encouraging fact," Thoreau wrote in *Walden*, "than the unquestionable ability of man to elevate his life by a conscious endeavor. It is something to be able to paint a particular picture, or to carve a statue, and so to make a few objects beautiful; but it is far more glorious to carve and paint the very atmosphere and medium through which we look, which morally we can do. To affect the quality of the day, that is the highest of arts." His own days were infused with "conscious endeavor" from the moment they began—with the conscious effort to see the natural world with fresh eyes—both because it was inherently fascinating, and because each part of it was a window on eternity, a microcosm of the cosmos. Thoreau quotes Confucius's instructions, "Renew thyself completely each day; do it again, and again, and forever again," and comments, "I can understand that. Morning brings back the heroic ages. I was as much affected by the faint hum of a mosquito making its invisible and unimaginable tour through my apartment at earliest dawn, when I was sitting with door and windows open, as I could be by any trumpet that ever sang of fame. It was Homer's requiem; itself an Iliad and Odyssey in the air, singing its own wrath and wanderings. There was something cosmical about it; a standing advertisement, till forbidden, of the everlasting vigor and fertility of the world." What Thoreau does so brilliantly throughout the book is evoke vivid concrete scenes of the sights and smells and sounds and feel of nature that also serve as vivid metaphors for the world beyond sensory perception—in short, for apprehensions of the divine. Making these intuitive connections was central to the Transcendentalist project of grasping the intimations of the Over-soul. But whereas others, such as Emerson, wrote philosophical tracts about Nature as a window on the world beyond the senses, Thoreau opened the window and climbed out, pulling the reader along on the adventure.

The project of writing *Walden* was less spontaneous than it looks. It began as journal entries—thousands of pages of them—which Thoreau then reshaped and revised into the text that he published years after he had ceased to live in his cabin in the woods. Typical of his artful method is this meditation that moves from a real snake to the spiritual side of man, and back to snake again, without missing a beat. On one of those "pleasant spring days" when "the winter of man's discontent was thawing as well as the earth, and the life that had lain torpid began to stretch itself," Thoreau repaired his broken axe with a wedge of fresh-cut green hickory, and "placed the whole to soak in a pond hole in order to swell the wood." Then, he writes, "I saw a striped snake run into the water, and he lay on the bottom, apparently without inconvenience, as long as I stayed there, or more than a quarter of an hour; perhaps because he had not yet fairly come out of the torpid state. It appeared to me that for a like reason men remain in their present low and primitive condition; but if they should feel the influence of the spring of springs arousing them, they would of necessity rise to a higher and more ethereal life. I had previously seen the snakes in frosty mornings in my path with portions of their bodies still numb and inflexible, waiting for the sun to thaw them."

Living "deliberately" for Thoreau requires noticing, probing, challenging, connecting, and understanding. "My instinct tells me that my head is an organ for burrowing," he writes, "as some creatures use their snout and fore-paws, and with it I would mine and burrow my way through these hills. I think that the richest vein is somewhere hereabouts; so by the divining rod and thin rising vapors I judge; and here I will begin to mine." All is what it seems—and more than it seems; everything is both itself and a metaphor for something else. But Thoreau insists on both halves of the equation all along the way—and the result is a book filled with meticulous observations of animal and plant life that often serve simultaneously as refreshing insights into one quirky human being named Henry David Thoreau, and, by extension, into the human condition. Like the (then) clear water of Walden Pond, Thoreau's often sparkling prose first quenches our thirst, and then quenches our thirst for self-knowledge. Whether we drink it or let it wash over us or gaze at the reflections on its surface, we emerge refreshed.

He combines his allegory with his agriculture in ways that allow both to keep their integrity. "This further experience also I gained. I said to myself, I will not plant beans and corn with so much industry another summer, but such seeds, if the seed is not lost, as sincerity, truth, simplicity, faith, innocence, and the like, and see if they will not grow in this soil, even with less toil and manurance, and sustain, me, for surely it has not been exhausted for these crops. Alas! I said this to myself; but now another summer is gone, and another, and another, and I am obliged to say to you, Reader, that the seeds which I planted, if indeed they *were* the seeds of those virtues, were wormeaten or had lost their vitality, and so did not come up." Later on in this passage, Thoreau makes clear what he really hopes to harvest: Why shouldn't the New Englander "not lay so much stress on his grain, his potato and grass crop, and his orchards," and "raise other crops than these? Why concern ourselves so much about our beans for seed, and not be concerned at all about a new generation of men? We should really be fed and cheered if when we met a man we were sure to see that some of the qualities which I have named . . . had taken root and grown in him. Here comes such a subtile and ineffable quality, for instance, as truth or justice. . . . Our ambassadors should be instructed to send home such seeds as these, and Congress help distribute them all over the land."

Thoreau's detailed observation—and recounting—of what he sees and what he does constantly vies with the task of improvement he has set out for himself and his reader. That the one does not force the collapse of the other is a testimony to the delicate balance he achieves in his artful prose. Watch where he goes with this description of a night of "midnight fishing from a boat by moonlight, serenaded by owls and foxes, and hearing, from time to time, the creaking note of some unknown bird close at hand." While he is drifting in the pond, "anchored in forty feet of water, and twenty or thirty rods from the shore," dragging a sixty-foot fishing line, he becomes lost in cosmic thought; now and then he feels a "slight vibration" along his line "indicative of some life prowling about its extremity, of dull uncertain blundering purpose there, and slow to make up its mind. At length you slowly raise, pulling hand over hand, some horned pout squeaking and squirming to the upper air. It was very queer, especially in dark nights, when your thoughts had wandered to vast and cosmogonal themes in other spheres, to feel this faint jerk, which came to interrupt your dreams and link you to Nature again. It seemed as if I might next cast my line upward into the air, as well as downward into this element, which was scarcely more dense. Thus I caught two fishes as it were with one hook."

Walden moves between superficial surfaces and measureless depths with a playfulness that belies its complexity. "I can assure my readers that Walden has a reasonably tight bottom a not unreasonable, though an unusual, depth," Thoreau writes.

"I fathomed it easily with a cod-line and a stone weighing about a pound and a half, and could tell accurately when the stone left the bottom, by having to pull so much harder before the water got underneath to help me. The greatest depth was exactly one hundred and two feet; to which may be added the five feet which it has risen since, making one hundred and seven. This is a remarkable depth for so small an area; yet not an inch of it can be spared by the imagination. What if all ponds were shallow? Would it not react on the minds of men? I am thankful that this pond was made deep and pure for a symbol."

"The life in us is like the water in the river," he writes. "It may rise this year higher than man has ever known it, and flood the parched uplands." His best metaphors are truly organic, made of found natural materials that surround him; they use felicities of the language itself (the word "higher," for example, having both physical and spiritual connotations) to achieve their end. They vivify his vision of an interdependent ecological system of many life forms of which humans are just one.

While the grace with which Thoreau celebrates the natural world as a source of physical and spiritual sustenance has won him many admirers and disciples, the arrogance and hypocrisy of some of his rants against the work ethic and the materialism that allegedly drives it, and against technology, have led others to question whether *Walden* may be less self-aware and honest than its author aspired to make it. For example, one of Thoreau's favorite topics is the life of "quiet desperation" he sees his fellow citizens living all around him, their lives driven by the need to acquire money to purchase goods that they don't really need. Another favorite topic is the way in which technological advances may not be advances after all, but impositions instead. But pause for a moment to recall all those allusions to the classics that dot every page of *Walden*, all those allusions to literature and philosophy and natural history and political history. Where did Thoreau learn all this? At Harvard College. Who paid for Thoreau's Harvard education? His father, who ran a pencil factory; his mother, who took in boarders to help make ends meet; and his older brother and sister—both schoolteachers who had not had the privilege of going to Harvard themselves, but who contributed money from their teaching salaries to pay their brother's expenses—which at the time were about $180 a year. Thoreau studied Latin and Greek and also took classes in English, history, mathematics, philosophy, Italian, French, German, and Spanish. He was wont to complain about the teaching methods. Supposedly, when Emerson observed that most of the branches of learning were taught at Harvard, Thoreau is supposed to have replied, "Yes, all of the branches and none of the roots." But grumble as he might, he learned a great deal from his years at college. The contempt he shows for the hard work on the part of his parents and siblings who earned the money that allowed him to attend college is ungenerous.

For Thoreau's Harvard education gave him more than a basic grounding in subjects that he would draw on for the rest of his life as a writer: it gave him access to the University Library—a truly priceless privilege. Emerson recalled (in his eulogy for Thoreau) that on one occasion Thoreau "went to the University Library to procure some books. The Librarian refused to lend them. Mr. Thoreau repaired to the President, who stated to him the rules and usages which permitted the loan of books to resident graduates, to clergymen who were alumni, and to some others resident within a circle of ten miles' radius from the college. Mr. Thoreau explained to the President that the railroad had destroyed the old scale of distances." The rules made no sense, Thoreau maintained, in the face of this fact. And his need for books—many books—was imperative. Emerson tells us that "the President found the petitioner so formidable and the rules getting to look so ridiculous, that he ended by giving him a privilege which in his hands proved unlimited thereafter." Note that the same Thoreau known for having complained that "the panting of the locomotive" interrupted his dreams, here cited it as a welcome technological advance, a means by which distances cease to have the meaning they once had—and a means of arguing for his right to borrow books from the Harvard library.

Far from being hostile to technological innovation, Thoreau was, instead, responsible for some notable ones himself. He invented a machine that ground graphite into a very fine powder, developed a formula for mixing ground graphite and clay, and improved the method for enclosing the graphite in a casing. The result was a pencil that wrote in smooth lines—the best pencil in America, and the only one that came up to the standards of those made by the leading European manufacturer, the German company Faber. As a result of these technological innovations, the Thoreau family pencil business flourished. The food on the table at the many meals that Thoreau ate at home while he was supposedly "living" in Walden Woods, as well as during the years after his experiment was concluded, was purchased with what his family earned from the pencil factory—the fruits of both technology and that much-maligned work ethic.

Thoreau's contempt for material goods has struck many readers as appealing and engaging: clearly most of us have much that we do not need, and could manage just as well with less. ("Most of the luxuries, and many of the so-called comforts of life, are not only not indispensable, but positive hindrances to the elevation of mankind," he writes.) But Thoreau has some blind spots on this front. "When I have met an immigrant tottering under a bundle which contained his all—looking like an enormous wen which had grown out of the nape of his neck—I have pitied him, not because that was his all, but because he had all *that* to carry." He then asserts the virtue of traveling light. But what if selling bits of "all *that*" is all the immigrant can do to feed his family, lacking (unlike Thoreau), literacy, language skills, connections, land to farm, and all the other things that ease one's way in this world? By ignoring the priceless advantages that are his by virtue of being born into a middle-class, English-speaking, well-connected, manufacturing family in Concord that can afford to send him to college, Thoreau can be blithely dismissive of material goods that might mean the difference between starving or surviving for a less-favored individual. He can also be less than forthcoming about his own material circumstances: despite the meticulous accounts he kept of his food budget ("Rice $1.73 1/2; Molasses $1.73; Rye meal $1.04 3/4"), he fails to even mention, let alone price, the value of the frequent meals he ate at his family's home and at the homes of friends, ignoring the role they played in his nutrition (supplying variety his normal diet did not) as well as in his budget.

It is striking that also absent from *Walden* is any reference to an embarrassing incident that occurred one year before Thoreau began to build his cabin. In April 1844, Thoreau accidentally set fire to Concord Woods and burned down three hundred acres. The incident—which was widely covered in the local press, which chastised Thoreau severely for his carelessness—was especially awkward for a young man aspiring to be a budding naturalist and respectful interpreter of nature. It is rather startling that a Thoreau determined to "require of every writer, first or last, a simple and sincere account of his own life" finds it so easy to fail to mention, much less discuss, this act of destruction on a rather massive scale. The author of the most famous tribute to Concord woodlands turns out also to have been responsible for one of the most damaging forest fires Concord had ever seen.

Yet despite the hypocrisy and the arrogance, despite all the pride and posturing and pretentiousness, *Walden* has managed to be a book that does exactly what it sets out to do—encourage us to "live deliberately," and to be aware of the miraculous freshness of every day. No other book in American literary history has provided as much impetus for the "conscious endeavor" of fronting the "essential facts" of nature in all their concrete as well as symbolic dimensions. *Walden* and Thoreau's other works have inspired generations of American writers to front the facts of the world around them and commit to paper what they see, what they feel, and what they learn, however nonconformist and individualistic those lessons may be. (*Walden* asserts, "If a man does not keep pace with his companions, perhaps it is because he hears a different drummer. Let him step to the music which he hears, however measured or far away.") Thoreau's influence extends beyond the United States as well: Russian novelist Leo Tolstoy, for example, who was instrumental in publishing the first Russian translations of Thoreau's works, was known to refer to *Walden* daily.

Thoreau was a key precursor for John Burroughs, the country's leading essayist on nature at the turn of the century, as well as for a host of late-twentieth-century writers. Autobiographical narratives inspired by Thoreau include Edward Abbey's 1968 *Desert Solitaire* (set in Utah), Annie Dillard's 1974 *Pilgrim at Tinker Creek* (set in Virginia's Blue Ridge Mountains), and Anne LaBastille's 2000 *Woodswoman II: Beyond Black Bear Lake* (set in the Adirondacks). Many other American writers also chose to follow Thoreau's example in their writing lives, if not in their personal lives, creating essays, novels, poems, and book-length nonfiction narratives informed by his respect for the ecology of the natural world and his attentiveness to the details of plant and animal life. Thoreau helped inspire twentieth-century nature writers Peter Matthiessen and Terry Tempest Williams, essayist E. B. White, and poet-novelists N. Scott Momaday and Linda Hogan, among others.

When American writers extol simplicity, eschew materialism, and urge their readers to live in harmony with nature; when they urge readers to avoid falling into mental ruts, to learn to perceive the world around

Henry David Thoreau (1817–1862). *Walden*, Thoreau's artfully crafted and deceptively simple account of his efforts to "live deliberately, to front only the essential facts of life" on the shores of Walden Pond, continues to have an impact on how Americans view the natural world and the importance of preserving it for future generations. PHOTO CREDIT: COURTESY OF THE NATIONAL PORTRAIT GALLERY, SMITHSONIAN INSTITUTION/ ART RESOURCE, NY.

them freshly each day; when they behold animals with rapt attentiveness; when they celebrate the restorative power of paying attention to all that grows, of taking time to observe the seasons, the weather, the details of landscape and the multiple life forms that fill it, and of letting those observations propel the metaphors that make their work worth reading—chances are an early encounter with *Walden* or other work by Thoreau may be lurking in the background, quietly encouraging them along this path. We might listen for echoes of Thoreau in William Carlos Williams's poem "Spring and All," where the poet explores in vividly concrete terms ("the stiff curl of wildcarrot leaf") the miracle of rebirth—of new shoots pushing their way up through dead, brown leaves and leafless vines as the roots of the plant world "grip down and begin to awaken" in spring; or in Wendell Berry's sense that

"In the stillness of the trees / I am at home" in his poem "Stay Home." We might find resonances of some of what Thoreau has learned about himself by paying close attention to animals, in Annie Dillard's meditation on weasels in *Teaching a Stone to Talk*, or in Aldo Leopold's response to watching "the green fire die" in the eyes of a wounded wolf in *Sand County Almanac*, or in Wallace Stevens's meditations in "Thirteen Ways of Looking at a Blackbird." When we read (in the poem "Peril of Hope") Robert Frost's lines, "It's right in there / Betwixt and between / The orchard bare / And the orchard green, / When the boughs are right / In a flowery burst / Of pink and white / That we fear the worst," we might recall Thoreau's deep belief in nature as a source of insight into the human soul and psyche. And we might sense some of Thoreau's disdain for the materialism that drives Western culture in Barry Lopez's urgent call, in *The Rediscovery of North America*, that our survival requires moving beyond "the quest for personal possessions" that fueled the European exploration of North America. (In *Walden*, Thoreau had urged his reader to "Be a Columbus to whole new continents and worlds within you, opening new channels, not of trade, but of thought.")

Thoreau may have had as great an impact on American nonfiction prose in general as he did on nature writing. William Howarth credits Thoreau with having launched an American tradition of creative journalism that has produced writers as different as James Agee, John McPhee, Joan Didion, and Norman Mailer. "His career," Howarth writes, "stands as a reminder to readers that no fact is trivial, if seen in the proper light—and with an observant eye."

One reader attracted by both Thoreau's message and his method was E. B. White. Scott Elledge, White's biographer, tells us that White referred to Thoreau "more often than to any other writer," and often "echoed him in thought and style." White himself tells us that he had a relationship to *Walden* that he had to no other book on his shelves. He shared Thoreau's belief in the importance of taking the time to "observe and feel" the world around you. He viewed *Walden*, Elledge tells us, "not as a sermon or an attempt to rearrange society," but (as White put it in his essay, "A Slight Sound at Evening") "the best youth's companion yet written in America." It is, White writes, "like an invitation to life's dance, assuring the troubled recipient that no matter what befalls him in the way of success or failure he will always be welcome at the party—that the music is played for him, too, if he will but listen and move his feet." A hundred years after Walden was published, White wrote that he still reread "with undiminished excitement" Thoreau's "famous invitation," which "will beckon as long as this remarkable book stays in print."

And if White was attracted to what Thoreau said, he was equally attracted to Thoreau's way of saying it. In one of his "Notes and Comment" essays, White once wrote, "May 6th is the saddest day in the year for us, as it is the day of Thoreau's death—a grief from which we have not recovered. Henry Thoreau has probably been more wildly misconstrued than any other person of comparable literary stature. He got a reputation for being a naturalist, and he was not much of a naturalist. He got a reputation for being a hermit, and he was no hermit. He was a writer, is what he was." White's own writing—and his philosophy of writing—demonstrate how much he learned from Thoreau. When White was invited in 1957 to revise a booklet on writing published decades earlier by his old college professor William Strunk Jr., White extolled ideals of writing that he had thought about in connection with Thoreau. The novice, White wrote, "should begin by turning resolutely away from all devices that are popularly believed to indicate style—all mannerisms, tricks, adornments. The approach to style is by way of plainness, simplicity, orderliness, sincerity." Like *Walden*, *The Elements of Style* by Strunk and White was a deceptively simple book that blended sharp observation, clear prose, humor, and insight to help readers learn to become better writers. By the early 1980s, the book had sold more than five and a half million copies and was required reading in literally thousands of college English courses across the country. Thus students who may or may not have read Thoreau themselves ended up encountering him—through White's slim, ubiquitous book about writing—as their freshman writing teacher.

Thoreau wrote in *Walden*, "Sometimes, in a summer morning, having taken my accustomed bath, I sat in my sunny doorway from sunrise till noon, rapt in a revery, amidst the pines and hickories and sumachs, in undisturbed solitude and stillness, while the birds sing around or flitted noiseless through the house, until by the sun falling in at my west window, or the noise of some traveller's wagon on the distant highway, I was reminded of the lapse of time. I grew in those seasons like corn in the night, and they were far better than any work of the hands would have been. They were not time subtracted from my life, but so much over and above my usual allowance. . . . This was sheer idleness to my fellow-townsmen, no doubt; but if the birds and flowers had tried me by their standard, I should not have been found wanting." Almost a century and a half since Thoreau wrote those words, the challenge of viewing ourselves as part of a larger ecological system of plant and animal life is still fresh; far from being a simple or idle project, learning how to live in harmony with nature turns out to be both necessary for our survival and more complicated than we supposed.

OLD CONCORD JAIL MARKER

CORNER OF MAIN AND LOWELL, CONCORD MONUMENT
SQUARE HISTORIC DISTRICT, CONCORD, MASSACHUSETTS

One day in July 1846, while he was living at Walden Pond, Henry David Thoreau went into town to pick up a pair of shoes he was having resoled and found himself arrested and thrown in jail for nonpayment of the poll tax that every Concord voter was required to pay. A relative quickly paid the tax for him (much to his irritation), but since the jailer had already retired for the night, Thoreau spent the night in the jail that stood on the corner of Main and Lowell in Concord (a plaque marks the spot where it stood). He was released the next day.

In 1848, Thoreau pondered the rationale for the act that led to his night in jail in a lecture on "The Rights and Duties of the Individual in Relation to Government" that he gave at the Concord Lyceum to an attentive audience. Several months later, he published a version of his lecture as "Resistance to Civil Government." Readers in the twentieth century would come to know it as "Civil Disobedience." It would be one of the most influential essays by an American, and would play a key role in shaping both the independence movement in India and the civil rights movement in the United States.

Thoreau tells us that he refused to pay the poll tax because he did not want his money to be used to support a government that supported slavery and that would use tax money to support the Mexican War, which would extend slavery even further. Technically, the poll tax was a local Concord tax, rather than one that would support the national government—but as the passage of the Fugitive Slave Law a few years later clearly showed, all the layers of government, from local to national, were interconnected when it came to upholding and enforcing the law, affirming the reasoning behind Thoreau's boycott of a local tax to protest a national policy. He was not the first person in Concord to refuse to pay the poll tax, nor was he the first member of his family to express opposition to slavery. Several years earlier, his friend and neighbor Bronson Alcott had refused to pay the poll tax, noting that "this act of non-resistance . . .does not rest on the plea of poverty," but rather "is founded on the moral instinct which forbids every moral being to be a party, either actively or permissively, to the destructive principles of power and might over peace and love." Thoreau's mother, Cynthia, had been active in local antislavery activities. But the eloquence with which Thoreau articulated the rationale behind his passive resistance to government policy would give his essay the impact it has had for more than 150 years.

"Must the citizen ever for a moment, or in the least degree, resign his conscience to the legislator?" he asked. "Why has every man a conscience then? I think that we should be men first, and subjects afterward." The notion that each individual had the responsibility of listening to his conscience as well as to his government was one that would strike a responsive chord for many in the century that followed—including, most notably, Mahatma Gandhi and Martin Luther King Jr. "How does it become a man to behave toward the American government today? I answer, that he cannot without disgrace be associated with it. I cannot for an instant recognize that political organization as my government which is the slave's government also," he maintained.

Writing from Concord, the cradle of the American Revolution, Thoreau felt particularly confident in asserting, "All men recognize the right of revolution; that is, the right to refuse allegiance to, and to resist, the government, when its tyranny or its inefficiency are great and unendurable." He argued that citizens could not absolve themselves of the evil perpetrated by their government by claiming no responsibility for their government's acts; if they paid taxes, they tacitly supported those acts.

> Practically speaking, the opponents to a reform in Massachusetts are not a hundred thousand politicians at the South, but a hundred thousand merchants and farmers here, who are more interested in commerce and agriculture than they are in humanity. . . . There are thousands who are in opinion opposed to slavery and to the war, who yet in effect do nothing to put an end to them; who, esteeming themselves children of Washington and Franklin, sit down with their hands in their pockets, and say that they know not what to do, and do nothing; who even postpone the question of freedom to the question of free trade, and quietly read the prices-current along with the latest advices from Mexico, after dinner, and, it may be, fall asleep over them both.

Thoreau did not believe that it was "a man's duty, as a matter of course, to devote himself to the eradication of any, even to most enormous, wrong; he may still properly have other concerns to engage him; but it is his duty, at least, to wash his hands of it, and, if he gives it no thought longer, not to give it practically his support. If I devote myself to other pursuits and contemplations, I must first see, at least, that I do not pursue them sitting upon another man's shoulders. I must get off him first, that he may pursue his contemplations too." We are complicit in each other's lives, and fates, he insisted. If our tax dollars support injustice, then we ourselves help perpetrate that injustice. "Unjust laws exist," he asserted. "Shall we be content to obey them, or shall we endeavor to amend them, and obey them until we have succeeded, or shall we transgress them at once?" If injustice is "of such a nature that it requires you to be the agent of injustice to another, then I say, break the law." Thoreau chose to break the law and pay the penalty (a night in jail), thereby modeling for future generations a strategy for challenging both unjust laws and the system that supports them.

Mahatma Gandhi wrote to his friend Henry S. Salt that he had been introduced to Thoreau's ideas on this subject around 1907, when he was "in the thick of" the "passive resistance struggle" for India's independence. "A friend sent me Thoreau's essay on civil disobedience. It left a deep impression upon me. I translated a portion of that essay for readers of *Indian Opinion* in South Africa which I was then editing, and I made copious extracts from that essay for that paper." Gandhi found the essay "so convincing and truthful" that he sought out other work by Thoreau, including *Walden* and other short essays, which he "read with great pleasure and equal profit." Thoreau helped inspire the massive resistance movement that Gandhi organized against the British occupation of India. "Civil Disobedience" also helped inspire Rev. Martin Luther King Jr. to launch the many acts of passive resistance that helped mobilize national support for the civil rights movement in the 1950s and 1960s. In addition, Thoreau's ideas played a role in antiwar movement during the Vietnam War, framing the terms in which many of the conscientious objectors to the war articulated their dissent. Often invoked whenever individuals are moved to protest unjust laws by breaking them and accepting the penalty of going to jail, Thoreau has continued to bear out the truth of a comment the critic F. O. Matthiessen made about him in 1941: "His vitality as a revolutionary is still unexhausted."

RELATED SITES

➥ Thoreau-Alcott House
255 Main Street, Concord, Massachusetts

Henry David Thoreau moved here in 1850, several years after he concluded his experiment at Walden Pond, and the year that he published his first book, *A Week on the Concord and Merrimack Rivers*. He lived in this house until his death in 1862. It was while he was living here that he wrote and published *Walden*, as well as the

1854 essay "Slavery in Massachusetts." In 1877, Louisa May Alcott used some of the money she had earned as an author to purchase the house in which her old friend had lived and install her family here. She was living here when she wrote *Jo's Boys* (1886), a sequel to *Little Women* (1868). Both Thoreau and Alcott took an active role in designing, supervising, and, in the case of Thoreau, actually building, additions to the house that may still be seen there today.

John Thoreau and his son Henry completely renovated and refurbished the two-story clapboard house on Main Street when they bought it. The original structure (built by a prominent Concord builder named Josiah Davis) was almost square; it had two inside chimneys and four rooms on each floor. Henry and his father built a portico supported by Doric columns over the front door and an elegant mahogany railing for the main staircase; they added a new two-story wing to the south of the house with a fieldstone foundation, finished basement, and attached shed. Their pencil factory was housed in the new wing. They also added doors connecting the south wing to the rest of the house. With four bedrooms, a large kitchen, two parlors, and a reception room, this was the grandest house the Thoreaus ever lived in, one that the success of the family pencil business allowed them to buy. Henry planted a flower and vegetable garden at the back of the house and gave annual melon parties for friends and neighbors during the summer. He built bookshelves for his collections of arrowheads, birds' eggs, and wildflowers along the low walls of the third-floor attic, and set up his cot and simple furnishings there. It was here that he did his writing, during those times when his help was not required at the pencil factory. The pencils—each of which sold for twenty-five cents in Boston—were completed via a secret process in the privacy of the second floor of the south wing. Henry and his sister Sophia were the only business employees allowed to finish the pencils, which were regarded as the finest in the country.

This was a highly productive period in Thoreau's life as a writer. In addition to *Walden*, he also published both "Excursion to Canada" (1853) and "Cape Cod" (1855) in *Putnam's Monthly*, as well as other articles in the *Atlantic Monthly* and the *Liberator*, while giving lectures around Concord, and in Philadelphia, Providence, and Nantucket. He delivered his strongest criticism of slavery in 1854 in his lecture "Slavery in Massachusetts," and developed intense admiration for militant abolitionist John Brown, who visited him here in 1857. Thoreau was devastated by Brown's hanging two years later following the raid he masterminded on the federal arsenal at Harpers Ferry, Virginia (now West Virginia). Thoreau's essay "The Last Days of John Brown" appeared in 1860. (The small green desk on which Thoreau wrote *Walden* and other works is on display at the Concord Museum, 200 Lexington Road, Concord, Massachusetts.)

When Louisa May Alcott helped her widowed sister Anna Alcott Pratt buy the house in 1877, the family consisted of her sister Anna and her children; her father, the philosopher Bronson Alcott; and her ailing mother (the "Marmee" of *Little Women*), who died here within the year. Although Louisa May Alcott maintained a residence in Boston during this period, she spent a lot of time in this house as well, and added a new wing, as the Thoreaus had. Alcott supervised the building of a two-story wing to the west of the original portion of the house, which contained a library on the first floor and a bedroom with an arched cathedral ceiling on the second floor. She also added a porch, which wrapped around the south wall of the new addition, converted the house's attic into four bedrooms, and made the second floor of the wing that had housed the pencil factory into a bedroom and storage space.

Her best-selling books enabled Alcott to buy this handsome house for her family—one to which she had additional sentimental attachment, given its connection to Thoreau. As a girl, she had idolized Thoreau, who was fifteen years her senior. She had looked forward to those occasions when the older writer lectured at the rustic, wooden School of Philosophy that her father had built behind Orchard House, the Alcotts' earlier Concord home, or when Thoreau shared his knowledge of Concord's rich plant and animal life with her.

Alcott's first national fame came with the publication of her 1863 book, *Hospital Sketches*, a wrenching, realistic account of her experiences as a nurse at the Union Hotel Hospital in Georgetown. (The book was a complete departure from both the lurid and violent "blood-and-thunder" stories she had published previously under the pseudonym A. M. Barnard, and her first book, *Flower Fables*, "legends of faery land," published in 1855 and dedicated to Ralph Waldo Emerson's daughter Ellen.) Alcott followed *Hospital Sketches* with her first novel, *Moods*, in 1865, a book whose title alluded to Emerson's comment, "Life is a train of moods like a string of beads."

Since her father—famed for his bold intellect and innovative ideas as an educator—was hopeless as a family provider, Alcott decided to assume the role of family breadwinner. In 1868, while she was editing a monthly magazine for children, a Boston publisher asked her to write a book for girls. *Little Women*, which appeared between 1868 and 1869, was her response. It was a huge success. While autobiographical in many ways, the household Alcott portrayed in *Little Women* was less quirky and more stable than her own precarious living arrangements had been during her childhood. The wholesome, engaging, realistic, and psychologically astute portrait of the growth and development of four sisters, based on Alcott and her own sisters, was a dramatically new departure in juvenile literature and appealed to young women all over the country, allowing Alcott to pay off her family's debts. She continued to publish other books based loosely on her (real or imagined) family life until her death in 1888, although none approached *Little Women* in popularity. The so-called Little Women series included *An Old-Fashioned Girl* in 1870; *Aunt Jo's Scrap Bag*, six volumes of which appeared between 1872 and 1883; *Little Men* (1871); *Eight Cousins* (1875); *Rose in Bloom* (1876); and *Jo's Boys* (1886). In 1873, Alcott published *Work: A Story of Experience*, a protofeminist novel that came out of her efforts to support herself as a seamstress, a domestic, a teacher, and a companion to an invalid before hitting her stride as a professional author who would pen nearly three hundred books, articles, poems, and stories, including some gothic fiction not brought to print until the 1990s.

A supporter, like Thoreau, of the antislavery movement, Alcott was also a supporter of women's suffrage, and was the first woman to cast a ballot in Concord—a symbolic act only: it could not be counted, because women were denied the vote until 1920.

Both wings of the Thoreau-Alcott house look much as they did when they were first built—Thoreau's portico is still there, as is Alcott's graceful porch. Most of the windows contain the original glass through which Thoreau and Alcott observed the changing seasons and the comings and goings of family and friends.

•❖ Sleepy Hollow Cemetery
Bedford Street, Massachusetts Route 62, Concord, Massachusetts

Henry David Thoreau, who died on May 6, 1862, is buried here, on Authors' Ridge, alongside other members of his family and the Hawthorne, Emerson, and Alcott families. The plain, eight-by-seven-inch gravestone reads simply, "Henry."

•❖ Orchard House
399 Lexington Road, Concord, Massachusetts

Louisa May Alcott wrote the first volume of *Little Women* in this house between May and July 1868. Her father, Bronson Alcott, had bought this property for his family in 1857 with money donated by Ralph Waldo Emerson and other friends. The ten-acre property included a seventeenth-century farmhouse and a tenant house, which Bronson Alcott connected into one house. His book-lined study was located to the left of the front center hall, while a front parlor was on the right; behind the study was a north-facing studio with skylights for the artistic youngest daughter, May. Feverish and dangerously ill as a result of her work in a Union hospital during the Civil War, Louisa returned to Orchard House to recuperate. After her chills and pain had subsided (she would never recover completely), she began writing again. At the semicircular shelf-desk in the wall between the two front windows in her bedroom, she edited her Washington letters into *Hospital Sketches* and wrote the first volume of *Little Women*. (She wrote the second volume in a furnished room in Boston's South End, where the burdens of running Orchard House didn't intrude.) She had been living here when Thoreau died in 1862. She wrote in a poem titled "Thoreau's Flute," "our Pan is dead; / His pipe hangs mute / . . . The Wisdom of a just content / Made one small spot a continent." (The flute itself is on permanent display at the Concord Museum, 200 Lexington Avenue, Concord.) Alcott presciently predicted to a friend "that though his life seemed too short, it would blossom and bear fruit long after he was gone." Louisa May Alcott reshingled Orchard House with some of the money she earned from *Hospital Sketches*, and few years later, the commercial success of *Little Women* brought her enough money to buy a furnace to heat it. Most of the furnishings on display belonged to the Alcott family.

❧ Ralph Waldo Emerson House

28 Cambridge Turnpike, near intersection with Lexington Road, Concord, Massachusetts

In 1835, at the time of his second marriage, the Transcendentalist essayist, poet, and philosopher Ralph Waldo Emerson purchased this large, two-story frame and clapboard house built in 1828–1829 by John T. Coolidge. He lived here until his death in 1882, and it was here, in his ground-floor study, that he wrote all of his best-known works, including *Nature* (1836), "The American Scholar" (1837), the two-volume *Essays* (1841, 1844), *Representative Men* (1850), and *English Traits* (1856). In these and other writings, he explored the idea of a world in which self-reliant, free individuals would be guided by their immediate and intuitive apprehension of the divine within themselves and in the world around them.

His books often urged his readers to be skeptical of books, encouraging them to seek truth on their own: "Meek young men grow up in libraries, believing it their duty to accept the views, which Cicero, which Locke, which Bacon, have given, forgetful that Cicero, Locke, and Bacon were only young men in libraries, when they wrote these books. . . . Books are for the scholar's idle times. When he can read God directly, the hour is too precious to be wasted in other men's transcripts of their readings." Books, Emerson believed, "are for nothing but to inspire. I had better never see a book, than to be warped by its attraction clean out of my own orbit, and made a satellite instead of a system." Sitting in his first-floor study, he wrote books designed to push his readers out into the world beyond books, with such comments as: "The world,—this shadow of the soul, or other me, lies wide around. Its attractions are the keys which unlock my thoughts and make me acquainted with myself. . . . I do not see how any man can afford, for the sake of his nerves and his nap, to spare any action in which he can partake. It is pearls and rubies to his discourse."

Thoreau, who would become his most famous disciple, was an almost daily visitor here, as well as a sometime handyman and gardener. He also lived in the house for several months during two winters when Emerson was out of town, and the Emerson children came to think of him as a member of the family. The garden behind the house looks much as it did when Emerson lived here, and the wooden barn is the original structure. Emerson's study is on the ground floor of the house, along with the dining room, kitchen, and guest room (where his four children were born), and there are four bedrooms upstairs. Writers who visited Emerson here included, in addition to Thoreau, Nathaniel Hawthorne, Margaret Fuller, and Emma Lazarus. When a fire that started in the attic damaged much of the house in 1872, Emerson's friends donated funds to completely rebuild it. (Most of the contents had been rescued.) All of the rooms remain furnished today as they were after the 1872–1873 restoration, with the exception of Emerson's study, which is furnished with duplicates of the original pieces (the originals are preserved at the Concord Museum).

☙ Margaret Fuller House
71 Cherry Street, Cambridge, Massachusetts

Margaret Fuller, author of the feminist classic *Woman in the Nineteenth Century* (1845), editor of the Transcendalist publication the *Dial*, and a friend and colleague of both Thoreau and Emerson, lived in this three-story, Federal-style house until age sixteen. It is now a community center.

☙ Yosemite National Park
Yosemite Village, California

Thoreau never traveled to Yosemite. But his words played a key role in inspiring naturalist and writer John Muir to work tirelessly for the preservation of this area of natural beauty, which became the second National Park in 1890. Muir read *Walden* when a friend sent him the book as a gift in 1872. He returned to it often over the course of his life, filling it with underlining and annotations. His friend Henry Fairfield Osborn called Muir "a very firm believer in Thoreau" and thought the two men had many qualities in common. But while Muir shared Thoreau's passion for wilderness preservation, Muir's focus was on preserving a place much wilder than Walden Pond, as is clear from this description he wrote of Yosemite Falls:

Reading *Walden* helped inspire naturalist John Muir to devote his life to preserving wilderness. Muir is pictured here with Theodore Roosevelt on Glacier Point, Yosemite Valley, California, in 1903.

Now and then one mighty throb sends forth a mass of solid water into the free air far beyond the others, which rushes alone to the bottom of the fall with long streaming tail, like combed silk, while the others, descending in clusters, gradually mingle and lose their identity. But they all rush past us with amazing velocity and display of power. . . . The heads of these comet-like masses are composed of nearly solid water, and are dense white in color like pressed snow. . . . At the bottom of the fall . . . is mostly a hissing, clashing, seething, upwhirling mass of scud and spray, through which the light sifts in gray and purple tones, while at times when the sun strikes at the required angle, the whole wild and apparently lawless, stormy, striving mass is changed to brilliant rainbow hues, manifesting finest harmony.

Thoreau's prose was a constant inspiration to the man who did so much to make it possible for us to visit Yosemite today. One can also honor the memory of this visionary naturalist with a visit to the towering grove of coastal redwoods named for him, the Muir Woods National Monument near San Francisco, and the John Muir National Historic Site in Martinez, California, Muir's home from 1890 until his death in 1914.

●◆ Bryce Canyon National Park
Utah Route 63, Bryce Canyon, Utah

Henry David Thoreau is a living presence in today's national parks. Two framed quotations from Thoreau's journals hang permanently in the kiosk along the Bristlecone Trail in Bryce Canyon National Park in southern Utah, on a hilltop overlooking a wilderness that includes cliffs and pinnacles, vast forests of ancient pines, and thousands of stone hoodoos as far as the eye can see: "I need solitude. I have come forth to this hill . . . to see the forms of the mountains on the horizon—to behold and commune with something grander than man" (*Journals*, August 14, 1854); and "Silence alone is worthy to be heard" (*Journals*, January 21, 1853).

FOR FURTHER READING

The Writers: Works and Words

Abbey, Edward. *Desert Solitaire*. Tucson: University of Arizona Press, 1988.

Alcott, Louisa May. *Alternative Alcott*. Edited by Elaine Showalter. New Brunswick, NJ: Rutgers University Press, 1988.

———. *Little Women*. Edited by Valerie Anderson. New York: Oxford University Press, 1994.

Anderson, Lorraine, Scott Slovic, and John P. Grady, eds. *Literature and the Environment: A Reader on Nature and Culture*. New York: Longman, 1999.

Berry, Wendell. *New Collected Poems*. Berkeley, CA: Counterpoint, 2012.

Burroughs, John. *The Art of Seeing Things: Essays*. Edited by Charlotte Zoe Walker. Syracuse, NY: Syracuse University Press, 2001.

Dillard, Annie. *Pilgrim at Tinker Creek*. New York: Harper's Magazine Press, 1974.

———. *Teaching a Stone to Talk*. New York: Harper and Row, 1982.

Emerson, Ralph Waldo. *Essays and Lectures*. Edited by Joel Porte. New York: Library of America, 1983.

Frost, Robert. *The Poetry of Robert Frost: The Collected Poems*. Edited by Edward Connery Lathern. 2nd rev. ed. New York: Holt, 2002.

Fuller, Margaret. *The Essential Margaret Fuller*. Edited by Jeffrey Steele. New Brunswick, NJ: Rutgers University Press, 1992.

LaBastille, Anne. *Woodswoman II: Beyond Black Bear Lake*. New York: W. W. Norton, 2000.

Leopold, Aldo. *A Sand County Almanac*. New York: Oxford University Press, 1949.

Lopez, Barry. *The Rediscovery of North America*. Lexington: University Press of Kentucky, 1990.

Muir, John. *The Wilderness World of John Muir*. Edited by Edwin Way Teale. Boston: Houghton Mifflin, 1954.

Snyder, Gary. *Earth House Hold*. New York: W. W. Norton, 1969.

———. *Turtle Island*. New York: W. W. Norton, 1974.

Strunk, William. *The Elements of Style: With Revisions, an Introduction, and a New Chapter on Writing by E. B. White*. New York: Macmillan, 1959.

Thoreau, Henry David. *Collected Essays and Poems*. Edited by Elizabeth Hall Witherell. New York: Library of America, 2001.

———. *A Week, Walden, The Maine Woods, Cape Cod*. Edited by Robert F. Sayre. New York: Library of America, 1985.

———. *The Writings of Henry David Thoreau: Journal*, Vol. 1: *1837–1844*. Edited by Elizabeth Witherell, William L. Howarth, Robert Sattelmeyer, and Thomas Blanding. Princeton, NJ: Princeton University Press, 1981.

———. *The Writings of Henry David Thoreau: Journal*, Vol. 2: *1842–1848*. Edited by Robert Sattelmeyer. Princeton, NJ: Princeton University Press, 1984.

Williams, William Carlos. *Collected Poems of William Carlos Williams*. Vol. 1, *1909–1939*. Edited by A. Walton Litz and Christopher MacGowan. Reprint ed. New York: New Directions, 1991.

Backgrounds and Contexts

Barksdale, Maynard. *Walden Pond: A History*. New York: Oxford University Press, 2004.

Buell, Laurence. *The Environmental Imagination: Thoreau, Nature Writing, and the Formation of American Culture*. Cambridge, MA: Harvard University Press, 1995.

Cain, William E., ed. *A Historical Guide to Henry David Thoreau*. New York: Oxford University Press, 2000.

Elledge, Scott. *E. B. White: A Biography*. New York: W. W. Norton, 1984.

Harding, Walter. *The Days of Henry Thoreau.* 1965, rev. 1982. Reprint, with new afterword, Princeton, NJ: Princeton University Press, 1992.

Henley, Don, and Dave Marsh, eds. *Heaven Is under Our Feet: A Book for Walden Woods.* Stamford, CT: Longmeadow Press, 1991.

Howarth, William. *The Book of Concord: Thoreau's Life as a Writer.* New York: Viking Press, 1982.

Myerson, Joel, ed. *The Cambridge Companion to Henry David Thoreau.* New York: Cambridge University Press, 1995.

———. *Critical Essays on Henry David Thoreau's "Walden."* Boston: G. K. Hall, 1988.

———. *A Historical Guide to Ralph Waldo Emerson.* New York: Oxford University Press, 2000.

Richardson, Robert D., Jr. *Henry Thoreau: A Life of the Mind.* Berkeley: University of California Press, 1986.

Salt, Henry S.. *Life of Henry David Thoreau.* Edited by George Hendrick, Willene Hendrick, and Fritz Oehlschlaeger. Urbana: University of Illinois Press, 1993.

Stern, Philip Van Doren, ed. *Th Collected Poems of William Carlos Williams Annotated "Walden."* New York: Clarkson N. Potter, 1970.

The Rotch-Jones-Duff House, 396 County Street, New Bedford, Massachusetts. This Greek Revival mansion, one of the "brave houses and flowery gardens" that Melville describes in *Moby-Dick*, was built in 1834 for a whaling merchant with strong antislavery sympathies. It is the only whaling mansion in New England that is open to the public.

3

Freedom's Port

From the start, the sea had played a role in Frederick Douglass's sense of what freedom meant—or could mean—for a slave like himself. In his 1845 *Narrative of the Life of Frederick Douglass, an American Slave*, he recalls that when he was boy in Baltimore, his "house stood within a few rods of the Chesapeake Bay, whose broad bosom was ever white with sails from every quarter of the habitable globe." "Those beautiful vessels, robed in purest white, so delightful to the eye of freemen," Douglass writes, "were to me so many shrouded ghosts, to terrify and torment me with thoughts of my wretched condition." His soul would cry out to the ships, "You are loosed from your moorings, and are free; I am fast in my chains, and am a slave! You move merrily before the gentle gale, and I sadly before the bloody whip! You are freedom's swift-winged angels that fly round the world; I am confined in bands of iron! O that I were free!"

Douglass learned the caulking trade and spent much of his early life gazing with envy at the ships that were so much freer than he was. When he finally made his break for freedom in 1838, he did it disguised as a sailor, with borrowed seaman's papers from a sympathetic American merchantman. "In my clothing I was rigged out in sailor style. . . . My knowledge of ships and sailor's talk came much to my assistance, for I knew a ship from stem to stern, and from keelson to cross-trees, and could talk sailor like an 'old salt.'" He traveled to Wilmington, Delaware, by train, then to Philadelphia by steamboat, then to New York by train, then on to Newport by steamer, then finally continued by carriage to the city where he would make his first home as a free man, New Bedford.

"I was quite disappointed at the general appearance of things in New Bedford," Douglass writes in his *Narrative*, recalling his arrival there. He had assumed that "in the absence of slaves, there could be no wealth, and very little refinement."

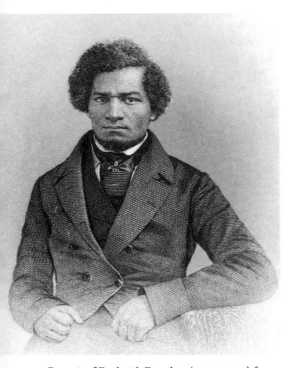

Portrait of Frederick Douglass (c. 1818–1895) from the frontispiece of his autobiography, *My Bondage and My Freedom*, published in 1855, in which Douglass observes that in New Bedford "the black man's children—although anti-slavery was then far from popular—went to school side by side with the white children, and apparently without objection from any quarter."

PHOTO CREDIT: COURTESY OF THE NATIONAL PARK SERVICE.

Upon coming to the North (as he later recalled), he "expected to meet with a rough, hard-handed, and uncultivated population, living in the most Spartan-like simplicity, knowing nothing of the ease, luxury, pomp, and grandeur of southern slave-holders." But New Bedford failed to live up to those expectations. "From the wharves," Douglass writes, "I strolled around and over the town, gazing with wonder and admiration at the splendid churches, beautiful dwellings, and finely-cultivated gardens; evincing an amount of wealth, comfort, taste, and refinement, such as I had never seen in any part of slaveholding Maryland. . . . But the most astonishing as well as the most interesting thing to me was the condition of the colored people, a great many of whom, like myself, had escaped thither as a refuge from the hunters of men. I found many, who had not been seven years out of their chains, living in finer houses, and evidently enjoying more of the comforts of life, than the average of slaveholders of Maryland."

One such person was Nathan Johnson, whose house at 17–21 Seventh Street still stands today. "I will venture to assert that my friend Mr. Nathan Johnson lived in a neater house; dined at a better table; took, paid for, and read, more newspapers; better understood the moral, religious, and political character of the nation, than nine tenths of the slaveholders in Talbot county, Maryland," Douglass writes. Johnson, listed as a "trader" in the city directory at the time Douglass arrived in New Bedford, was one of the city's leading black abolitionists, and the only black member of the local library society. As Kathryn Grover notes in *The Fugitive's Gibraltar: Escaping Slaves and Abolitionism in New Bedford*, he also worked with his wife in a family confectionary and catering business that advertised "Fresh Bordeaux Almonds; superior (French) Olives, Olive Oil, Prunes, Cocoa Nuts, Oranges, Lemons, Lemon Syrup, shelled Almonds, Spices, &c. &c. Confects, Jellies, Ice Cream, Cake, Candies &c. as usual Refreshments served up in the best manner, and charges moderate." She goes on to recount:

The number of people of color in New Bedford, proportionate to the city's population as a whole around the middle of the nineteenth century exceeded that of New York, Boston, and Philadelphia. They were dockworkers, sailors, captains, stewards, owners of small businesses and boardinghouses, caterers, and blacksmiths. . . . They worked on ships that plied the coastal trade, transporting raw materials and manufactured goods up and down the eastern seaboard, and they manned vessels that circumnavigated the globe. They built sturdy, attractive homes in this prosperous whaling port, subscribed to newspapers and magazines, and established thriving churches and schools. But it was not the level of material comfort that made New Bedford so special for Douglass and the hundreds of other fugitive slaves who made their home there: it was the fresh air of freedom that they breathed in the city. For there is no record of any fugitive slave having ever been returned to slavery from New Bedford.

New Bedford's exemplary record when it came to shielding fugitive slaves did not mean that the town had completely eradicated racism: white caulkers, for example, refused to accept Frederick Douglass in their ranks on New Bedford's docks in the 1830s, and they would not allow George Teamoh to work among them some twenty years later, despite the fact that both ex-slaves were expert caulkers. But by the mid-1850s, when Teamoh was denied work because of racial prejudice, his protest in the local paper led to immediate change. He tells us that he "published a short article in the *New Bedford Standard*, defending the colored caulkers of that city from the unjust proscription under which they had been placed." The article "had the desired effect, as we were all given employment the next day after its publication." New Bedford's commitment to reject racism allowed young black men with energy and ambition to enjoy a level of independence and freedom unequaled anywhere in the country.

New Bedford, often called the Whaling Capital of the World, was a city of fresh starts and new beginnings. It was the place where hundreds of fugitives fleeing slavery made new lives for themselves as free men and women. And it was the point of departure for thousands of voyages that took Americans far from home both physically and mentally, delivering them into realms they could hardly have imagined before. It was the city where fugitive slave Frederick Douglass made his first home on free soil and from which Herman Melville embarked on a series of voyages that would open his mind and unfetter his imagination.

From the 1830s to the 1860s, New Bedford and the nearby island of Nantucket lit the world. Sailing ships out of these ports pursued one of the most lucrative quarries then known to man: the sperm whale, whose blubber was rendered at high temperatures aboard ship into an oil that fueled lamps and was turned into smokeless, odorless candles. In the middle of the nineteenth century, New Bedford was considered by many to be the wealthiest city in the nation—some even said the wealthiest in the world. When petroleum-based alternatives such as kerosene and gas replaced spermaceti oil, the profitability of whaling declined. Today New Bedford is still one of the nation's most active seaports, although it is scallops and other fish—not whales—that the ships bring in. But standing on the cobblestone streets of the New Bedford Whaling National Historic Park, amid buildings built in the 1830s and 1840s, feeling the sea breeze that wafts up from the waterfront, and gazing across the docks out to the ocean that stretches as far as the eye can see, one can catch a scent of the fresh air of freedom that made the town Melville's portal to the world beyond these shores and that helped Douglass and so many of his fellow fugitives know that when they reached New Bedford they had come to a place where they were free to reinvent themselves without fear of being returned to slavery.

The thirteen-block area of the downtown adjacent to the waterfront, as well as other landmarks and historic sites throughout the city, preserve much of the early- to mid-nineteenth-century New Bedford that Frederick Douglass and Herman Melville knew in the 1830s and 1840s. Both men would have often passed the U.S. Customs House at the corner of William and North Second Streets, the oldest continuously operated customs house in the country. Built in 1836 with a granite facade and four Doric columns, the Greek Revival building was designed by the architect of the Washington Monument, Robert Mills. They probably strolled by the handsome Federal-style Benjamin Rodman house down the street. (Melville may have had the Rodman house, with its decorative iron fence, in mind when he wrote in *Moby-Dick*, "Go and gaze upon the iron emblematical harpoons round yonder lofty mansion.") It is likely they would have glanced at the vertical sundial on the Union Street exterior of the Sundial Building, in which clocks and chronometers were made. Seamen set their instruments to "New Bedford Time" by consulting the sundial on this 1820 brick-and-stone building. Frederick Douglass worked for a time at Rodman Candleworks on Water Street, which produced some of the finest smokeless, odorless spermaceti candles in the world. He and Melville would have walked past the Mariners' Home on Johnny Cake Hill, originally built in 1787, and Seamen's Bethel next door, which Melville visited in 1841, and later immortalized in a memorable scene in *Moby-Dick*.

Both men probably wandered past the imposing Greek Revival mansion and garden built in 1834 for William Rotch Jr., a whaling merchant with strong antislavery sympathies, at 396 County Street. Both Douglass and Melville undoubtedly stood on New Bedford's wharves, looking both out to sea, and back to the city that rose up from the water, walked through the junction of Union and Water Streets, and took in the bustling activities of the waterfront and the town's busy hive of boardinghouses, rum shops, restaurants, clothing stories, bread and biscuit bake-shops, coopers' and blacksmiths' shops, and the lighthouse in the harbor.

Although Canada was generally thought to be the safest destination for fugitive slaves, New Bedford exerted a strong pull for many runaways. Friends urged fugitive slave Samuel Nixon to run for Canada when he escaped slavery in 1855, but, as William Still recalls in *The Underground Railroad* (1872), "it was in vain to attempt to convince 'Sam' that Canada or any other place on this Continent was quite equal to New Bedford." In addition to figuring centrally in Douglass's three autobiographies (his *Narrative, My Bondage and My Freedom,* and *The Life and Times of Frederick Douglass*) the town features in fugitive slave narratives by Henry "Box" Brown, George Teamoh, Harriet Jacobs, Leonard Black, William Grimes, John S. Jacobs, Thomas H. Jones, Edmund Kelley, and John W. Thompson. The hundreds of slaves who made their way to New Bedford from the 1830s through the 1860s found the city appealing because the wealthy whaling port was always in need of workers. As Jeffrey Bolster notes in *Black Jacks: African American Seamen in the Age of Sail*, the maritime trades had always been more open to hiring African Americans than many other fields, and whaling had been particularly welcoming. Also appealing was the atmosphere of liberalism and tolerance that were among the legacies of the Quakers who had dominated the city's economic and political life through the 1820s, and the ways in which the city's large population of color welcomed new-comers—helping them find work and housing, and fiercely protecting them from being kidnapped and taken back into slavery. When Douglass arrived there, he was surprised by more than the material prosperity he encountered in the city's black population. He found the city's people of color "much more spirited than I had supposed they would be. I found among them a determination to protect each other from the blood-thirsty kidnapper, at all hazards."

In his *Narrative*, Douglass relates the following story, which illustrates the spirit of the people of color in New Bedford: "A colored man and a fugitive slave were on unfriendly terms. The former was heard to threaten the latter with informing his master of his whereabouts. Straightway a meeting was called among the colored people, under the stereotyped notice, 'Business of importance!' The betrayer was invited to attend. The people came at the appointed hour, and organized the meeting by appointing a very religious old gentleman as president, who, I believe, made a prayer, after which he addressed the meeting as follows: *'Friends, we have got him here, and I would recommend that you young men just take him outside the door, and kill him!'* With this, a number of them bolted at him; but they were intercepted by some more timid than themselves, and the betrayer escaped their vengeance, and has not been seen in New Bedford since. I believe there have been no more such threats." "No colored man is really free in a slaveholding state," Douglass wrote in 1855. "He wears the badge of bondage while nominally free, and is often subjected to hardships to which the slave is a stranger; but here in New Bedford, it was my good fortune to see a pretty near approach to freedom on the part of the colored people." In *My Bondage and My Freedom*, Douglass expanded on this point, observing that "the colored people in that city are educated up to the point of fighting for their freedom, as well as speaking for it."

Shortly after fugitive slave George Teamoh arrived in the mid-1850s, he tells us in his narrative *God Made Man, Man Made the Slave*, New Bedford's "good citizens gathered around me with charitable offerings and a protest of eternal hatred to slavery and all its alliances." Life was not easy there for Teamoh: winters were cold, and the only work available to him was low-paying and hard. Nonetheless, citizens there valued what he cared for most "with a zeal which knew no bounds." "Long long years ago, [they] laid down as a principle and nailed to the mast-head of their little bark that had crossed so many rugged waters,—the full and untrammeled possession of one's ownership of himself." Because of New Bedford's unwavering commitment to this principle, Teamoh called the city "the fugitive's Gibraltar."

New Bedford was a multiracial, multilingual, multicultural city, peopled by individuals of every color and hue from all over the world. On its streets, sailors with ritual scarring and traditional tattooing were a common sight; both Melville and Douglass probably saw a number of mariners with tattoos as elaborate as those of the harpooner Queequeg in *Moby-Dick*. African Americans brushed shoulders with sailors of African descent from the Azores, Cape Verde, the Caribbean, Africa, and Europe. At a time when most printed channels of communication—newspapers, magazines, and broadsheets—addressed the concerns of white Americans and represented their interests and their views, the oral culture of the maritime world of black seamen allowed people of African descent to learn important news of people of color around the globe. The docks of the Eastern Seaboard and the streets that surrounded them became communication hubs for the black Atlantic world, forging bonds of community among people of color in distant locales.

The sea, the site of the dread Middle Passage of the slave ships, and the scene of more than 155 shipboard slave rebellions, became for many, after the slave trade was ended, a site associated with escape from slavery and with freedom from slave-catchers. African American journalist and novelist Martin Delany captures the attitude of many black sailors toward the freedom of the seas in this black sailors' song that he quotes in his novel of the early 1860s, *Blake; or, The Huts of America:* "Hurra for the sea and its waves! / Ye billows and surges, all hail! /My brothers hence-forth—for ye scorn to be Slaves, / As ye toss up your crests to the gale; / Farewell to the land of the bloodhound and chain, / My path is away o'er the fetterless main." Racism was by no means absent from the sailors' world, and exploitation was prob-ably the rule rather than the exception; but the dangerous nature of the work and the interdependence it required often gave black sailors more autonomy, equality, and opportunities for self-assertion than other lines of work. The proprietor of a black boardinghouse observed that in whaling, unlike other industries, "A coloured man is only known and looked upon as a man, and is promoted in rank according to his ability and skill to perform the same duties as the white man."

This level of equality caught some white seamen by surprise. As Jeffrey Bolster relates in *Black Jacks*, shortly after joining the crew of the *Cachelot* in New Bedford, a white sailor named Frank Bullen was questioned by an impressive-looking black seaman. Bullen recalls that he had responded to one of the seaman's questions by saying "'yes' very curtly, for I hardly liked his patronizing air; but he snapped me up short with 'yes, *sir,* when yew speak to me, yew blank limejuicer. I'se de fourf mate ob dis yar ship, en my name's Mistah Jones, 'n yew jest freeze on to dat ar, ef yew want ter lib long 'n die happy. See, sonny.' I *saw,* and answered promptly, 'I beg your pardon, sir, I didn't know.'" In a world of very limited employment options, the sea held out the promise of earning a living at a trade that was at least as honorable as it was hard—and of being paid the same wages as one's white counterparts, however low those wages might be. During the first half of the nineteenth century, close to a fifth of the men who manned the nation's ships were of African descent, and most, but not all, were free.

The sea also came to be associated with fresh perspectives and more fluid identi-ties. The sea was the means by which African Americans like Frederick Douglass and Paul Laurence Dunbar could travel to countries like England, where one's race played less of a role in shaping how one was treated. ("I gaze around in vain for one who will question my equal humanity," Douglass wrote about his stay in Britain. "I meet nothing to remind me of my complexion.") It was also the means by which Americans like Herman Melville could learn firsthand that the so-called savages of Polynesia were, in many ways, more civilized than the so-called civilized citizens back home.

The fugitive slave Frederick Augusta Washington Bailey decided to change his name to Frederick Johnson when he was married in New York to his fiancée, Anna, by Rev. James W. C. Pennington. When the newlyweds arrived by stagecoach at Nathan and Mary Johnson's house at 17–21 Seventh Street in New Bedford in

September 1838 with no money to pay the driver, the Johnsons advanced them what they owed. But Nathan Johnson, one of the town's leading black abolitionists, would give his guest much more than stagecoach fare. At breakfast the next morning in the Federal-style, wood-frame house that would be Frederick and Anna's first home on free soil, Nathan Johnson told Frederick that New Bedford was teeming with people of color named "Johnson," and that choosing another surname would be wise. Frederick decided to give his generous host the privilege of choosing one for him. Sir Walter Scott's *The Lady of the Lake* inspired him to suggest the name by which his guest would be known thenceforth: Frederick Bailey may have been "born in Tuckahoe, near Hillsborough, and about twelve miles from Easton, in Talbot county, Maryland" (as he tells us in his *Narrative*), but Frederick *Douglass* was born in the Johnson House on Seventh Street in New Bedford (now a National Historic Landmark).

Despite the unusual degree of equality that black residents of New Bedford enjoyed, some of the prejudice that was more familiar in the rest of the country existed here as well. When white caukers refused to let him ply his trade among them, Douglass tells us that he "sawed wood—dug cellars—shoveled coal—swept chimneys . . . rolled oil casks on the wharves,—helped to load and unload vessels—worked in Ricketson's candle works—in Richmond's brass foundry, and elsewhere." He also became licensed to preach by the New Bedford African Methodist Episcopal Church and often preached in a "little school-house on Second Street . . . where we worshipped."

In the summer of 1841, having worked hard all spring and summer in Richmond's brass foundry, Douglass decided to take a brief holiday by attending a large antislavery convention held on the nearby island of Nantucket. It was there that a prominent abolitionist who had heard Douglass speak in church in New Bedford invited him to address the convention. Douglass claimed he was unable to "remember a single connected sentence" that he spoke that night. "It was with the utmost difficulty that I could stand erect, or that I could command, and articulate two words without hesitation and stammering. I trembled in every limb. I am not sure that my embarrassment was not the most effective part of my speech, if speech it could be called." The next speaker, the abolitionist William Lloyd Garrison, took Douglass himself "as his text," giving a particularly powerful speech. At the close of the meeting, Douglass was approached by the general agent of the Massachusetts antislavery society, who urgently pressed him to become an agent of the society, making public speeches against slavery, for which he would receive a salary.

Douglass, just three years out of slavery and still a fugitive wary of being arrested by his master, was reluctant to say yes. But, he tells us, the man "was not to be put off, and I finally consented to go out for three months, for I supposed that I should have got to the end of my story and my usefulness, in that length of time." Douglass began traveling through New England describing what it had been like to be a slave and advocating the nonviolent agitation against slavery for which the Society stood. It was the start of a stunning new career for him—one that would occupy him for the next fifty-four years, and it was the beginning of his transformation into the most respected and influential black leader in the nation. He would publish his first autobiography (the *Narrative*) in 1845, and leave for a lecture tour of Britain that year. After his freedom was purchased by British friends, he began publishing his own newspaper, the antislavery weekly the *North Star*, the first of several periodicals he launched. In sharp, clear, compellingly eloquent language, Douglass tirelessly chastised America for failing to live up to its promise, for the hypocrisy that allowed its citizens to think of themselves as good, upright, and religious while keeping fellow human beings in chains.

During the Civil War, Douglass lobbied President Abraham Lincoln to let black men serve in the Union Army, and he went on to recruit a number of black troops himself, including two of his sons. After the war, he held a number of government posts, including president of the short-lived Freedman's Savings and Trust Company, U.S. marshal for the District of Columbia, recorder of deeds for the District of Columbia, and consul general to Haiti. His moral vision, passionate and lucid prose, and commitment to making real the ideals to which his country paid lip service infused his three autobiographies, one short story, and scores of articles and speeches, and helped make him one of the most admired American writers of the nineteenth century.

Before he went to New Bedford in 1841, Herman Melville had worked as a bank clerk, a farmer, a bookkeeper, and a teacher. He had also had—like Ishmael in *Moby-Dick*—some experience in the merchant marine. Reading Richard Henry Dana Jr.'s *Two Years before the Mast* (1840) helped ignite Melville's curiosity about what it would be like to sail the Pacific. A story he may have read in a magazine around this time about the killing of a great white sperm whale named Mocha Dick in the Pacific may have further piqued his interest. Like Ishmael, he had come to New Bedford to join the crew of a whaling ship. He signed on as a seaman on the *Acushnet* for a voyage that was to last at least three years and left New Bedford for the South Seas on January 3, 1841. A year and a half later, weary of the tyranny and cruelty he encountered on the ship, Melville deserted the *Acushnet* in the

Herman Melville (1819–1891) left New Bedford on the whaling ship *Acushnet* in 1841 on a voyage that would inspire his novel *Moby-Dick*.

PHOTO CREDIT: COURTESY OF THE RARE BOOK AND SPECIAL COLLECTIONS DIVISION, THE LIBRARY OF CONGRESS, WASHINGTON, DC.

Marquesas, along with a friend, and spent a month in a valley inhabited by a tribe known as the Typees. He left the island on an Australian whaler, the *Lucy Ann*, which stopped by seeking additional crew members; conditions on board the *Lucy Ann* turned out to be even worse than on the *Acushnet*. He was sent ashore with other shipmates as a mutineer, escaped his captors, and explored Tahiti and Eimeo with a shipmate. He spent six months as a harpooner on a Nantucket whaling ship, the *Charles and Henry*, which took him to Lahina on the island of Maui; from there he went to Honolulu, where he got a job as a bookkeeper and clerk in a store, signing a contract to work for a year. But his original ship, the *Acushnet*, unexpectedly arrived in port, and perhaps fearing that he would be prosecuted as a deserter, Melville cut short his stay on shore and enlisted in the U.S. Navy in August 1843, shipping out on the frigate the *United States*. Discharged soon after the *United States* anchored in Boston Harbor on October 3, 1844, Melville returned home, having been away for nearly four years. He began sharing his stories with his family, who urged him to write them down.

Melville's early novels *Typee, Omoo, Mardi, Redburn,* and *White-Jacket,* all feature settings, characters, themes, and plots drawn partly from his experiences at sea; partly from his reading of popular literature, history, and travel narratives; and partly from his rich imagination. In the exotic, remote islands in the South Seas, in books like *Typee: A Peep at Polynesian Life* (1846), Melville's characters encounter human societies that challenge their familiar assumptions—about the nature of Christian and heathen, of white and nonwhite; or about the nature of selfhood and individuality, of colonialism and imperialism, of authority, and of freedom itself. In these early books, he spins romantic travel adventures that captured his readers' imaginations while also implicitly challenging them to question a system in which the "savage" islanders were "civilized into draft horses and evangelized into beasts of burden." (Douglass reprinted a section on tattooing from *Typee* in the *North Star* in 1848. Although Douglass was familiar with some of Melville's writing, and, as Robert Wallace suggests, Melville was probably aware of some of Douglass's work, there is no record of the two having met in New Bedford or elsewhere.) The popularity of *Typee* led Melville to follow it with a sequel, *Omoo*, which was also a popular success. In *Mardi*, subtitled, "a chartless voyage," he focuses more on ideas and on his own creative process than he had in the earlier popular travel romances; he was disappointed when it failed to sell. *Redburn* and *White-Jacket* represent returns to Melville's earlier successful style. The first book fictionalizes his voyage to Liverpool on the trading ship *St. Laurence* in 1839 (where he endured oppressive working conditions he would remember all his life), while the second has its roots in his experience in the U.S. Navy on the man-of-war *United States* (where conditions were equally tyrannical and despotic). In a letter to his father-in-law, Judge Lemuel Shaw, in 1849, Melville shared his low opinion of these last two books: "They are two *jobs*, which I have done for money—being forced to it, as other men are to sawing wood."

It was his sixth effort to transmute his seagoing days into fiction that would result in his most memorable novel, *Moby-Dick*. "To produce a mighty book," Ishmael tells the reader in *Moby-Dick*, "you must choose a mighty theme. No great and enduring volume can ever be written on the flea, though many there be who have tried it." Melville's sense of humor comes through here. But so does his sense of purpose: the book engages questions and ideas as "mighty" and powerful as a whale—and as disconcerting and troubling as that freak of nature, a *white* whale. Melville's genius in *Moby-Dick* manifests itself in his ability to ponder profound and complex issues about man and nature and reality itself while simultaneously spinning a magnificently concrete and vividly realized adventure story of a whale hunt. In the vast, open seas of the imagination into which *Moby-Dick* pulls its reader, everything is up for grabs—including basic assumptions about one's society. Some critics suggest that in this book about an eerily malevolent great white whale Melville may have been challenging the idealizing of "whiteness" in his society, recognizing that "whiteness" elevated into an ideology could be both savage and evil.

While his earlier sea novels drew on Melville's experiences after he deserted the *Acushnet*, *Moby-Dick* takes the reader to the events leading up to his signing on for his first whaling voyage. It all begins in New Bedford, on a dark night, with Ishmael searching for a place to sleep near the waterfront. He settles on "The Spouter-Inn." When he enters he finds a number of young seamen gathered about a table, examining in the dim light diverse specimens of scrimshaw—complicated carvings made out of whale's teeth, whalebone, and baleen that sailors made to pass the time during the interminable voyages. The kinds of things they were examining may be seen at the New Bedford Whaling Museum in the Historic District. Scrimshaw objects ranging from elaborate boxes to ornate pie-crimpers to love-letter-inscribed corset stays—meant to be seen by one's sweetheart and no one else—are arrayed in the museum's glass cases on the second floor.

The Spouter-Inn's proprietor, Peter Coffin, tells Ishmael that if he is willing to share his bed with a harpooner, he can spend the night. Ishmael assents without knowing much about his bedfellow. When the man appears, Ishmael is taken aback: "Such a face! It was of a dark purplish, yellow color, here and there stuck over with large, blackish looking squares." At first Ishmael thinks his roommate has been in a fight. But then he realizes he is covered with tattoos, and decides that "he must be some abominable savage or other shipped aboard of a whaleman in the South Seas, and so landed in this Christian country. I quaked to think of it." Initially terrified to find that he will be sharing his bed with a "cannibal," Ishmael finds that there is much more to the harpooner Queequeg than meets the eye. The two become fast friends—inseparable—and sign up for the whaling voyage together. Much as Melville's experiences in the South Seas shook up his understandings of what it meant to be "savage" and "civilized," Queequeg challenges Ishmael's views of the meaning of these terms by proving himself a more devoted and generous friend, a more gifted harpooner, and a more selfless human being than any "civilized" white man of Ishmael's acquaintance.

CANNIBALS AND CHRISTIANS

AN EARLY SCENE FROM *MOBY-DICK*

Having boarded the New Bedford schooner that will take them to Nantucket (where they will board the whaling ship *Pequod*), Ishmael and Queequeg attract "jeering glances of the passengers"—not because of Queequeg's tattoos, a sight that was not uncommon in cosmopolitan New Bedford, but because the passengers "marvelled that two fellow beings should be so companionable; as though a white man were anything more dignified than a whitewashed negro." When a rude young man is caught by Queequeg mimicking him behind his back, "the brawny savage" dropped his harpoon, caught him in his arms, and sent him high up bodily into the air. When the fellow "landed bursting lungs upon his feet," while "Queequeg, turning his back upon him, lighted his tomahawk pipe and passed it to [Ishmael] for a puff," the winded sailor calls the captain in outrage:

> "Capting! Capting!" yelled the bumpkin, running towards that officer; "Capting, Capting, here's the devil."
>
> "Hallo, you sir," cried the Captain, a gaunt rib of the sea, stalking up to Queequeg, "what in thunder do you mean by that? Don't you know you might have killed that chap?"
>
> "What him say?" said Queequeg, as he mildly turned to me.
>
> "He say," said I, "that you came near kill-e that man there," pointing to the still shivering greenhorn.
>
> "Kill-e," cried Queequeg, twisting his tattooed face into an unearthly expression of disdain, "ah! him bevy small-e fish-e; Queequeg no kill-e so small-e fish-e; Queequeg kill-e big whale!"
>
> "Look you," roared the Captain, "I'll kill-e you, you cannibal, if you try any more of your tricks aboard here; so mind your eye."

But it so happened just then, that it was high time for the Captain to mind his own eye. The prodigious strain upon the main-sail had parted the weather-sheet, and the tremendous boom was now flying from side to side, completely sweeping the entire after part of the deck. The poor fellow whom Queequeg had handled so roughly, was swept overboard; all hands were in a panic; and to attempt snatching at the boom to stay it, seemed madness. It flew from right to left, and back again, almost in one ticking of a watch, and every instant seemed on the point of snapping into splinters. Nothing was done, and nothing seemed capable of being done; those on deck rushed towards the bows, and stood eyeing the boom as if it were the lower jaw of an exasperated whale. In the midst of this consternation, Queequeg dropped deftly to his knees, and crawling under the path of the boom, whipped hold of a rope, secured one end to the bulwarks, and then flinging the other like a lasso, caught it round the boom as it swept over his head, and at the next jerk, the spar was that way trapped, and all was safe. The schooner was run into the wind, and while the hands were clearing away the stern boat, Queequeg, stripped to the waist, darted from the side with a long living arc of a leap. For three minutes or more he was seen swimming like a dog, throwing his long arms straight out before him, and by turns revealing his brawny shoulders through the freezing foam. I looked at the grand and glorious fellow, but saw no one to be saved. The greenhorn had gone down. Shooting himself perpendicularly from the water, Queequeg now took an instant's glance around him, and seeming to see just how matters were, dived down and disappeared. A few minutes more, and he rose again, one arm still striking out, and with the other dragging a lifeless form. The boat soon picked them up. The poor bumpkin was restored. All hands voted Queequeg a noble trump; the captain begged his pardon. From that hour I clove to Queequeg like a barnacle; yea, till poor Queequeg took his last long dive. Was there ever such unconsciousness? He did not seem to think that he at all deserved a medal from the Humane and Magnanimous Societies. He only asked for water—fresh water—something to wipe the brine off; that done, he put on dry clothes, lighted his pipe, and leaning against the bulwarks, and mildly eyeing those around him, seemed to be saying to himself— "It's a mutual, joint-stock world, in all meridians. We cannibals must help these Christians."

"In this same New Bedford there stands a Whaleman's Chapel, and few are the moody fishermen, shortly bound for the Indian Ocean or Pacific, who fail to make a Sunday visit to the spot. I am sure I did not," Ishmael tells us in *Moby-Dick*. The Whaleman's Chapel to which Ishmael refers was Seamen's Bethel on Johnny Cake Hill, which still stands today. It is believed that Melville himself paid a visit there before he sailed on the *Acushnet*. Seamen's Bethel has served as a meeting place for religious services since 1832, when it was built by the New Bedford Port Society for the Moral Improvement of Seamen. Located at the center of the area that in Melville's day was the waterfront's tavern and boardinghouse district, the Seamen's Bethel was to be a religious haven where young seamen could resist the temptations of the tap room and the brothel. It is still used as a house of prayer, and memorials to New Bedford whalemen and fisherman who lost their lives at sea appear on the walls inside and on a plaque out front. The memorials Ishmael describes in chapter 7 of *Moby-Dick*—to an eighteen-year-old who "was lost overboard, Near the isle of Desolation, off Patagonia," or to crew members of "The Ship Eliza, Who were towed out of sight by a Whale, On the Off-shore Ground in the Pacific," or to a captain "Who in the bows of his boat was killed by a Sperm Whale on the coast of Japan," are chilling to a man about to ship out on a whaling vessel himself. They prompt Ishmael to contemplate his own death: "It needs scarcely be told, with what feelings . . . I regarded those marble tablets, and by the murky light of that darkened, doleful day read the fate of the whalemen who had gone before me. Yes, Ishmael, the same fate may be thine."

The terrifying sermon Ishmael hears Father Mapple preach in Seamen's Bethel—taking as his text the story of Jonah and the Whale—probably only added to the trepidation Ishmael felt on the eve of his maiden voyage on a whaling chip. Visitors to Seamen's Bethel today will see a pulpit exactly like the one from which Father Mapple preached in *Moby-Dick*: "its paneled front was in the likeness of a ship's bluff bows, and the Holy Bible rested on a projecting piece of scroll work, fashioned after a ship's fiddle-headed beak." But the pulpit in Seamen's Bethel today is testimony not to the power of preservation, but to the power of imagination: it was built in 1959, inspired by the fictional pulpit Melville imagined in his greatest novel.

If the pulpit testifies to Melville's capacity for fantasy, the New Bedford Whaling Museum at 18 Johnny Cake Hill testifies to his capacity to recall and evoke the world of fact. The museum houses the largest collection of whaling artifacts in the world—and any number of those artifacts will strike a visitor who has read *Moby-Dick* as familiar, because Melville allows the reader to visualize them so accurately and to understand their function so fully. There are cases of harpoons, for example, like those cast by Queequeg and his fellow harpooners in the novel. (There is also a display case about a local man whose invention of the iron toggle harpoon in 1848 revolutionized whaling—African American whaleman and inventor Lewis Temple, whose invention made many New Bedford fortunes, though not his own.) There is the *Lagoda*, an eighty-nine-foot half-scale replica of a whaling ship. There are whaling implements; captains' logbooks; paintings, prints, drawings, and photographs of whale ships, whalemen, and whaling; ship models; figureheads; scrimshaw objects; souvenirs whalemen brought back from the Pacific; navigational instruments; lamps and lighting devices using whale oil; the skeleton of a young humpback whale; and a 1,275-foot "Panorama of a Whaling Voyage 'Round the World," which may have helped inspire Melville to write *Moby-Dick*.

Chapters of New Bedford local history come alive, as well, as the objects of daily life in this whaling town—furniture, glassware, household implements, signs, toys, needlework—help evoke the lives of those who stayed on shore. The thousands of whale-related artifacts, manuscripts, photographs, paintings, models, and miscellaneous objects in the museum's collection serve as a fascinating physical complement to the eclectic array of "Extracts" about whales and whaling with which Melville opens *Moby-Dick*.

Melville would return to the sea in "Benito Cereno," a tense and dramatic story about a shipboard slave uprising, and in the meditative *Billy Budd*, a novella that pondered the nature of good and evil and justice and injustice, which was published after his death. In these works, as in all of Melville's fiction set on the sea, the fully rendered details of the mariner's trade helped make the ambitious and complex issues explored in his fiction live and breathe in ways that continue to rivet the reader's attention.

In the twentieth century, some of Melville's most attentive and appreciative readers have been fellow writers. Poets including Robert Lowell, Hart Crane, and W. H. Auden, as well as novelists like Edward Dahlberg and John Updike all engaged Melville in a conversation across time, so to speak, writing work of their own that responds explicitly to his. Other writers have used Melville more playfully: The opening line of Philip Roth's *Great American Novel* (1973)—"Call me Smitty"—and the first line of Kurt Vonnegut Jr.'s novel *Cat's Cradle* (1963)—"Call me Jonah"—parody the opening line of chapter 1 of *Moby-Dick*: "Call me Ishmael." Science fiction writer Philip José Farmer begins his novel *The Wind Whales of Ishmael* (1971) where *Moby-Dick* ends, with Ishmael clinging to Queequeg's coffin until he is rescued, while Sena Jeter Naslund takes as her central character in *Ahab's Wife; or, The Star-Gazer* (1999) a woman who goes to sea disguised as a cabin boy, gets shipwrecked, marries one of her fellow survivors, and then falls in love with a sea captain named Ahab who is obsessed with a white whale.

But it is perhaps in the work of writers shaped by *both* of New Bedford's favorite literary sons, Melville and Douglass, that each writer's most lasting and profound literary legacies may be found. Douglass's eloquent autobiographies, speeches, and essays—with their unswerving focus on the gap between the promise of equality on which the nation was founded and the country's failure to live up to that promise—shaped every African American writer who followed him, challenging each to equal his stunning blend of eloquence and earthiness, of anger and art. Twentieth-century black writers who were fortunate enough to be swept away by Melville's genius, as well, include Ralph Ellison, who introduced his novel *Invisible Man* with an epigraph from "Benito Cereno"; David Bradley, who "read and reread *Moby-Dick* and used it as a master text" for key lessons in how to tell a story when he was writing his multi-layered ambitious novel *The Chaneysville Incident*; and Charles Johnson, whose novel *Middle Passage* blends fugitive slave narrative with a sea story and adds to the brew a slave revolt as well as extended philosophical meditations about self-knowledge, good and evil, poverty and wealth, slavery and freedom. More than a century and a half after Douglass and Melville breathed the fresh air of freedom on the wharves of New Bedford, their work helped inspire some of the twentieth century's most original African American writers to craft books that ventured, with boldness and daring, out of the safe harbor of the familiar into waters that were uncharted and new.

RELATED SITES

● Frederick Douglass National Historic Site
1411 W Street, SE, Washington, DC (Anacostia)

Douglass defied the District of Columbia's racist housing laws when he purchased this attractive two-story brick house in a segregated neighborhood in 1877 when he took office as U.S. marshal of the District of Columbia. He called the home and the fifteen acres on which it sat (for which he paid $6,700) Cedar Hill after the cedar trees that shaded the house when he moved there. While he was living here, Douglass wrote his third autobiography, *The Life and Times of Frederick Douglass*, published in 1881, a book in which he addresses with bitter candor his disappointment at the fate of black rights in the post-Reconstruction debacle: "To-day, in most of the Southern States, the fourteenth and fifteenth amendments are virtually nullified. The rights which they were intended to guarantee are denied and held in contempt. The citizenship granted in the fourteenth amendment is practically a mockery, and the right to vote, provided for in the fifteenth amendment, is literally stamped out in face of government. The old master class is to-day triumphant, and the newly-enfranchised class in a condition but little above that in which they were found before the rebellion." From the veranda of his graceful home, Douglass could look down on the U.S. Capitol dome some five miles away and ponder how so much promise had been transformed into so much disappointment. In *The Life and Times* he hazards an answer:

> Do you ask me how, after all that has been done, this state of things has been made possible? I will tell you. Our reconstruction measures were radically

Frederick Douglass's study and library at Cedar Hill, his home in Washington, DC, from 1878 until his death in 1895.

PHOTO CREDIT: COURTESY OF THE NATIONAL PARK SERVICE.

defective. They left the former slave completely in the power of the old master, the loyal citizen in the hands of the disloyal rebel against the government. . . . In the hurry and confusion of the hour, and the eager desire to have the Union restored, there was more care for the sublime superstructure of the republic than for the solid foundation upon which it could alone be upheld. To the freedmen was given the machinery of liberty, but there was denied to them the steam to put it in motion.

Douglass's sense of accomplishment during the years he lived here was diminished by his sense of all that remained undone. Material signs of what he had achieved however, were present in each room of Cedar Hill—tasteful and elegant furnishings (including a gilded mirror, a marble fireplace, and a gracefully carved wooden, mirror-backed sideboard on which an elaborate silver coffee service sits); gifts from admirers (including a desk given to him by Harriet Beecher Stowe, and a walking stick that had belonged to President Abraham Lincoln, a gift from Lincoln's widow); Greco-Roman sculptures; and paintings (including one in the front hall of the Fifty-Fourth Massachusetts, in which his sons, Lewis and Charles, had served, storming Fort Wagner).

The home has been restored to look as it did when Douglass lived here. Ninety percent of the furnishings are original, and the house still contains many of his personal belongings, including family photographs, the exercise dumbbells that were part of Douglass's regular fitness regimen, and his personal library of more than a thousand books. He lived here until his death in 1895.

☙ Frederick Douglass–Isaac Myers National Maritime Park
Thames and Caroline Streets, Baltimore, Maryland (Fells Point Historic District)

This park celebrates Maryland's African American maritime history and shipbuilding tradition. The renovated Sugar House, a warehouse dating to the 1810s that is Baltimore's oldest waterfront industrial building, was in use when Frederick Douglass—then a young slave named Frederick Bailey—worked on the wharves here as a cauker and laborer. In his later years, Douglass served on the board of directors of Isaac Myers's Chesapeake Marine Railway and Drydock Company, the first black-owned shipyard in the United States. Opened here in 1868, this enterprise pioneered in employing blacks and whites together in the workplace. Myers later founded the Colored Caukers' Trade Union Society and helped organize the Colored National Labor Union.

☙ Rockledge, William Lloyd Garrison House
125 Highland Street, Boston, Massachusetts

This was the home of the distinguished abolitionist who first enlisted Douglass as a lecturer for the Massachusetts Anti-Slavery Society.

☙ Sgt. William H. Carney House
128 Mill Street, New Bedford, Massachusetts

A former slave who, like Douglass, fled to New Bedford, Carney was a member of the Fifty-Fourth Massachusetts Regiment. Carney rescued the American flag from the fallen standard-bearer during the attack on Fort Wagner in South Carolina on July 18, 1863, and carried it to safety under intense Confederate fire. He became the first African American to earn the Congressional Medal of Honor (although it was not awarded until nearly four decades after his heroic act). Frederick Douglass had tirelessly recruited black men to join the Fifty Fourth. After the war, Carney worked in the U.S. Post Office housed in the old customs house on 2nd and William Streets in New Bedford.

☙ Rotch-Jones-Duff House
396 County Street, New Bedford, Massachusetts (County Street Historic District, roughly bounded by Acushnet, Page, Middle, and Bedford Streets)

"Nowhere in all America will you find more patrician-like houses; parks and gardens more opulent, than in New Bedford," Melville wrote in *Moby-Dick*. "Yes; all these brave houses and flowery gardens came from the Atlantic, Pacific, and Indian Oceans. One and all, they were harpooned and dragged up hither from the bottom of the sea." Typical of the "brave houses and flowery gardens" to which he referred is the Greek Revival Rotch-Jones-Duff House at 396 County Street. Built in 1834 by William Rotch Jr., this is the only whaling mansion open to the public in New England. The historic gardens feature a formal boxwood rose garden and a wildflower walk, while the house displays family furnishings and personal items. Rotch was involved in a number of maritime-related businesses, including oil refining, banking, and candle manufacturing. He was also a dedicated antislavery activist. Rotch funded a successful lawsuit against the owner of the brigantine *Hope*, who was convicted of having violated the law that ended the slave trade in Massachusetts. The suit charged that the *Hope* left Boston as a slaver in 1788 three months after that law was passed and sold 116 slaves in the West Indies before returning with other cargo to the United States. Rotch also tirelessly collected information about incidents of cruelty to slaves and crew members on New England ships, and he deeply believed that the freedom struggle of African Americans was as just as the fight for liberty that had fueled the American Revolution.

☙ Palmer Light Station
New Bedford Harbor, Massachusetts

Both Frederick Douglass and Herman Melville saw the light shining from this historic light station, designed by Charles M. Pierce, as they walked along the waterfront here.

❦ Arrowhead, Herman Melville House

780 Holmes Road, Pittsfield, Massachusetts

Herman Melville moved with his family to this 1780 white-frame farmhouse in the Berkshires, surrounded by apple orchards, hayfields, and a pasture in 1850. He named it "Arrowhead" because of the Indian arrowheads he turned up when he plowed the fields for the first time. The farm, which he bought from a widowed aunt with the help of a loan from his father-in-law, had been the site of many pleasant vacations during his childhood. Formerly an inn on the stagecoach route from Hartford, Connecticut, to Bennington, Vermont, the farmhouse features a huge, square, central fireplace that, according to Melville, "swallowed cords of wood as a whale does boats." (It inspired his sketch "I and My Chimney," about a wife's efforts to remodel an ancient farmhouse much like this one.) He planned to combine farming and writing but showed little talent for the former, raising only enough food for his family's table, and his horse and cow. His writing flourished here, however. It was in the second-floor study, in this house run by women (Melville's wife, mother, and four unmarried sisters), near a window that looked out on Mount Greylock that he wrote most of *Moby-Dick*. He lived and breathed the novel with total concentration: "I look out my window in the morning when I rise as I would out of a port-hole of a ship in the Atlantic. My room seems a ship's cabin; & nights when I wake up & hear the wind shrieking, I almost fancy there is too much sail on the house." In the writer's imagination, Mount Greylock came to look like a surfacing whale. Fellow Berkshire County resident Nathaniel Hawthorne often visited Melville here. Melville dedicated *Moby-Dick* to his close friend, owing to his "admiration for his genius." The long, wooden porch or "piazza" he built in the back of the house helped inspire his *Piazza Tales*. Melville also wrote *Pierre*, *Israel Potter*, and *The Confidence-Man* while living here, along with stories including "Benito Cereno," "Bartleby, the Scrivener," and "The Paradise of Bachelors and the Tartarus of Maids." Because none of his literary endeavors was a financial success, he had to sell off farmland to pay his debts and support his family. He sold the house and all the land that remained to his brother in 1863. Today Arrowhead, a National Historic Landmark, is a museum that is open to the public.

❦ The *Charles W. Morgan*

Mystic Seaport, 75 Greenmanville Avenue, Mystic, Connecticut

The last of the nineteenth-century wooden whaling vessels, the *Charles W. Morgan* was launched at New Bedford in 1841. It sailed thirty-seven voyages in pursuit of whales over eighty years, traveling more leagues of the world's oceans than any other whaler. A full-rigged, double topsail bark weighing more than three hundred tons, the *Charles W. Morgan* measured more than a hundred feet from stem to stern and carried six or more six-man whaleboats, used to chase, harpoon, kill, and tow whales back to the ship. The oil was rendered from whale blubber on board in cast-iron try-pots set into a brick, iron, and wood furnace, and the ship transported the thousands of gallons of rendered oil back to port. The public may board the ship, which is a National Historic Landmark vessel.

Some six hundred boats are known to have been built and launched between 1784 and 1919 from the five shipyards that once lined this portion of the Mystic River. Located halfway between New York and Boston, Mystic Seaport occupies the site of three of those five shipyards. It is the nation's leading maritime museum and home to the largest collection of nineteenth- and early twentieth-century watercraft and maritime artifacts in the United States. Galleries include exhibits of figureheads and ship carvings, ship's models, and scrimshaw.

●◆ Nantucket Historic District
Nantucket Island, Nantucket, Massachusetts

Nantucket was the world's leading whaling port from about 1740 to 1840, and the town of Nantucket remains a fine example of an early New England seaport. Douglass gave his first major antislavery speech here in 1841. In *Moby-Dick*, Ishmael and Queequeg board the *Pequod* here. In addition to containing an important collection of scrimshaw, the Whaling Museum at 15 Broad Street features items that Nantucket whalers brought back from their many voyages to the South Pacific.

FOR FURTHER READING

The Writers: Works and Words

Andrews, William L., and Henry Louis Gates Jr., eds. *Slave Narratives*. New York: Library of America, 2000.

Bradley, David. *The Chaneysville Incident*. 1981. New York: Harper Perennial, 1990.

———. "Our Crowd, Their Crowd: Race, Reader, and *Moby-Dick*." In *Melville's Evermoving Dawn: Centennial Essays*, edited by John Bryant and Robert Milder, 119–146. Kent, OH: Kent State University Press, 1997.

Delany, Martin. *Blake; or, The Huts of America, a Novel*. Introduction by Floyd J. Miller. Boston: Beacon Press, 1970.

Douglass, Frederick. *Autobiographies.* Edited by Henry Louis Gates Jr. New York: Library of America, 1994.

Ellison, Ralph. *Invisible Man.* 1952. Reprint, New York: Vintage Books, 1989.

Farmer, Philip José. *The Wind Whales of Ishmael.* New York: Ace Books, 1971.

Johnson, Charles. *Middle Passage.* New York: Atheneum, 1990.

Melville, Herman. *Pierre, Israel Potter, The Piazza Tales, The Confidence-Man, Billy Budd, Uncollected Prose.* Edited by Harrison Hayford. New York: Library of America, 1984.

———. *Redburn, White-Jacket, Moby-Dick.* Edited by G. Thomas Tanselle. New York: Library of America, 1983.

———. *Typee, Omoo, Mardi.* Edited by G. Thomas Tanselle. New York: Library of America, 1983.

Naslund, Sena Jeter. *Ahab's Wife: Or, The Star-Gazer: A Novel.* New York: William Morrow, 1999.

Neill, Peter, ed. *American Sea Writing.* New York: Library of America, 2000.

Roth, Philip. *The Great American Novel.* New York: Holt, Rinehart and Winston, 1973.

Still, William. *The Underground Railroad.* 1872. Reprint, Chicago: Johnson Publishing Co., 1970.

Teamoh, George. *God Made Man, Man Made the Slave: The Autobiography of George Teamoh.* Edited by Nash Boney, Rafia Zafar, and Richard L. Hume. Macon, GA: Mercer University Press, 1990.

Vonnegut, Kurt. *Cat's Cradle.* New York: Holt, Rinehart and Winston, 1973.

Backgrounds and Contexts

Bolster, W. Jeffrey. *Black Jacks: African American Seamen in the Age of Sail.* Cambridge, MA: Harvard University Press, 1997.

Bryant, John, ed. *A Companion to Melville Studies.* Westport, CT: Greenwood Press, 1986.

Bryant, John, and Robert Milder, eds. *Melville's Evermoving Dawn: Centennial Essays.* Kent, OH: Kent State University Press, 1997.

Grover, Kathryn. *The Fugitives' Gibraltar: Escaping Slaves and Abolitionism in New Bedford, Massachusetts.* Amherst: University of Massachusetts Press, 2001.

Jehlen, Myra, ed. *Herman Melville: A Collection of Critical Essays.* Englewood Cliffs, NJ: Prentice Hall, 1994.

Karcher, Carolyn L. *Shadow over the Promised Land: Slavery, Race, and Violence in Melville's America.* Baton Rouge: Louisiana State University Press, 1980.

Levine, Robert S., and Samuel Otter, eds. *Frederick Douglass and Herman Melville: Essays in Relation.* Chapel Hill: University of North Carolina Press, 2008.

McFeely, William. *Frederick Douglass.* New York: W. W. Norton, 1991.

Parker, Hershel. *Herman Melville: A Biography.* Vol. 1, *1819–1851.* Baltimore: Johns Hopkins University Press, 1996.

Stauffer, John. *The Black Hearts of Men: Radical Abolitionists and the Transformation of Race.* Cambridge, MA: Harvard University Press, 2002.

———. *Giants: The Parallel Lives of Frederick Douglass and Abraham Lincoln.* New York: Twelve, 2009.

Sundquist, Eric, ed. *Frederick Douglass: New Literary and Historical Essays.* Cambridge: Cambridge University Press, 1990.

Wallace, Robert K. *Douglass and Melville: Anchored Together in Neighborly Style.* New Bedford, MA: Spinner Publications, 2005.

The house at 73 Forest Street, Hartford, Connecticut, that Harriet Beecher Stowe purchased with royalties she earned from her books. The book that bankrolled its purchase was, like the house, an amalgam of different subjects and styles, including Gothic and Rustic elements.

PHOTO CREDIT: PHOTO BY TODD VAN HOOSEAR.

4

The House That
Uncle Tom's Cabin Bought

HARRIET BEECHER STOWE HOUSE
73 FOREST STREET, HARTFORD, CONNECTICUT

In 1885, a welcome package arrived at the graceful, white wood–trimmed house at 73 Forest Street: a new illustrated edition of *Uncle Tom's Cabin*, published by Houghton and Mifflin. Harriet Beecher Stowe, then seventy-four years old, was delighted to receive it. "So pretty a book, at so cheap a price ought to command a sale," Stowe wrote to her publisher, noting that "from the letters constantly coming to me in every mail I judge the interest in it is unabated." The only writing Stowe was doing at that time tended to be notes to friends. But the money that her books continued to bring in was the main support not only of Stowe and her aged husband, but also of her twin daughters, who helped look after both of them.

The name of the architect who designed the house at 73 Forest Street in 1871 remains unknown. But there was nothing anonymous about the author who bought the house two years later and lived in it for the next twenty-three years, until the end of her life. She bought it with the proceeds from another house—one she herself had designed, in her imagination—the most famous house in American literature, *Uncle Tom's Cabin*. By the time Stowe moved to the Forest Street house in 1873, she was the best-known American author in the world. President Abraham Lincoln had called her "the little woman who wrote the book that started this great war." The book had unprecedented sales in both the United States and England; it kept fourteen power printing presses running around the clock and sold more copies than any book but the Bible ("There has been nothing like it in the history of bookmaking," one English reviewer wrote.) It was translated into dozens of languages, and stage plays based on the novel (without Stowe's involvement or permission) were produced so often both before and after the Civil War that *Uncle Tom's Cabin* became widely known as "the world's greatest hit."

With its bay windows, several porches, and steep roof, the house was a cross between different architectural styles—Rustic cottage and Gothic villa. The book that bankrolled its purchase was also an amalgam of different subjects and styles. One could find in its pages both gothic hauntings and rustic fireside talk. Part sentimental novel, part realist novel, part political satire, and part sermon, Stowe's book blended plainspoken simplicity with tear-jerking sentimentality and lush romantic effusions, much as the unknown architect mixed styles in what would be Stowe's final home.

Her first home when she returned to Hartford was an elaborate Gothic Revival villa called Oakholm, which she moved her family into in 1864, after having supervised every aspect of its construction. It was around this time that she began writing "House and Home" columns for the *Atlantic Monthly* on how to build, decorate, and manage sensible, easy-to-maintain homes. But Stowe had not taken her own advice: the rambling, drafty, eight-gabled house proved too costly to maintain, and in 1873 she and her husband moved into the much more modest dwelling on Forest Street on the western edge of Hartford. One attraction was the neighborhood, called "Nook Farm" (after the bend or "nook" in a river that bordered the area at the time), an enclave of accomplished writers and reformers that included, in addition to her celebrated next-door neighbor, Mark Twain, her suffragist sister Isabella Beecher Hooker, *Hartford Courant* editor and novelist Charles Dudley Warner, and the actor William Gillette. It was here that she would finish her last novel, *Poganuc People*, which drew on her Connecticut childhood. (Other books she wrote while living in the Forest Street home include *Palmetto Leaves, Betty's Bright Idea, Footsteps of the Master, A Dog's Mission*, and *Women in Sacred History*.)

The house reflected many of the principles laid out in an influential chapter on "home decoration" that Stowe had contributed to the home management book she coauthored with her sister Catharine, *The American Woman's Home* (1869). The simplicity and grace of the house's exterior had played a role in Stowe's selection of it as her home. It was not marred by a jumble of the kinds of superfluous architectural ornaments that Stowe referred to as "'curlywurlies' and 'whigmaliries,' which make the house neither prettier nor more comfortable, and which take up a good deal of money" (one wonders what she thought about the ornate exterior of the Twain house soon to be built next door). Some houses, she went on, in "Home Decoration," feature "a very ugly, narrow, awkward porch on the outside. . . . The only use of this porch was to cost money, and to cause every body who looked at it to exclaim as they went by, 'What ever induced that man to put a thing like that on the outside of his house?'" The porches outside Forest Street house, by way of contrast, are graceful and utilitarian. Choices like these were more than merely matters of taste in Stowe's view: they were reflections of character. (In a novel she published two years before moving into the house, *Pink and White Tyranny*, Stowe renders harsh judgment on the shallowness and unworthiness of a new wife who redecorates her husband's comfortable old country house according to what she construes as the dictates of French fashion.)

The American Woman's Home advocated decorating strategies that allowed homemakers to spend less time on housework. In place of the hard-to-clean heavy carpeting common in many middle-class Victorian homes, Stowe and Beecher advocated putting rush mats on bedroom floors. In place of the heavy drapes that made the rooms of most Victorian homes dark and stuffy, they urged women to let the sunlight in, filtered through a light screen of ferns, ivy, and other plants. The conservatory of the home Mark Twain built next door was constructed according to that plan. (During Stowe's final years, as her faculties dimmed and she roamed the neighborhood absentmindedly picking wildflowers, she would often wander into Twain's yard and cut blooms that she found growing there, to the consternation of his gardener. As Kenneth Andrews tells us in *Nook Farm*, the family hung scissors "at convenient points to remind her not to injure the plants by breaking off the stems.")

In the Forest Street house, Stowe practiced what she preached, infusing the rooms with the "harmony of color" she praised in *The American Woman's Home*, where she also laid out for housewives precise calculations of the price of simple white muslin curtains, chintz fabric to be used for upholstery and table-coverings, and appealing, inexpensive "chromos" of works by "some of our best American artists." Stowe filled her house with art that ranged from graceful landscapes that she painted herself to a reproduction of a Renaissance painting (Raphael's *Madonna of the Goldfinch*) and of an ancient Greek sculpture (the Venus de Milo). Her interest in painting and design can be seen not only in the watercolors and oils by Stowe that hang in several rooms, but also in the pieces of furniture she decorated herself that are in the sitting room off her bedroom, and the violet-patterned china dinnerware she designed that is in the dining room. The kitchen was organized for maximum efficiency and cleanliness, with a worktable in the middle, and with canisters of staples in easy reach—a very sensible and convenient design. Unlike Dinah's kitchen in *Uncle Tom's Cabin*, which "looked as if it had been arranged by a hurricane blowing through it," with "about as many places for each cooking utensil as there were days in the year," Stowe's kitchen is a model of order and good organization.

Stowe designed the efficient kitchen of her Forest Street home in Hartford according to principles laid out in the home management guide she coauthored with her sister Catharine, *The American Woman's Home*.

PHOTO CREDIT: COURTESY OF THE HARRIET BEECHER STOWE HOUSE, HARTFORD, CT.

Stowe's attraction to decorating with plants was not limited to the house's interior. She was increasingly absorbed, during her later years, in her elaborate outdoor gardens—her beds of tulips, daffodils, chrysanthemums, roses, delphiniums, foxgloves, and jack-in-the-pulpits. She spent many a happy hour gardening, as well as painting watercolors of her favorite plants and flowers. The garden today includes many plants of the same varieties she cultivated, and some of her paintings of them still hang on the wall. While Gertrude Stein would later write that "a rose is a rose is a rose," for Stowe, the roses in her garden—and the flowers in the watercolors she painted and hung on her walls—had a broader significance. "Of so great dignity and worth is this holy and sacred thing, that the power to create a HOME ought to be ranked above all creative faculties," she wrote. "The sculptor who brings out the breathing statue from cold marble, the painter who warms the canvas into a deathless glow of beauty, the architect who built cathedrals and hung the world-like dome of St. Peter's in mid-air, is not to be compared, in sanctity and worthiness, to the humblest artist, who, out of the poor materials afforded by this shifting, changing world, creates the secure Eden of a home." A well-run home, for Stowe—the repository of key moral values—would come to represent nothing less than the potential moral regeneration of the nation.

The young girl who had gone to school in Hartford decades before her return to the city in 1864 had not planned to write a book that would change the world. Indeed, had someone suggested that she would, young Harriet undoubtedly would have politely challenged them. And if anyone had predicted that her seventieth birthday in 1881 would be a school holiday for children in Hartford, the modest, thirteen-year-old student-teacher at her sister Catharine's Hartford Female Seminary in 1824 undoubtedly would have scoffed. Later in life, she professed some puzzlement as to how it all had happened.

Born in Litchfield, Connecticut, in 1811 to the Reverend Lyman Beecher and his first wife, Roxana Foote Beecher, Harriet was the seventh child in her family—and the fourth daughter. Roxana Beecher, who died in 1816, was remembered as an angelic and saintly mother and wife; she was also a young woman who wrote poetry and was fascinated by science (she wrote to a relative about her excitement at the "discovery that the fixed alkalies are metallic oxyds"). Her influence on Harriet was limited by the fact that Harriet was only five when she died; but Roxana was an important influence on her eldest child, Catharine, who was sixteen at the time of her mother's death. Catharine in turn would shape her younger sister Harriet's life in key ways.

Lyman Beecher, a Congregationalist minister and one of the most famous clergymen in America, represented a strange mix of playfulness, gentle guidance, and terror for his children. On the one hand, he was a father who let his children wake him up each morning by climbing onto his bed and pulling his nose, and who refused to get out of bed before the children checked under it for savage beasts and reassured him that there were none to be found. He was a father who patiently taught his children how to poke holes in weak religious arguments, and how to frame strong ones, and who guided their intellectual and moral development with devotion and care. But he was also a rigid and demanding father who required his children to accept his own interpretation of the Bible, and who terrorized them with visions of eternal damnation if they veered from the course. All of his sons became ministers, whether they were suited to the job or not. That career option was not open to his daughters, since the church excluded women in that role.

Harriet had the good fortune to attend Litchfield Female Academy, a school whose director, Sara Pierce, believed not only in teaching the music, dancing, singing, and embroidery requisite for "marriageable" young women of the day, but also in "vindicating the equality of the female intellect" by exposing girls to history, geography, moral philosophy, composition, grammar, arithmetic, Latin, astronomy, chemistry, and botany. Located a block from the Beecher home in Litchfield, the school attracted young women from across the United States, Canada, and the West Indies, and gave them an education not unlike the best schools of the time for young men. Although its aim was to prepare young women to assume traditional social roles, through competitions and prizes it also fostered pride in individual achievement.

In 1823, Catharine decided to open a school for girls in Hartford, the Hartford Female Seminary, starting out with seven girls in a single room. The following year, when Harriet was thirteen, she moved to Hartford to help her sister with the school. She was the same age as many of the pupils—including Sarah Willis, who would go on to a stellar writing career of her own under the pseudonym Fanny Fern. Sometimes Harriet found herself reading one chapter ahead of the class she was to teach the next day. She remained in Hartford until she followed her father to his new job as head of Lane Theological Seminary in Cincinnati in 1832.

It was in Cincinnati, across the river from slaveholding Kentucky, that the evils of slavery forced themselves on Harriet's awareness. Although she ventured into the slave South only once, in 1833, on a brief visit to Kentucky, Cincinnati itself was a hotbed of antislavery activity. Black and white abolitionists, runaway slaves, bounty hunters, Underground Railroad operatives, fearful freedmen, and equally fearful whites all figured in the drama that played itself out there in the 1830s and 1840s, as Stowe watched the city and the nation lurch fitfully toward the conflict that would rip it apart decades later.

Harriet published her first story in 1834 in *Western Monthly Magazine*. She was twenty-three years old. Two years later, she married a teacher at the seminary, Calvin Stowe, "a man rich in Greek and Hebrew and Latin and Arabic, and alas, rich in nothing else," as she once put it. During the first decade of her marriage, Stowe gave birth to five children; two more would follow shortly thereafter. By the time Harper Brothers invited her to publish a collection of her stories in 1843, she was deep into juggling career and family obligations. Anticipating by nearly a century Virginia Woolf's comments on the importance of "a room of one's own" for a woman writer, Stowe wrote to her husband, "If I am to write, I must have a room to myself which shall be *my* room." Already favoring the profusion of plants that would be central to her decorating philosophy, she wrote that she wanted to keep her plants in the room she was fixing up with a stove and a cheap carpet as her writing room, "and then I shall be quite happy." A letter she would write a few years later conveys a good sense of the formidable challenges she faced as she tried to write amid the demands of domesticity: "Since I began this note I have been called off at least a dozen times; once for the fishman to buy a codfish—once to see a man who had brought me some barrels of apples—once to see a book man—then to Mrs. Upham to see about a drawing I promised to make for her—then to nurse the baby—then into the kitchen to make a chowder for dinner & now I am at it all again for nothing but deadly determination enables me ever to write—it is rowing against wind and tide." (Because Calvin Stowe's earnings as a biblical scholar were scarcely adequate to support his growing family, Harriet took in boarders to help make ends meet. Her husband encouraged her, in a letter he wrote to her in 1847 while she was taking the "water cure" at a sanitarium in Brattleboro, Vermont, for her health, to continue to try to "pick up a little pocket money" through her writing.)

Stowe's growing abolitionist sympathies come across in a sketch she published in 1845 titled "Immediate Emancipation," in which a runaway slave from Kentucky seeks refuge in a Cincinnati home—an occurrence familiar to residents of the day. In her story, however, the plot takes a less familiar twist: the Quaker in whose home the fugitive has taken refuge manages to persuade the slave's master who comes to reclaim him to give him his freedom instead. The story was a rehearsal, of sorts, for scenes Stowe would later paint in *Uncle Tom's Cabin*. Despite her growing sympathy for the antislavery cause, however, she was not actively involved in abolitionism before she wrote her most famous novel. (Members of her family were, however: her brother Edward, for example, had been friends with the outspoken abolitionist editor Elijah Lovejoy, who was murdered by a mob in Alton, Illinois, for publishing his antislavery newspaper.)

The watershed period for Stowe was 1849–1850, a period that brought about changes in her personal life, and in the nation's life, that converged to push her along the road to *Uncle Tom's Cabin*. In 1849, her eighteen-month-old son "Charley" (Samuel Charles), her sixth child, died in Cincinnati's cholera epidemic. Charley had been Stowe's happiest, healthiest, and most easygoing child ("the most beautiful and most loved" of her children, as she later put it), a source of unalloyed pleasure and joy. Crushed by his death, her pain also gave her a sense of connection with every slave mother whose child was torn from her arms by the cruelties of a slave system that inflicted similarly devastating heartbreak. "It was at *his* dying bed and at *his* grave," she later wrote, "that I learnt what a poor slave-mother may feel when her child is torn away from her. In those depths of sorrow which seemed to me immeasurable, it was my only prayer to God that such anguish might not be suffered in vain. . . . I felt that I could never be consoled for it unless this crushing of my own heart might enable me to work out some great good to others."

The following year, in 1850, the year Calvin Stowe was hired to teach at Bowdoin College in Brunswick, Maine, and moved the family there, the passage of the Fugitive Slave Law made the whole country complicit in the institution of slavery, a partner in the evil business of splitting families apart and destroying lives. The law made anyone who helped a runaway in any way—with food, shelter, or advice— liable to a substantial prison term and a thousand-dollar fine. What was once a "southern" problem now became the nation's problem, as "The Government Kidnapping Act" (as some abolitionists called it) made free blacks, as well as slaves who had run to the North to seek their freedom, vulnerable to being kidnapped and sold into slavery. Still raw from the personal pain of losing Charley, Stowe wrote to her brother Henry that she felt "as if my heart would burn itself out in grief and shame" as she watched fugitives forcibly reenslaved all around her.

A letter from her sister-in-law Isabella (her brother Edward's wife) helped solidify her resolve: "if I could use a pen as you can," Isabella wrote to her, "I would write something that would make this whole nation feel what an accursed thing slavery is." Stowe decided to do just that by writing a series of sketches about slavery for a magazine, the *National Era*. She had already published several pieces in this publication (including a response to the Fugitive Slave Law), but now she proposed to do something new: she would turn vivid storytelling to rhetorical, political ends. She wrote the editor, "There is no arguing with *pictures*, and everybody is impressed by them, whether they mean to be or not."

When a writing room of her own was hard to come by in her busy household, she wrote in her husband's office at the college, spurred on by a vision she had in church one Sunday of a saintly slave being beaten to death. She wrote as a woman possessed, and would later say of the novel, "God wrote it." From June 5, 1851, to April 1, 1852, the *National Era* ran weekly installments of *Uncle Tom's Cabin*. It appeared book form in 1852, and sold three hundred thousand copies within a year. It would also inspire a multitude of stage productions on both sides of the Atlantic.

Harriet Beecher Stowe (1811–1896), author of *Uncle Tom's Cabin* (1852), which sold more copies than any book of its time but the Bible, and the book that President Abraham Lincoln credited with having started the Civil War.
PHOTO CREDIT: COURTESY OF THE LIBRARY OF CONGRESS, PRINTS AND PHOTOGRAPHS DIVISION, WASHINGTON, DC.

More than twenty different stage adaptations of *Uncle Tom's Cabin* were mounted in London alone between 1852 and 1855, as Sarah Meer notes in her book, *The Uncle Tom Mania.*

The "pictures" that Stowe painted exposed the brutal realities of slavery for a reading audience accustomed to rhetoric and diatribe but not to the blend of sentiment and sermon that Stowe presented. The melodramatic Christian martyrdom of Uncle Tom and little Eva moved her readers to tears, and those dimensions of the book, combined with its repeated attack on the institution of slavery, moved many of her countrymen to action. Slavery, Stowe demonstrated, subverted Christianity, attacked the family, and threatened the social fabric of the nation. Writing for an audience already prepared for stories of the lives of runaway slaves by the publication of the many slave narratives that preceded Stowe's novel, her unforgettable tale blended antislavery polemic with the emotional appeal of the sentimental novel in new and powerful ways.

In addition to fueling the fires of abolitionism, the book would indelibly shape the portrayal of African Americans in American fiction for several generations—mainly for the worse. Her novel may have attacked the institution of slavery, but it also perpetuated racial stereotypes. Stowe believed, as she wrote in *A Key to Uncle Tom's Cabin*, that "the Negro race is confessedly more simple, docile, childlike, and affectionate, than other races." She meant it as a compliment (as a reason for why "the divine graces of love and faith, when in-breathed by the Holy Spirit, find in [the] natural temperament [of Negroes] a more congenial atmosphere"). But for many African Americans during the century and a half since the publication of the book, it was a compliment they were loath to accept. Stowe's "romantic racialism" was a far cry from a view of actual equality among the races—from the recognition that black and white were alike in their moral and intellectual aptitude. Similarly, her endorsement of the idea of black emigration to Africa ran counter to a vision of the United States as a nation that had a place for black citizens as well as white. Black writers in the twentieth century would come to view Stowe's vision of the "nature" of the black race as a burdensome stereotype they had to overturn.

From the start, the book ignited heated debate, and it would become, as Langston Hughes put it, "the most cussed and discussed book of its time." While northern abolitionists celebrated it, southern slaveholders challenged its veracity. The anti–*Uncle Tom* literature that began to appear shortly after the novel was published featured benevolent plantation owners who looked after their slaves with kindness and generosity. Slave masters in anti–*Uncle Tom* literature used their whips only reluctantly, when all other forms of discipline failed, and were surrounded by slaves who were happy, loyal, contented, and in no way desirous of their freedom. Some southern writers charged Stowe outright with being a liar. She fought back, reaffirming the book's basis in fact when she published *A Key to Uncle Tom's Cabin* in 1853. Allegedly a compilation of her sources, it was actually a compilation of sources she assembled after her novel was published. Meanwhile, the deluge of stage productions, games, songs, poems, busts, figurines, dioramas, plates, engravings, and other items representing characters in Stowe's novel—referred to today as "Tomitudes"—that appeared after the book came out led Stephen Hirsch to call Uncle Tom "in his various forms, the most frequently sold slave in American history." Some of the "Tomitudes" that were presented to Stowe are on display in the house on Forest Street.

Stowe's work elicited a wide range of responses from African American writers. Some ex-slaves—most notably Lewis Clarke and Josiah Henson—put themselves forth as the models for George Harris and Uncle Tom, respectively. Both Frances Ellen Watkins Harper in her poem "Eliza Harris," and Paul Laurence Dunbar in his poem "Harriet Beecher Stowe," endorse Stowe's efforts and their effects, and Langston Hughes, in an introduction to the novel, refers to it as "a moral battle cry."

But the slave narrative of Solomon Northup—*Twelve Years a Slave*, published in 1853—takes exception to the view that the patient forbearance Tom represents is in any way typical of the slave's perspective on his condition. "Men may write fictions portraying lowly life as it is, or as it is not . . ." Northup wrote, "but let them toil with [the slave] in the field—sleep with him in the cabin—feed with him on husks; let them behold him scourged, hunted, trampled on, and they will come back with another story in their mouths. Let them know the *heart* of the poor slave—learn his secret thoughts—thoughts he dare not utter in the hearing of the white man; let them sit by him in the silent watches of the night—converse with him in trustful confidence, of 'life, liberty, and the pursuit of happiness,' and they will find that ninety-nine out of every hundred are intelligent enough to understand their situation, and to cherish in their bosoms the love of freedom, as passionately as themselves."

Richard Wright titled his first collection of short stories *Uncle Tom's Children* but later decided that the title had been a mistake, linking his book, as it did, to the tear-drenched culture of sentiment in which Stowe had been so successful, but which he was at pains to reject. He wrote that he "had written a book which even bankers' daughters could read and weep over and feel good about." He swore to himself "that if I ever wrote another book, no one would weep over it; that it would be so hard and deep that they would have to face it without the consolation of their tears." The result was the wrenching and compelling novel *Native Son*, a book no-body would dare simply "weep over and feel good about."

Other twentieth-century African American writers—including James Baldwin and Ishmael Reed—questioned the legacies of the racial politics of *Uncle Tom's Cabin* and its impact on the nation's views of African Americans. In 1949, in an essay titled "Everybody's Protest Novel," James Baldwin wrote that Stowe was "not so much a novelist as an impassioned pamphleteer," author of "a very bad novel" whose sticky sentimentality gave life to racial stereotypes while denying life and complexity to its black characters; the book, Baldwin believed, promoted rather than challenged prejudice based on color and race: the only black characters in the novel who manifest intelligence, initiative, and independence, he reminds us, do so in direct proportion to the lightness of their skin. In 1976, Ishmael Reed published his wildly out-of-control satirical novel, *Flight to Canada*, which begins with a section called "Naughty Harriet," which ponders (among other things) the relationship between Stowe's book and ex-slave Josiah Henson's own story. Reed writes, "Harriet made enough money on someone else's plot to buy thousands of silk dresses and a beautiful home."

The disadvantageous royalty agreements Stowe had signed, however, prevented the enormous popularity of *Uncle Tom's Cabin* from providing her with enough of an estate to keep that "beautiful home" on Forest Street in the family after she died. "The home" may have been the center of the family and of the moral universe of the nation for America's best-known author, but neither her faith in the saving powers of domesticity nor the money she earned from her most famous novel were enough to let her grown daughters Eliza and Hatty (who had shared the house with her for many years) maintain the house after her death. Stowe's grandniece, Katharine Seymour Day, later purchased and restored the home and turned it into the museum and educational center that it is today—a monument to Stowe's efforts to change the world with her words.

JOHN P. PARKER HOUSE

300 FRONT STREET, RIPLEY, OHIO

Living less than one hundred feet from the bank of the Ohio River, John P. Parker had a good, unobstructed view of activity along the water's edge—useful if you were engaged in helping the fugitive slaves who crossed the river in the dark of night, and protecting them from the slave-catchers.

Parker didn't leave his mark on American literary history until nearly a hundred years after his death, in 1996, when his remarkable narrative, *His Promised Land: The Autobiography of John P. Parker, Former Slave and Conductor on the Underground Railroad*, edited by Stuart Seely Sprague, was published. By 1996, the house in which he had lived from 1853 until his death in 1900 had fallen into serious disrepair: part of the tin roof was badly rusted, the chimney was missing, the walls were dilapidated, and signs of deterioration were everywhere. By 2010, however, the house had been restored, and today it operates as a museum that celebrates the ingenuity and sheer chutzpah of a man who not only outwitted the enemy but lived to tell the tale in vivid, delicious detail.

Born a slave himself in Norfolk, Virginia, in 1827, Parker was the son of a black woman and a white man. When he was eight, he was bound to another slave and forced to walk to Richmond. In Richmond he was sold and marched in chains to Mobile, Alabama. Parker became a skilled ironworker. He bought his freedom in 1845 with money he earned in the foundry and moved to Cincinnati. When the man with whom he was boarding in Cincinnati wanted Parker to help him rescue his family from slavery, he was initially reluctant. But the success he encountered when he decided to help encouraged him to rescue many others. He started a family of his own and moved to Ripley, Ohio, a center of abolitionist activity. His daring rescues earned him the respect of fellow abolitionists and the enmity of slavery's defenders. During the Civil War, Parker managed to smuggle hundreds of slaves into the Union Army. Shortly after his death, a Cincinnati newspaper opined that "a more fearless creature never lived. He gloried in danger. . . .He would go boldly over into the enemy's camp and filch the fugitives to freedom."

In 1865, he became part owner of a foundry that manufactured engines, reapers, and other machinery, and in 1890 he built the Phoenix Foundry, one of the largest foundries in Ohio at the time. Parker was awarded several patents for iron agricultural implements he invented. A number of iron objects

The home of abolitionist, inventor, and writer John Parker (1827–1900), 300 Front Street, Ripley, Ohio. Born into slavery, Parker became a key Underground Railroad operative who helped hundreds of slaves to freedom through this house, a story he tells in *His Promised Land: The Autobiography of John P. Parker, Former Slave and Conductor on the Underground Railroad.*

PHOTO CREDIT: PHOTO BY ALBERTA HEMSLEY.

manufactured at his foundry are on display on the grounds of the Parker House in Ripley.

Parker's memoir, *His Promised Land*, is distinctive in part because of its author's candor and openness about the Underground Railroad, a subject that before the end of the war tended to be treated by those involved with it with the utmost reticence. But it is also a special book because Parker's courage, intelligence, and lucid style make it particularly readable and engaging—a welcome addition to the literature of abolition and slavery, and to nineteenth-century black autobiography.

At one point in the book, a black man Parker has never met knocks on his door at midnight one night and claims that he had run away to Canada, leaving his wife behind, but now wants to rescue her with Parker's help. Parker's intuitions make him suspicious. When he threatens "that unless he told me the truth I would shoot him," the man "confessed he was only a decoy, sent by four men who were . . . lying behind a log on the riverbank waiting for him to bring me down to the skiff. He said that the men planned to kidnap me, if I resisted, to kill me. They were determined to earn the reward of $1,000 dead or alive. He pleaded he was there against his will, as one of the men was his master, and had threatened to kill him if he had not come and told the story he did." Parker decides to "[run] the slave off to Canada, as a good joke on his master." "[T]he slave pleaded he did not want to go to Canada . . . but I shook my head and said we would run him away whether [he wished it] or no. The man begged and pleaded, but I was more interested now in sending a warning on [to] my enemies than I was in the wishes of this man." He sent the man out the back door in the care of an Irish neighbor who stayed "close on [the man's] back swearing dire threats unless he went along peaceably to Canada."

"With the decoy gone," Parker writes,

I foolishly determined to seek my would-be kidnappers in their wooden log lair. By this time it was getting towards daylight as it was in July. . . . Having waited [until] the last minute, placing two pistols in my jacket, carrying my hunting knife openly in my hand, with a large English mastiff at my heels, I started over the bank to confront my enemies. . . . Coming opposite the log, I drew my pistol and called for the men to come out. As there was no answer, for a moment the thought came to my mind perhaps the slave had deceived me. All such notions left me when I saw the gleam of a gun over the top of the log. I needed no further evidence to establish the sinister ambush that had been prepared for me.

A second time I called the men, warning them that I knew of their hiding place. Furthermore I had summoned my friends, who were at the top of the bank, ready to shoot them down if any injury came to me. Of course, the only force present was myself, my wife, and my dog. The only response to this statement was the ominous click of a rifle as it was cocked, made ready to fire. My faithful dog came to my rescue as he now leaped on the top of the log and began barking furiously.

The diversion no doubt saved my life, for the four men, seeing their hiding place was known, now came out in the open and confronted me. They were armed with rifles and pistols in their belts, as the dawn now began to break over the eastern hills. They were threatening and furious, demanding their slave. I was perfectly oblivious of any man and demanded to whom they referred, what was his name, and where was he going. . . . As they persisted in wanting to know where their man was, I kept asking, "What man?" determined to force a confession out of their own perfidy. Finally one of the men confessed they had sent a man to my house. I replied that there was a runaway at my house who wanted to go to Canada, and that the last I saw of him he was going that way.

Then Parker writes, "a neighbor whom my wife had aroused called me by name from the top of the bank. I answered, saying I was talking to four men, giving their names, saying I was coming at once. Backing away from the party. I kept my face toward them, as I did not propose to be shot down without defending myself. I backed away, until I reached a point of safety, leaving four men standing helplessly by with a hatred that but for their own safety would have prompted them to shoot me down in my tracks." Once he is "out of the range of their guns," Parker runs to safety, watching "the skiff with the four men pull away, fairly beside themselves with rage, and one of them less a slave for their futile night's raid." He worried that the slave he had forcibly run away might jeopardize all their safety "because all he had to do was raise an outcry and the law would be back of him." But his Irish neighbor came back and "reported that the man decided that it was too good a chance to lose, and agreed to go on via the Underground Railway. So far as I ever knew he must have reached his promised land."

RELATED SITES

❧ Litchfield Historic District
Intersection of U.S. Route 202 and Connecticut Route 63, Litchfield, Connecticut

The Litchfield Historic District is the best surviving example in the country of a typical late-eighteenth-century New England town and contains many buildings that Harriet Beecher (born here in 1811) would have seen during her childhood here.

❧ Harriet Beecher Stowe House
2950 Gilbert Avenue and Foraker Avenue, Cincinnati, Ohio

Harriet Beecher moved to this simple, two-story brick house in 1832, when her father came to Cincinnati to head Lane Seminary. It was here that she began her publishing career, met her husband, and first learned about the evils of slavery from fugitive slaves and abolitionists. She lived in this house until 1836, and in the neighborhood until 1850. Today the house is a community center and museum.

John Rankin House
6152 Rankin Road, Ripley, Ohio

Presbyterian minister John Rankin, author of the influential 1826 book, *Letters on American Slavery*, was an abolitionist actively involved in Underground Railroad activities in Ohio. He and his wife and children reputedly assisted as many as two thousand slaves to escape from 1822 to 1865. Stowe visited him in this one-and-a-half-story, 1828 brick Federal-style house while she was living in Cincinnati, and it was here that she heard the story of a fugitive slave that would shape Eliza's story *Uncle Tom's Cabin*. Rankin's house is open to the public.

Early Stone Buildings of Central Kentucky
Some of the fugitive slaves Stowe encountered in Cincinnati had fled plantations in neighboring Kentucky, where they might have lived in stone slave quarters like the ones that can be seen today at the Albert Knox Farm, U.S. Route 150, Danville; Bayless Quarters, Kentucky Route 13, North Middletown; the Stone Quarters on Burgin Road, Kentucky Route 152, Harrodsburg; the James Briscoe Quarters, off U.S. Route 25, Delaplain; the Ash Emison Quarters, off U.S. Route 25, Delaplain; the Joseph Patterson Quarters, off U.S. Route 421, Midway; the John Leavell Quarters, off Kentucky Route 753, Bryantsville; the Hogan Quarters, off Kentucky Route 33, Versailles; and the Andrew Muldrow Quarters, Griers Creek Road, Tyrone. The plot of *Uncle Tom's Cabin* is set in motion when a Kentucky farmer decides to deal with his financial troubles by selling two of his slaves. Stowe mentions in *A Key to Uncle Tom's Cabin* that she based the physical description of Eliza in *Uncle Tom's Cabin* on a beautiful young enslaved woman whom she had once met while she was traveling in Kentucky.

Harriet Beecher Stowe House
63 Federal Street, Brunswick, Maine

Stowe lived in this frame house with her husband and children from 1850 to 1852. It was here that she wrote *Uncle Tom's Cabin*. The house, which has been extensively altered, is owned by Bowdoin College and is not open to the public.

●◆ Laura Plantation
2247 Louisiana Route 18 (River Road), Vacherie, Louisiana

At this plantation on the banks of the Mississippi River run by four generations of Creole women, one can still visit four extant ramshackle wooden slave cabins that were constructed in the 1840s at the edge of the sugar cane fields, as well as the manor house and other buildings, also built by enslaved people. In *Uncle Tom's Cabin*, Uncle Tom dies on a rural Louisiana plantation.

FOR FURTHER READING

The Writers: Works and Words

Baldwin, James. *Collected Essays*. Edited by Toni Morrison. New York: Library of America, 1998.

Beecher, Catharine, and Harriet Beecher Stowe. *The American Woman's Home; or, Principles of Domestic Science*. 1869. Edited by Nicole Tonkovich. New Brunswick, NJ: Rutgers University Press, 2002.

Dunbar, Paul Laurence. "Harriet Beecher Stowe." In *The Collected Poetry of Paul Laurence Dunbar*. Edited by Joanne M. Braxton. Charlottesville: University of Virginia Press, 1993.

Fields, Annie. *Life and Letters of Harriet Beecher Stowe*. Boston: Houghton Mifflin, 1897.

Gates, Henry Louis, Jr. and Nellie Y. McKay, gen. eds. *The Norton Anthology of African American Literature*. New York: W. W. Norton, 1997.

Harper, Frances E. W. "Eliza Harris." In *Complete Poems of Frances E. W. Harper*. Edited by Maryemma Graham. Schomburg Library of Nineteenth-Century Black Women Writers. New York: Oxford University Press, 1988.

Northup, Solomon. *Twelve Years a Slave* 1853. Edited by Sue Eakin and Joseph Logsdon. Baton Rouge: Louisiana State University Press, 1968.

Parker, John P. *His Promised Land: The Autobiography of John P. Parker, Former Slave and Conductor on the Underground Railroad*. Edited by Stuart Seely Sprague. New York: W. W. Norton, 1996.

Rankin, John. *Letters on American Slavery*. Boston: I. Knapp, 1838.

Reed, Ishmael. *Flight to Canada*. New York: Random House, 1976.

Stowe, Harriet Beecher. *The Harriet Beecher Stowe Reader*. Edited by Joan D. Hedrick. New York: Oxford University Press, 1999.

———. *A Key to Uncle Tom's Cabin*. Bedford, MA: Applewood Books, 1998.

———. *Pink and White Tyranny*. Boston: Roberts Brothers, 1871.

———. *Uncle Tom's Cabin: Authoritative Text, Backgrounds and Contexts, Criticism*. Edited by Elizabeth Ammons. New York: W. W. Norton, 1994.

Wright, Richard. *Native Son*. 1940. In *Richard Wright: Early Works: Lawd Today! / Uncle Tom's Children / Native Son*. Introduction by Arnold Rampersad. New York: Library of America, 1991.

———. *Uncle Tom's Children*. 1938. New York: Harper and Row, 1960.

Background and Contexts

Ammons, Elizabeth. *Critical Essays on Harriet Beecher Stowe.* Boston: G. K. Hall, 1980.

Andrews, Kenneth. *Nook Farm: Mark Twain's Hartford Circle.* Cambridge, MA: Harvard University Press, 1950.

Birdoff, Harry. *The World's Greatest Hit: "Uncle Tom's Cabin."* New York: S. F. Vanni, 1947.

Brown, Gillian. "Getting in the Kitchen with Dinah: Domestic Politics in *Uncle Tom's Cabin.*" *American Quarterly* 36, no. 4 (Autumn 1984): 502–523.

Gossett, Thomas F. *"Uncle Tom's Cabin" and American Culture.* Dallas: Southern Methodist University Press, 1985.

Hedrick, Joan D. *Harriet Beecher Stowe: A Life.* New York: Oxford University Press, 1994.

Hirsch, Stephen A. "Uncle Tomitudes: The Popular Reaction to *Uncle Tom's Cabin.*" In *Studies in the American Renaissance*, edited by Joel Myerson, 303–330. Boston: Twayne, 1978.

Meer, Sarah. *The Uncle Tom Mania: Slavery, Minstrelsy, and Transatlantic Culture in the 1850s.* Athens: University of Georgia Press, 2005.

Sundquist, Eric J., ed. *New Essays on "Uncle Tom's Cabin."* Cambridge: Cambridge University Press, 1986.

The ornate and elegant Tiffany-designed front entrance hall of the Mark Twain House, 351
Farmington Avenue, Hartford, Connecticut.

5

The Irony of American History

THE MARK TWAIN BOYHOOD HOME AND MUSEUM
206-208 HILL STREET, HANNIBAL, MISSOURI

THE MARK TWAIN HOUSE AND MUSEUM
351 FARMINGTON AVENUE, HARTFORD, CONNECTICUT

The small, white clapboard house on Hill Street in Hannibal, Missouri, is as different from the ornate mansion on Farmington Avenue in Hartford, Connecticut, as the line drawing of the barefoot, grinning Huck who peers out from the first frontispiece of *Huckleberry Finn* is from the photograph of the elegant bust of Mark Twain that appears as a second frontispiece on the page opposite it. But the two houses are bound to each other as tightly as the pages of the double frontispiece in the first American edition of Mark Twain's most celebrated novel. The millions of tourists who make the journey from all over the world to the little house in Hannibal come because of the books Twain wrote while living in the sumptuous home in Hartford, books in which "the Matter of Hannibal," as Henry Nash Smith once put it, often takes center stage.

THE MARK TWAIN BOYHOOD HOME AND MUSEUM, HANNIBAL, MISSOURI

The simple, two-story house on Hill Street has a far from simple story to tell—one that involves the challenge of balancing nostalgia for the innocence of youth with knowledge of the injustice, bigotry, and hypocrisy that the blinders of youth occluded. This complex story—one that Sam Clemens struggled all his life to tell—is also the complex story of his country.

In front of the house stands a sign that reads, "TOM SAWYER'S FENCE. HERE STOOD THE BOARD FENCE WHICH TOM SAWYER PERSUADED HIS GANG TO PAY HIM FOR THE PRIVILEGE OF WHITEWASHING. TOM SAT BY AND SAW

THAT IT WAS WELL DONE." The sign, like so much of Mark Twain's hometown, blends history and fiction with abandon. The boy who grew up in this house would become famous for blending history and fiction as well, binding the two together with an inimitable sense of humor that won him the gratitude of generations of readers.

But Mark Twain's humor had a serious purpose at its heart. When he accepted an honorary degree from Yale in 1888, he wrote to Yale's President Timothy Dwight that he wanted to remind the world that the line of business he was in "is a useful trade, a worthy calling; that with all its lightness and frivolity it has one serious purpose, one aim, one specialty, and it is constant to it—the deriding of shams, the exposure of pretentious falsities, the laughing of stupid superstitions out of existence; and that whoso is by instinct engaged in this sort of warfare is the natural enemy of royalties, nobilities, privileges and all kindred swindles, and the natural friend of human rights and human liberties."

Mark Twain (1835–1910) in front of his boyhood home on Hill Street in Hannibal, Missouri, 1902.
PHOTO CREDIT: PHOTO BY HERBERT TOMLINSON; COURTESY OF THE MARK TWAIN PAPERS, THE BANCROFT LIBRARY, UNIVERSITY OF CALIFORNIA, BERKELEY.

The hodgepodge of fact and fiction on the "historical marker" for "Tom Sawyer's Fence" has a serious purpose behind it as well—but one that has nothing to do with deriding shams, exposing pretentious falsities, or laughing stupid superstitions out of existence: it's about money. Twain-related tourism has been the mainstay of the town's economy since the 1930s.

From early in the twentieth century, when the lumber industry that had driven much of its economy largely abandoned the town, Hannibal discovered that it had one resource that would prove to be infinitely renewable: its status as the place that furnished the setting for the adventures of Tom Sawyer and Huck Finn. Hannibal is not "on the way to" anywhere. It is a drive from any major airport, and passenger trains don't run there. But hundreds of thousands of tourists every year make the pilgrimage anyway, pumping millions of dollars into Hannibal's economy annually by eating meals in the Mark Twain Dinette, buying tickets to enter the Mark Twain Cave, and stocking up on Twain-related souvenirs. In addition to the Mark Twain Boyhood Home, original buildings associated with Sam Clemens in the Mark Twain Historic District include the Becky Thatcher House, home of his childhood sweetheart, Laura Hawkins; John Marshall Clemens's Justice of the Peace Office; and Grant's Drug Store. (Some twenty buildings in the Mark Twain Historic District date back to the period when the Clemens family lived in the town.)

The Clemens family had moved to Hannibal in 1839, when Sam was four years old, and lived in several houses in the general vicinity of Hill Street and Main Street. John Marshall Clemens moved his family into this modest white house in 1843 or 1844. The furnishings a visitor sees there today may be authentic period pieces, but one would have been more likely to find them in wealthier homes than that of the downwardly mobile John Clemens. At a low point in the family's fortunes, Sam's brother printed his failing newspaper in the front room of the house, while his sister gave piano lessons there, and his mother took in boarders. Declining fortunes finally forced the family to move in with a local pharmacist (above Grant's Drug Store), supplying meals in exchange for rent in 1846.

In 1847, John Marshall Clemens died, and eleven-year-old Sam soon began taking odd jobs in local stores. He took a full-time job as printer's devil in 1848 and continued working for newspapers for the next several years, occasionally publishing short squibs under his own name and under various inventive pseudonyms. He left Hannibal in 1853 to work as a journeyman printer for the next two years in St. Louis, New York, Philadelphia, Washington, DC, and other cities. He would go on to become a steamboat pilot, a prospector, a journalist, a lecturer, and a world-famous writer. But the town of Hannibal, where he spent most of his formative years, would never be far from his mind.

Located about 120 miles above St. Louis on the Mississippi River in northeastern Missouri, Hannibal was well situated for steamboat landings. When Sam Clemens lived here, there were two churches, two schools, a library, several saloons, and two hotels. The economy was dominated by slaughterhouses, a distillery, sawmills, and plants for processing pork, leather, tobacco, and hemp. From the time of Hannibal's founding in 1819 by a slave owner named Moses Bates, slaves played an important role in the town's economy—one that only grew in significance as the region was increasingly settled by other slaveholders from Kentucky, Virginia, and Tennessee. As Terrell Dempsey observes, "Because slaves could be leased, even white people of very modest means—people as poor as the Clemens family—had slaves in their households." Dempsey goes on to note that "Slaves were also an extremely important source of revenue for local and state governments. Slaves, like land, were taxed, and they constituted a substantial portion of the taxable wealth. In 1847, taxes on slaves accounted for more than 10 percent of Marion County revenue. . . . But the impact of slavery was not merely economic. Government, law, religion, economics, and social status were all inextricably tied to slavery, and just as each institution was supported, in some fashion, by slavery, so each institution had a stake in its perpetuation." Despite the fact that slavery pervaded nearly every aspect of the world of Sam Clemens's childhood, it was far from his mind when he wrote his first novel set in that world.

Several years before he began to write that book, he got a letter from a childhood friend, Will Bowen, that set in motion a stream of nostalgic memories: "The old life has swept before me like a panorama; the old days have trooped by in their glory again," Twain wrote to his friend. He fondly recalled playing Robin Hood, the town pump, the schoolhouse, his crush on the girl who lived across the street. Those memories fed directly into *Tom Sawyer*, a book that captured a sun-drenched summertime of juvenile fantasies, freedom, and friendships—an exuberant adventure story that encased a gently ironic portrait of small-town life. One can imagine Twain smiling to himself as he penned the skirmishes of the poodle and the pinch bug, or as he described the treasures that Tom bartered for that mass of Sunday school tickets, or as he related Tom's insistence that he had to stay home from school because his sore toe was "mortified." Twain wrote most of the book in Elmira, New York, where the gently rolling wooded hills and the Chemung River in the distance brought back memories of the woods and river of his youth. In the benign, reassuring world of *Tom Sawyer*, danger was satisfactorily vanquished, the misbehaving scamps were forgiven by the indulgent adults who surrounded them, and the ultimate buried treasure fantasy actually came true.

On the surface, the strange sketch that Twain published in 1876 would seem to have nothing to do with the novel *Adventures of Tom Sawyer*, which appeared the same year. "Facts Concerning the Recent Carnival of Crime in Connecticut" was a dark, surreal fantasy about a man who (literally) kills his conscience. Later that summer, when he wrote to Will Bowen, the same friend whose earlier letter had brought back all those pleasant memories, Twain tore into his old friend for not relegating "the dreaminess, the melancholy, the romance, the heroics" of adolescence to the rubbish heap. "All this," he ranted, "is simply mental & moral masturbation" belonging "eminently to the period usually devoted to *physical* masturbation, & should be left there & outgrown." What an odd comment from an author who had just published a novel about the dreaminess, melancholy, romance, and heroics of youth!

Perhaps on some level Twain knew that only someone prepared to kill, or at least suppress, that troublesome thing called a "conscience" could write a book set in the world of his childhood that ignored so completely the fact that Hannibal had been a slaveholding town. The "Carnival of Crime" and that second letter to Bowen were written by a man who now recognized that the world in which that innocent idyll had been set had not been so innocent after all. Scenes that were bathed in sunlight in *Tom Sawyer* would take on increasingly darker hues in later works as he became aware of how much he had failed to see before. As an adult, Twain would become a searing critic of the racism that shot through every aspect of his Hannibal childhood—and of the racism that persisted in American society long after slavery was ended.

Twain's growing awareness of the fact that he had lived his relatively happy youth in a society that had failed to question the injustice and immorality of slavery posed a problem: could he ever evoke the innocence of childhood again now that he knew all that he knew about the moral bankruptcy of the society in which he had enjoyed that childhood? The solution he hit upon in *Huckleberry Finn* involved channeling his double vision into satire, making sure that the reader knew that behind the boy in ragged overalls telling the story was an author who understood what was really going on.

Those in charge of presenting the Mark Twain Boyhood Home to tourists face the challenge of conveying the difference between the boy who accepted the town's racial hierarchies and the adult who was embarrassed and appalled by the racism that went unquestioned in the world of his youth. Although throughout the twentieth and early twenty-first century the fact that Hannibal had been a slaveholding town had no place in the narratives it told about itself, since 2005 the existence of slavery in Hannibal and in the Clemens household are acknowledged in the home and museum, as are specific slaves who served as models for Twain's fictional characters.

A book sits on an easel in the house open to a page that reads:

Hannibal was a slave-holding town in a slave-holding state when Sam Clemens lived here (1839–1853). Indeed, his parents were born in an America where slavery existed all around them and was rarely questioned. Although the Clemens family was not considered well to do, they did rent or own slaves when they could afford to do so. Mark Twain identified two such slaves, Lewis and Sandy, who would have been slaves in this house. Sandy became a model for "Jim," a young slave boy in *The Adventures of Tom Sawyer*. A middle-aged slave at Sam's Uncle John Quarles' farm in Florida, Missouri, was Uncle Dan'l. He became the model for another "Jim," the young adult slave in *Adventures of Huckleberry Finn*, and a beloved literary character.

The "Slavery in Hannibal" section of the exhibit in the museum adjacent to the house notes that "About a quarter of Hannibal's county—around 2,800—were enslaved African-Americans. Forty-four percent of the county's white families owned slaves, and others, including the Clemens family, paid owners to rent slaves." Another panel notes that "Sam spent plenty of time around enslaved African Americans in his childhood. He may have had misgivings about their treatment, but his opposition to slavery didn't surface until later in his life." It also includes this quote from Twain's autobiography: "We lived in a slaveholding community: indeed, when slavery perished my mother had been in daily touch with it for sixty years. Yet, kind-hearted and compassionate as she was, I think she was not conscious that slavery was a bald, grotesque, and unwarrantable usurpation. She had never heard it assailed in any pulpit, but heard it defended and sanctified in a thousand." The exhibit also includes the story of the slave child named Sandy that Twain included in his autobiography:

We had a little slave boy whom we had hired from some one, there in Hannibal. He was from the Eastern Shore of Maryland, had been brought away from his family and his friends, half-way across the American continent, and sold. He was a cheery spirit, innocent and gentle, and the noisiest creature that ever was, perhaps. All day long he was singing, whistling, yelling, whooping, laughing—it was maddening, devastating, unendurable. At last, one day, I lost all my temper, and went raging to my mother, and said Sandy had been singing for an hour without a single break, and I couldn't stand it, and wouldn't she please shut him up. The tears came into her eyes, and her lip trembled, and she said something like this—"Poor thing, when he sings, it shows that he is not remembering, and that comforts me; but when he is still, I am afraid he is thinking, and I cannot bear it. He will never see his mother again; if he can sing, I must not hinder it, but be thankful for it. If you were older, you would understand me; then that friendless child's noise would make you glad."

After that, "Sandy's noise," Twain wrote, "was not a trouble to me any more." A simple pallet on which an enslaved child like Sandy would have slept appeared in the exhibit briefly in the 1990s but mysteriously disappeared shortly thereafter. It was back in 2001 and is on the floor in the kitchen now.

The Boyhood Home's decision to acknowledge the existence of slavery in Hannibal is tremendously important, and the staff and board members who made that happen deserve credit for overruling the opposition and making the right choice. But the exhibit panels about slavery have a hermetically sealed, cordoned-off quality to them that distorts not only Hannibal's history but also the achievement of its most famous native son. Racism, not slavery, was the subject that Mark Twain struggled with as a writer and as a citizen for the last four decades of his life. From his writings in the 1870s about racism toward the Chinese to his attacks on ideas of white privilege and white superiority during the last decades of his life, the subject of racism was never far from his mind. His 1870s satires, "Disgraceful Persecution of a Boy" and "Goldsmith's Friend Abroad Again," took aim at the racism that led California courts to convict the Chinese not just when guilty, but always; that allowed the Chinese to be mugged by gangs of young white hoodlums while white policemen stood idly by; and that forbade the Chinese to testify against their white abusers in court. The target of his satire in *Huckleberry Finn* in 1885 was not slavery, which had been gone for two decades: it was the racism that had allowed upstanding, respectable citizens to be blind to what was morally indefensible about buying and selling other human beings; it was also the racism that allowed those same respectable citizens to effectively reenslave the ex-slaves in the 1880s by snatching away from them the hard-won rights they had been granted during Reconstruction. In the 1890s, in *Pudd'nhead Wilson*, Twain called into question the very the idea of "race," calling it but a "fiction of law and custom"; and in *Following the Equator*, as he witnessed the devastation of indigenous populations by white settler-colonists in Australia and New Zealand, Twain challenged the idea that white people have a monopoly on "civilization." "There are many humorous things in the world," he quipped—"among them, the white man's notion that he is less savage than the other savages."

Some of Twain's most intriguing explorations of racism remained unpublished at his death, reaching audiences only in the late twentieth and early twenty-first centuries. In "The Stupendous Procession," for example, written in 1901, Twain rewrote familiar texts, inserting references to the implied but unstated racial ideology that lay behind then, imagining a phantasmagoric parade that featured banners with phrases such as "'ALL WHITE MEN ARE BORN FREE AND EQUAL.' *Declaration of Independence*" or "'GOVERNMENTS DERIVE THEIR JUST POWERS FROM THE CONSENT OF THE GOVERNED WHITE MEN.' *Declaration of Independence*."

In "A Family Sketch" Twain returned to the theme of the meaninglessness of race. He notes that when he entered the Century Building in New York City with his friend George Griffin, the array of clerks in the counting-room glanced up with curiosity" at the sight of "a 'white man' & a negro walking together. . . . The glances embarrassed George, but not me, for the companionship was proper; in some ways he was my equal, in some my superior, & besides, deep down in my interior I knew that the difference between any two of those poor transient things called human beings that have ever crawled about this world & then hid their little vanities in the compassionate shelter of the grave was but microscopic, trivial, a mere difference between worms." Mark Twain knew, however, that although race might be a "fiction of law and custom," if society behaved as if it was much more than that, the results would shape the lived experience of its members in profound ways.

While Twain the author explored such issues obliquely, often through satire, citizen Twain tackled them more directly, taking a number of concrete actions to help aspiring African Americans get the education they needed to achieve their goals. In 1885, for example, when lecturing at Yale, he met Warner T. McGuinn, one of the first black students at the Yale Law School. McGuinn was holding down three part-time jobs—as a waiter, a clerk in a lawyer's office, and a bill collector—and was having trouble finding enough time for his studies. Twain was impressed by the young man and wrote a letter to Francis Wayland, dean of the Yale Law School, expressing his desire to help. The letter, sent on Christmas Eve 1885, the year that *Huck Finn* was published, provided a succinct comment on racism's shameful legacies: "We have ground the manhood out of them," he wrote, referring to black people, "& the shame is ours, not theirs, & we should pay for it." Twain ended up paying for McGuinn's board for the rest of his law school career, making it possible for him to make the most of his education and even to win a top prize at graduation. Twain's confidence in McGuinn turns out to have been well placed: in later years, he went on to win a major victory in federal court that helped lead to the desegregation of American cities; he also became a mentor to a young lawyer who worked in the office next door in Baltimore—Thurgood Marshall. Marshall, of course, would argue *Brown v. Board of Education* before the U.S. Supreme Court, winning a verdict that would result in the desegregation of the nation's schools—including the schools of Hannibal, Missouri. (Marshall, who would later become the first black Supreme Court justice, remembered McGuinn with admiration when asked about him in

1985. "Warner McGuinn," he said, "was the greatest lawyer who ever lived. If he'd been white he'd have been a judge.")

Some influential friends of Twain's—like *Hartford Courant* editor Charles Dudley Warner—argued that higher education for African Americans was a waste and a mistake. Twain disagreed. Twain's friend William Dean Howells observed that Twain "held himself responsible for the wrong which the white race had done the black race in slavery, and he explained, in paying the way of a negro student through Yale, that he was doing it as part of the reparation due from every white man to every black man." In addition to supporting Warner McGuinn, Twain gave financial assistance to A. W. Jones, a theology student at Lincoln University. He also served as co-chair of a fundraiser for Booker T. Washington's Tuskegee Institute and helped lead the effort to get the State of Connecticut to give a pension to an early pioneering Quaker educator named Prudence Crandall, who had opened the first private boarding school in New England for "young ladies and little misses of color." Twain also worked to help talented African Americans in the arts achieve the visibility and success that they desired. He wrote a publicity blurb for the Fisk Jubilee Singers that helped ensure the success of their first European tour. And he was a prominent patron of the Hartford painter Charles Ethan Porter, promoting his work, purchasing it himself, and sending him off with a letter of introduction designed to open doors for him when he headed to Paris to study art.

It was while he was living in Hartford that Twain paid many of these installments on the debt he said that every white man owed every black man in America. One can understand the temptation, on the part of the managers of the Mark Twain Boyhood Home in Hannibal, to leave those stories to their Hartford colleagues to tell. But that would be a mistake. One reason is the extent to which Twain's thinking about race and racism always circled back to Hannibal. No matter how far he traveled, Hannibal was never far from his mind. In Bombay in the 1890s, for example, the sight of a German abusing a native servant vividly called up the chilling image of a slave in Hannibal being murdered by his master for some trifling offense. All his life, Twain kept mining scenes from his childhood for fresh insights into the human heart and mind.

Black speakers from his Missouri childhood were central to the process by which Sam Clemens became Mark Twain. He would recall, half a century after he heard them, the "impressive pauses and eloquent silences" of the stories Daniel Quarles told him during summer nights. He would also recall being awestruck by the rhetorical performances of Jerry, a "gay and impudent and satirical and delightful young black man—a slave, who daily preached sermons from the top of his master's woodpile, with me for the sole audience. To me he was a wonder. I believed he was the greatest man in the United States." All his life Twain would emulate the lessons in storytelling and satire he learned from Daniel Quarles and Jerry, striving to reach an audience as effectively as these master-talents managed to reach him.

Black voices continued to shape the writer Twain became in key ways throughout his life. It was two black speakers in the North—Mary Ann Cord in Elmira, New York, and a child named William Evans in Paris, Illinois—who stimulated him to understand in fresh ways the power and vitality of vernacular storytelling. In "A True Story, Repeated Word for Word as I Heard It" (1874), published in the *Atlantic Monthly*, Mary Ann Cord ("Aunt Rachel" in the story) told Clemens ("Misto C——" in the story) in her own eloquent language the story of being separated from her child on the auction block and of being reunited years later. The sketch won Twain critical acclaim. William Evans, a talkative and engaging black child he met on December 30, 1871, whom he profiled three years later in a *New York Times* piece titled "Sociable Jimmy," helped spark his awareness of the potential of a child-narrator, and contributed significantly to the voice with which he would endow Huck Finn.

At a time when the speech of African Americans was widely ridiculed in the nation at large, Twain recognized that African American vernacular speech and storytelling manifested a literary potential that was rich, powerful, and largely untapped in print. He went on to change the course of American literature by infusing it with lessons he had learned from African American speakers. And at a time when African Americans themselves were classified as inferior specimens of humanity by pseudoscientists and so-called educators, Mark Twain's awareness of black individuals of courage and talent impelled him to challenge this characterization in fiction, nonfiction, quips, quotes, and unpublished meditations that he wrote from the 1870s until his death.

Daniel Quarles, the gifted storyteller young Sam so admired, comes into his own at "Jim's Journey: The Huck Finn Freedom Center," Hannibal's newest museum. While the Boyhood Home notes that Twain cites him as a model for Jim in *Huckleberry Finn*, here visitors learn more: that he was born in Kentucky in 1805, and was "only a few years older than his master, John Quarles" (Sam Clemens's uncle), who brought him to Florida, Missouri, in 1834; that he was emancipated by his master in 1855; that he and his family "stayed on or near the farm until 1873, when he and some of his family moved to Hannibal." The life that his son, Harre Quarls, lived under slavery and after, receives its due, as well. Born in Florida, Missouri, to Daniel and Hannah Quarles, Harre was sold to a master in Texas who "treated us jus''bout like you would a good mule"; the comment was meant as praise for a master who treated him well. Harre Quarls was proud of the fact as a slave in Texas, he learned to read and write, skills that allowed him to teach school there after slavery ended. Visitors can read about the efforts that a descendant, Larry McCarty, made to track the Quarls family genealogy through multiple branches separated during slavery and after; and they can learn about recent archaeological excavations at the Quarles farm in Florida, Missouri, that may shed further light on the houses in which Daniel and Hannah Quarles lived and worked.

Visitors can also see a photograph of Henry Dant, who was born into slavery on a farm about fifteen miles from Florida, Missouri, in 1835, the same year Sam Clemens was born. He worked hard on Judge Kendrick's farm, driving hogs to nearby towns, looking after the horses and mules when stages stopped at the farm, making brooms and baskets, and often plowing corn and cutting wheat until midnight. When he was set free at the end of the war, Henry Dant was married and had a child. But all his master gave him to start his new life was "a side of meat and a bushel of meal." He lived to be 105, passing away in Hannibal in 1939. Nine years later, in 1948, his grandson Melvin bought a sixty-acre farm off of what is now New London Gravel Road, where he and his family raised horses, cows, chickens, and pigs. Henry Dant's great-grandson, Joel Dant, was born the year his father purchased the farm. He attended school in a nearby one-room schoolhouse and then left the farm for college and graduate school and a career as a corporate executive in Chicago. But in 2009 he came back to Hannibal, where he and his wife, Faye (also a Hannibal native), built a comfortable home for themselves on the family land. Both of them played a key role in developing the museum that reconnects the history of African Americans in Hannibal with the life and work of the writer who learned much of his art by listening appreciatively to the voices of a gifted storyteller and a brilliant satirist who also happened to be slaves.

The museum tells the stories of other former slaves with connections to Hannibal, and sons of slaves, such as Blanche Kelso Bruce and George Coleman Poage, both of whom set national records, in politics and sports, respectively. Born a slave in Virginia, Bruce taught school in Hannibal in 1864. He later moved to Mississippi, where he became the first ex-slave to serve a full term in the U.S. Senate. During his time in the Senate he was an advocate for desegregating the U.S. Army and treating Native Americans more equitably; in 1878, he spoke out against a Chinese Exclusion Act that the Senate was debating. He was also the first former slave to preside over the U.S. Senate, which he did on February 14, 1879. George Coleman Poage, born in Hannibal to a former slave and a free woman in 1880, became the first African American to win a medal in the Olympics. He won two bronze medals for track at the 1904 Olympic Games in St. Louis.

Scores of photos line the walls. One haunting, sepia-tinted photo shows an infantryman in a World War I uniform staring resolutely into the camera. The picture is displayed against the backdrop of a black velvet American Legion post banner bearing the soldier's name: Clarence Woodson. Woodson was killed in the last battle on the last day of World War I. He is buried in a military cemetery in Thiaucourt, France. The following year, 1919, twenty-four black veterans from Hannibal organized an American Legion post in town named for him, the Clarence Woodson American Legion Post 155—not to be confused with the Emmette J. Shields American Legion Post 55, which was for local white veterans. Senator Blanche Bruce's dream of a desegregated U.S. Army was finally realized more than half a century ago. But the black and white American Legion posts in Hannibal remained separate until the late 1990s.

The museum tells the story of the African American community in segregated Hannibal in the early twentieth century—the black-owned barbershops, beauty shops, fraternal organizations, nightclubs, and funeral homes; the seven black-owned grocery stores; and the two black newspapers—all gone now. Businesses like these fill a 1927 "Colored Directory" that is exhibited in a glass case in the museum. "Local African Americans developed, defined and created this separate, resilient community, often hidden from the eyes of white residents," Faye Dant writes in *Missouri Passages*, a newsletter of the Missouri Humanities Council. "They depended on each other for survival and found strength in adversity, excelling despite numerous hurdles."

A display case devoted to "Jim Crow Laws" evokes the past for visitors too young to remember what segregation looked like. An exhibit card explains that "Jim Crow was more than insulting public signs and ads. It was the systemic degrading of African Americans." "Jim Crow was alive and well in Hannibal," Dant notes in *Missouri Passages*, recalling her Hannibal childhood. "While the schools were integrated Blacks still had to use the back door for take-out in Hannibal restaurants. The local movie theater welcomed blacks—Balcony seating only. Black kids had to take their own skates to the local skating rink. In later years it changed—giving Blacks Tuesday night all to themselves." Dant recalls that during her childhood the Ku Klux Klan was a visible presence, as well. Some of the kitsch racist figurines that proliferated during the Jim Crow era are on display in the museum, along with other offensive memorabilia—including a bizarre public marker, which Dant remembers seeing often when she grew up here, whose mention of "Niggar Jim" [*sic*] was the only public "reference to Black people in 'Mark Twain's town'" during her childhood.

There are also scores of photos of the small, proud, segregated Douglass High School, which gave generations of Hannibal's black children the skills to make their way in a white-run world that assumed they'd never to amount to very much. The medals, honors, and clippings about their achievements that line the display shelves attest to the foolishness of white Hannibal's low expectations of its black children. Students who attended Douglass became dedicated teachers, doctors, dentists, and lawyers; talented musicians and athletes; successful businessmen. And committed public servants—such Donald L. Scott, who would become deputy librarian and chief operating officer of the Library of Congress.

Douglass High School closed in 1955, following court-ordered desegregation, but black students at Hannibal High continued to face various forms of discrimination for decades. Joe Miller, who integrated Hannibal High during his senior year, recalled that more than two hundred white students boycotted the first day of school that year in protest. Hannibal High had been integrated for seven years by the time Larry Thompson graduated in 1963. The bright young black man had been elected

Sign near the entrance to Jim's Journey: The Huck Finn Freedom Center in Hannibal, Missouri: "In order to live in the present and prepare for the future, we must first understand and appreciate the past. Welcome!!"
PHOTO CREDIT: PHOTO BY SHELLEY FISHER FISHKIN.

class president. But he wasn't allowed to attend the graduation parties: they were held at the segregated country club. Undaunted, Thompson went on to become deputy attorney general of the United States, where he was in charge of investigating cases of corporate fraud, including the investigations of Enron, WorldCom, and the Arthur Anderson accounting firm.

The framed sign that greets visitors when they enter Jim's Journey reads, "In order to live in the present and prepare for the future, we must first understand the past. Welcome!!" The new museum offers Hannibal a remarkable opportunity. If the town embraces the stories told here as a part of the story it tells about itself, encouraging visitors to explore the newest museum in town as well as the oldest, it could make history as a community willing to reimagine, in bold and constructive ways in the twenty-first century, what it means to be "America's Hometown." Hannibal could find itself held up as a model for how a community can make a genuine effort to come to terms with its past—all of it. If it chooses to do so.

THE MARK TWAIN HOUSE, HARTFORD, CONNECTICUT

Hartford was abuzz in 1874 with the home that Mark Twain was building for his family at 351 Farmington Avenue. The *Hartford Daily Times* opined on March 23 that "it is one of the oddest looking buildings in the State ever designed for a dwelling, if not the whole country." To Mark Twain, however, the house would become a living part of the family. As he would write in 1896, "To us, our house was not unsentient matter—it had a heart, and a soul . . . it was of us, and we were in its confidence and lived in its grace and in the peace of its benediction. We never came from an absence that its face did not light up and speak out its eloquent welcome—and we could not enter unmoved."

Twain had moved to Hartford in 1871 with his wife, Olivia, and his infant son, Langdon, having visited the city three years earlier to meet with his publisher Elisha Bliss, whose American Publishing Company published *The Innocents Abroad* in 1869. Twain was impressed by the city's beauty and by its intellectual vitality—particularly in the thriving literary community at its western edge called Nook Farm, where he rented a house on Forest Street, and then bought land. In 1873, he engaged architect Edward Tuckerman Potter to design a home for his family to be paid for

The Mark Twain House, 351 Farmington Avenue, Hartford, Connecticut. Twain produced his most important work during the period when this was his home, 1874 to 1891. He cherished the "all-pervading spirit of peace and serenity and deep contentments" that he and his family found here.
PHOTO CREDIT: PHOTO BY JOHN GROO; COURTESY OF THE MARK TWAIN HOUSE AND MUSEUM, HARTFORD, CT.

with his wife's inheritance. His neighbors included Charles Dudley Warner, editor of the *Hartford Courant*, with whom Twain coauthored his first novel in 1873 (*The Gilded Age*); the Reverend Joseph Hopkins Twichell, Twain's minister and closest friend; and the aged Harriet Beecher Stowe.

The nineteen-room Victorian Gothic Revival house had seven bedrooms and seven bathrooms, a library, drawing room, dining room, and billiard room. Although Potter designed it, Twain and Olivia made preliminary sketches for the layout of the rooms, oversaw the construction, and added and changed many features. Twain had a patch of tin put on the roof, for example, so that he could hear the rain drumming, and had the dining-room fireplace constructed with a divided flue that rose on either side of a window, so that he could watch the snow falling outside as flames danced in the fireplace below. Reflecting Twain's lifelong fascination with technology, the house boasted one of the first telephones in a private home, a battery-powered burglar alarm, flush toilets, central heating, hot-and-cold running water, and a speaking tube intercom system. Rambling, decklike porches circled the outside of the many-gabled house, which was decorated with dramatic patterns of black and vermilion brick. Louis Comfort Tiffany and his associates Lockwood de Forest and Candace Wheeler decorated the first floor in 1881, coming up with a dramatic style that borrowed freely from American, Oriental, Turkish, and Indian styles and adapted designs from native American flowers and plants. With its mosaic tiles, oriental carpets, and banister of deep, rich, polished walnut; ornamental details carved by Leon Marcotte of New York and Paris; and silver-stenciled wall coverings done by Tiffany's design firm, it was gorgeous and unique—and vastly more expensive than predicted.

In the midst of the construction, Twain wrote to his mother-in-law, Olivia Langdon, "I have been bullyragged all day by the builder, by his foreman, by the architect, by the tapestry devil who is to upholster the furniture, by the idiot who is putting down the carpets, by the scoundrel who is setting up the billiard-table (and has left the balls in New York), by the wildcat who is sodding the ground and finishing the driveway (after the sun went down), by a book agent whose body is in the back yard and the coroner notified. Just think of this thing going on the whole day long, and I am a man who loathes details with all my heart." But if the process frustrated him, he was delighted with the result: "How ugly, tasteless, repulsive are all the domestic interiors I have ever seen in Europe compared with the perfect taste of this ground floor, with its delicious dream of harmonious color, and its all-pervading spirit of peace and serenity and deep contentments." The period in which Twain enjoyed the "deep contentments" of Farmington Avenue with his wife and three daughters (his son had passed away as an infant) was the most productive time of his life. During the years he lived here, from September 1874, when the house was completed, to

1891, when financial setbacks forced him to move his family to Europe, he published "A True Story" (1874), "Sociable Jimmy" (1874), *Sketches, New and Old* (1875), *The Adventures of Tom Sawyer* (1876), *A Tramp Abroad* (1880), *The Prince and the Pauper* (1881), *The Stolen White Elephant, Etc.* (1882), *Life on the Mississippi* (1883), *Adventures of Huckleberry Finn* (1885), *A Connecticut Yankee in King Arthur's Court* (1889), and a host of additional sketches, stories, and essays.

He did most of his writing in the billiard room on the third floor, across the hall from the room of George Griffin, his butler, a smart and savvy black man who kept unwanted interruptions away and served as a willing sounding board for Twain's ideas. In "A Family Sketch" (1906), Twain tells us that Griffin "was a Maryland slave by birth; the Proclamation set him free, & as a young fellow he saw his fair share of the Civil War as body servant to General Devens," a distinguished officer in the Union Army. Griffin showed up one day in 1875 to wash windows and ended up staying for close to two decades. In "A Family Sketch" Twain called him "handsome, well built, shrewd, wise, polite, always good-natured, cheerful to gaiety, honest, religious, a cautious truth-speaker, devoted friend to the family, champion of its interests." George Griffin's bedroom in the Mark Twain House has been fully restored and is open to visitors who tour the house. The billiard room served not only as Twain's study, office, and private lair, but also as a favorite place to relax and entertain friends when he wasn't writing. On Friday evenings, Twain and a small group of friends would play billiards, tell stories, drink hot scotch, and smoke cigars until late into the night. Twain was always the last one to call it a night, often knocking billiard balls about until total exhaustion set in.

When guests arrived, they would have their hats and coats taken by George Griffin in the sumptuous entry hall and then would proceed to one or the other of the first floor's luxurious public rooms—the drawing room, in which a Tiffany craftsman had stenciled silver East Indian motifs over a salmon pink background; the library, graced by a mantel carved in Scotland for the dining room at Ayton Castle; or the dining room, with wall-coverings designed to look like embossed leather, where Twain would wine and dine them with grace and style, all the while regaling them with perfectly timed anecdotes. Guests might include William Dean Howells, Matthew Arnold, Bret Harte, Sir Henry Morton Stanley, George Washington Cable, Thomas Nast, Edwin Booth, Thomas Bailey Aldrich, and virtually anyone of note who was traveling from New York to Boston or to anywhere, for that matter. A brass smoke shield in the library was emblazoned with an apt quote from Ralph Waldo Emerson: "The ornament of a house is the friends who frequent it."

Twain may have enjoyed poking fun at pompous art critics and insufferable museum guides, but he also came to take genuine pleasure in purchasing and commissioning art, and he counted many artists as his friends. On the wall of the dining room is an oil painting, *Still Life with Peonies* by Charles Ethan Porter, an African American painter with a studio in Hartford whom Twain admired, supported, and considered a friend. Sculptures by another artist whose work Twain supported, Karl Gerhardt, are in the front hall (a bust of Twain) and the drawing-room (*Seated Mercury*). These friendships may have helped fuel Twain's ire at the fact that the work of dead artists automatically tended to be valued more highly than that of living artists. His best-known work on this theme is the wild, over-the-top, cross-dressing satire he wrote in 1898, the play *Is He Dead?* Written shortly after Twain emerged from bankruptcy, *Is He Dead?* centers on a fictionalized version of the real-life artist, Jean-François Millet. (Owing to bad luck, bad timing, the play's rough edges, and the sprawling cast it would have required—as well as its irreverence toward a venerated figure in the arts—Twain failed to get it produced in his lifetime. It finally debuted on Broadway in 2007, to great acclaim.)

The family's private rooms upstairs were no less distinctive than the public rooms. Twain and his wife brought back from Venice the ornately carved bed in the master bedroom, and Twain kept it all his life, moving it from house to house in the United States, as he changed residence—"the most comfortable bedstead that ever was," Twain wrote, "with space enough in it for a family and carved angels enough ... to bring peace to the sleepers and pleasant dreams." Sam, Olivia, and their three daughters, Susy, Clara, and Jean, shared the rambling, three-story brick home with numerous cats and collies—as well as the seven servants required to keep the house running and to handle the constant stream of guests at what amounted to a nearly continuous celebrity dinner party. Twain did most of his writing in these years during the summers in Elmira, New York, at Quarry Farm, his sister-in-law's home, in the graceful octagonal study she built for him in the woods adjacent to the house.

In 1891, financial problems forced Twain to move his family to Europe, where living in hotels cost less than maintaining the beloved house in Hartford, with its staff of seven. Three years later he would file for bankruptcy. The family never lived in the Hartford house again. Lovingly restored with meticulous attention to detail and accuracy, the Mark Twain House in Hartford is one of the most beautifully preserved Victorian homes in America today.

The guides who take visitors through the home do a fine job of exploring links between the rooms in the home and the writing Twain did while living there, as well as conveying the texture of daily life in the bustling household. The story they tell has changed over time, responding to new research by scholars. They have been particularly attentive to issues of race in Mark Twain's work and the controversies they have sparked: they have run workshops on this topic for high school teachers for more than twenty-five years; their tours foreground the story of Twain's friendship with George Griffin, his support of Warner McGuinn (Twain wrote the famous McGuinn letter to the dean of the Yale law school while living here), and the assistance he gave Charles Ethan Porter; they have hosted talks on Twain and race by prominent black figures in the arts such as the award-winning novelist David Bradley and the celebrated comic Dick Gregory; and they have sponsored an exhibit examining Twain's journey from "a childhood where slavery was accepted as God's law, to a celebrity old age during which he railed against lynching and racial bias."

It is ironic that in the twenty-first century the Mark Twain House has been plagued by financial problems not unlike those that Twain himself had faced a century earlier. Twain had never been good at estimating expenses or evaluating investments and their likely returns or finding trustworthy employees to handle his money. He had to leave the beloved Hartford house for Europe to save money; his overly optimistic investments in the Paige Typesetter and his publishing company forced him into bankruptcy; and during the final years of his life, the dishonesty of two employees trusted with the management of his household nearly defrauded his heirs of their inheritance. In 2003, the Mark Twain House opened a lavish, strikingly beautiful, and technologically sophisticated new visitors' center that ended up costing some nineteen million dollars—significantly more than had been estimated. Through support from the state of Connecticut, foundations, and private individuals, combined with drastic cutbacks, layoffs, and retrenchment, the institution narrowly avoided bankruptcy. By 2010, it became evident that a long-time, trusted employee, Donna Gregor, the institution's comptroller, had been embezzling funds for years. In November 2011, she was convicted of having embezzled more than a million dollars and was sentenced to three and a half years in prison. Those who had preserved with such devotion the home belonging to the man who bragged that he'd "been swindled out of more money than there is on this planet" found themselves the victims of a swindle a century after his death.

Mark Twain is claimed by Missouri, Nevada, California, Connecticut, and New York, and historic sites in each of those states honor his memory. He was a bridge between North and South—a Confederate sympathizer who after the Civil War would toast General U. S. Grant at banquets of Union veterans, and later publish Grant's memoirs. And he was a bridge between East and West—a brash, outrageous westerner who also knew how to behave in the drawing rooms of Europe or the salons of Boston—most of the time. Twain was a man able to admit he had been wrong, unafraid to change. A man who made fun of women's rights early in his career, but who came to support them later on. A child of slaveholders who went on to write one of the greatest antiracist novels by an American.

He participated in so many key chapters of the nation's life—and went on to influence how we recall and understand them—that it's easy to see why he came to be viewed, in many ways, as the embodiment of his country. His adventures as an unsuccessful prospector out west helped him understand the very American get-rich-quick mentality he wrote about in *Roughing It*. His stint as a Washington correspondent got him thinking about the corrosive role of money in politics, a subject he would tackle when he wrote the first Washington novel, a book that would give an entire era its name: *The Gilded Age*. His awareness of mechanical disasters—like the steamboat explosion that killed his brother—prompted him to think about the promises and pitfalls of technology, a subject central to *A Connecticut Yankee in King Arthur's Court*. As Twain watched European nations carve up Africa, and as he observed his own country's imperialist designs on the Philippines, he thought about the arrogance of the idea of white superiority—a subject he explored in the polemical pamphlets and other writings during his later years, and in his travel book *Following the Equator*. His frequent targets were hypocrisy, misplaced pride, and self-delusion on the part of individuals and nations. His countrymen were not always ready to listen to what he had to say. One such case was his scorching satire, "The War-Prayer," which exposes the lies and half-truths that allow a country to wage war swaddled in the self-righteous belief that God is on its side; Twain was unable to publish it during his lifetime. A satirist so subtle his meanings were often missed, and a polemicist so direct his messages were sometimes pointedly ignored, Twain did not have all the answers. But he earnestly struggled with the right questions—and they are questions we are still struggling with today.

A who's who of prominent twentieth-century authors acknowledge his importance to them—American writers including Russell Banks, David Bradley, Ralph Ellison, William Faulkner, Dick Gregory, Ernest Hemingway, Ursula Le Guin, Bobbie Ann Mason, Arthur Miller, Kurt Vonnegut, and Ralph Wiley, and writers outside the United States, such as Argentina's Jorge Luis Borges, Cuba's José Martí, Japan's Kenzaburō Ōe, Britain's George Bernard Shaw, and China's Lu Xun. Twain's words combined with Hal Holbrook's genius as a writer and actor transformed the possibilities of solo performance in American theatre. As Kent Rasmussen's book *Dear Mark Twain: Letters from His Readers* makes clear, ordinary readers—cheese merchants and children, railroad clerks and retired soldiers, farmers and foremen—all felt as if the famous author was speaking to them personally—and they spoke back in the letters they sent him.

Hannibal was where it all began. But Hannibal was not where it ended. The Mark Twain of whitewashed fence fame that Hannibal celebrates every Fourth of July during "Tom Sawyer Days," and all year long at the Boyhood Home and other sites in the Mark Twain Historic District is only a small part of why millions of visitors come here. They come because of the questions that Sam Clemens asked after he left Hannibal, when he grew up. They come because of his humor and irreverence, his honesty, his candor, his generosity, his imaginative vision, and his appreciation of the ironic and absurd. They come because Mark Twain restores to us some part of ourselves that deep down we believe is worth preserving.

SCENES OF "A TRUE STORY, REPEATED WORD FOR WORD AS I HEARD IT"

SLOVER-BRADHAM HOUSE
201 Johnson Street, New Bern, North Carolina

SLOVER DEPENDENCY
521 East Front Street, New Bern, North Carolina

QUARRY FARM
131 Crane Road, Elmira, New York

One evening in the summer of 1874, as the sun set over the Chemung River valley, a former slave named Mary Ann Cord, the cook at Quarry Farm (where Mark Twain and his family spent summers), told Twain, his wife, Olivia, and others assembled on the porch, the story of how she was forcibly separated from her husband and seven children on the auction block and eventually reunited with her youngest child during the war.

Nothing is left of the Richmond slave market where Mary Ann Cord and her son Henry were sold to different masters in 1852. But the house in which they were reunited in North Carolina more than a decade later is still there, preserved not for its place in American literary history but as the headquarters of General Ambrose E. Burnside during the Civil War, and, a little more than half a century later, as the home of Caleb Davis Bradham, the inventor of Pepsi-Cola.

Mary Ann Cord was bought by Charles Slover of New Bern, North Carolina, a prosperous merchant, bank president, and shipper in the West Indies trade, who built an elegant mansion for his family around 1848 on the southwest corner of East Front and Johnson Streets in New Bern. The Slover-Bradham House (201 Johnson Street) is New Bern's grandest Renaissance Revival–style residence, built by one of its most prosperous and respected citizens. It was to this stately three-story brick house that Slover brought Mary Ann Cord.

Cord lived in the Slover Dependency, next door (at 521 East Front Street), a very large, detached outbuilding that served as the kitchen, slave quarters, and smokehouse, where she cooked for a household that by 1861 included Charles Slover and his wife, their eight children, and ten slaves. Sometime before New Bern was captured by Union troops in 1862, Slover moved his family to High Point, North Carolina, for safety. Mary Ann Cord was left behind in the house, along with other slaves.

The succession of Union generals who made the Charles Slover House their headquarters and home—first, General Ambrose Burnside of Rhode Island, then Major General John G. Foster of New Hampshire—may have appreciated the fact that the building, with its gracefully columned, classical Greek entrance, resembled homes built by prosperous merchants in New England (the part of the country from which Slover's wife originally came). The house (a National Historic Landmark, now used as a private residence) served as headquarters for all U.S. military operations in North Carolina. (As Cord observed, "Dey wa' n't no small-fry officers, mine you, dey was dey biggest dey *is*.") Visible from the street, the house and dependency remain much the way they looked when Mary Ann Cord lived there.

Six years after being separated from his mother, Henry Washington followed the North Star to freedom in 1858 when he was sixteen, and ended up in Elmira, New York, where he learned to be a barber. Sometime after the Civil War began, Henry "went to whah dey was recruitin'" (as his mother later told the story) and hired himself out as a servant to the commanding officer of one of many infantry and artillery units that were organized in Elmira. Henry "went all froo de battles everywhah, huntin' for his ole mammy," hiring himself out "to fust one officer an' den another, tell he'd ransacked de whole Souf." Black soldiers were allowed to enlist in the Union Army in 1863, and in June of that year, Henry Washington's name appears in the records of individuals subject to military service in New York's 27th Congressional District, where he is listed as a twenty-three-year-old "married," "colored" "laborer" from Elmira, born in Maryland, which is where his mother was from. (He may have been connected with the 110th Regiment, New York Infantry, Company F, which lists a Henry Washington as an "under cook.") Washington evidently joined a black regiment that had garrison duty in New Bern, where he was reunited with his mother.

The ground floor of the two-story Slover Dependency is a huge kitchen with two large fireplaces—a room more than big enough to hold dances in, as Cord remembers ("de sojers dah at Newbern was always havin' balls an' carryin' on. Dey had 'em in my kitchen, heaps o' times, 'ca'se it was so big"). It was there, leaning over the stove with "de pan o' hot biscuits in my han,'" that Cord saw "a black face come aroun' under mine, an' de eyes a'lookin' up into mine. . . ." The scar on his forehead told her it was her son.

The Slover Dependency, 521 East Front Street, New Bern, North Carolina. In the large, open kitchen of these slave quarters, Mary Ann Cord was reunited with the son from whom she had been separated on the auction block, when he came to New Bern with the U.S. Colored Troops during the Civil War. Cord's story inspired Mark Twain's first contribution to the *Atlantic Monthly* and influenced his delineation of Jim in *Huckleberry Finn*.

PHOTO CREDIT: PHOTO BY CURTIS BLAKE.

The story she told the Clemens family was Cord's extended response to "Misto C——'s" mistaken impression that because "it was no more trouble for her to laugh than it is for a bird to sing," she must have "never had any trouble" in her life. "Oh, no, Misto C——," she said, recalling the moment she was reunited with Henry, "*I hain't had no trouble. An' no joy!*" Twain wrote that "she had the best gift of strong & simple speech that I have known in any woman except my mother. She told me a striking tale out of her personal experience, once, & . . . I wrote [her words] down before they were cold." He found Cord's story "a shameful tale of wrong & hardship," but also "a curiously strong piece of literary work to come unpremeditated from lips untrained in literary art." It became the basis for the first piece Twain published in the *Atlantic Monthly*, "A True Story, Repeated Word for Word as I Heard It."

Aunt Rachel, the name Twain gives Cord in the piece, tells her story with great power and directness.

Dey put chains on us an' put us on a stan' as high as dis po'ch—twenty foot high— . . . An' dey'd come up dah an' look at us all roun', an' squeeze our arm, an' make us git up an' walk, an' den say, "Dis one too ole," or

Mary Ann Cord, the former slave who was the cook at Quarry Farm, in Elmira, New York, whose "vigorous eloquence" left a deep impression on Mark Twain.

"Dis one lame," or "Dis one don't 'mount to much." An' dey sole my ole man, an' took him away, an' dey begin to sell my chil'en an' take *dem* away, an' I begin to cry; an' de man say, "Shet up yo' damn blubberin'," an' hit me on de mouf wid his han'. An' when de las' one was gone but my little Henry, I grab' him clost up to my breas' so, an' I ris up an' says, "You sha'n't take him away," I says; "I'll kill de man dat teches him!" I says. But dey got him—dey got him, de men did; but I took and tear de clo'es mos' off of 'em an' beat 'em over de head wid my chain; an' *dey* give it to *me*, too, but I didn't mine dat.

Unlike typical dialect tales of the time, which presented black dialect to be condescended to or ridiculed, here the dialect was presented respectfully, as a vehicle for communicating raw pain, strong emotion, and harsh truth. Cord's story condensed the pain of the thousands of other ex-slaves who tried—and often failed—to reunite their families. Sitting among his own beloved children, Twain found in Cord's image of children being wrenched from their mothers' arms on the auction block a reminder of the agony inflicted by slavery and the enigma of human cruelty.

Cord's grief and despair at being separated from her family, and the language in which she expressed those emotions, would find their way into Jim's despair at his separation from his own cherished children in *Huck Finn*. Perhaps the most important thing Mary Ann Cord taught Twain was that the vernacular—in her case, the ungrammatical dialect of a woman with no formal education—could move a narrative forward dramatically and effectively, suggesting to him the potential of a vernacular voice as the scaffolding of compelling fiction—a key step on the road to *Adventures of Huckleberry Finn*.

Before he left for the war, Henry Washington had established himself as one of the best-known barbers in Elmira, and Elmira's elite—including Jervis Langdon (who would become Twain's father-in-law) and his son Charlie—had their own shaving mugs on the wall at his shop. He brought his mother back to Elmira after the war, where she took a job as the cook at Quarry Farm, the home of Susan Crane, Mark Twain's sister-in-law, where Twain and his family would spend most summers from 1871 to 1889. Henry Washington, who

Henry Washington's Barber Shop, 424 East Water Street, Elmira, New York. The older man, on the sidewalk, is Henry Washington Sr., the son from whom Mary Ann Cord was separated on the auction block in Richmond, Virginia ("A True Story, Repeated Word for Word as I I Ieard It"). The young man in a vest in the doorway is probably his son, Henry Washington Jr., born in 1873, who also became a barber. Henry Washington Sr. was Mark Twain's barber during the more than twenty summers the author spent in Elmira. The photo was taken between 1887 and 1895. The building no longer exists. PHOTO CREDIT: COURTESY OF THE CHEMUNG COUNTY HISTORICAL SOCIETY.

Quarry Farm, Elmira, New York, where the Clemens family spent summers and where Twain began *Tom Sawyer*, *Huck Finn*, and many other books. Mary Ann Cord told her story on the front steps pictured here.

became Mark Twain's barber, too, had cut his famously unruly hair many times before Twain heard his mother's story that memorable evening in 1874. (Before opening his own barber shop on East Water Street, Henry Washington worked in the barber shop of the Rathbun Hotel, where Twain was a regular customer during the summer.)

Sam Clemens and his family spent more than twenty summers at Quarry Farm as the guests of Susan Crane and her husband, Theodore. Through the generosity of Irene and Jervis Langdon Jr., Quarry Farm is now a home for visiting Twain Scholars, administered by the Center for Mark Twain Studies at Elmira College.

RELATED SITES

⚬◆ Mark Twain's Study

Elmira College Campus, 1 Park Place, Elmira, New York

This octagonal, glass-enclosed study was built for Twain by his sister-in-law, Susan Crane and her husband, Theodore. It originally stood about a hundred yards from the main house at Quarry Farm on a wooded hillside overlooking the Chemung River valley.

It was in this study that he wrote major portions of *The Adventures of Tom Sawyer*, *A Tramp Abroad*, *Adventures of Huckleberry Finn*, *The Prince and the Pauper*, and *A Connecticut Yankee in King Arthur's Court*, as well as many short pieces. It was moved from Quarry Farm to the campus of Elmira College in 1952, where it has been carefully preserved.

Mark Twain looking out the window of the octagonal study in which he did all his writing during summers at Quarry Farm.

PHOTO CREDIT: COURTESY OF THE MARK TWAIN ARCHIVE, GANNETT-TRIPP LIBRARY, ELMIRA COLLEGE, ELMIRA, NY.

❧ Mark Twain Birthplace State Historic Site
Mark Twain State Park, 37352 Shrine Road, Florida, Missouri

Sam Clemens was born in Florida, Missouri, in 1835 in a small, white frame house that probably resembled the one preserved here, which was allegedly moved from its original site to the Mark Twain State Park in 1930. The house's authenticity has long been a subject of debate. The actual cabin in which Sam Clemens was born may have been a structure destroyed piece-by-piece by literary relic-seekers during the first third of the twentieth century. (As Hilary Lowe notes, "According to a 1934 account of the 1904 exposition in the Paris *Mercury*, 'a frame house was cut up into canes, which were sold at the St. Louis World's Fair as having been made from the timber in the house where Mark Twain was born.'") The Quarles farm, where Clemens spent summers, was in this area.

❧ Jubilee Hall
Campus of Fisk University, 1000 Seventeenth Avenue North, Nashville, Tennessee

This imposing, six-story Victorian Gothic structure, the oldest remaining permanent building in the United States dedicated to the education of African Americans, was built with funds that the Fisk Jubilee Singers—all former slaves or children of slaves—raised to save their school, Fisk University, from bankruptcy. The publicity blurb Twain wrote for them helped ensure the success of their first European tour, in 1873. The haunting melodies the group sang introduced many white Americans to the beauty of African American music for the first time. Soon after Twain had entertained the Fisk Jubilee singers in his home in Lucerne, Switzerland, in 1897, he wrote to a friend, "I think that in the Jubilees and their songs America has produced the perfectest flower of the ages; and I wish it were a foreign product so that she would worship it and lavish money on it and go properly crazy over it."

❧ Prudence Crandall Museum
1 South Canterbury Road, Canterbury, Connecticut

When, in 1832, Prudence Crandall admitted a young black woman named Sarah Harris to her Canterbury Female Boarding Academy, a successful school patronized by wealthy local families, white parents withdrew their daughters. The Quaker schoolteacher's response was to open the first private boarding school for "young ladies and little misses of color" in New England. It attracted students from Connecticut, Boston, Providence, and New York. Angry townspeople harassed Crandall and her students, pelted the school with stones and eggs, set fire to it, broke its windows, and got the Connecticut General Assembly to pass a law that restricted African American students from coming into the state to get an education and forbade the opening of schools for African Americans in Connecticut. Crandall spent a night in jail and took her struggle to the courts. Arguments from her trials would later be used in the *Brown v. Board of Education* case in 1954 and helped spark a national debate about racism and prejudice. In 1848, she moved to Illinois with her husband. She started a school for Native Americans in Elk Falls, Kansas, in 1877. In 1886, Mark Twain helped lead the successful effort to get the Connecticut legislature to grant Crandall a pension. Twain also offered to lease her former home in Canterbury for her retirement. Crandall, who admired Twain's writings, appreciated the offer, but chose to remain in Kansas. Crandall's photo hangs in Twain's billiard room in Hartford. The Prudence Crandall Museum honors its namesake as an early advocate for equal education.

❦ Old Louisiana State Capitol
100 North Boulevard, Baton Rouge, Louisiana

When Mark Twain returned to the Mississippi River in 1882, having been away from it for two decades, the one building that brought forth the most memorable commentary on architecture in all of his writings was the Old Louisiana State Capitol building in Baton Rouge. Built in 1849, this castlelike structure was undergoing restoration when he saw it. Twain didn't think that was a good idea. In *Life on the Mississippi* (1883), he wrote:

> Sir Walter Scott is probably responsible for the Capitol building; for it is not conceivable that this little sham castle would ever have been built if he had not run the people mad, a couple of generations ago, with his medieval romances. The South has not yet recovered from the debilitating influence of his books. . . . It is pathetic enough, that a whitewashed castle, with turrets and things—materials all ungenuine within and without, pretending to be what they are not—should ever have been built in this otherwise honorable place; but it is much more pathetic to see this architectural falsehood undergoing restoration and perpetuation in our day, when it would have been so easy to let dynamite finish what a charitable fire began, and then devote this restoration-money to the building of something genuine.

Twain's hatred for this building stems from his sense of what it represents: a dangerous, self-deluding, and false self-image that mires the South in a romantic past that blinds it to all that is wrong with southern culture in the present and stops it from moving forward. As his friend William Dean Howells noted, "no one has ever poured such scorn upon the second-hand, Walter-Scotticized, pseudo-chivalry of the Southern ideal."

Woodlawn Cemetery
Walnut and Davis Streets, West Hill and Bancroft Roads, Elmira, New York

Woodlawn Cemetery is the final resting place of Samuel Langhorne Clemens; his wife, Olivia Langdon Clemens; his infant son, Langdon; his daughters Susy, Jean, and Clara; his only grandchild, Nina Gabrilowitsch; and Clara's two husbands, Ossip Gabrilowitsch and Jacques Samoussoud (Samoussoud's grave is unmarked). The Clemens family plot is adjacent to that of the Jervis Langdon family, which includes the graves of Twain's father-in-law and also Clemens's grandnephew, who, with his wife, Irene, gave Quarry Farm to Elmira College to preserve as a residence for visiting Twain scholars. Mary Ann Cord, the former slave who became the cook at Quarry Farm, and whose "vigorous eloquence" so impressed Twain, is buried here, as well.

FOR FURTHER READING

The Writers: Works and Words

Banks, Russell. Introduction to *The Gilded Age*. In Fishkin, *The Oxford Mark Twain*.

Borges, Jorge Luis, and Ester Zemborain de Torres. *An Introduction to American Literature*. Lexington: University of Kentucky Press, 1971.

Bradley, David. Introduction to *How to Tell a Story and Other Essays*. In Fishkin, *The Oxford Mark Twain*.

Ellison, Ralph. Interview with Fishkin quoted in Fishkin, *Was Huck Black? Mark Twain and African American Voices*. New York: Oxford University Press, 1993.

Faulkner, William. Transcript and recording of speech at Washington and Lee University, 15 May 1958. http://faulkner.lib.virginia.edu/display/wfaudio31.

Federal Writers Project. *Born in Slavery: Narratives from the Federal Writers Project*. http://memory.loc.gov/ammem/snhtml.

Fishkin, Shelley Fisher, ed. *The Mark Twain Anthology: Great Writers on His Life and Work*. New York: Library of America, 2010.

———. *The Oxford Mark Twain*. 29 vols. New York: Oxford University Press, 1996.

Gregory, Dick (with Sheila P. Moss). *Callus on My Soul* (2000). In Fishkin, *The Mark Twain Anthology*.

Hemingway, Ernest. *The Green Hills of Africa*. New York: Charles Scribner's Sons, 1935.

Lu, Xun. "A Short Introduction to 'Eve's Diary.'" 1931. Translated by Gongzhao Li. In Fishkin, *The Mark Twain Anthology*.

Martí, José. "North American Scenes." 1884. Translated by Rubén Builes and Cintia Santana. In Fishkin, *The Mark Twain Anthology*.

Mason, Bobbie Ann. Introduction to *The American Claimant*. In Fishkin, *The Oxford Mark Twain*.

Miller, Arthur. Introduction to *Chapters from My Autobiography*. In Fishkin, *The Oxford Mark Twain*.

Ōe, Kenzaburō. "An American Traveler's Dreams—Huckleberry Finn Who Goes to Hell." 1966. Translated by Hiroaki Sato. In Fishkin, *The Mark Twain Anthology*.

Shaw, George Bernard. "Letter to Samuel L. Clemens." 1907. In Fishkin, *The Mark Twain Anthology*.

Teems, Scott, director. *Holbrook/Twain: An American Odyssey*. Laura D. Smith, executive producer, 2014.

Twain, Mark. *Adventures of Huckleberry Finn*. Edited by Victor Fischer and Lin Salamo. The Mark Twain Project. Berkeley: University of California Press, 2001.

———. *Is He Dead? A Comedy in Three Acts by Mark Twain*. Edited by Shelley Fisher Fishkin. Berkeley: University of California Press, 2003.

———. *Mark Twain at the Buffalo Express: Articles and Sketches by America's Favorite Humorist*. Edited by Joseph B. McCullough and Janice McIntire-Strasburg. DeKalb: Northern Illinois University Press, 1999.

———. *Mark Twain: Collected Tales, Sketches, Speeches, & Essays*. Edited by Louis J. Budd. 2 vols. New York: Library of America, 1992.

———. *The Oxford Mark Twain*. Edited by Shelley Fisher Fishkin. 29 vols. New York: Oxford University Press, 1996.

Twain, Mark, Livy Clemens, and Susy Clemens. *A Family Sketch and Other Private Writings*. Edited by Benjamin Griffin. Berkeley: University of California Press, 2014.

Vonnegut, Kurt. "Some Comments on Mark Twain's *A Connecticut Yankee in King Arthur's Court* by Kurt Vonnegut at the Age of Seventy-Two." In Fishkin, *The Oxford Mark Twain*.

Wiley, Ralph. *Dark Witness: When Black People Should Be Sacrificed (Again)*. New York: One World/Ballantine Books, 1996.

Zwick, Jim, ed. *Mark Twain's Weapons of Satire: Anti-imperialist Writings on the Philippine-American War*. Syracuse, NY: Syracuse University Press, 1992.

Backgrounds and Contexts

Camfield, Gregg. *The Oxford Companion to Mark Twain*. New York: Oxford University Press, 2003.

Courtney, Steve. *"The Loveliest Home That Ever Was": The Story of the Mark Twain House in Hartford*. Introduction by Hal Holbrook. Mineola, NY: Dover Publications, 2011.

Dant, Faye. "Hannibal African American Life History: Hannibal's Invisibles." *Missouri Passages: Missouri Humanities Council News* 10 (March 2012). http://www.mohumanities.org/news-updates/missouri-passages/march-2012-vol-10-no-2/hannibal-african-american-life-history-hannibals-invisibles.

Darr, Bev. "Hannibal Middle School Students Will Compete in National Contest." *Hannibal Courier-Post*, June 6, 2008. http://www.hannibal.net/article/20080606/News/306069880.

Dempsey, Terrell. *Searching for Jim: Slavery in Sam Clemens's World*. Columbia: University of Missouri Press, 2003.

Faden, Regina. "Museums and Race: Living Up to the Public Trust." *Museums & Social Issues* 2, no. 1 (Spring 2007).

———. "Museums and the Story of Slavery: The Challenge of Language." In *Politics of Memory: Making Slavery Visible in the Public Space*, edited by Ana Lucia Araujo. New York: Routledge, 2012.

———. "Presenting Mark Twain: Keeping the Edge Sharp." *Mark Twain Annual* (2008).

Fishkin, Shelley Fisher. "False Starts, Fragments, and Fumbles: Mark Twain's Unpublished Writing on Race." *Essays in Arts and Sciences* 20 (October 1991): 17–31.

———. *Lighting Out for the Territory: Reflections on Mark Twain and American Culture*. New York: Oxford University Press, 1997.

———. "Mark Twain." In *From Fact to Fiction: Journalism and Imaginative Writing in America*, 55–84. New York: Oxford University Press, 1988.

———. *Was Huck Black? Mark Twain and African American Voices*. New York: Oxford University Press, 1993.

Fishkin, Shelley Fisher, ed. *Historical Guide to Mark Twain*. New York: Oxford University Press, 2002.

Greene, Lorenzo J., Gary R. Kremer, and Antonio F. Holland. *Missouri's Black Heritage*. 1980. Rev. ed. Columbia: University of Missouri Press, 1993.

Hagood, J. Hurley, and Roberta Hagood. *Hannibal, Too: Historical Sketches of Hannibal and Its Neighbor*. Marceline, MO: Walworth, 1986.

Hand, Bill. *A Walking Guide to North Carolina's Historic New Bern*. Charleston, SC: History Press, 2007.

Jerome, Robert D., and Herbert A. Wisbey Jr., eds. *Mark Twain in Elmira*. Elmira, NY: Mark Twain Society, 1977.

Kaplan, Justin. *Mr. Clemens and Mark Twain*. New York: Simon and Schuster, 1966.

King, Wilma. *Stolen Childhood: Slave Youth in Nineteenth-Century America*. Bloomington: Indiana University Press, 1998.

Lowe, Hilary Iris. *Mark Twain's Homes and Literary Tourism*. Columbia: University of Missouri Press, 2012.

Marks, Ken, and Lisa Marks. *Hannibal, Missouri: A Brief History*. Charleston, SC: History Press, 2012.

Poletti, Mary. "Rediscovering the Past: Hannibal Woman Searches for Clues to Black History." *Quincy Herald-Whig*, March 15, 2011. http://www.thelocalq.com/node/2173.

Powers, Ron. *Dangerous Water: A Biography of the Man Who Became Mark Twain*. New York: Basic Books, 1999.

———. *Mark Twain: A Life*. New York: Free Press, 2005.

———. *White Town Drowsing*. New York: Anchor Books, 1992.

Rasmussen, R. Kent, ed. *Dear Mark Twain: Letters from His Readers*. Berkeley: University of California Press, 2013.

————. *Mark Twain A to Z*. New York: Facts on File, 1995.

Rasmussen, R. Kent, with critical commentary by John H. Davis and Alex Feerst. *Critical Companion to Mark Twain: A Literary Reference to His Life and Work*. New York: Facts on File, 2007.

Robinson, Forrest, ed. *The Cambridge Companion to Mark Twain*. New York: Cambridge University Press, 1995.

Sandbeck, Peter B. *Historic Architecture of New Bern and Craven County, North Carolina*. New Bern, NC: Troyon Palace Commission, 1988.

Shelden, Michael. *Mark Twain: The Man in White: The Grand Adventures of His Final Years*. New York: Random House, 2010.

Strane, Susan. *A Whole-Souled Woman: Prudence Crandall and the Education of Black Women*. New York: W. W. Norton, 1990.

Wecter, Dixon. *Sam Clemens of Hannibal*. Boston: Houghton Mifflin, 1952.

Welch, Marvis Olive. *Prudence Crandall: A Biography*. Manchester, CT: Jason Publishers, 1983.

Williams, Donald E. *Prudence Crandall's Legacy: The Fight for Equality in the 1830s, Dred Scott, and Brown v. Board of Education*. Wesleyan, CT: Wesleyan University Press, 2014.

Zwick, Jim. *Confronting Imperialism: Essays on Mark Twain and the Anti-imperialist League*. West Conshohocken, PA: Infinity Publishing, 2007.

————. "Mark Twain and Imperialism." In *A Historical Guide to Mark Twain*, edited by Shelley Fisher Fishkin, 227–255. New York: Oxford University Press, 2002.

What's Left of Big Foot's Band. Group of Miniconjou Lakota Sioux, 1891.

6

Native American Voices
Remember Wounded Knee

WOUNDED KNEE NATIONAL HISTORIC LANDMARK
PINE RIDGE INDIAN RESERVATION,
WEST OF BATESLAND, SOUTH DAKOTA

On May 28, 1903, Joseph Horn Cloud made his way across the desolate rolling grasslands of the Pine Ridge Indian Reservation in southwestern South Dakota until he reached the top of a hill at Wounded Knee, his thoughts circling back to that bleak December day, thirteen years earlier, when he had watched the U.S. Army kill so many of his relatives and friends. They had been unarmed. They hadn't stood a chance against the rifles of the Seventh Cavalry. Joseph Horn Cloud climbed the hill with some fellow survivors to place a granite monument at the unmarked mass grave where some 150 men, women, and children who had perished in the 1890 massacre were buried.

There is still debate today about the number killed at Wounded Knee, as Gail Brown notes in "Wounded Knee: The Conflict of Interpretation." Some sources put the number of Lakotas killed as high as three hundred or even four hundred. But while the precise number of deaths may be uncertain, the significance of the event is not: Wounded Knee—the violent climax of decades of white duplicity, greed, murder, theft, and revenge—was the last armed encounter of the nineteenth century between Native Americans and the United States government.

For Native Americans, it quickly became an emblem, as Mario Gonzalez and Elizabeth Cook-Lynn put it in *The Politics of Hallowed Ground*, of "the deliberate genocide of a people by European invaders of this continent who called themselves Americans." The events of December 29, 1890, were precipitated by a pan-Indian messianic religious movement—the "Ghost Dance"—that the government felt threatened by, but which held out to Native Americans the hope that these lands would once again be theirs and not the white man's. The Wounded Knee massacre

Burial of the Dead at the Battlefield [sic] *at Wounded Knee, S.D., 1891.*
PHOTO CREDIT: NORTHWESTERN PHOTO CO., CHADRON, NE; COURTESY OF THE
HUNTINGTON LIBRARY, SAN MARINO, CA.

marked the end of that hope. From 1890 to the present, Native American writers
have struggled with the challenge of how to best to remember what happened at
Wounded Knee, how to honor the dead, and how to let the past inform the present.
They have struggled with the question that contemporary Oneida poet Roberta
Hill Whiteman asked when she occupied Wounded Knee in 1973: "How can I mark
this sorrow?"

Marking the sorrow of Wounded Knee has been central to much Native
American autobiography, fiction, and poetry ever since the terrible events occurred there in 1890. Much as the "Ghost Dance" was the first truly pan-Indian movement, Wounded Knee became a pan-Indian site for memorializing the
dead, recalling the pain, remembering the Indians' hopes for a different kind of
world, mourning the death of those hopes, and mobilizing to protest contemporary conditions that are the legacies of white Americans' war of genocide against
the Indian tribes that peopled North America before they got there. The Native Americans who witnessed all or part of the massacre and its aftermath—including Nicholas Black Elk, Charles Eastman, and Alice Ghost Horse—passed

on their versions of what had happened. The Wounded Knee massacre figures prominently in the first novel written by a woman of American Indian descent, *Wynema: A Child of the Forest*, by S. Alice Callahan, published in 1891. In the twentieth century, Wounded Knee has figured in poetry, fiction, and nonfiction by Native American writers including Elizabeth Cook-Lynn, Mary Crow Dog, Vine Deloria Jr., Roberta Hill Whiteman, N. Scott Momaday, and Wendy Rose, while themes that Wounded Knee brings to the surface figure in poetry by James Welch, Zitkala-Ša, and others. The place and its multiple meanings reverberate through more than a century of Native American letters.

Wounded Knee National Historic Landmark is located near the Stronghold Unit of Badlands National Park on the Pine Ridge Indian Reservation, an area comanaged by the Oglala Sioux Tribe and the National Park Service. The names that the Lakota and early French trappers gave the area—*mako sica* and *les mauvaises terres a traverser*—both mean "bad lands," reflecting the place's relative lack of water and desolate loneliness. The rugged landscape of the park is marked by native short prairie grasses, scattered pine trees, occasional small streams, and a large numbers of spires, peaks, and buttes carved by erosion—extraordinary rock formations that a mid-nineteenth-century explorer quoted in a geological survey of the upper Midwest refers to as "some magnificent city of the dead, where the labor and the genius of forgotten nations had left behind them a multitude of monuments of art and skill." In 1935, architect Frank Lloyd Wright was struck by the "indescribable sense of mysterious elsewhere" of the Dakota Badlands, "a distant architecture" that struck him as "an endless supernatural world more spiritual than earth but created out of it." Peopled first by ancient mammoth hunters, by the mid-eighteenth century the area had become home to the Lakota Sioux, who considered the Black Hills sacred. The Second Treaty of Fort Laramie in 1868 (between the Sioux and the U.S. government) set aside the area for exclusive use by the Indians, as a part of the Great Sioux Reservation. The United States promised that no unauthorized persons "shall ever be permitted to pass over, settle upon, or reside in [this] territory." But the discovery of gold in the Black Hills in 1874 led whites to rush to the area in unprecedented numbers in violation of the treaty, precipitating the violent clash at Little Bighorn in 1876, in which the Sioux prevailed over the Seventh Cavalry. Nearly a quarter-century later, on the chill, windswept hills near Wounded Knee Creek, the Seventh Cavalry would take its revenge.

By the fall of 1883, whites had killed most of the bison herds, and, as the decade wore on, increasing efforts were made to confine Indian tribes to reservations. Nicholas Black Elk, the great Sioux spiritual leader whose story (as he told it to John G. Neihardt) would be published in 1932 as *Black Elk Speaks*—puts it bluntly:

There was hunger among my people before I went away across the big water, because the Wasichus did not give us all the food they promised in the Black Hills treaty. They made that treaty themselves; our people did not want it, and did not make it. . . . [I]t was worse when I came back. My people looked pitiful. There was a big drouth, and the rivers and creeks seemed to be dying. Nothing would grow that the people had planted, and the Wasichus had been sending less cattle and other food than ever before. The Wasichus had slaughtered all the bison and shut us up in pens. It looked as though we might starve to death. We could not eat lies.

Black Elk recalls a time when Indians had lived in harmony with the animals and each other: "Once we were happy in our own country and we were seldom hungry, for then the two-leggeds and the four-leggeds lived together like relatives, and there was plenty for them and for us. But the Wasichus came, and they have made little islands for us . . . and always these islands are becoming smaller, for around them surges the gnawing flood of the Wasichu; and it is dirty with lies and greed."

During the years leading up to the Wounded Knee massacre, the Indians' lands were confiscated by the U.S. government and overrun by government troops, the promised rations were cut to starvation levels, and Indian protests and appeals were ignored. "Never was more ruthless fraud and graft practiced upon a defenseless people than upon these poor natives by the politicians!" recalls Sioux writer Charles A. Eastman (whose Santee Sioux name was Ohiyesa, "the winner") in *From the Deep Woods to Civilization: Chapters in the Autobiography of an Indian.* "Never were there more worthless 'scraps of paper' anywhere in the world than many of the Indian treaties and Government documents! Sickness was prevalent and the death rate alarming, especially among the children." "Trouble from all these causes had for some time been developing, but might have been checked by humane and conciliatory measures," Eastman writes, but such measures were not forthcoming. Like many a troubled and despairing group before them, the Indians sought hope in a religious revival movement—in the preachings of a Paiute Indian named Wovoka who fashioned himself as the messiah who would bring an end to the Indians' sufferings if they followed his teachings and danced the religious dance he taught them, the "Ghost Dance." "My people were groping blindly after spiritual relief in their bewilderment and misery," Eastman continues. "The 'Messiah craze' in itself was scarcely a source of danger," he notes, adding that it was about as dangerous as the preachings of a well-known Christian evangelist whom no one found especially threatening: "One might almost as well call upon the army to suppress Billy Sunday and his hysterical followers," Eastman wryly suggests.

THE GHOST DANCE
AT WOUNDED KNEE
FROM BLACK ELK SPEAKS

In 1931, Nebraska poet John Neihardt interviewed the great Oglala Sioux holy man Nicholas Black Elk (then in his late sixties) with his daughter, Enid Neihardt, an adept stenographer. Neihardt edited the transcript into *Black Elk Speaks: Being the Life Story of a Holy Man of the Oglala Sioux as Told through John G. Neihardt (Flaming Rainbow)*. This wide-ranging book—part autobiography, part religious vision, part history, and part prophecy—became perhaps the most widely read Native American text in the twentieth century and played a key role in the modern revival of Native American religion. Contemporary scholars have looked at the book as a blending of Native American and Christian religious ideas (not only because of John Neihardt's role as amanuensis, but because Black Elk himself had converted to Catholicism in 1904); as a modernist effort to incorporate many voices into a single text (Black Elk often turns the narrative over to eyewitnesses other than himself); as an example of the *testimonio*, a contemporary genre of communal autobiography (such as *I, Rigoberta Menchu: An Indian Woman from Guatemala*); and as an invaluable window on Lakota culture and history. Born in the 1860s (his exact date of birth is unknown), Black Elk grew up at a time when the Lakota lived off of the abundant buffalo herds that roamed the Great Plains. After gold was discovered in the Black Hills when he was a child, he witnessed the Lakota's successful resistance to the white invaders at Little Bighorn in 1876, and in 1890, he witnessed both the Ghost Dance at Wounded Knee Creek and the massacre that followed it. Here is a selection from his comments on the Ghost Dance:

> The Wasichus had slaughtered all the bison and shut us up in pens. It looked as though we might all starve to death. We could not eat lies, and there was nothing we could do. . . . Our people were pitiful and in despair.
>
> But early that summer when I came back from across the big water (1889) strange news had come from the west, and the people had been talking and talking about it. . . . There was a sacred man among Paiutes who had talked to the Great Spirit in a vision, and the Great Spirit had told him how to save the Indian peoples and make the Wasichus disappear and bring back all the bison and the people who were dead and how there would be a new earth. . . . [H]is name was Wovoka. He told

them that there was another world coming, just like a cloud. It would come in a whirlwind out of the west and would crush out everything on this world, which was old and dying. In that other world there was plenty of meat, just like old times; and in that world all the dead Indians were alive, and all the bison that had ever been killed were roaming around again. . . .

This was all that was heard the whole winter. . . . [I]t was a very bad winter, with much hunger and sickness. Afterwhile I heard that north of Pine Ridge at the head of Cheyenne Creek, Kicking Bear had held the first ghost dance, and that people who danced had seen their dead relatives and talked to them. The next thing I heard was that they were dancing on Wounded Knee Creek just below Manderson.

. . . For awhile I kept from going, but at last I could not any more. So I got on my horse and went to this ghost dance on Wounded Knee Creek below Manderson.

I was surprised, and could hardly believe what I saw; because so much of my vision seemed to be in it. The dancers, both women and men, were holding hands in a big circle, and in the center of the circle they had a tree painted red with most of its branches cut off and some dead leaves on it. This was exactly like the part of my vision where the holy tree was dying, and the circle of the men and women holding hands was like the sacred hoop that should have power to make the tree to bloom again. . . .

When I went to the dance, I went only to see and to learn what the people believed; but now I was going to stay and use the power that had been given me. The dance was over for that day, but they would dance again next day, and I would dance with them.

Before we started dancing next day, Kicking Bear offered a prayer, saying: "Father, Great Spirit, behold these people! They shall go forth to-day to see their relatives, and yonder they shall be happy, day after day, and their happiness will not end."

Then we began dancing, and most of the people wailed and cried as they danced, holding hands in a circle; but some of them laughed with happiness. Now and then some one would fall down like dead, and others would go staggering around and panting before they would fall. While they were lying there like dead they were having visions, and we kept on dancing and singing, and many were crying for the old way of living and that the old religion might be with them again.

. . . I was dancing with my eyes closed, as the others did. Suddenly it seemed that I was swinging off the ground and not touching it any longer. . . . It seemed I would glide forward like a swing, and then glide back again in longer and longer swoops. There was no fear with this, just a growing happiness. . . . My body did not move at all, but I looked ahead and floated fast toward where I looked. . . . I could see a beautiful land where many, many people were camping in a great circle. I could see that they were happy and had plenty. Everywhere there were drying racks full of meat. The air was clear and beautiful with a living light that was everywhere. All around the circle, feeding on the green, green grass, were fat and happy horses; and animals of all kinds were scattered all over the green hills, and singing hunters were returning with their meat.

I floated over the tepees and began to come down feet first at the center of the hoop where I could see a beautiful tree all green and full of flowers. When I touched the ground, two men were coming toward me, and they wore holy shirts made and painted in a certain way. They came to me and said: "It is not yet time to see your father, who is happy. You have work to do. We will give you something that you shall carry back to your people, and with it they shall come to see their loved ones."

I knew it was the way their holy shirts were made that they wanted me to take back. They told me to return at once, and then I was out in the air again, floating fast as before. . . .

Then I fell back into my body, and as I did this I heard voices all around and above me, and I was sitting on the ground. Many were crowding around, asking me what vision I had seen. I told them just what I had seen, and what I brought back was the memory of the holy shirts the two men wore.

That evening some of us got together at Big Road's tepee and decided to use the ghost shirts I had seen. So the next day I made ghost shirts all day long and painted them in the sacred manner of my vision. . . . And I thought that if this world would do as the vision teaches, the tree could bloom here too. . . .

. . . Because of my vision and the power they knew I had, I was asked to lead the dance next morning. We all stood in a straight line, facing the west, and I prayed: "Father, Great Spirit, behold me! The nation that I have is in despair. The new earth you promised you have shown me. Let my nation also behold it."

In her 1891 novel, *Wynema: A Child of the Forest*, S. Alice Callahan, a writer of Muscogee (Creek) descent, also uses the occasion of the Ghost Dance to compare Indian and Christian notions of religious tolerance when she quotes from debates in the newspapers shortly before the outbreak of violence at Wounded Knee. In the novel, an Indian reader comments that "If our Messiah does come, we will not try to force you into our belief. We will never burn innocent women at the stake, or pull men to pieces with horses because they refuse to join with us in our ghost dances." But the newspaper's editorial opines, "If the United States army would kill a few thousand or so of the dancing Indians there would be no more trouble." Gerald, a white character in the novel who is sympathetic to the plight of the Indians, says, "Just think, the poor things are starving to death and are praying to their Messiah to relieve them, as nobody on earth will. And because of this, the white people want them killed."

Anthropologist James Mooney's 1896 book, *The Ghost-Dance Religion*, which quoted at length from conversations with Indians that Captain J. M. Lee recorded in 1890, would become one of the most widely cited accounts of the beliefs that animated the messianic movement: Wovoka told the Indians that if they only danced the Ghost Dance and sang the Ghost Dance songs, the buffalo would come back, and the Indians' dead ancestors would return to life—"young again"; and when the "Great Spirit" came, "all the Indians [would] go to mountains, high up away from whites," and while they were in these high places, a big flood would drown all the white people. After that, the world would belong to the Indians again, and wild game would be thick again everywhere. It was a vision of the coming of the messiah in some ways not unlike Judeo-Christian messianic visions. It did not require the Indians to engage the whites in battle (although the special shirts worn in the Ghost Dance were said to protect wearers from bullets), or to take an active role in ridding the world of white people. The "Great Spirit" would look after details like that; all one had to do now was "dance, everywhere, keep on dancing." And one had to dance wearing Ghost Dance garments—fringed shirts and dress that were ritually prepared and that bore distinctive designs—including crescents, stars, birds, dots, rings, human figures, and multicolored rainbow lines called "trails," drawn around the torso, arms, legs, etc. Ghost Dancers believed that the crow feathers they wore on their heads would serve as wings to help them fly away from the dying world below (where white people would perish) to the new earth above where Indians would live in freedom and autonomy.

Ghost Dance fervor spread, holding out the illusion of hope to a despairing people. The U.S. government chose to deny the followers of the Ghost Dance the religious freedom that the country's first white settlers had sought, and on which the country was founded. They chose to interpret what was essentially a religious movement as a sign that Indians were preparing to go to war against the United

States. The army was instructed to stop the Ghost Dance. Militia and army troops began to converge on the area as tensions built.

On December 15, 1890, Sitting Bull, the renowned Hunkpapa Sioux leader and medicine man, was murdered at the Standing Rock Agency while being arrested by Indian policemen working for the federal government. In *Wynema*, the title character, an Indian woman who has been educated by whites, and her white friends, are disturbed to read in "one of our great dailies" the story of what happened to the renowned Sioux chief: "It was reported to the Indian police that Sitting Bull proposed starting to the Bad Lands; so they started out at once, followed by a troop of cavalry . . . to arrest him and bring him back. When the police reached Sitting Bull's camp they found him making preparations for departure. So they immediately arrested him and started back." Some of Sitting Bull's followers clashed with the Indian police and Sitting Bull was shot by the police in the scuffle. "Poor fellows!" says one of *Wynema's* white friends. "They are starved almost to death, and in the attempt to crawl off to themselves are slaughtered like cattle." Another white friend says that it is "indeed a great crime, for which my people will be made to answer." The novel is not a great work of art—but in its efforts (one year after the massacre) to use fiction to give voice to Indian perspectives on the escalating tensions leading up to Wounded Knee, it is unique in literary history. How can one "make peace with a Government whose only policy is to exterminate my race?" asks an Indian in the novel named Wildfire. "What is life to a caged bird, threatened with death on all sides? The cat springs to catch it and hangs to the cage looking with greedy eyes at the victim. Strange, free birds gather round its prison and peck at its eyes, taunting it with its captivity until it beats its wings against the cage and longs for freedom, yea, even the freedom of *death*. So it is with us. The white man has caged us, here, for his greedy brothers to devour."

The death of Sitting Bull prompted Chief Big Foot to seek shelter for his Minneconjou band of followers (along with Chief Red Cloud) at the Pine Ridge Agency. The army—the Seventh Cavalry, as bad luck would have it, still smarting, years later, from the Sioux victory at Little Bighorn—escorted the group of some 350 Indians to Wounded Knee. Years later (as Mario Gonzalez and Elizabeth Cook-Lynn note in *The Politics of Hallowed Ground*), a South Dakota politician testified before Congress that a man who had served under the son of the commanding officer of the Seventh Cavalry told him, "The Seventh Cavalry went to Pine Ridge with the full intent of getting even for the loss of Custer at the Little Bighorn 14 years before." An Indian witness, Joseph Horn Cloud, reported having heard a similar motive discussed the night before the massacre took place, as one of his descendants reported in an interview with the National Park Service. Joseph Horn Cloud, a young man who had learned English in school, was curious about what the cavalrymen were saying, so on the evening of December 28 he visited their campfires and eavesdropped. He told his father that he overheard the men talking about this group of Indians having killed Custer, adding that they wanted to do something about it. On the morning of December 29, after a night spent drinking and toasting the capture of Chief Big Foot, the officers gathered the Indians in a circle and came to disarm them.

Dee Brown notes in *Bury My Heart at Wounded Knee* that an eyewitness named White Lance recalled, "They called for guns and arms, so all of us gave the guns and they were stacked up in the center." The soldiers thought there must be more arms hidden in the camp. Alice Ghost Horse/Kills the Enemy/War Bonnet was a twelve-year-old child who witnessed what happened next (years later she told the story to her son, John War Bonnet, who wrote it down in Lakota). After some cavalrymen had searched "the wagons for axes, knife, guns, bow and arrows, and awls" and confiscated them, they "continued to argue with the Lakotas." "During the heated discussion," she tells us, "a medicine man by the name of Yellow Bird appeared from nowhere and stood facing the east right by the fire pit which was now covered up with fresh dirt. He was praying and crying. He was saying to the eagles that he wanted to die instead of his people. He must sense that something was going to happen. He picked up some dirt from the fireplace and threw it in the air and said this is the way he wanted to go back . . . to dust." Lt. John C. Gresham, who was there, suspected Yellow Bird of sending a signal of some sort when he threw the dirt—an opinion shared by the majority of the cavalrymen. But Lt. W. W. Robinson, another eyewitness, observed that the fact that many small children were playing among the nearby teepees suggests that the Indians had no hostile intent. Yellow Bird threw the dirt, a Minneconjou survivor tells us, not as a signal, but as a prayer.

The search of the teepees and wagons yielded only two rifles, one of which belonged to a young Minneconjou named Black Coyote, who raised the new Winchester over his head and shouted that he had paid a lot of money for it and that it belonged to him. Wasumaz, one of Big Foot's band who later changed his name to Dewey Beard, recalled that Black Coyote was deaf. "If they had left him alone," Beard wrote, "he was going to put his gun down where he should. They grabbed him and spun him in the east direction. He was still unconcerned, even then. He hadn't his gun pointed at anyone. His intention was to put that gun down. They came on and grabbed the gun that he was going to put down. Right after they spun him around there was the report of a gun, was quite loud." The accidental discharge of a deaf man's gun may have triggered the indiscriminate firing from the soldiers that followed, as the air became thick with the smoke from their carbines.

"We tried to run but they shot us like we were a buffalo," Louise Weasel Bear remembered. "I know there are some good white people, but the soldiers must be mean to shoot children and women. Indian soldiers would not do that to white children." A young woman named Hakiktawin recalled, "My grandfather and grandmother and brother were killed as we crossed the ravine, and then I was shot on the right hip clear through and on my right wrist where I did not go any further as I was not able to walk." The Seventh Cavalry lost twenty-five men, most of them killed by their fellow-soldiers' bullets or shrapnel since they had stood in a circle, completely surrounding the Indians. Many of cavalrymen were awarded Congressional Medals of Honor for their "bravery."

"I did not know then how much was ended," Black Elk said. "When I look back now from this high hill of my old age, I can still see the butchered women and children lying heaped and scattered all along the crooked gulch as plain as when I saw them with eyes still young. And I can see that something else died there in the bloody mud, and was buried in the blizzard. A people's dream died there. It was a beautiful dream. . . . The nation's hoop is broken and scattered. There is no center any longer, and the sacred tree is dead."

Charles Eastman witnessed the immediate aftermath of the massacre as a physician searching for survivors in the snow. Eastman writes:

On the day following the Wounded Knee massacre there was a blizzard. On the third day it cleared, and the ground was covered with an inch or two of fresh snow. We had feared that some of the Indian wounded might have been left on the field, and a number of us volunteered to go and see. I was placed in charge of the expedition of about a hundred civilians, ten or fifteen of whom were white men. We were supplied with wagons in which to convey any of whom we might find still alive. Of course a photographer and several reporters were of the party.

Fully three miles from the scene of the massacre we found the body of a woman completely covered with a blanket of snow, and from this point on we found them scattered along as they had been relentlessly hunted down and slaughtered while fleeing for their lives. Some of our people discovered relatives or friends among the dead, and there was much wailing and mourning. . . . I counted eighty bodies of men who had been in the council and who were almost as helpless as the women and babes when the deadly fire began, for nearly all their guns had been taken from them. . . .

It took all of my nerve to keep my composure in the face of this spectacle, and of the excitement and grief of my Indian companions, nearly every one of whom was crying aloud or singing his death song.

There were a few dozen survivors. "All this was a severe ordeal for one who had so lately put all his faith in the Christian love and lofty ideals of the white man," writes

Eastman, who had converted to Christianity and found his faith severely tested by Wounded Knee. Three days after the massacre, Eastman and other rescuers carried the wounded and dying into a church that served as a makeshift hospital. Christmas decorations still hung on the walls—including a banner that read, "PEACE ON EARTH, GOOD WILL TO MEN."

At the cemetery at Wounded Knee the mass grave that holds the victims of the massacre is surrounded by more recent graves of Indians who died fighting for the United States in World War I and World War II—proof that some Indians were willing to give their lives for a country that had so little regard for theirs that less than thirty years before World War I it had gunned them down here in cold blood. That irony probably would have been appreciated by W. A. Prather, the regimental poet of the Ninth Cavalry, a black unit that stayed on at Wounded Knee long after all of the white troops had been sent home. In a poem he published in *Army and Navy Journal* on March 7, 1891, two and a half weeks before his unit was allowed to leave, he wrote:

> The rest have gone home,
> And to meet the blizzard's wintry blast,
> The Ninth, the willing Ninth,
> Is camped here till the last. . . .

> In warm barracks
> Our recent comrades take their ease,
> While we, poor devils,
> And the Sioux are left to freeze. . . .

The sense of promises broken and hopes betrayed that comes across in Charles Eastman's and Nicholas Black Elk's narratives is echoed in work by later Native American writers. Zitkala-Ša, for example, a Sioux writer who grew up on the Yankton Reservation in South Dakota and who would write and edit important collections of Indian stories, published a poem titled "The Red Man's America" in 1918, whose lines and rhyme scheme parallel the words to a familiar patriotic hymn:

> My country! 'tis to thee,
> Sweet land of Liberty,
> My pleas I bring.
>   Land where OUR fathers died,
>   Whose offspring are denied
>   The Franchise given wide,
>   Hark, while I sing.

James Welch, a poet and novelist of Blackfeet descent, also addressed, as Zitkala-Ša had, the exclusion of Native Americans from the rights and liberties other American enjoyed. His 2004 poem "The Man from Washington" captures the duplicity with which the government habitually dealt with the Indians—signing treaties violated with impunity and promising rations that never materialized.

The end came easy for most of us.
Packed away in our crude beginnings
in some far corner of a flat world.
We didn't expect much more
than firewood and buffalo robes
to keep us warm. The man came down,
a slouching dwarf with rainwater eyes,
and spoke to us. He promised
that life would go on as usual,
that treaties would be signed, and everyone
man, woman, and child—would be inoculated
against a world in which we had no part,
a world of wealth, promise, and fabulous disease.

The story of what happened at Wounded Knee was passed on orally by survivors to their children and grandchildren, many of whom wrote it down. Many Indians would make pilgrimages to the sacred site where their ancestors had been massacred. Vine Deloria Jr., who would become a leading American Indian spokesman, and would write books including *Custer Died for Your Sins* (1969) and *We Talk, You Listen: New Tribes, New Turf* (1970), recalls that "The most memorable event of my early childhood was visiting Wounded Knee.... The people were simply shot down much as was allegedly done, according to newspaper reports, at Songmy," Deloria wrote in 1970, referring to the Vietnamese village also known as My Lai, where American infantrymen reportedly massacred hundreds of civilians in March 1968. "The massacre was vividly etched in the minds of many of the older reservation people, but it was difficult to find anyone who wanted to talk about it." But if the generation of Deloria's parents rarely

Zitkala-Ša (a.k.a. Gertrude Simmons Bonnin) (1876–1938). This gifted Yankton Sioux writer, who was fourteen when the Wounded Knee Massacre took place, viewed all Sioux across the region as family ("Either by marriage, by blood, or by adoption every member of the tribe bore some relation to the rest," she wrote) and did not object to the press's calling her "Sitting Bull's Granddaughter" (although it is unlikely that she was a blood relation). The stories about Indian life that she published in prominent national magazines like *Harper's* and the *Atlantic Monthly* and the sharp essays and blunt poems like "The Red Man's America" that she published in *American Indian Magazine* eloquently took America to task for its indefensible treatment of Native Americans. PHOTO CREDIT: PHOTO BY GERTRUDE KÄSEBIER; COURTESY OF THE DIVISION OF CULTURE AND THE ARTS, NATIONAL MUSEUM OF AMERICAN HISTORY, BEHRING CENTER, SMITHSONIAN INSTITUTION, WASHINGTON, DC.

wanted to talk about Wounded Knee, their children had no such reticence. In fact, the massacre is central to much of the poetry and fiction that they would write in the late twentieth century, a period marked by a renaissance of Native American letters.

The acclaimed Native American poet and novelist N. Scott Momaday (of Kiowa descent) was moved by the photographs of the massacre's aftermath to write this poem, titled "December 29, 1890":

Wounded Knee Creek
In the shine of photographs
Are the slain, frozen and black
on a simple field of snow,
They image ceremony:
women and children dancing,
    old men prancing, making fun.
    In autumn there were songs, long
    since muted in the blizzard.
In summer the wild buckwheat
shone like fox fur and quillwork,
and dusk guttered on the creek.
Now in serene attitudes
of dance, the dead in glossy
death are drawn in ancient light.

In Momaday's poem, the contrast between the lyrical "before" summer scenes and the grim "after" winter scenes underlines the ways in which the Wounded Knee massacre has come to symbolize the annihilation of Native American hopes, dreams, and ways of life in a world in which only photographs of the dead reflect "ancient light."

In her book *Bone Dance: New and Selected Poems 1965–1993*, Wendy Rose, who is of Hopi and Miwok descent, begins her poem titled "I Expected My Skin and My Blood to Ripen" with an extract from an auction catalog advertising items plundered from dead Indians at Wounded Knee. The catalog extract and the poem that follows it—in which the poet enters the mind of a woman killed in the massacre—make clear the poet's view that Indian art and artifacts get more respect than the Indians themselves did:

When the blizzard subsided four days later [after the massacre in 1890 at Wounded Knee], *a burial party was sent. . . . [A] long trench was dug. Many of the bodies were stripped by whites who went out in order to get the Ghost shirts and other accoutrements the Indians wore. . . . [T]he frozen bodies were thrown*

*into the trench stiff and naked.... [O]nly a handful of items remain in private
hands.... [E]xposure to snow has stiffened the leggings and moccasins, and all the
objects show the effects of age and long use.... [Items pictured for sale] moccasins
$140; hide scraper $350; buckskin shirt $1200, women's leggings $275, bone breastplate
$1000.....—Kenneth Canfield's 1977 Plains Indian Art Auction Catalog*

I expected my skin and my blood
to ripen, not to be ripped from my bones;
fallen fruit I am peeled, tasted,
discarded. My seeds open
and have no future. Now there has been no past.
My own body gave up the beads,
my own hands gave the babies away
to be strung on bayonets,
to be counted one by one
like rosary stones and then
tossed to the side of life
as if the pain of their birthing
had never been. My feet were frozen to the leather,
pried apart, left behind—bits of flesh
on the moccasins, bits of paper deerhide
on the bones. My back was stripped
of its cover, its quilling intact,
was torn, taken away.
My leggings were taken like in a rape
and shriveled to the size
of stick figures
like they had never felt the push
of my strong woman's body
walking in the hills.
It was my own baby
whose cradleboard I held—
would've put her in my mouth like a snake
if I could, would've turned her into a bush
or rock if there'd been magic enough
to work such changes.
Not enough magic
to stop the bullets, not enough magic

> to stop the scientists, and not enough magic
> to stop the money.

In her book *To Seek the House of Relatives*, Elizabeth Cook-Lynn, a member of the Crow Creek Sioux Tribe, published a poem titled "A Poet's Lament: Concerning the Massacre of American Indians at Wounded Knee." Cook-Lynn believes that it "is the responsibility of a poet like me to 'consecrate' history and event, survival and joy and sorrow, the significance of ancestors and the unborn; and I use one of the most infamous crimes in all of human history, which took place against a people who did not deserve to be butchered, to make that responsibility concrete." "Anger," Cook-Lynn tells us, "is what started me writing. Writing, for me, then, is an act of defiance born of the need to survive. I am me. I exist. I am Dakotah. I write. It is the quintessential act of optimism born of frustration. It is an act of courage, I think. And, in the end," she writes (paraphrasing a comment by Acoma Pueblo writer Simon Ortiz), "it is an act that defies oppression."

By the end of the nineteenth century, Wounded Knee had become an emblem of Indian defeat at the hands of white authorities and a symbol of the death of the traditional Indian way of life. But 1890 would not be the last armed encounter between the government and Indians at Wounded Knee. In February 1973, the trading post at Wounded Knee was seized by members of the American Indian Movement and Lakota Sioux in a radical act of resistance. They occupied it for seventy-one days. The list of demands they presented began with the statement: "We are operating under the Provisions of the 1868 Sioux Treaty. This is an act of war initiated by the United States. We are only demanding our country." The list included the demand that the Senate Foreign Relations Committee hold hearings on treaties made with American Indian Nations, that the Senate Subcommittee on Administrative Practices and Procedures immediately investigate the Bureau of Indian Affairs, and that the Senate Sub-Committee on Indian Affairs immediately investigate all Sioux Reservations in South Dakota. By the late twentieth century, Wounded Knee would become an emblem of Indian militancy, a symbol of the resurgence of red power and Indian pride that put a national spotlight Native American rights. Once again, the Ghost Dance was danced. And once again, gunfire rang out in the hills. Once again there were bodies to bury. As Osage writer Robert Warrior and Comanche writer Paul Chaat Smith commented in *Like a Hurricane*, "Wounded Knee seemed to be a place where everything happened twice. At times, the Ghost Dance and the machine guns, the army and the political agendas seemed like ghostly apparitions or cheap imitations of historical events. Political theater, some called it. Destiny and prophecy, countered the militants."

Mary Crow Dog's memoir, *Lakota Woman*, captures some of the pride with which the Indians reclaimed Indian traditions during the occupation. "After I had my baby during the siege of Wounded Knee they gave me a special name—Ohitika Win, Brave Woman, and fastened an eagle plume in my hair, singing brave-heart songs for me. I am a woman of the Red Nation, a Sioux woman." The past infuses the present as Mary Crow Dog, like the young mothers in Big Foot's band in 1890, tries to protect her baby from being shot: "I had my first baby during a firefight, with the bullets crashing through one wall and coming out through the other. When my newborn son was only a day old and the marshals really opened up upon us, I wrapped him up in a blanket and ran for it. We had to hit the dirt a couple of times, I shielding the baby with my body, praying, 'It's all right if I die, but please let him live.'" Mary Crow Dog's baby survived—but the memory prompts her to recall her sister's loss. Her sister Barbara chose to go to the government hospital in Rosebud to have her baby. But, "when she came out of anesthesia [she] found that she had been sterilized against her will. The baby lived only for two hours, and she had wanted so much to have children." Her sister's loss that day resonated with the visions of genocide that filled the minds of the survivors of the Wounded Knee massacre of 1890.

Wounded Knee has become an emblem of the war of words that has such power to shape both history and reality. Its official name—"Wounded Knee Battlefield"—incites anger, given that there was no battle here, but a massacre of Indians whose arms had already been confiscated by the U.S. Army. One of the most contested sites on the National Register, Wounded Knee is a touchstone of competing versions of the American past, and competing visions of the American future. Mario Gonzalez and Elizabeth Cook-Lynn's important 1999 book, *The Politics of Hallowed Ground: Wounded Knee and the Struggle for Indian Sovereignty*, documents, through first-person narratives, the efforts of Minneconjou and Oglala Sioux to establish a Native American monument at the site of the Wounded Knee massacre. "This effort, taking place at the close of the twentieth century, is in recognition of the fact that there is no national monument anywhere in the United States that honors the history of an indigenous nation's *defense of itself*. There is no place for Lakota tribal heroism to be recognized in the United States. *The failure to take note of this indigenous inalienable right is at the heart of America's racism*," Gonzalez and Cook-Lynn write. The proposed Native American monument at Wounded Knee would do more than honor the Lakota dead, as the granite monument currently at the site does. It would honor the Lakota people's resistance to those who would steal their land, colonize them, and destroy their way of life. Coming to terms with what happened at Wounded Knee turns out to be a task not just for poets and novelists and historians, but for every American who wants to understand what the United States is—and what it might become.

RELATED SITES

❧ Sand Creek Massacre National Historic Site
Kiowa County, Colorado (County Road W, a mile east of County Road 54);
supervisor's office: 910 South Wansted Street, Eads, Colorado

The group of some seven hundred peaceful Cheyenne and Arapaho men, women, and children camped on a bend in Sand Creek in southeastern Colorado did not fear the soldiers of the Colorado volunteer militia forces, because a flag of truce flew over their camp, a flag, in fact, that had been presented the previous year by President Abraham Lincoln to one of their principal Cheyenne elders, Black Kettle.

Earlier in the fall of 1864, Black Kettle had told the both the governor of the state, John Evans, and the head of the militia, Colonel John W. Chivington, "I want you to give all these chiefs of the soldiers here to understand that we are for peace, that we may not be mistaken for enemies." But at this site on November 29, 1864, nearly two hundred women, children, and older men were ruthlessly slaughtered by Colorado volunteers under Chivington's command. Chivington had ordered the soldiers to take no prisoners; a number of babies were among those butchered. The soldiers subsequently dishonored the dead by parading through the streets of Denver with their mutilated remains.

Acoma Pueblo poet Simon Ortiz memorializes the victims—and the betrayal and brutality that took place here—in his 1981 collection of poetic sketches and meditations, *From Sand Creek: Rising in This Heart Which Is Our America*, a book that opens out to explore in broader terms both the injustices inflicted on Native Americans in the name of Manifest Destiny, and how that history shapes what it means to be a United States citizen and an Indian today. In his preface to the book, Ortiz writes, "For Indian people, I would like *From Sand Creek* to be a study of that process which they have experienced as victim, subject, and expendable resource. For people of European heritage, I want it to be a study . . . which looks at motive and mission and their own victimization. I hope, finally, we will all learn something from each other. We must. We are all with and within each other."

In *From Sand Creek* Ortiz alternates brief (sometimes one-line) prose poems with free verse glimpses into the present and the past, evoking some of the alienation and dislocation experienced by Indians in Fort Lyons, Colorado—the site of both a contemporary Veterans Administration Hospital (where Ortiz himself underwent treatment from 1974 to 1975), and, in 1864, the headquarters of the U.S. troops who, along with Chivington's Volunteers, perpetrated the Sand Creek massacre. Through fragments that read almost like haikus, Ortiz evokes the entire tragic history of the clash of Native and European peoples ("Buffalo were dark rich clouds moving upon the rolling hills and plains of America. And then the flashing steel came upon bone and flesh").

Ortiz's poems do not flinch from the horror of what happened here ("They were amazed / at so much blood. / Spurting, / sparkling, / splashing, bubbling, steady / hot arcing streams. / Red / and bright and vivid / unto the grassed plains"). Nor do they resist laying the blame on the self-righteous arrogance of the Europeans: "And onward, / westward / they marched, / sweeping aside the potential / of dreams which could have been / generous and magnificent / and genius for them. / It is / no wonder / they deny regret / for the slaughter/ of their future"). And they underline the importance of remembering shameful episodes of American history, linking, for example, what happened at Sand Creek with what would happen during the Vietnam War at My Lai ("Remember My Lai. / In fifty years, / nobody knew / what happened. / It wasn't only the Senators. / Remember Sand Creek").

But Ortiz's book, which won the Pushcart Prize for Poetry in 1981, endeavors to transform despair into hope: "This America / has been a burden / of steel and mad / death, / but, look now, / there are flowers / and new grass / and a spring wind / rising / from Sand Creek."

Historian Ned Blackhawk writes, "We commemorate 'discovery' and 'expansion' with Columbus Day and the Gateway arch . . . but nowhere is there national recognition of the people who suffered from those 'achievements,'—and have survived." He suggests that a "symbolic but necessary first step" might be "a National Day of Indigenous Remembrance and Survival, perhaps on Nov. 29, the anniversary of Sand Creek."

Simon J. Ortiz (1941–). In *From Sand Creek: Rising in This Heart Which Is Our America* and other works, Simon Ortiz (Acoma Pueblo) explores the injustices done to Native peoples in the name of Manifest Destiny and probes what it means to be an American, a U.S. citizen, and an Indian. The acclaimed Native American writer is the author of more than twenty books of poems, stories, and essays.
PHOTO CREDIT: PHOTO BY DAVID L. BURCKHALTER.

❧ Little Bighorn Battlefield National Monument
Junction of Interstate 90 and U.S. Route 212, near Hardin, Montana

At this site on June 25 and 26, 1876, the Seventh Cavalry under the command of Lt. Col. George Armstrong Custer was defeated by Lakota Sioux and Cheyenne. The dead included Custer and nearly everyone in his immediate command. The massacre of Lakota Sioux at Wounded Knee fourteen years later by the Seventh Cavalry was in part retaliation for the Seventh Cavalry's defeat at the hands of the Sioux at Little Bighorn. Poet and novelist James Welch (Blackfeet) evokes this history in *Killing Custer: The Battle of Little Bighorn and the Fate of the Plains Indians* (coauthored with Paul Stekler). Crazy Horse, the leader of the Oglala Sioux tribe who helped annihilate the troops under Custer's command, has figured prominently in books by American writers including Joseph Bruchac, Larry McMurtry, Peter Matthiessen, N. Scott Momaday, John Neihardt, and Mari Sandoz, who have been intrigued and inspired by his determined resistance to the white invasion of the northern Great Plains.

❧ Big Hole National Battlefield
16425 Montana Route 43, Wisdom, Montana

❧ Nez Perce National Historical Park
39063 U.S. Route 95, Spalding, Idaho

Sites in Oregon, Washington, and Montana
Five groups of Nez Perce fleeing from the U.S. Army sustained an overwhelming loss of life at Big Hole National Battlefield during the summer of 1877, a turning point in the Nez Perce War of that year. This history is evoked through museum exhibits, guided hikes, and interpretive talks. An annual commemoration of the battle takes place every August 9. One can read a Nez Perce perspective on the Battle of Big Hole in *Yellow Wolf: His Own Story*, a book based on conversations that Yellow Wolf (or He-Mene Mox Mox), a Nez Perce warrior who fought in the Nez Perce war of 1877, had with Lucullus Virgil McWhorter, a white man who wrote down his story. At the thirty-eight sites that constitute Nez Perce National Historical Park (designated 1965) and on the Nez Perce National Historic Trail (part of the park), which runs from the Wallowa Valley of east Oregon to Bear Paw Battlefield in northern Montana, Nez Perce culture and history are commemorated.

❧ Kaibab National Forest
Northern Arizona; supervisor's office: 800 South 6th Street, Williams, Arizona

Like many parts of the country originally inhabited by Native Americans, this 1.6 million-acre forest of ponderosa pine, Douglas fir, Engelmann spruce, aspen, blue spruce, piñon pine, oak, and juniper bordering the north and south rims of the Grand Canyon is now owned by the federal government. In his poem "Grand Canyon Christmas Eve, 1969" in his book *Woven Stone*, Acoma Pueblo poet Simon Ortiz meditates on the irony of now having to pay to gather firewood on his family's ancestral land. The poem includes the following lines:

> Nearby, a U.S. Forest Service
> sign reads:
> KAIBAB NATIONAL FOREST
> CAMP ONLY IN CAMPING AREAS
> NO WOOD GATHERING
> GO AROUND OTHER SIDE OF ENCLOSED AREA
> & DEPOSIT 85 CENTS FOR WOOD
> This is ridiculous.
> You gotta be kidding.
> Dammit, my grandfathers
> ran this place
> with bears and wolves. . . .
> And I got some firewood
> anyway from the forest,
> mumbling, Sue me. . . .

Ortiz explores a similar theme in regard to Montezuma Castle National Monument in his poem titled "A Designated National Park." (Montezuma Castle National Monument is on Montezuma Castle Road, Arizona; exit 289 on Interstate 17, ninety minutes north of Phoenix, forty-five minutes south of Flagstaff.) After Ortiz quotes the entrance fees on the sign at "Montezuma Castle in the Verde Valley, Arizona," he writes, "This morning, / I have to buy a permit to get back home."

John G. Neihardt State Historic Site
Northwest Corner of Washington and Grove Streets, Bancroft, Nebraska

Nebraska poet John G. Neihardt moved to this home in 1900. It was while living here that he first became acquainted with Indians. Neihardt, whom Oglala Sioux holy man Black Elk would call "Flaming Rainbow," would collaborate with Black Elk on *Black Elk Speaks: Being the Life Story of a Holy Man of the Oglala Sioux as Told through John G. Neihardt (Flaming Rainbow)*.

FOR FURTHER READING

The Writers: Works and Words

Black Elk. *Black Elk Speaks: Being the Life Story of a Holy Man of the Oglala Sioux as Told through John G. Neihardt (Flaming Rainbow)*. 1932. Introduction by Vine Deloria Jr. Lincoln: University of Nebraska Press, 1988.

Bruchac, Joseph, ed. *Survival This Way: Interviews with American Indian Poets*. Tucson: Sun Tracks and the University of Arizona Press, 1987.

Callahan, S. Alice. *Wynema: A Child of the Forest*. 1891. Edited with introduction by A. Lavonne Brown Ruoff. Lincoln: University of Nebraska Press, 1997.

Cook-Lynn, Elizabeth. *Notebooks of Elizabeth Cook-Lynn*. Sun Tracks. Tucson: University of Arizona Press, 2007.

———. *Seek the House of Relatives*. Marvin, SD: Blue Cloud Quarterly Press, 1983.

———. *Why I Can't Read Wallace Stegner and Other Essays: A Tribal Voice*. Madison: University of Wisconsin Press, 1996.

Crow Dog, Mary, and Richard Erdoes. *Lakota Woman*. New York: Grove Weidenfeld, 1990.

Deloria, Vine, Jr. *Custer Died for Your Sins: An Indian Manifesto*. New York: Macmillan, 1969.

———. *We Talk, You Listen: New Tribes, New Turf*. New York: Macmillan, 1970.

Eastman, Charles. *From the Deep Woods to Civilization: Chapters in the Autobiography of an Indian*. 1916. Lincoln: University of Nebraska Press, 1977.

Holler, Clyde, ed. *The Black Elk Reader*. Syracuse, NY: Syracuse University Press, 2000.

Jensen, Richard E., R. Eli Paul, and John E. Carter. *Eyewitness at Wounded Knee*. Lincoln: University of Nebraska Press, 1991.

Kilcup, Karen L. *Native American Women's Writing, 1800–1924: An Anthology*. Oxford: Blackwell Publishers, 2000.

LaDuke, Winona. *Recovering the Sacred: The Power of Naming and Claiming*. Brooklyn, NY: South End Press, 2005.

McWhorter, Lucullus Virgil. *Yellow Wolf: His Own Story*. Caldwell, ID: Caxton Press, 1940.

Momaday, N. Scott. *In the Presence of the Sun: Stories and Poems, 1961–1991*. New York: St. Martin's Press, 1992.

———, ed. *American Indian Authors*. Boston: Houghton Mifflin, 1972.

Niatum, Duane, ed. *Carriers of the Dream Wheel: Contemporary Native American Poetry*. San Francisco: Harper and Row, 1981.

Ortiz, Simon J. *From Sand Creek: Rising in This Heart Which Is Our America*. New York: Thunder's Mouth Press, 1981.

———. *Woven Stone*. Tucson: University of Arizona Press, 1992.

Purdy, John L., and James Ruppert, eds. *Nothing but the Truth: An Anthology of Native American Literature*. Upper Saddle River, NJ: Prentice Hall, 2001.

Rose, Wendy. *Bone Dance: New and Selected Poems, 1965–1993*. Tucson: University of Arizona Press, 1994.

Smith, Paul Chaat, and Robert Allen Warrior. *Like a Hurricane: The Indian Movement from Alcatraz to Wounded Knee*. New York: New Press, 1996.

Welch, James. *Riding the Earthboy*. New York: Penguin, 2004.

Welch, James, with Paul Stekler. *Killing Custer: The Battle of Little Bighorn and the Fate of the Plains Indians*. New York: W. W. Norton, 2007.

Whiteman, Roberta Hill. *Star Quilt*. Minneapolis: Holy Cow! Press, 1984.

Zitkala-Ša, *American Indian Stories, Legends, and Other Writings*. Edited by Cathy N. Davidson and Ada Norris. New York: Penguin, 2003.

Backgrounds and Contexts

Blackhawk, Ned. "Remember Sand Creek Massacre." *New York Times*, November 27, 2014. http://www.nytimes.com/2014/11/28/opinion/remember-the-sand-creek-massacre.html?_r=0.

Brown, Dee. *Bury My Heart at Wounded Knee: An Indian History of the American West*. New York: Holt, Rinehart and Winston, 1970.

Brown, Gail. "Wounded Knee: The Conflict of Interpretation." In *Myth, Memory, and the Making of the American Landscape*, edited by Paul A. Shackel, 103–118. Gainesville: University of Florida Press, 2001.

Coleman, William S. E. *Voices of Wounded Knee*. Lincoln: University of Nebraska Press, 2000.

Foote, Kenneth E. *Shadowed Ground: America's Landscapes of Violence and Tragedy*. Austin: University of Texas Press, 1997.

Gonzalez, Mario, and Elizabeth Cook-Lynn. *The Politics of Hallowed Ground: Wounded Knee and the Struggle for Indian Sovereignty*. Urbana: University of Illinois Press, 1999.

Krupat, Arnold. *The Voice in the Margin: Native American Literature and the Canon*. Berkeley: University of California Press, 1989.

Lincoln, Kenneth. "A Contemporary Tribe of Poets" (review essay). *American Indian Culture and Research Journal* 6, no. 1 (1982): 79–101.

———. *Native American Renaissance*. Berkeley: University of California Press, 1983.

Linenthal, Edward. *Sacred Ground: Americans and Their Battlefields*. Urbana: University of Illinois Press, 1991.

Mintz, Steven, ed. *Native American Voices: A History and Anthology*. 2nd enlarged ed. St. James, NY: Brandywine Press, 2000.

Mooney, James. *The Ghost-Dance Religion: Extract from the Fourteenth Annual Report of the Bureau of Ethnology*. Washington, DC: Government Printing Office, 1896.

Owen, David Dale. *Report of a Geological Survey of Wisconsin, Iowa, and Minnesota; and Incidentally of a Portion of Nebraska Territory*. Philadelphia: Lippincott, Grambo, and Co., 1852.

Ruoff, LaVonne Brown. *American Indian Literatures: An Introduction, a Bibliographic Review, and Selected Bibliography*. New York: Modern Language Association of America, 1990.

Wright, Frank Lloyd, and Lewis Mumford. *Frank Lloyd Wright and Lewis Mumford. Thirty Years of Correspondence*. Princeton, NJ: Princeton University Press, 1935.

The handsome parlor in the Paul Laurence Dunbar House in Dayton, Ohio. Luxuries such as a velvet settee, an artfully framed oil painting, and the photographic portrait of the author reflect the wealth that Dunbar's books and readings brought him.

PHOTO CREDIT: PHOTO BY SHELLEY FISHER FISHKIN.

7

"I Know Why the Caged Bird Sings"

THE PAUL LAURENCE DUNBAR HOUSE
219 PAUL LAURENCE DUNBAR STREET, DAYTON, OHIO

On the flyleaf of the high school chemistry textbook on the bookshelf in the cozy, second-floor study, alongside notes on the properties of carbonic acid, are two signatures—"Paul L. Dunbar" and "P. Laurence Dunbar"—evidence that book's teenaged owner was trying out different versions of who he wanted to be. The name was key to his future, since he had determined to be a writer. He was gifted, glib, and quick. He was president of the high school literary club, editor of the school newspaper, and author of the school song. Journalism and poetry came easily to him. He had a sense of humor and a ready wit; he was personable, and he was ambitious. He hit the pavement to look for a job after graduation in the spring of 1891, convinced that with his track record of talent and responsibility, some local newspaper or law office would surely hire him in some clerical position. He was offered one job. It was in the Callahan Building—one of the more impressive office buildings in downtown Dayton. He was hired to run the elevator (salary: four dollars a week). Nobody wanted to hire a black man in Dayton for a nonmenial job in 1891, no matter how good he was.

By 1903, however, when Dunbar bought this pleasing nine-room, two-story brick house in his hometown for his mother, he was one of the best-known writers in the country. The comfortable, well-designed home (a cross between Italianate and Queen Anne style) in a tree-lined, middle-class neighborhood, with its graceful wrought-iron columns and neat green shutters, an electric chandelier in the dining room (a new and extravagant luxury), green velvet upholstery in the parlor, state-of-the-art laundry facilities off the kitchen, and tasteful wall-coverings and art throughout, represented a level of material success that few Dayton law clerks—much less elevator operators—could have imagined for themselves.

But if the well-appointed parlor and dining room reflected the money he had earned from his poetry and fiction, the books in his upstairs study—his "Loafin'

Holt" as he called it—reflected the prestige his writing had won him. There was a volume of President Theodore Roosevelt's speeches inscribed to Dunbar with the president's "regards," as well as an autographed gift copy of lawyer Clarence Darrow's essays. Poets, playwrights, statesmen, and journalists from around the country and around the world sent their books to him inscribed "with admiration"—books that would nestle up against that old high school chemistry text on his study's shelves.

But the questions Dunbar implicitly played with on his textbook's flyleaf stayed with him throughout his life: Who did he want to be? How ought he to present himself to the world? While the high school youth weighed the relative merits of "Paul L." versus "P. Laurence," the writer he grew up to be asked himself whether he should write in standard English or black dialect, whether he should be concentrating on poetry or on fiction, focusing on white characters or black ones, criticizing his society directly or obliquely—or all of the above. One goal remained clear throughout: he wanted to earn his way through life as a professional poet and fiction writer. No African American had yet achieved that goal, and the increasingly bitter state of race relations in the country made it all the more elusive; but these facts seemed merely to strengthen his resolve. Perhaps a sentence that he marked in one of those books that would end up in his study—D. Augustus Straker's *The New South Investigated*—may have helped spur him on: "When we cannot climb the mountain, let us tunnel the rock."

Dunbar bought this house for his mother, Matilda Dunbar, in 1903 with money he earned from the sale of his many books of poetry and fiction. The tuberculosis that had plagued him throughout much of his adult life was taking its toll, and now, recognizing that he was ailing and failing at a mere thirty-one years old, he wanted to be sure that his mother had a comfortable place to live after he was gone. Although he had not lived in this part of town when he was growing up, he knew it well, having come here often to visit his classmates Orville and Wilbur Wright, who lived in the neighborhood and tinkered in their bicycle shop down the road. At the time Dunbar bought this house, most of the neighbors were white, and racial prejudice in the country was at a dangerous high. But Dunbar had earned such respect and prominence as a writer that he was welcomed with pride. He lived in this house with his mother from 1903 until his death in 1906, and she lived there for another twenty-eight years, until her death in 1934. All those years she kept his study exactly the way he had left it, leaving on the desk the poem he was completing when he died, and a scrap of paper on which he had written, "It is one of the peculiar phases of Anglo-Saxon conceit to refuse to believe that every black man does not want to be white."

The opera singer Sissieretta Jones came to visit here, as did the writer James

Weldon Johnson. But along with the famous and talented, there were visitors who shyly admitted that they couldn't read. Dunbar bought a book on education methods, pulled his old McGuffey's Readers off the shelves, and endeavored to teach them; he taught no formal classes, but word got out: if you came and wanted to learn, he would help you. In 1936, when the state of Ohio purchased it, the house became the first publicly owned African American historic site in the nation. In 1962, it became the second national landmark registered in Ohio.

It is in part because of Matilda Dunbar's devotion to her son's memory that the Dunbar House is as evocative as it is of the man who lived there. She allowed nothing to be changed in his study, preserving it as a shrine to her extraordinary son, and kept the furnishings and family heirlooms in the rest of the house in good condition—bending to modernity only by updating some of the kitchen appliances. In the dining room, where every morning for twenty-eight years after his death Matilda Dunbar would put on the table two eggs for Paul—the same breakfast she had served him every day he lived in the house—there were clear reminders both of where she had come from and where she had arrived. The handsome table, the delicate china platters, and the electric chandelier were emblems of the solid middle-class comfort in which her famous son had left her, while the distinctive piece of furniture called a "mammy's bench" across the back wall recalled her roots in slavery. She had taken the bench with her through her many moves in the city, but it fit so

Paul Laurence Dunbar had this comfortable, nine-room brick house at 219 Summit Street (now Paul Laurence Dunbar Street), in Dayton, Ohio, built for himself and his mother with earnings from his books and readings.

PHOTO CREDIT: FROM THE COLLECTIONS OF DAYTON HISTORY.

perfectly against the back wall of the dining room on Summit Street that it looked as if it had always belonged right there. She had appreciated the ingeniousness of the long rocking bench with the removable gate across half its length as she juggled household tasks, her work as a laundress, and the challenge of minding young Paul, and later his baby sister. The clever piece of furniture allowed a mother to rock her baby safely in the gated section while having room on the other half of the bench for herself and the things she needed to do—folding laundry, shelling peas, and so on. Matilda had been introduced to a bench like this as part of her work as a house slave near Shelbyville, Kentucky. There were no more babies in the house by the time she moved to Summit Street in 1903, but that didn't stop Matilda from keeping, in a prominent place, this big and bulky reminder of her slave past. Like her son, she knew that not *everything* from the slave past deserved to be forgotten: alongside the pain and humiliation and degradation there was occasionally something worth savoring or saving—melodies, moments of laughter, and ingenious furniture for minding babies.

Matilda Dunbar—then Matilda Glass Murphy—had come to Dayton in 1866. She was a young widow with two young sons from her marriage to a slave on a nearby plantation. Her grandmother, Rebecca Porter, who had been freed by a Dayton abolitionist, settled in the city in 1839, and her mother had arrived in the 1860s when her master had set her free. In Dayton, Matilda met and married Joshua Dunbar, a plasterer who had also been a slave in Kentucky, and who had escaped to Canada on the Underground Railroad before settling in Ohio. Joshua Dunbar served in the Fifty-Fifth Massachusetts Regiment of Volunteers (Company F), reenlisted in the Fifth Massachusetts Cavalry, and rose to the rank of sergeant in the U.S. Colored Troops who served in the Union Army. Paul was born in 1872.

His parents separated shortly after his birth and later divorced. Paul's mother raised him in a series of houses around the city in which she lived with Paul's two half-brothers from her previous marriage, and his baby sister, who died when she was two. Paul's father continued to live in Dayton, at the Old Soldiers' Home, until his death in 1885. Family members and family friends, many of whom, like his parents, had been raised in the slave South, undoubtedly told Paul stories of their lives under slavery, and he listened with the avid attentiveness of a young man who was interested in everything. Matilda Dunbar, who earned a living as a laundress, taught herself to read by propping up passages from the Bible over her washtub. Paul, a precocious child from the start, managed to learn to read at the same time, as he helped her with her work. As he told the *Philadelphia Times* in 1902, "My mother, who had no education except what she picked up herself, and who is generally conceded to be a very unusual woman, taught me to read when I was four years old. Both my father and herself were fond of books and used to read to us as we sat around the fire at night."

He recalled having written his first poem before he started school, at age six, and he recited his first original poem in public when he was twelve, at a program at the Eaker Street A.M.E. Church. From that point on, he would recall that "the fever took me and I wrote ream upon ream of positive trash when I should have been studying Euclid. Plays, verses, stories, everything I could think or dream turned out. Fortunately I seldom tried to publish."

As Ann Honious notes in *What Dreams We Have*, Dunbar looked back on his days at Dayton's Central High School with fondness: seven years after graduation he wrote, "I was the only Negro in the class and apparently popular. My chums encouraged me. My teachers encouraged me." He was elected president of the school literary club, the Philomathean Society, and served as editor in chief of his school's newspaper, the *High School Times*. "I set earnestly to work to live up to these honors and succeeded in bringing out the paper a month late every time," Dunbar

The Class of 1890 at Central High School, Dayton, Ohio. Paul Laurence Dunbar is standing on the left in the back row; his friend and classmate Orville Wright is standing in the middle of the back row. Dunbar was president of the literary club, editor of the school newspaper, and author of the school song at Central High. This picture was taken in 1889, when Dunbar was seventeen or eighteen years old.

PHOTO CREDIT: COURTESY OF SPECIAL COLLECTIONS AND ARCHIVES, WRIGHT STATE UNIVERSITY LIBRARIES, DAYTON, OH.

remembered, but he wrote editorials that "are still pointed to as marvels of school-boy—well—audacity." He became friends with Orville Wright, a classmate. Orville appreciated Dunbar's way with words, much as Dunbar appreciated Orville's way with machines. When Orville and his brother Wilbur decided to publish a neighborhood newspaper, the *Westside News*, on a printing press they rigged up in their bicycle shop, they relied on Dunbar to supply much of the copy. When Dunbar decided to publish a paper of his own for the black community, the *Dayton Tattler*, the Wright brothers printed it on their press.

Dunbar observes, in a matter-of-fact tone jarring for its lack of bitterness, that "after graduation there was nothing for me to do save to go into menial employment as other Negroes did. I took the nearest thing—an elevator." Dunbar, who had worked briefly as a janitor at the American Cash Register company before finding work as an elevator operator in the Callahan Building, put his time to good use and always had a copy of *Century Magazine*, a dictionary, a writing tablet, a pencil, and a stack of books to read as he waited for elevator calls. He also observed details of character and dress, of cadence and accent, as he ferried passengers from floor to floor, noting the differences between broad New England A's and the kind of Hoosier twang that poet James Whitcomb Riley's poems made famous. In between trips, he jotted down notes, ideas, poems, and sketches, some of which he would send off to newspapers to try to get published. Some were direct imitations of other poets he admired—like Riley, for whom he wrote an appreciative few stanzas in the Indiana dialect for which Riley's own work was best known. Occasionally a newspaper in the Midwest or in the East would print one of the poems that he submitted. His poem, "Christmas Is a-Comin'," for example, ran in the *Rochester Herald* on Christmas Eve that winter. The "elevator boy poet," as he would come to be known, wrote a poem that he was invited to deliver as an address of welcome on the occasion of a meeting of the Western Association of Writers in Dayton. The poem greatly impressed many of the writers assembled, and several sought Dunbar out the next day in the elevator. One in particular encouraged him to continue writing and helped give him the courage to try to self-publish a book of poems.

When he found out that it would cost more to publish a slim book of poems than he earned in six months as an elevator operator, Dunbar was crestfallen; but William Blacher, the business manager of the Press of United Brethren Publishing House, liked his pluck and admired his poems and advanced him the $125 he needed. Shortly before Christmas 1892, five hundred copies of a neatly printed sixty-two-page book titled *Oak and Ivy* were delivered to the Dunbar house. Within two weeks, Dunbar had sold enough books to passengers going up and down in his elevator to repay William Blacher the money he had lent him.

His first book of poems represented a remarkable range of subjects, styles, and tones. There were poems that celebrated nature in carefully crafted literary language influenced by poets such as Longfellow, Shakespeare, Tennyson, Keats, Poe, and Shelley—such as "October" or "The Meadow Lark." There were earnest declarations of love of that marched in sprightly rhythms and regular rhymes—such as "Night of Love," "Love's Pictures," "Nora: A Serenade," and "My Love, Irene." There were poems imitative of James Whitcomb Riley's Hoosier dialect, including "A Summer Pastoral," "The Old Apple Tree," "My Sort o' Man," and "James Whitcomb Riley from a Westerner's Point of View." And there were solemn poems of homage to figures Dunbar admired or to whom he was indebted—including, in addition to Riley, Dr. James Newton Matthews of Illinois, an early mentor, and John Greenleaf Whittier. Dunbar celebrated Whittier's songs for being "sublime in their simplicity," and he echoed that theme in the poem "Common Things," which reiterated the virtue of forsaking the lofty and exotic in favor of subjects closer to home: "We like the man who soars and sings, / With high and lofty inspiration; / But he who sings of common things / Shall always share our admiration." The one poem written entirely in black dialect, "A Banjo Song," touched on a theme to which Dunbar would return frequently: an older person's nostalgia for the pleasures of youth—whether the first flush of love, or the site of the diversions of one's childhood and young adulthood. In this category would be "The Old Apple Tree," "The Ol' Tunes," "Goin' Back," and "The Old Homestead" ("For 'twas there I spent the moments / Of my youth, life's happy spring").

Several poems touched on questions of racial justice and on issues of racial pride. The short poem titled "Justice" invokes the ideal of a literally blind Justice who is unconscious of the "creed or race" of the man whose cause she hears, while "To Miss Mary Britton" looks forward to a time when "liberty" will be made "real"—a dream being sabotaged by the passage of Jim Crow legislation, as Dunbar's headnote to the poem signals: "When the legislature of Kentucky was discussing the passage of a separate-coach bill, Miss Mary Britton, a teacher in the Schools of Lexington, Kentucky, went before them, and in a ringing speech protested against the passage of the bill. Her action was heroic, though it proved to be without avail." The poet pleads,

Grant thou, O gracious God,
That not in word alone
Shall freedom's boon be ours,
While bondage-galled we moan!
But condescend to us
In our o'erwhelming need;

Break down the hind'ring bars,
And make us free indeed.
Give us to lead our cause
More noble souls like hers,
The memory of whose deed
Each feeling bosom stirs;
Whose fearless voice and strong
Rose to defend her race,
Roused Justice from her sleep,
Drove Prejudice from place.

The poet's admiration of Mary Britton's protest ends up displacing the fact that she failed: justice was not roused; prejudice was not driven away—an early example of Dunbar's efforts to use poetry to imbue his readers with hope in the face of starkly discouraging facts.

"Ode to Ethiopia" is a proud hymn to the glory of black America, which predicts its "continuous rise." Here Dunbar prophesies that the story of black people's triumphant achievements would be told by "bards which from thy root shall spring"—that is, by black poets like himself. Among all of the upbeat expressions of hope and victory in *Oak and Ivy* one can catch glimpses of the frustration Dunbar himself must have felt at the necessity of being a "bard" who could hone his craft only in found moments between elevator calls. In "A Career," for example, the speaker expresses his desire to break out of the forces that constrain him:

Break me my bounds, and let me fly
To regions vast of boundless sky;
Nor I, like piteous Daphne, be
Root-bound. Ah, no! I would be free
As yon same bird that in its flight
Outstrips the range of mortal sight. . . .

Writing at his post—or "perch"—in the elevator of the Callahan Building—a little cage, really, with a door that he had to open and close scores of time each day as he dreamed of being a soaring poet in a world that had assigned him to ride up and down an elevator shaft all day—Dunbar could identify with the plight of a caged songbird. That image would be central to one of his best-known works today, "Sympathy." Alice Dunbar-Nelson, who was Dunbar's wife at the time he wrote "Sympathy" in 1899, recalled after his death that the "iron grating of the book stacks in the Library of Congress," where he was working at the time, "suggested to him the bars of the bird's cage. June and July days are hot. All out of doors called and the trees of the shaded streets of Washington were tantalizingly suggestive of his beloved streams and fields. . . . He understood how the bird felt when it beat its wings against its cage." Yet while the stacks of the library may have been the most proximate source of the metaphor, Dunbar's earlier dream of breaking his bounds and flying like a bird—a dream written in an elevator "cage"—may have shaped his vision in the poem, as well.

Sympathy

I know what the caged bird feels, alas!
   When the sun is bright on the upland slopes;
When the wind stirs soft through the springing grass,
And the river flows like a stream of glass;
   When the first bird sings and the first bud opes,
And the faint perfume from its chalice steals—
I know what the caged bird feels!

I know why the caged bird beats his wing
Till its blood is red on the cruel bars;
For he must fly back to his perch and cling
When he fain would be on the bough a-swing;
And a pain still throbs in the old, old scars
And they pulse again with a keener sting—
I know why he beats his wing!

I know why the caged bird sings, ah me,
When his wing is bruised and his bosom sore,—
When he beats his bars and he would be free;
It is not a carol of joy or glee,
But a prayer that he sends from his heart's deep core,
But a plea, that upward to Heaven he flings—
I know why the caged bird sings!

At age twenty-one, in 1893, after his *Oak and Ivy* had been favorably reviewed in the *Toledo Blade*, Dunbar set out for Chicago, where the World's Columbian Exposition had just opened, and where many young men sought jobs. Frederick Douglass, who was in charge of the Haitian Pavilion at the fair, gave Dunbar a

Paul Laurence Dunbar (1872–1906). The author of hundreds of poems, stories, plays, novels, and articles, Dunbar was nation's first black writer to achieve great national success as an author. He was also a progenitor of spoken-word poetry in America. His performances of his poetry were popular among white audiences as well as black. Dunbar was born in Dayton, grew up in Dayton, and died there, as well.

PHOTO CREDIT: COURTESY OF THE OHIO HISTORY CONNECTION.

job as a clerical assistant, paying him out of his own pocket a salary that was a dollar more per week than he had earned as an elevator operator. On "Colored People's Day" at the fair—a highly contested occasion that many African Americans thought demeaning—Douglass made sure that black excellence in the arts was showcased with the respect it deserved. Dunbar recited several of his poems and won new admirers. (He would later memorialize Douglass in a poem he wrote after his death.)

With the help of generous friends, Dunbar continued to publish. *Majors and Minors* came out in 1895. To his delight and surprise, William Dean Howells, dean of American literary critics and editor of *Harper's Weekly*, reviewed *Majors and Minors* in *Harper's* in June of the following year. Although not blind to the merits of Dunbar's poems in "literary English," as he put it, Howells was much more taken with Dunbar's poems in black dialect. "It is when we encounter the dialect poems that we find ourselves in the presence of a man with a direct and fresh authority do the kind of thing he is doing." Howells wrote that he would have been impressed by the "uncommon quality" of the dialect poems even if they had been written by a white man. "But since they are the expressions of a race-life from within the race, they seem to me infinitely more valuable and significant."

Overnight, Dunbar found himself famous. His printer, Hadley and Hadley, was deluged with orders for the book. Hundreds of readers wrote him letters, and he secured the services of a manager—Major James B. Pond, who also managed the lecture tours of Mark Twain. Pond booked Dunbar on a tour of readings and introduced him to various New York publishers, including Dodd, Mead, who published *Lyrics of Lowly Life* later that year; he also arranged for him to give a lecture tour of England the following year. The 1896 volume, which also included an introduction by William Dean Howells, would become Dunbar's most famous book.

Howells's well-meaning introduction reflects the unwitting condescension typical of so many white readers—even liberal ones. Howells notes that Dunbar "charmingly" reveals in these poems "a finely ironical perception of the negro's limitations, with a tenderness for them which I think so very rare as to be almost quite new. I should say, perhaps, that it was this humorous quality which Mr. Dunbar added to our literature, and it would be this which would most distinguish him, now and hereafter." Howells, to his credit, writes that "in more than one piece he has produced a work of art." But the art for Howells consists principally in dialect poems that express "the negro's limitations." Nowhere in his introduction is the reader prepared for the impressive cadences of "Ere Sleep Comes Down to Soothe the Weary Eyes" or for the poignant fear of belatedness in "Unexpressed." Nowhere is there a recognition of the plea embedded in "Not They Who Soar" for appreciating those unknown African Americans who built the country with their sweat and blood and who W.E.B. Du Bois would invoke seven years later in his preface to *Souls of Black Folks*: "Not they who soar, but they who plod. Their rugged way, unhelped, to God / Are heroes; they who higher fare, / And, flying, fan the upper air, / Miss all the toil that hugs the sod. / 'Tis they whose backs have felt the rod, / Whose feet have pressed the path unshod, / May smile upon defeated care, / Not they who soar."

Nowhere is there a glimpse of Dunbar's paean to the bravery of "The Colored Soldiers" who fought in the Civil War in the poem by that name ("And where'er the fight was hottest, / Where the bullets fastest fell, / There they pressed unblanched and fearless / At the very mouth of hell"). Nowhere is there an awareness of Dunbar's efforts to bear witness in that same poem to the cruelty those soldiers suffered at the hands of Confederate soldiers at sites like Fort Pillow, where many ex-slaves were shot down in cold blood while trying to surrender. Nowhere does Howells prepare the reader for the impassioned elegy for Frederick Douglass, whom Dunbar praises as "no soft-tongued apologist" but as someone who "spoke straightforward, fearlessly uncowed," who gave "sin and crime" "their proper hue, / And hurled at evil what was evil's due," who "dared the lightning in the lightning's track, / And answered thunder with his thunder back." Nor did Howells appreciate that even some of the poems he valued most for the appealing quality of their dialect were, in the context of the rest of the book, and of the moment in history when Dunbar published them, signifying more than their "charming" surface revealed. (In addition, Howells erred when he assumed that the word "minors" in the title of the book referred to Dunbar's dialect poems, as David Bradley points out in "Factoring Out Race." Although the dialect poems appeared in a section marked "Humor and Dialect" along with some nondialect poems, nothing in the book suggests that the poet considered them less important than the other poems in the book. Bradley suggests that the terms "majors and minors" in the book's title refer metaphorically to the musical keys that best fit the various poems.)

Dunbar's career took off during a period when the horizon of expectations for most of his fellow black Americans was constricting in alarming, and sometimes harrowing ways. During the 1890s, the middle of the period known as the "nadir" in American race relations, racially motivated lynchings reached epidemic proportions, sowing terror around the country. The convict-lease system effectively reenslaved thousands of free black men throughout the South who were convicted of "vagrancy" charges, or, if poor, on charges of "intent to steal," only to be leased out as cheap labor for extended periods of time. Blacks were disenfranchised in ever-growing proportions through a variety of means, including violent intimidation. Jim Crow laws were passed across the country, green-lighting separate Bibles for blacks and whites in courtrooms and segregated classrooms, railroad cars, waiting rooms, hospitals, water fountains, and cemeteries. Meanwhile pseudoscientists of varying persuasions argued that the black race was an inferior race, and destined first to lose out to the superior Anglo-Saxons, and eventually to simply disappear. It would be hard to imagine a less auspicious time for a young black man to aspire to be a professional author. But these obstacles only seemed to strengthen Dunbar's resolve.

Far from being oblivious to what was going on around him, Dunbar addressed contemporary racism in hard-hitting newspaper articles like one he published in the *Toledo Journal* in 1898. With a sarcasm and daring that would have surprised readers used to reading his poems singing the praises of hot corn-pone and banjo music or his eloquent elegies for fallen black soldiers, Dunbar asks why the whites don't just say to the blacks, "We don't like you. We do not want you in certain places. Therefore when we please we will kill you. We are strong people; you are weak. What we chose to do we will do, right or no right." He wrote this piece shortly after the Spanish-American War, where many African Americans served bravely, and in the wake of the election-related Wilmington race riots, where a number of African Americans were killed. He writes, "The new attitude may be interpreted as saying, 'Negroes, you may fight for us, but you may not vote for us. You may prove a strong bulwark when the bullets are flying, but you must stand from the line when the ballots are in the air.'"

He wrote impassioned prose on the new forms of slavery that the freed slaves were forced to suffer at the turn of the century. In a 1903 piece called "The Fourth of July and Race Outrages" that he published in the *New York Times*, he notes:

The papers are full of the reports of peonage in Alabama. A new and more dastardly slavery there has arisen to replace the old. For the sake of re-enslaving the Negro, the Constitution has been trampled under foot, the rights of man have been laughed out of court, and the justice of God has been made a jest. . . . Every wire, no longer in the South alone, brings us news of a new hanging or a new burning, some recent outrage against a helpless people, some fresh degradation of an already degraded race. . . . Like a dark cloud, pregnant with terror and destruction, disenfranchisement has spread its wings over our brethren of the South. Like the same dark cloud, industrial prejudice glooms above us in the North.

In his poetry, as well, Dunbar sometimes addressed the sense of betrayal that the "nadir" brought to African Americans: "What, was it all for naught, those awful years / That drenched a groaning land with blood and tears?" He asks in a 1901 poem, "To the South—ON ITS NEW SLAVERY":

Was it to leave this sly convenient hell,
That brother fighting his own brother fell?
When that great struggle held the world in awe,
And all the nations blanched at what they saw,
Did Sanctioned Slavery bow its conquered head
That this unsanctioned crime might rise instead?
Is it for this we all have felt the flame,—
This newer bondage and this deeper shame?

He doesn't pull any punches here. In four devastatingly accurate words—"this sly convenient hell"—he sums up his anger at the injustice he sees around him and indicts the infuriatingly easy mode of denial that white America so "conveniently" can hide behind. How do you jolt your fellow citizens into an awareness of "this newer bondage and this deeper shame" if they are determined to deny its existence? (Dunbar didn't seem to be aware of this fact, but two years before this poem appeared in print, Mark Twain had actually published an essay that gave this phenomenon a name: "the lie of silent assertion" Twain called it—the "silent assertion that nothing is going on which fair and intelligent men are aware of and are engaged by their duty to try to stop.") How do you break through that lie of silent assertion? Dunbar must have wondered. How do you get them to feel the pain and shame and frustration of the black child who learns how very narrow are the opportunities open to him in life? How do you counter the mounting pseudoscientific so-called evidence about the inferiority of black people when you know that black people are as smart and kind and creative and talented and attractive and capable as white people are? And how do you instill a measure of hope in black people when all the forces around them conspire to stamp it out?

The singing of the caged bird can be interpreted by less empathetic souls as a song of "joy or glee," as Dunbar puts it in the poem "Sympathy." But Dunbar knows it is a song of pain and frustration. In his brilliant poem, "We Wear the Mask," which appeared in *Lyrics of Lowly Life* but which Howells seems not to have noticed, he spells out this phenomenon, unmasks it, so to speak, decoding the real meaning of what is going on, and dares the reader to ever mistake the mask for the reality again.

We Wear the Mask
We wear the mask that grins and lies,
It hides our cheeks and shades our eyes,—
This debt we pay to human guile;
With torn and bleeding hearts we smile,
And mouth with myriad subtleties.
Why should the world be over-wise,
In counting all our tears and sighs?
Nay, let them only see us, while
    We wear the mask.
We smile, but, O great Christ, our cries
To thee from tortured souls arise.
We sing, but oh the clay is vile
Beneath our feet, and long the mile;
But let the world dream otherwise,
    We wear the mask!

Writing at a time when the legacies of minstrelsy led to the proliferation on the stage and in fiction of cheerful and happy-go-lucky paper-thin black characters who grinned their way through life, Dunbar took pains here to identify the "grin" as a "lie," as a "mask" that covered the "torn and bleeding hearts" beneath. The image of the "mask," the layers of pretense often required for survival in a racist society, went on to become a major trope among African American writers in the twentieth century.

Although "We Wear the Mask" is widely read today, it was not among Dunbar's best-known poems in his own day. During his lifetime, he was most famous for his dialect poems, in part because of Howells's early rave review. His dialect poetry was in great demand, and he had a well-booked schedule of readings. Lavishly illustrated gift books of his dialect poems—*Candle-Lightin' Time; Li'l Gal; Howdy, Honey, Howdy; Joggin' Erlong; Poems of Cabin and Field*; and *When Malindy Sings*—sold well at Christmastime. These poems were lively, rhythmic, colorful, and charming. Beneath the surface and between the lines, however, they were often mounting sharp and subtle challenges to the culture's assumptions about race. Some have charged Dunbar with having written poems that were part of the "Plantation Tradition," a commercially successful late-nineteenth-century nostalgia for the days "befo' de war." There is no political agenda, for example, to "The Party," perhaps the most widely recited of his dialect poems. But rather than trying to conform to known models of commercial success, one could just as easily say that Dunbar was simply being faithful to the stories his parents and their friends had told him. Matilda and Joshua Dunbar and their friends had not liked being slaves, to be sure. But they also were able to recall fleeting periods of pleasure, often involving music, or family, or early love or food—and those memories were just as real as the memories of being whipped and exploited. For unlike white Plantation Tradition writer Thomas Nelson Page, whose loyal slaves had no lives of their own and lived to serve their beloved masters, slaves in Dunbar's dialect poems of plantation life are vibrant and alive individuals with likes and dislikes, energy and agency and special talents. Can we blame Dunbar for not wanting to cede to white authors propping up the Plantation Tradition the right to write about the complexity of his parents' lives and those of their friends? Ultimately, in his most memorable dialect poems, far from imitating the Thomas Nelson Pages of his day, Dunbar is doing something far more subversive: he is celebrating the genius and beauty of his people, a radical act in a society that in dozens of subtle and unsubtle ways, every day, declares them stupid and ugly.

"We Wear the Mask" may be read as a stunningly compressed treatise on psychology—as well as a gloss on how to read behavior that led to demeaning stereotypes of black people in the popular arts. "Sympathy" is a poignant expression of frustration. In all of these poems, Dunbar was countering the mainstream "lie of silent assertion" that accepted without question the idea that black people were inherently inferior, and that there was nothing wrong with a status quo that made a mockery of equality of opportunity and that was deeply suspicious of "difference."

At a time when promises made to African Americans were flagrantly betrayed and hopes were smashed, as the country embarked on a shameful bad-faith denial of the rights it had extended at the close of the Civil War, Dunbar crafted a subtle and luminous beacon of hope, a poem called "An Ante-Bellum Sermon."

An Ante-Bellum Sermon

WE is gathahed hyeah, my brothahs,
   In dis howlin' wildaness,
Fu' to speak some words of comfo't
   To each othah in distress.
An' we chooses fu' ouah subjic'
   Dis—we'll 'splain it by an' by;
"An' de Lawd said, 'Moses, Moses,'
   An' de man said, 'Hyeah am I.'"

Now ole Pher'oh, down in Egypt,
   Was de wuss man evah bo'n,
An' he had de Hebrew chillun
   Down dah wukin' in his co'n;
'Twell de Lawd got tiahed o' his foolin',
   An' sez he: "I'll let him know—
Look hyeah, Moses, go tell Pher'oh
   Fu' to let dem chillun go."

"An' ef he refuse to do it,
   I will make him rue de houah,

Fu' I'll empty down on Egypt
   All de vials of my powah."
Yes, he did—an' Pher'oh's ahmy
   Was n't wuth a ha'f a dime;
Fu' de Lawd will he'p his chillun,
   You kin trust him evah time.

An' yo' enemies may 'sail you
   In de back an' in de front;
But de Lawd is all aroun' you,
   Fu' to ba' de battle's brunt.
Dey kin fo'ge yo' chains an' shackles
   F'om de mountains to de sea;
But de Lawd will sen' some Moses
   Fu' to set his chillun free.

An' de lan' shall hyeah his thundah,
   Lak a blas' f'om Gab'el's ho'n,
Fu' de Lawd of hosts is mighty
   When he girds his ahmor on.
But fu' feah some one mistakes me,
   I will pause right hyeah to say,
Dat I'm still a-preachin' ancient,
   I ain't talkin' 'bout to-day.

But I tell you, fellah christuns,
   Things 'll happen mighty strange;
Now, de Lawd done dis fu' Isrul,
   An' his ways don't nevah change,
An' de love he showed to Isrul
   Was n't all on Isrul spent;
Now don't run an' tell yo' mastahs
   Dat I's preachin' discontent.

'Cause I is n't; I'se a-judgin'
   Bible people by deir ac's;
I'se a-givin' you de Scriptuah,
   I'se a-handin' you de fac's.
Cose ole Pher'oh b'lieved in slav'ry,
   But de Lawd he let him see,
Dat de people he put bref in,—
   Evah mothah's son was free.

An' dahs othahs thinks lak Pher'oh,
   But dey calls de Scriptuah liar,
Fu' de Bible says "a servant
   Is a-worthy of his hire."
An' you cain't git roun' nor thoo dat,
   An' you cain't git ovah it,
Fu' whatevah place you git in,
   Dis hyeah Bible too 'll fit.

So you see de Lawd's intention,
  Evah sence de worl' began,
Was dat His almighty freedom
  Should belong to evah man,
But I think it would be bettah,
  Ef I'd pause agin to say,
Dat I'm talkin' 'bout ouah freedom
  In a Bibleistic way.

But de Moses is a-comin',
  An' he's comin', suah and fas'
We kin hyeah his feet a-trompin',
  We kin hyeah his trumpit blas'.

But I want to wa'n you people,
  Don't you git too brigity;
An' don't you git to braggin'
  'Bout dese things, you wait an' see.

But when Moses wif his powah
  Comes an' sets us chillun free,
We will praise de gracious Mastah
  Dat has gin us liberty;
An' we'll shout ouah halleluyahs,
  On dat mighty reck'nin' day,
When we 'se reco'nised ez citiz'—
  Huh uh! Chillun, let us pray!

With sly wit, Dunbar's "Ante-Bellum Sermon" reminds his readers that two equally grim periods of enslavement both ended in eventual liberation.

In addition to publishing more than a dozen volumes of poetry, Dunbar also published four novels, numerous song lyrics, dramatic sketches, newspaper articles, and more than a hundred short stories. He peopled his fiction with white mid-westerners, slaves, former slaves, Reconstruction office-seekers, lynchers, lynching victims, post-Reconstruction southern blacks arriving in northern cities, porters, politicians, preachers, lawyers, law clerks, reporters, dancers, waiters, and striking miners. Dunbar was a commercial writer, an author who sought to sell his work in the marketplace. Yet he was also a self-aware writer who understood that his work was entering a highly charged and often offensive cultural conversation about African Americans that was going on around it. Was it possible to write commercial fiction that also redirected that conversation in productive ways? To what extent could a black writer at the turn of the century destabilize stereotypes—about black writers, and about black people generally—and still find a lucrative market for his fiction? His stories reveal a writer aware that the nation's media often painted African Americans in broad brushes dipped in racist bigotry while whitewashing any moral lapse on the part of whites. For example, in "The Lynching of Jube Benson," Dunbar writes dryly that the lynching of a blameless black man "was very quiet and orderly. There is no doubt that it was as the papers would have said, a gathering of the best citizens." He tackles media bias again in "The Tragedy at Three Forks," where two unlucky innocent black men who happen to be passing through the area are summarily lynched by the "law-abiding citizens of Barlow County." Following the lynching, he writes, "conservative editors wrote leaders about it in which they deplored the rashness of the hanging but warned the negroes that the only way to stop lynching was to quit the crimes of which they so often stood accused."

In addition to challenging "the papers" through sly irony, his stories also displace, disrupt, or directly challenge stereotypes of African Americans that the media commonly promulgated. For example, in dozens of turn-of-the-century stories and sketches in magazines such as *Century*, *Scribner's*, and *Harper's*, African American religion was ridiculed, and black preachers were presented as ignorant, pompous, self-important blowhards. Dunbar, by way of contrast, shows us black characters sincerely seeking faith ("Anna'Lizer's Stumblin' Block"), black ministers sincerely devoted to communal uplift ("The Ordeal at Mt. Hope"), and black preachers preaching cogent, articulate, and effective sermons ("The Trial Sermons on Bull-Skin"). And at a time when degrading, minstrelsy-inflected stereotypes of black men as "sambos" or "zip coons" infested the popular media and entertainment, he presented black men in a broad array of roles and relationships—such as a father surprised by the love he feels for his baby daughter ("Jimsella"), and a con-man who becomes the secret benefactor of an elderly woman who reminds him of his mother ("Aunt Mandy's Investment"). And at a time when "mammy" and the "jezebel" stereotypes often defined the scope of roles assigned to black women in popular culture, Dunbar presented black women, as well, in a wide range of different roles: such as a psychologically abused wife who gains the courage to stand up to her husband and demand respect ("The Emancipation of Evalina Jones"). In his short stories, he explores themes involving black people that were absent from the columns of the nation's newspapers, the nostalgic Plantation Tradition tales that were so popular in the nation's magazines, or the ubiquitous latter-day versions of minstrel shows—such as the discrimination black youth encountered in the job market ("One Man's Fortunes"), or the intricacies of black political life ("The Scapegoat"). He also explores the complexities of black-white relations among characters of a range of ages and occupations in multiple regions of the country and in varied venues—relations between children, between college students, or between employer and employee; relations in a private home, a law office, a political campaign, and a court of law.

His last novel, *Sport of the Gods*, which appeared in 1902, a wrenching naturalistic story of the fate of a black family that migrates to New York at the turn of the century, has the distinction of being the first urban novel of the black experience. Despite the fact that Dunbar worked in a wide range of genres and styles, and explored a broad array of themes and characters, the vast popularity of his dialect poetry sentenced most of his other work to relative obscurity—although the full range of his writing has received increasing attention since the centenary of his death in 2006.

Dunbar felt trapped by the public's demand that he continue producing dialect poetry when other forms came to interest him equally or more. As Dunbar put it in a poem he called "The Poet," "He sang of life, serenely sweet, / With, now and then, a deeper note," but found in the end that the world had praise not for the sweet or deep songs he sang but only for "a jingle in a broken tongue." Dunbar himself wrote dialect poetry that was much more than "a jingle in a broken tongue," but these lines may suggest his fears about how the world increasingly might come to view his achievement in those poems. Readers often failed to recognize the continuities among the many forms of poetry he produced. As the poet Elizabeth Alexander observed in 2006, "When you look at the dialect and the standard poems side by side, their sense of verse, line, and meter is not at all dissimilar. And I would argue that as Dunbar's dialect poems are shaped by literary sensibilities, his literary poems are enlivened by vernacular energy and a rhythmic mastery that also emanates from that same source. The greatest of his standard verses are clearly not written out of a solely Anglo-American tradition. Perhaps that is Dunbar's genius, that high-low fusion that is also the greatest possibility of African American poetry."

Dunbar served as a key inspiration to generations of African American poets in the twentieth century who appreciated the boldness and audacity of what he ventured and the originality and success of what he achieved. He recognized the potential of African American vernacular speech as the stuff of which poetry is made and celebrated the artistry inherent in black folk expression. He modeled the possibility of being a professional African American writer, and he gave writers permission to move back and forth between standard English and vernacular dialects, demonstrating, in the process, an ear attuned to the nuanced rhythms of speech as well as a finely honed sensitivity to the subtle cadences of poetry. Twentieth-century black poets Countee Cullen, Michael Harper, Robert Hayden, Ishmael Reed, Anne Spencer, and Margaret Walker would all write poems about Dunbar. Maya Angelou, who was riveted by Dunbar when she read him as a child, took the title of her autobiography as well as the title of a poem from a line in Dunbar's poem, "Sympathy": "I Know Why the Caged Bird Sings." Langston Hughes, who read him avidly as he developed his own inimitable poetic talents, would pick up where Dunbar left off and transform American poetry in the process. Since Dunbar was the first African American poet to perform his poetry on stage, delighting white and black audiences around the world with the vitality of black vernacular performance, he could also be viewed as the progenitor, as well, of hip-hop, rap, and poetry slams.

Elizabeth Alexander recalled in 2006 that her father often recited Dunbar's poem "The Party" and notes that it was "always a thrill" when he did: the poem helped give her access to the cadences of "black communal speech that he grew up with" but that were less a part of her own experience. Only as she prepared to speak about Dunbar's influence on contemporary poets at a conference held on the centennial of his death at Stanford University did she realize that a poem of her own called "The Party" had "borrowed, stolen, and paid homage" to Dunbar's poem by the same title. Alexander views Dunbar as "the significant beginnings of our tradition, the first black poet to do it 'as a job,' if you will," and "a great-grandfather to today's practicing poets," embodying "the very idea of the black poet with attendant issues and contradictions in the life lived and in the aesthetics that remain relevant for us today." When she queried some five hundred contemporary black poets about Dunbar's impact on them, they "wrote back swiftly and forcefully of 'their Dunbar.'" She observes, "Those of a more experimental vein saw Dunbar as someone to play with, to riff on, to deform. Formalists were in awe of his capacities, consistently sounding the note that his fluency and mastery as a formalist has been underestimated. . . . Many poets talked about the formal challenges of dialect, that writing dialect is not at all easy. Over and over they said that he was learned orally; there were many poets who, like me, never saw Dunbar on the page until long after we knew his poems." They made it abundantly clear to Alexander that "Dunbar matters very much to contemporary African American poets."

He has mattered to other American poets, as well. Reminding us, for example, that "William Carlos Williams recalls in his autobiography that his father read to him from Dunbar's dialect verse," Aldon Lynn Nielson believes that "there can be little doubt that Dunbar played a role in Williams's desire to root his poetics in identifiably American inflections and rhythms." Dunbar's lyric poetry also had an impact on twentieth-century music and film. Greg and Lillian Robinson note that Paul Robeson "commissioned and performed musical settings of 'L'il Gal' and 'Down Lover's Lane.' William Grant Still cited verses from Dunbar in the score of his 1935 Afro-American Symphony as epigraphs for the four movements. In the 1940s, Thomas Kerr composed a song cycle of Dunbar's verse, and Janice Brown Johnson wrote orchestral settings of his poem "The Pool."" Nielson reminds us that the celebrated jazz vocalist Abbey Lincoln performed versions of Dunbar's poems "Sympathy" and "When Malindy Sings" set to music composed by Oscar Brown Jr. In the hands of "these late 20th-century artists," Nielson tells us, "Malindy" becomes a "prayer flung up to heaven out of a sore breast as the poem's rhythms beat against the bars for freedom." Meanwhile Alexander observes that Dunbar's poems have done compelling cultural work in contemporary films such as *The Rosa Parks Story*, directed by Julie Dash, in which a recitation of "We Wear the Mask" plays a subtle and dramatic role.

"We Wear the Mask" has long been considered by critics "one of Dunbar's most specifically racial poems," as David Bradley observes in his introduction to Dunbar's poetry in an anthology of Dunbar's works. But Bradley then goes on to remind us that white midwestern poet James Whitcomb Riley had written a poem that began, "We are not always glad when we smile." Bradley is not claiming "that Dunbar was not referring to the angst of the American Negro; indeed, given the racial horrors of the era, it is hard to believe he did not have that somewhere in his mind." Rather, Bradley means to point out that reading "We Wear the Mask" as a poem about race alone is both "not evidenced by the text" and is also "subtly limiting."

Bradley notes that "ironically, but perhaps not surprisingly, it seems it was Ohioans who saw Dunbar most clearly, despite their own arguable bias." Howells—who hailed from Martin's Ferry, Ohio—called Dunbar's dialect poems evidence of "the essential unity of the human race, which does not think or feel black in one and white in another, but humanly in all." And Toledo mayor Brand Whitlock, who had objected to one of Dunbar's most political poems, "The Haunted Oak," wrote in a eulogy: "There was nothing foreign in Paul's poetry, nothing imported, nothing imitated: it was all original, native, and indigenous. Thus he became not the poet of his race alone—I wish I could make people see this—but the poet of you, and of me, and of all men everywhere."

The home in Dayton that honors his memory—a home in which he wrote, read, taught others to read, shared his final years with his mother, and corresponded with fans of his work around the globe—allows us a glimpse into the tragic and luminous life he led, and the rich legacy that he left.

PAUL LAURENCE DUNBAR'S CIVIL WAR

FORT PILLOW STATE PARK
3122 Park Road, Henning, Tennessee

OLUSTEE BATTLEFIELD, STATE HISTORIC PARK
5815 Battlefield Trail Road, Olustee, Florida

ROBERT GOULD SHAW MEMORIAL
Boston Common, Boston, Massachusetts

Paul Laurence Dunbar's father, Joshua Dunbar, joined the Fifty-Fifth Massachusetts Regiment of Volunteers (Company F) in the Civil War and told his son stories of the fellow soldiers who had served bravely with the U.S. Colored Troops in that war. Dunbar wrote two poems about black soldiers like his father—one in standard English and one in dialect, "The Colored Soldiers," and "When Dey 'Listed Colored Soldiers." He also wrote a poem titled "Robert Gould Shaw," about the young white officer who commanded the black troops of the Fifty-Fourth Massachusetts Regiment.

Black soldiers were not allowed into the Union Army until 1863, when pressure from black and white abolitionists led to the formation of one of the first black regiments, the Fifty-Fourth Massachusetts Regiment. The Fifty-Fourth distinguished itself at Fort Wagner, South Carolina, in July 1863, where many of its members, including Shaw, were killed. "The Colored Soldiers" is Dunbar's tribute to these men, as well as to those who fought alongside his father in the Fifty-Fifth. His allusions to "Wagner," "Olustee" and "Pillow" reference three sites of Union defeat—Fort Wagner in South Carolina, Olustee in Florida, and Fort Pillow in Tennessee—where black soldiers performed admirably and suffered horrendous casualties.

The Colored Soldiers

If the muse were mine to tempt it
And my feeble voice were strong,
If my tongue were trained to
    measures,
I would sing a stirring song.
I would sing a song heroic

Of those noble sons of Ham,
Of the gallant colored soldiers
Who fought for Uncle Sam!
In the early days you scorned
    them,
And with many a flip and flout

Said "These battles are the white
    man's,
And the whites will fight them
    out."
Up the hills you fought and
    faltered,
In the vales you strove and bled,
While your ears still heard the
    thunder
Of the foes' advancing tread.
Then distress fell on the nation,
And the flag was drooping low;
Should the dust pollute your
    banner?
No! the nation shouted, No!
So when War, in savage triumph,
Spread abroad his funeral pall—
Then you called the colored
    soldiers,
And they answered to your call.
And like hounds unleashed and
    eager
For the life blood of the prey,
Sprung they forth and bore them
    bravely
In the thickest of the fray.
And where'er the fight was hottest,
Where the bullets fastest fell,
There they pressed unblanched
    and fearless
At the very mouth of hell.
Ah, they rallied to the standard
To uphold it by their might;
None were stronger in the labors,
None were braver in the fight.
From the blazing breach of Wagner
To the plains of Olustee,
They were foremost in the fight

Of the battles of the free.
And at Pillow! God have mercy
On the deeds committed there,
And the souls of those poor
    victims
Sent to Thee without a prayer.
Let the fulness of Thy pity
O'er the hot wrought spirits sway
Of the gallant colored soldiers
Who fell fighting on that day!
Yes, the Blacks enjoy their freedom,
And they won it dearly, too;
For the life blood of their
    thousands
Did the southern fields bedew.
In the darkness of their bondage,
In the depths of slavery's night,
Their muskets flashed the dawning,
And they fought their way to light
They were comrades then and
    brothers,
Are they more or less to-day?
They were good to stop a bullet
And to front the fearful fray.
They were citizens and soldiers,
When rebellion raised its head;
And the traits that made them
    worthy,—
Ah! those virtues are not dead.
They have shared your nightly
    vigils,
They have shared your daily toil;
And their blood with yours
    commingling
Has enriched the Southern soil.
They have slept and marched and
    suffered
'Neath the same dark skies as you.

They have met as fierce a foeman,   Every blot of Slavery's shame.
And have been as brave and true.   So all honor and all glory
And their deeds shall find a record   To those noble sons of Ham—
In the registry of Fame;   The gallant colored soldiers
For their blood has cleansed   Who fought for Uncle Sam!
    completely

"God have mercy on the deeds committed there," Dunbar wrote of Fort Pillow. This Confederate fort on the Chickasaw Bluffs overlooking the Mississippi River in Tennessee was occupied by Union troops in 1862, and recaptured in 1864 by Confederate troops under the command of General Nathan Bedford Forrest (who would later become the first Grand Wizard of the Ku Klux Klan). About half of the 570 Union troops were former slaves recruited in Alabama (the First Battalion of the Sixth U.S. Colored Heavy Artillery and Company D of the Second U.S. Colored Light Artillery). Two-thirds of the black soldiers there were killed (compared with a little more than one-third of the white soldiers). A number of them were killed while trying to retreat or surrender, leading the battle to become widely known as a massacre. The angry cry, "Remember Fort Pillow!" helped rally black soldiers throughout the rest of the war.

If the tone of "The Colored Soldiers" is heroic, Dunbar's poem, "When Dey 'Listed Colored Soldiers," strikes a more personal note, as the excerpt below reveals. The speaker in the poem is the sweetheart of a soldier who enlists:

Oh, I hugged him, an' I kissed him, an' I baiged him not to go;
But he tol' me dat his conscience, hit was callin' to him so,
An' he coul n't baih to lingah w'en he had a chanst to fight
For de freedom dey had gin him an' de glory of de right.
So he kissed me, an' he lef' me, w'en I'd p'omised to be true;
An' dey put a knapsack on him, n' a coat all colo'ed blue.
So I gin him pap's ol' Bible f'om de bottom of de draw',—
W'en dey 'listed colo'ed sojers an' my 'Lias went to wah.

In Dunbar's poems, as Joanne Braxton reminds us, black soldiers "are almost always depicted as silent heroes who fought bravely and without question to solve the quarrels of northern and southern white men who took them for granted; yet these poems are also filled with strategic silences, a negotiation with an audience that did not want to know too much." "'When Dey 'Listed Colored Soldiers' follows 'Lias into war through the eyes of his sweetheart," Braxton notes, "but begs the question of the manner of his death and burial." 'Lias, like so many other black soldiers, never came home.

The experience of the black soldiers like Joshua Dunbar is memorialized at the Robert Gould Shaw Memorial on the Boston Common, a stunning sculpture by Augustus Saint-Gaudens that almost seems to ripple with the movement of men and horses. Dedicated on Memorial Day in 1897 in ceremonies that included veterans of the Fifty-Fourth and Fifty-Fifth Massachusetts Regiments and the Fifth Cavalry, the sculpture captures the quiet courage of the young men who marched off to fight for a country that would continue to deny their children basic rights. As Dunbar put it in a newspaper article in 1898, they were to be "a strong bulwark when the bullets were flying," but were "to stand from the line when the ballots are in the air." His poem "Robert Gould Shaw," published in 1903, concludes with an angry reminder of the nation's failure to honor the memory of these brave soldiers by making real for the next generation the freedoms for which they gave their lives. The grim and ultimate irony of the sacrifice Shaw and his men represent—"This cold endurance of the final pain"—is the idea that "thou and those who with thee died for right / Have died, the Present teaches, but in vain!"

RELATED SITES

•◆ Wright Cycle Company and Wright Printing Shop
22 South Williams Street, Dayton, Ohio

It was in this bicycle shop that Orville and Wilbur Wright had some of their earliest experiences tinkering with machines. They manufactured their own brand of bicycles here from 1895 to 1897. Their experience of working with sprockets, spokes, chain drives, metals, lathes, drills, and tires stood them in good stead when they designed and built their first gliders and flying machines. A bicycle that Orville Wright gave Dunbar is on display at the Dunbar House visitors' center. Wilbur and Orville Wright would leave their mark on history by inventing "the world's first power-driven, heavier-than-air machine in which man made free, controlled and sustained flight" (as their achievement is described in the National Air and Space Museum, where their legendary plane is on permanent display). The print shop on the second floor of this building recalls the printing technology that the Wright brothers had rigged up to print the two neighborhood newspapers that they and their friend Dunbar tried to launch when they were still in high school This site is part of the Dayton Aviation Heritage National Park, which also includes the Dunbar House, the Huffman Prairie Flying Field, and the John W. Berry Sr. Wright Brothers Aviation Center.

◗◆ James Whitcomb Riley Homestead
250 West Main Street, Greenfield, Indiana

This white clapboard country house surrounded by a white picket fence, where James Whitcomb Riley (1849–1916) spent his childhood, is the setting of some of Riley's most popular poems. He left home at age sixteen to join a traveling medicine show, where he roped in customers by playing the banjo and reciting his own verse. His first book of poetry, published in 1883, and the other hugely popular collections he would publish, celebrated country life in rural Indiana towns like this one.

◗◆ James Whitcomb Riley House
523 Lockerbie Street, Indianapolis, Indiana

"Hoosier poet" James Whitcomb Riley lived in this large, two-story, brick Italianate Victorian house as a paying guest from 1893 to his death in 1916. It was during the 1890s that he helped inspire Paul Laurence Dunbar to pursue his own experiments in writing poetry in dialect. The house contains memorabilia of Riley's life and career.

◗◆ Will Marion Cook House
221 West 138th Street, New York City

Pioneer composer Will Marion Cook (1869–1944), who helped open Broadway to musical comedy shaped by African American folk traditions, collaborated with Paul Laurence Dunbar on the successful 1898 production *Clorindy: The Origin of the Cakewalk*. Cook lived in this 1891 Victorian townhouse house from 1918 until his death in 1944. The fashionable neighborhood, home to many successful professionals like Cook, was known as "Strivers Row."

❧ World's Columbian Exposition Site
In the Jackson Park Historic Landscape District and Midway Plaisance, Chicago

When Dunbar came here to look for work in the spring of 1893, he would have often walked past the French Beaux Arts–style building designed by Charles Atwood, which was then the Palace of Fine Arts at the fair, and which is now Chicago's Museum of Science and Industry. "The buildings at the World's Fair are indeed a wonder in themselves," Dunbar wrote his friend Dr. James Newton Matthews shortly after he arrived, when the buildings were still under construction. The double-thick brick walls built to protect this building's art collection account for the structure's longevity.

❧ Woodland Cemetery and Arboretum
118 Woodland Avenue, Dayton, Ohio

This garden cemetery (one of the five oldest in the nation) in the heart of Dayton is the final resting place of Paul Laurence Dunbar. His mother and sister are buried next to him. The large willow tree that hangs over his grave was planted to honor the wish expressed in his poem, "A Death Song," that he be buried under a willow tree. The first verse of the poem is carved on his tombstone. The graves of Orville and Wilbur Wright are not far off.

FOR FURTHER READING

The Writers: Works and Words

Alexander, Elizabeth. "Dunbar Lives!" In Fishkin et al., eds., special issue, *African American Review* 41, no. 2 (Summer 2007): 395–401. Expanded version in Alexander, Elizabeth. *Power and Possibility: Essays, Reviews, and Interviews*, 9–19. Ann Arbor: University of Michigan Press, 2007. Alexander's presentation of this material at the Stanford Paul Laurence Dunbar Centennial Conference in 2006 may be viewed at http://www.youtube.com/watch?v=VS1pkUIWICk.

Dunbar, Paul Laurence. *Candle-Lightin' Time*. Illustrated. New York: Dodd, Mead, 1904.

———. *The Collected Novels of Paul Laurence Dunbar*. Edited by Herbert Woodward Martin, Ronald Primeau, and Gene Andrew Jarrett. Athens: Ohio University Press, 2009.

———. *The Collected Poetry of Paul Laurence Dunbar*. Edited and with an introduction by Joanne M. Braxton. Charlottesville: University Press of Virginia, 1993.

———. *The Complete Poems of Paul Laurence Dunbar*. New York: Dodd, Mead, 1913.

———. *The Complete Stories of Paul Laurence Dunbar*. Edited by Gene Andrew Jarrett and Thomas

Lewis Morgan. Foreword by Shelley Fisher Fishkin. Athens,: Ohio University Press, 2009.

———. *Howdy, Honey, Howdy.* Illustrated. New York: Dodd, Mead, 1905.

———. *In His Own Voice: The Dramatic and Other Uncollected Works of Paul Laurence Dunbar.* Edited by Herbert W. Martin. Athens: Ohio University Press, 2002.

———. *Joggin' Erlong.* Illustrated. New York: Dodd, Mead, 1906.

———. *L'il Gal.* Illustrated. New York: Dodd, Mead, 1904.

———. *Lyrics of Lowly Life.* New York: Dodd Mead, 1896.

———. *Majors and Minors.* New York: Dodd, Mead, 1897.

———. *Oak and Ivy.* Dayton, OH: United Brethren Publishing House, 1893.

———. *The Paul Laurence Dunbar Reader.* Edited by Jay Martin and Gossie H. Hudson. New York: Dodd, Mead, 1975.

———. *Poems of Cabin and Field.* Illustrated. New York: Dodd, Mead, 1904.

———. *"The Sport of the Gods" and Other Essential Writing by Paul Laurence Dunbar.* Edited and introduced by Shelley Fisher Fishkin and David Bradley. New York: Modern Library/Random House, 2005.

———. *When Malindy Sings.* Illustrated. New York: Dodd, Mead, 1906.

Backgrounds and Contexts

Bradley, David. "Factoring Out Race: The Cultural Context of Paul Laurence Dunbar." In Fishkin et al., eds., special issue, *African American Review* 41, no. 2 (Summer 2007): 357–366. Bradley's presentation of this material at the Stanford Paul Laurence Dunbar Centennial Conference in 2006 may be viewed at https://www.youtube.com/watch?v=OOmXp0oUFI4.

Braxton, Joanne M. "Dunbar: The Originator." In Fishkin et al., eds., special issue, *African American Review* 41, no. 2 (Summer 2007): 205–214. Braxton's presentation of this material at the Stanford Paul Laurence Dunbar Centennial Conference in 2006 may be viewed at http://www.youtube.com/watch?v=OvHVvfpFoqs (part 1) and http://www.youtube.com/watch?v=VQ6oMUoDR7A (part 2).

Cunningham, Virginia. *Paul Laurence Dunbar and His Song.* New York: Biblo and Tannen, 1969.

Fishkin, Shelley Fisher. "Race and the Politics of Memory: Mark Twain and Paul Laurence Dunbar." *Journal of American Studies* 40, no. 2 (August 2006): 283–309.

Fishkin, Shelley Fisher, and David Bradley. General introduction and section introductions, *The Sport of the Gods and Other Essential Writing by Paul Laurence Dunbar.* New York: Modern Library/Random House, 2005.

Fishkin, Shelley Fisher, Gavin Jones, Meta DeEwa Jones, Arnold Rampersad, and Richard Yarborough, guest eds. Special issue on Paul Laurence Dunbar. *African American Review* 41, no. 2 (Summer 2007). http://www.jstor.org/stable/i40001501.

Gerber, David A. *Black Ohio and the Color Line, 1860–1915.* Urbana: University of Illinois Press, 1976.

Honious, Ann. *What Dreams We Have: The Wright Brothers and Their Hometown of Dayton, Ohio.* Fort Washington, PA: Eastern National/NPS, 2003.

Jones, Gavin. *Strange Talk: The Politics of Dialect in Gilded Age America.* Berkeley: University of California Press, 1999.

Martin, Jay, ed. *A Singer in the Dawn: Reinterpretations of Paul Laurence Dunbar.* New York: Dodd, Mead, 1975.

Mullen, Harryette. "'When He Is Least Himself': Dunbar and Double Consciousness in African American Poetry." In Fishkin et al., eds., special issue, *African American Review* 41, no. 2 (Summer 2007): 277–282. Mullen's presentation of this material at the Stanford Paul Laurence Dunbar Centennial Conference in 2006 may be viewed at https://www.youtube.com/watch?v=VS1pkUIWlCk.

Nielson, Aldon Lynn. "'Purple Haze': Dunbar's Lyric Legacy." In Fishkin et al., eds., special issue, *African American Review* 41, no. 2 (Summer 2007): 283–288. Nielson's presentation of this material at the Stanford Paul Laurence Dunbar Centennial Conference in 2006 may be viewed at https://www.youtube.com/watch?v=VS1pkUIWlCk.

Revell, Peter. *Paul Laurence Dunbar.* Boston: Twayne Publishers, 1979.

Robinson, Lillian S., and Greg Robinson. "Paul Laurence Dunbar: A Credit to His Race?" In Fishkin et al., eds., special issue, *African American Review* 41, no. 2 (Summer 2007): 215–225. Lillian and Greg Robinson's presentation of this material at the Stanford Paul Laurence Dunbar Centennial Conference in 2006 may be viewed at https://www.youtube.com/watch?v=mFefpquXTyY.

Sapirstein, Ray. "Picturing Dunbar's Lyrics." In Fishkin et al., eds., special issue, *African American Review* 41, no. 2 (Summer 2007): 327–339. Sapirstein's presentation of this material at the Stanford Paul Laurence Dunbar Centennial Conference in 2006 may be viewed at https://www.youtube.com/watch?v=bdMf3F7nqbY.

Crowded neighborhood of Jewish immigrants on New York's Lower East Side in 1907. Lower East Side tenement buildings like the one that houses the Tenement Museum are the setting of fiction and poetry by writers including Abraham Cahan, Stephen Crane, Pietro di Donato, Mike Gold, Morris Rosenfeld, and Anzia Yezierska.

8

Leaving the Old World for the New

THE TENEMENT MUSEUM
97 ORCHARD STREET, NEW YORK CITY

When the writer Anzia Yezierska found herself in a hotel room for the first time, paid for by the Hollywood studio that wanted to make a film about her stories of life in the tenements of the Lower East Side, it was the bathroom that left her speechless with rapture: "Bathtub, washbowl, and toilet. My own. White-tiled walls. Sunlight streaming in through clean glass windows. . . ." In the fictionalized autobiography in which she limns this scene, *Red Ribbon on a White Horse*, she remembers the "iron sink in the hall on Hester Street. One faucet for eight families. Here were two faucets. Hot water, cold water, all the water in the world. I turned on both faucets and let them run for the sheer joy of it." But her joy was destined to be short-lived. For although she was exhilarated at first to be so far from the plumbing and poverty of the Lower East Side, she soon found that distance unbearable: she thought she had left behind an iron sink, but she had actually left behind the wellspring of her imagination as a writer. She soon went back to New York.

The tenement on Hester Street in which Yezierska had lived was not far from the building that houses the Tenement Museum today. In fact, she probably went past 97 Orchard Street often—but she wouldn't have noticed, for there was nothing unusual about it. No well-known figure lived there. No dramatic events took place there. Indeed, while this obscurity makes it unusual in the roster of American landmarks, that lack of distinctiveness—its typicality—makes it all the more representative of the world it reflects. For 97 Orchard Street is characteristic of the buildings that nearly two million Jews from eastern Europe moved into when they arrived in New York between 1881 and 1914.

Jews from eastern Europe were not the only residents of 97 Orchard Street—although they were clearly in the majority. Between 1873 and 1935, some ten thousand people from more than twenty nations lived in the building. In the spirit of its special status as the first American museum devoted to chronicling, interpreting, and commemorating the home and community life of ordinary, urban working-class and poor immigrants and migrants, the museum sponsors a variety of programs to promote tolerance and to provide historical perspective on immigrant life in Manhattan's Lower East Side.

Some immigrants came to avoid the brutal campaign of government-sponsored anti-Semitism against Russia's five million Jews after the assassination of Tsar Alexander II in 1881. Some came to avoid conscription in the tsar's army. Some sought a more auspicious economic future. All brought hopes and dreams for a better life in America than they could expect in the Old Country. In overcrowded apartments off dark and noisy hallways, where they confronted on a daily basis uncertainty about what precisely the New World demanded of them and what it had to offer, these immigrants reinvented themselves as "Americans." In the sweatshops of the Lower East Side where they earned their bread, in the settlement houses where many learned their English, in their crowded apartments, in their synagogues, and in their theaters, they pondered which of the old ways would survive here, and which ones would not; they fell in love and fell out of love; they were convivial, lonely, confident, and confused; they were plagued by poverty, disease, and exploitation and seduced by the promises held out to them. The museum evokes some of the texture of their lives by re-creating the spaces in which they moved and the physical objects that they used. But for a window onto their souls and psyches we must read the novels, poems, plays, and songs that they wrote.

With its storefront at street level and red-brick facade, the house on 97 Orchard Street between Broome and Delancy built in 1863–1864, is typical of the five- and six-story tenements erected on the Lower East Side during the first big wave of tenement construction in New York. They were built to pack the largest number of families into the smallest space with few amenities (such as private toilets, running water, heat, and rooms with windows) and were subject to little regulation. Built on narrow city lots designed for single-family row houses—twenty-five feet wide by one hundred feet deep—tenements often housed more than twenty families. In a report in 1862, the superintendent of buildings in New York called those buildings "tenements" where "the greatest amount of profit is sought to be realized from the least possible amount of space, with little or no regard for the health, comfort, or protection of the lives of the tenants." The city's Council of Hygiene and Public Health deemed that "such concentration and packing of a population has probably never been equaled in any city as may be found in particular localities in New York." The population density was even higher than in the slums of East London.

"... Long streamers of garments fluttered from fire escapes," writes Stephen Crane in his novel about tenement-dwellers on the Lower East Side, *Maggie: A*

Girl of the Streets (1893): "In all unhandy places there were buckets, brooms, rags and bottles. In the street infants played or fought with other infants or sat stupidly in the way of vehicles. Formidable women, with uncombed hair and disordered dress, gossiped while leaning on railings, or screamed in frantic quarrels. Withered persons, in curious postures of submission to something, sat smoking pipes in obscure corners. A thousand odors of cooking food came forth to the street. The building quivered and creaked from the weight of humanity stamping about in its bowels." Pietro di Donato described some of those "thousand odors" in his 1939 novel of tenement life, *Christ in Concrete*: "Each flat had its distinctive powerful odor," he writes. From "the large Farabutti family in one of the upper flats" came the smells of children savoring "the big potato-fried-egg sandwiches which they chewed while shouting," while from "the Jewish family who lived silently on the opposite side of the thin shadowy light-shaft" came "the smells of cabbage soup and chicken fat." The air in the tenement halls was "rubbery with greasy cooking and cut with cheap strong disinfectant."

Interior windows and hall toilets were added to 97 Orchard Street in response to the passage of the Tenement House Act of 1901, and in 1905 a wood-and-glass storefront replaced the first-floor facade, which looks today much as it looked then. Indeed, the upper floors of the building look much as they looked in 1905, when the varnished-burlap wall-coverings with their three-dimensional plaster ornaments were probably added. The indoor toilets in the center hall were also probably added in 1905 (the original building had toilets only in the backyard). The wooden stairs running through the center of the building are the original ones, from the 1860s, and the configuration of the three small rooms in each apartment—living room or front parlor, central kitchen, and inner bedroom—has stayed the same as well. The original building, like all tenements, was extremely dark, with forty of the sixty rooms receiving no direct light at all, which prompted the building's owners to increase light and ventilation by adding gas lights in the halls, translucent glass in some rooms, and a ventilating skylight over the stairs.

The Tenement Museum re-creates in careful and imaginative detail the apartments of specific Jewish, Italian, and Irish immigrant families who lived at 97 Orchard Street in the nineteenth and early twentieth centuries. For example, one apartment gives the visitor a window on the world of Nathalia and Julius Gumpertz, Jewish immigrants from East Prussia, an area now in Poland, who lived there with their children in the mid- to late 1870s. After the death of her husband, who was a seller of "wrappers" or dressing gowns, Nathalia earned a living as a dressmaker, working out of her third-floor flat. Another apartment captures the atmosphere in the home of Adolfo and Rosaria Baldizzi, Italian immigrants from Palermo, Sicily, who lived there with their children from the late 1920s to the early 1930s. Adolfo, trained as a cabinetmaker, had trouble finding steady work and sought jobs as a handyman when he could get them; meanwhile, Rosaria worked long hours—sometimes from 7 A.M. to 6 P.M.—sewing linings into coats in a garment factory.

In another apartment, a visitor enters the home of Abraham and Fannie Rogarshevsky and their six children ranging from six months to nine years old, as well as a six-month-old niece, Jewish immigrants from Telsh, Lithuania, who moved into the building sometime between 1907 and 1910. Abraham and his daughters Ida and Bessie all worked in the garment industry, Abraham as a "presser," Ida as a "baster," preparing the garments with temporary stitches, and Bessie as a sewing machine operator. Other children—Sam and Morris—went into business, Morris as a shipping clerk and fur salesman, and Sam as an undertaker and taxi driver. The museum freezes in time the days right after Abraham's death from tuberculosis on July 12, 1918, when the family was "sitting shiva," observing the traditional Jewish mourning ritual. Another apartment tells the story of Harris and Jennie Levine, who arrived from Poland in 1890, moved to 97 Orchard Street around 1892, and turned their apartment into a small garment factory in which they and three employees took in piecework, producing items of clothing for which they were paid by the piece. (Similar work took place in more than one hundred other apartments on Orchard Street between Broome and Delancy.) Because the workers were paid only four or five cents per piece that they sewed, they put in particularly long hours to make ends meet.

Another apartment evokes the lives of the Confino family, Sephardic Jewish immigrants from Kastoria, Turkey, who lived there starting around 1914. The sixth apartment (the most recently restored) explores the experience of the Irish Catholic Bridget and Joseph Moore, who lived in the building in 1869. Joseph Moore worked as a waiter and bartender. While they lived here, they coped with the illness and death of a child.

The building's first residents were largely German immigrants. By the 1880s, however, large numbers of Jewish immigrants, mainly from Russia, began moving in, and twenty years later, the residents would be almost entirely Russian-born immigrants and their children. The more the building deteriorated, the more people seemed to move into its twenty small apartments. While 72 people lived in the building in 1870, 111 lived there in 1900. An 1896 article in the *New York Times* described life in the tenements as characterized by "contracted quarters, lack of family privacy, and promiscuous toilet arrangements, inviting moral deterioration; lack of light and air, and of sanitary accommodations, insuring a large death rate, and danger from fire—that ever-present tenement horror. All of these are wickedly cruel when such houses are new; when they become old, dilapidated, infested with vermin and infected with disease germs, they are a disgrace to humanity and a menace, not only to the health of the unfortunate residents therein, but to the health of the whole community." (Allegra Confino, who lived on the top floor at 97 Orchard Street, recalled how her family, tormented by rats at night, would go after them with brooms. Allegra was once bitten on her toe by a rat when she lived here as a child.)

Mike Gold described tenement conditions there in 1930 in his autobiographical novel, *Jews without Money*:

> Our tenement was nothing but a junk-heap of rotten lumber and brick. It was an old ship on its last voyage; in the battering winter storms, all its seams opened, and wind and snow came through. The plaster was always falling down, the stairs were broken and dirty. Five times that winter the water pipes froze, and floods spurted from the plumbing, and dripped from the ceilings.
>
> There was no drinking water in the tenement for days. The women had to put on their shawls and hunt in the street for water. Up and down the stairs they groaned, lugging pails of water.

The poverty, the overcrowding, the lack of privacy, the primitive plumbing, and the decaying overburdened structures indelibly shaped the imaginations of the writers the tenements produced, as did their dreams, their sense of possibility, and their perplexity at the puzzle of a society that promised so much but often delivered so little.

Gold recalled a pressing question of his childhood: "Did God make bedbugs? One steaming hot night I couldn't sleep for the bedbugs. They have a peculiar nauseating smell of their own; it is the smell of poverty. They crawl slowly and pompously, bloated with blood, and the touch and smell of these parasites wakens every nerve to disgust." It wasn't due to any lack of cleanliness in his home; Gold adds that his mother

> worked herself to the bone keeping us fresh and neat. The bedbugs were a torment to her. She doused the beds with kerosene, changed the sheets, sprayed the mattresses in an endless frantic war with the bedbugs. What was the use; nothing could help; it was Poverty; it was the Tenement.
>
> The bedbugs lived and bred in the rotten walls of the tenement, with the rats, fleas, roaches; the whole rotten structure needs to be torn down; a kerosene bottle would not help.

It had been a frightful week of summer heat. I was sick and feverish with heat, and pitched and tossed, while the cats sobbed in the yard. The bugs finally woke me. They were everywhere. I cannot tell the despair, loathing and rage of the child in the dark tenement room, as they crawled on me, and stank.

I cried softly. My mother woke and lit the gas. She renewed her futile battle with the bedbugs. The kerosene smell choked me. My mother tried to soothe me back to sleep. But my brain raced like a sewing machine.

"Momma," I asked, "why did God make bedbugs?"

She laughed at her little boy's quaint question. I was often jollied about it later, but who has answered this question? Did the God of Love create bedbugs, did He also put pain and poverty into the world?

At the turn of the century, the walls of 97 Orchard Street reverberated with jokes and shouts and wails and imprecations and exclamations in Yiddish, the language spoken by virtually all of the Jews who came from eastern Europe. Some of the writers who came out of this milieu in the early twentieth century—the poet Morris Rosenfeld, for example—wrote American literature in Yiddish. Rosenfeld, who worked long hours in a sweatshop all day wrote poetry at night about the sweatshop and the toll it took on family life. His most famous poem is probably the poignant "Mayn Yingele":

נאָר זעלטן זעלטן זע איך אים,	*Nor zelten, zelten zey ikh im,*
מײַן שײנעם, װען ער װאַכט,	*Mayn sheynem ven er vakht,*
איך טרעף אים אימער שלאָפֿנדיק,	*Ikh tref im tomid shlufndik*
איך זע אים נאָר בײַנאַכט.	*Ikh zey ihm nor by nakht.*
די אַרבעט טרײַבט מיך פֿרי אַרױס	*Dih arbet traybt mikh frih aroys,*
און לאָזט מיך שפּעט צוריק;	*Un lozt mikh speyt turik,*
אַ פֿרעמד איז מיר מײַן אײגן לײַב!	*O, fremd iz mir mayn eygn leyb,*
אַ פֿרעמד מײַן קינדס אַ בליק!	*O, fremd mayn kinds ah blik!*
איך קום צעקלעמטערהײט אַהײם,	*Ikh kum tsuklemterhayt aheym*
אין פֿינצטערניש געהילט,	*In finsternish gehilt,*
מײַן בלײַכער פֿרױ דערצײילט מיר באַלד,	*Mayn bleykhe froy dertseylt mir bald*
װי פֿײַן דאָס קינד זיך שפּילט;	*Vih fayn dohs kind zikh spilt.*

Here is Aaron Kramer's translation:

> But seldom do I see him when
> he's wide awake and bright.
> I always find him sound asleep,
> I see him late at night.
>
> The time-clock drags me off at dawn,
> At night it lets me go.
> I scarcely know my flesh and blood,
> His eyes I hardly know.
>
> I climb the staircase wearily,
> a figure wrapped in shade,
> Each night my haggard wife describes
> how well the youngster played.

Subsequent verses depict the father's sadness at not being able to see his child begin to talk, at not being able to look into his eyes when he's awake. It ends with a thought the father cannot bear: "One morning, when you wake, my child / you'll find that I'm not there!" ("*Ven du vakst oyf amol, mayn kind, / Gefinst du mikh nit mer!*"). The poem is all the more heartrending given that the son the poet longs to see during waking hours in "Mayn Yingele," Joseph Rosenfeld, died at age fifteen in 1905.

In other poems, such as "The Sweatshop," Rosenfeld gives us a vivid sense of what the father was doing during all those days when he was separated from his child (the translation is Aaron Kramer's):

> So wild is the roar of machines in the sweatshop
> I often forget I'm alive, in that din!
> I'm drowned in the tide of the terrible tumult
> my ego is slain; I become a machine.
>
> I work and I work without rhyme, without reason,
> produce and produce and produce without end.
> For what? And for whom? I don't know, I don't wonder—
> Since when can a whirling machine comprehend?

Rosenfeld was a hugely popular poet on the Lower East Side, where his poems were recited in the tenements and sweatshops and at workers' gatherings. He reached an even wider audience when his poems were translated into English, and, eventually, many other languages, including Japanese.

While Morris Rosenfeld wrote moving Yiddish poetry and lyrics about the world of the tenement and the sweatshop, Israel Jacob Schwartz (who translated Walt Whitman and other poets into Yiddish) wrote a book-length, epic Yiddish poem about a Jewish immigrant who leaves the sweatshops of the Lower East Side for the Midwest, where he becomes an itinerant peddler. Schwartz recalled, "I came to America in 1906. It was the time of the great mass immigration. . . . We came here during a time of great hopes. . . . [A]n entire people moved to a new land, a new environment, under a free sky. . . . We were dazzled, we were winged." Out of that dazzlement came Schwartz's book, *Kentucky*, the first American epic poem in Yiddish, published in 1918.

The vibrant Yiddish cultural life that enveloped the Lower East Side at the turn of the century embraced popular genres, including musical theater. One of the most famous popular songs from the Yiddish stage was the ironic "Di Grine Kuzine," or "the green cousin." It was composed by Abe Schwartz, who would go on to write many of the songs central to musical comedies on the Yiddish stage; both Yacob Leiserovitz and Hyman Prizant claimed to have written the lyrics. It was published in 1921 and was an immediate hit. "Di Grine Kuzine" launched a whole category of songs about the disillusionment of working-class Jewish immigrants for whom the streets of the "golden land" turn out not to be paved with gold after all. In "Di Grine Kuzine" a rosy-cheeked young girl with "*fiselech, vos betn zich tsum tantsn*" (feet just begging to dance) comes to America filled with hope and excitement. Braiding Yiddish and English together into a language somewhere in between, the "greenhorn's" cousin and the song's narrator asks his neighbor who lives "*nekst-dorke*" (next door) for a job for his cousin in her "*milineri-storke*" (millinery shop), an establishment that both sells hats and makes them. He is delighted to get her a job there and exclaims, "*az lebn zol di goldena medina*" (so long live Golden Land!)—the Golden Land, of course, being America, where such things can happen. But by the next time he sees his cousin, after time has passed, years of working in the sweatshop have robbed her of her youth and zest for living. The song ends with his cursing Columbus: "*az brenen zol Kolumbuses medina!*" (that "Golden Land" of Columbus should go to hell!)

Despite the privations of crowded tenement living and the toll taken by the sweatshop, not all newcomers were as disappointed as the "greenhorn" cousin in "Di Grine Kuzine." A part of the great wave of Jewish immigration from eastern Europe at the turn of the century, ten-year-old Ettie Weitz arrived at Ellis Island in

Arriving at Ellis Island on July 17, 1909, from Delatyn, a village in the foothills of the Carpathian Mountains (then in the Austro-Hungarian Empire), the Weitz family moved into a tenement on Rivington Street, not far from the Tenement Museum at 97 Orchard Street in what is now the Lower East Side Historic District. Ettie Weitz (the tallest girl in the back row) wrote an unpublished memoir describing her life there. From left to right, an unnamed cousin who lived with them, father Meier Leib Weitz, baby brother Joe, Ettie Weitz, sister Rosie, sister Rae, mother Mariym (née Pauker), and brother Frank.

PHOTO CREDIT: PHOTO FROM THE AUTHOR'S PERSONAL COLLECTION.

1909 from a small town in a Polish-speaking part of the Austro-Hungarian Empire called Delatyn. She and her parents, her two brothers, three sisters, and a cousin lived in tenement on Rivington Street not far from the Tenement Museum in what would become the Lower East Side Historic District. Like the members of the ordinary families whose lives are documented in the Tenement Museum, she would not become famous; but, like them, she left us a glimpse into the world in which she lived: in her case, that record is an unpublished memoir.

Ettie Weitz described the tenement in which she lived as "dark" and "dismal." But she and her family filled that "dark, dismal" space with songs from the Yiddish stage like "Di Grine Kuzine" and Abraham Goldfaden's "Rozhinkes mit Mandlen" (from the operetta *Shulamis*), along with other Yiddish songs like M. M. Warshawsky's "Oif'n Pripitshik," and folk songs like "Az der Rebe Tanzt," "Lomir Zich

Ibebetn," and "Tum Balalaika"; with armloads of books from the public library (*Little Women, The Count of Monte Cristo, Les Misérables*, and novels by Jack London were her favorites); and, on special occasions, with the aroma of freshly baked *mandelbrot*.

Like the cousin in "Di Grine Kuzine," Ettie Weitz (as her memoir makes clear) had "*fiselach vus beyten sich tzum tantzen*." And like the cousin in "Di Grine Kuzine" who got a "*dzhob*" in a "*milineri-storke*," Ettie Weitz, too, got a job a millinery store when she was fourteen. But unlike the *grine kuzine* who ended up cursing Columbus, Ettie Weitz was so sure her family's decision to come to America was the right one that every now and then she said a little *blessing* on Columbus. Just how right that decision was became even more apparent in the decades that followed as the fate of family members who stayed behind and their children chillingly came to light. In October 1941, SS officer Ernst Varchmin ordered his subordinates to collect and kill the Jews of Delatyn and another nearby town. Nearly two thousand were buried in mass graves. Less than a year later, a Polish newspaper in Budapest reported that the entire region was *Judenrein*, literally, "cleansed of Jews." Meanwhile, Ettie Weitz's grandchildren and great-grandchildren—including the author of this book—continue to thrive in America.

Second Avenue was the center of Yiddish theater in America, where tenement dwellers would spend their hard-earned money to see their favorite actors and actresses perform. The Yiddish Art Theatre at 189 Second Avenue (at 12th Street) was the home of Maurice Schwartz's Yiddish Art Theatre Company, the longest continuously running repertory company in the history of Yiddish theater. Built in 1926—the only theater structure built on the East Side expressly for a Yiddish theater troupe—it is the only surviving theater from this period on the Lower East Side. Although it is now a movie theater, the Village East Cinema, many of its distinctive design elements remain: its opulent interior and exterior decorations inspired by Moorish design include a recessed ceiling dome containing a prominent Star of David, as well as other references to Judaism in the elaborate plaster ornamentation covering the boxes, the proscenium, and the underside of the balcony. It was designed by Harrison G. Wiseman, a prominent New York theater architect, in the Moorish Revival style popular in synagogues at this time. The auditorium seated 1,236. Yiddish theater, whose roots stretch back to the fifteenth and sixteenth centuries in Venice and northern, central, and eastern Europe, began in the United States in 1882 in New York. The Yiddish plays performed in the theaters that sprang up on the Lower East Side and in drama clubs and amateur groups affiliated with fraternal organizations and labor unions were usually melodramas centering on familiar Jewish folk characters. Joseph Lateiner and Moshe Hurwitz wrote more than two hundred plays for their rival theater companies, featuring such stars as Yiddish matinee idol Boris Thomaschevsky and Jacob Adler. From 1892 through 1902, playwright Jacob Gordin succeeded in moving the Yiddish theater beyond soap opera sentimentality to greater realism, enlisting it in the service of progressive social change.

The Yiddish Art Theatre's founder, Maurice Schwartz, was an actor who emigrated from the Ukraine and raised money for his company when it was in debt by accepting roles in vaudeville, in film, and on Broadway. The theater performed works by writers including Abraham Goldfaden, Jacob Gordin, Sholem Aleichem, Sholem Asch, I. L. Peretz, and Israel Joshua Singer. In 1932, Singer's play *Yoshe Kalb* ran for a record-breaking three hundred performances. The theater also occasionally performed works by Shakespeare, including a new translation of *Othello* by Mark Schweid presented in 1929 in which (as Joel Berkowitz notes) the translator not only "shifts from prose to verse whenever Shakespeare does, but even tries to find a Yiddish approximation for Shakespeare's rhymes." Jerome Robbins, who would go on to fame as a Broadway producer, director, and choreographer, made his debut here in 1937, dancing with his sister in a show called *The Brothers Askhenazi* that ran for almost a year. Albert Einstein attended a performance. Several actors who got their start on the Yiddish stage went on to achieve fame in Hollywood or on Broadway. This group includes Muni Meisenfreund, who as Paul Muni would become an Oscar-winning Hollywood actor, and the legendary Joseph Buloff, whose many Broadway roles would include the peddler Ali Hakim in the hit musical *Oklahoma!*

The Yiddish Art Theatre features in *A Red Ribbon on a White Horse*, where a Hollywood producer brags, "I got Schwartz from the Jewish Art Theatre to send us his star for the mother." It also figures prominently in Abraham Cahan's *The Rise of David Levinsky*, where David flirts with a young woman by talking of "the Jewish theater, a topic for which I knew her to have a singular weakness. The upshot was that I soon had her telling me of a play she had recently seen"—probably one of the sentimental melodramas popular in the early part of this century. The Yiddish Art Theatre remained open until 1950, by which time the Yiddish theater audience as well as its supply of actors and writers was depleted by the assimilation of American Jews into mainstream American culture and by Hitler's destruction of European Jewry in the Holocaust.

New York's National Yiddish Theatre–Folksbiene, the longest continually producing Yiddish theatre company in the world, continues to present Yiddish plays and readings at various locations. Founded in 1915 as the Folksbiene Theatre by socially conscious Yiddish actors to bring quality theater to the public, the Folksbiene opened with a Yiddish production of Henrik Ibsen's *Enemy of the People*. The theater developed a repertory of plays of Yiddish origin, which it performed alongside Yiddish translations of classic, mainstream non-Yiddish plays. In the 1980s, the Folksbiene began providing simultaneous translation in Russian and English to attract larger audiences. In the fall of 1999, the theater mounted Joseph Buloff's adaptation of *A Klezmer's Tale: Yoshke Muzikant*, by Ossip Dimov, a Polish-born playwright who came to the United States in 1913 and remained here until his death in 1958, writing more than twenty plays. Buloff reworked *Yoshke Muzikant* over the course of his long career, first in 1925, then in 1951, and lastly in 1972. The 1999 production drew on all these earlier versions to produce a play that received both critical and popular acclaim. In the 1990s, the theater marked the explosion of interest in Yiddish by commissioning and performing new Yiddish plays by contemporary American playwrights. In 2006–2007, the National Yiddish Theatre–Folksbiene received a "Special Achievement Drama Desk Award for preserving 92 consecutive seasons of the cultural legacy of Yiddish-speaking theatre in America."

Interest in American literature written in Yiddish throughout the twentieth century was reignited by the award of a Nobel Prize in 1978 to Isaac Bashevis Singer, most of whose fiction was originally written in Yiddish. And in the 1980s, poet Irena Klepfisz (who was born in 1941 in the Warsaw Ghetto) reclaimed the borders between Yiddish and English as a place from which a modern Jewish American poet can wrest lyrical and compelling art. In the post-Holocaust era, after six million Yiddish speakers were exterminated by the Nazis, Klepfisz's integration of English and *mameloshn*, or the mother tongue, takes on particular power and poignancy—as in the poem "Di Rayze Aheym / The Journey Home" in *A Few Words in the Mother Tongue* (the lines that follow come from the section of the poem called *Kashes*/Questions).

> *In velkhn yor?*
>   in what year?
> *mit vemen?*
>   with whom?
> *di sibes?*
>   the causes?
> *der rezultat?*
>   the outcome?
> *di geshikhte*
>   the history

fun der milkhome
   of the war
fun dem sholem
   of the peace
fun di lebn giblibene
   of the survivors
tsvishn fremde
   among strangers
oyf der zayt
   on this side
tsvishn meysim
   among ghosts
oyf der zayt
   on this side.

The early-twentieth-century Jewish writers from the world of the East Side tenements who were destined to leave the greatest mark on American letters in the decades that followed were those who endeavored to capture Yiddish inflections and intonations while writing in English: Abraham Cahan, Anzia Yezierska, and Henry Roth. In the following passage from Anzia Yezierska's prize-winning story "The Fat of the Land," Hannah Breineh may be speaking English, but the cadences of her speech are Yiddish to the core:

> In an air-shaft so narrow that you could touch the next wall with your bare hands, Hannah Breineh leaned out and knocked on her neighbor's window.
>
> "Can you loan me your wash-boiler for the clothes?" she called. Mrs. Pelz threw up the sash.
>
> "The boiler? What's the matter with yours again? Didn't you tell me you had it fixed already last week?"
>
> "A black year on him, the robber, the way he fixed it! If you have no luck in this world, then it's better not to live. There I spent out fifteen cents to stop up one hole, and it runs out another. How I ate out my gall bargaining with him he should let it down to fifteen cents! He wanted yet a quarter, the swindler. *Gottunieu!* My bitter heart on him for every penny he took from me for nothing."

(The word of Yiddish in this passage, the exclamation "*Gottunieu!*," means "My G-d!").

If Yezierska captured the cadences of Yiddish in English prose, Henry Roth in *Call It Sleep*, an ambitious, experimental novel shaped, in part, by James Joyce's challenging magnum opus *Ulysses*, shows immigrant children in a Lower East Side Hebrew school (*cheder*) shifting back and forth between the multiple dialects and languages in which they live. In the following passage, as the child is bantering with his friends about the fate of his handball ("hen'ball") in Yiddish-inflected English overlaid on a New York accent, he is simultaneously practicing to recite the four questions in Hebrew that the youngest child must ask at the Passover seder: "Yuh can't cover books wit' newspaper. My teacher don' let. An aftuh she took mine bean-shoooduh, she pinched me. . . . *Bein yoshvim uven mesubim*. So wad's de nex' woid? Mine hen'ball wend down duh sewuh!" In *Call It English: The Languages of Jewish American Literature*, Hana Wirth-Nesher explores the ways in which these and other language experiments involving accent, dialect, bilingual wordplay, and cross-cultural translations indelibly shaped the work of Jewish American writers such as Mary Antin, Saul Bellow, Bernard Malamud, Cynthia Ozick, Grace Paley, Philip Roth, and Delmore Schwartz—as well as Cahan, Yezierska, and Henry Roth.

Every immigrant and every immigrant writer was engaged in a constant set of negotiations between the Old World and the New as he or she made decisions about language, religion, work, love, food, ritual, and one's sense of identity at its most basic level. Every day was filled with choices. What should one eat? For some, like Hannah Breineh in Yezierska's story "The Fat of the Land," who defies her upwardly mobile daughter's strict prohibitions by marching through the lobby of her fancy uptown apartment building carrying a smelly basket of fish from the Lower East Side, the act of buying and cooking traditional foods in a kitchen from which they are banished becomes a gesture of defiance. And what of religious study and ritual? David Levinsky, in Abraham Cahan's magisterial novel, *The Rise of David Levinsky*, expected such questions to be unproblematic when he set off for the United States. When he tells his friend Reb Sender of his plan to "leave my native place and to seek my fortune in that distant, weird world," Reb Sender is "thunderstruck."

> "To America!" he said. "Lord of the World! But one becomes a Gentile there."
> "Not at all," I sought to reassure him. "There are lots of good Jews there, and they don't neglect their Talmud, either."

Levinsky is right: there are many good Jews in America, and many keep up their religious studies; but the obstacles are more challenging than he expected, and the lure of material success is more seductive. As he puts it later, looking back on his life,

I was born and reared in the lowest depths of poverty and I arrived in America—in 1885—with four cents in my pocket. I am now worth more than two million dollars and recognized as one of the two or three leading men in the cloak-and-suit trade in the United States. And yet, when I take a look at my inner identity it impresses me as being precisely the same as it was thirty or forty years ago. My present station, power, the amount of worldly happiness at my command, and the rest of it, seem to be devoid of significance.

The emptiness Levinsky feels, after having lived the classic rags-to-riches American success story, suggests the complexity of retaining a sense of who one is amidst the insidious attractions of what one might be.

LEFT: Abraham Cahan (1860–1951). In 1887, five years after arriving in the United States from the Russian Empire at age twenty-one, Cahan founded the legendary *Jewish Daily Forward*, a socialist newspaper based on the Lower East Side that would become the leading Yiddish publication in the United States and would be key to helping fellow immigrants negotiate the challenges of life in their adopted country. Contributors included "sweatshop poet" Morris Rosenfeld and Nobel Laureate Isaac Bashevis Singer. Cahan ran the paper until 1946. The author, as well, of fiction and journalism in English, his most famous novel is *The Rise of David Levinsky* (1917).
PHOTO CREDIT: NEW YORK WORLD-TELEGRAM AND THE SUN NEWSPAPER PHOTOGRAPH COLLECTION; COURTESY OF THE LIBRARY OF CONGRESS, PRINTS AND PHOTOGRAPHS DIVISION, WASHINGTON, DC.

RIGHT: Anzia Yezierska (1885–1970) and her family came to the United States from the Russian Empire around 1890, making their home on New York's Lower East Side in a tenement near the Tenement Museum. In a writing career that lasted more than a half century, Yezierska gave voice to the hungers and longings of her fellow Jewish immigrants from eastern Europe, particularly those of the women. Her most famous novel is *Bread Givers: A Struggle between a Father of the Old World and a Daughter of the New* (1925).
PHOTO CREDIT: UNDERWOOD & UNDERWOOD; COURTESY OF THE LIBRARY OF CONGRESS, PRINTS AND PHOTOGRAPHS DIVISION, WASHINGTON, DC.

Many of Anzia Yezierska's characters experience a similar emptiness as they try to understand the sense of dislocation that they feel, straddling two worlds, one foot in each, yet body and soul in neither. Rachel Ravinsky, for example, officiously corrects her mother's table manners at the start of "Children of Loneliness," imagining herself as an ambassador from the world of "real Americans," determined to help her mother slough off her telltale Old World habits. A handsome young American named Frank Baker appears on the scene, and Rachel soon aspires to blissful wedded assimilation. But when she figures out that Frank's interest in her and her world is not the interest of a suitor, but of a sociologist, she falls into despair, voicing the pain that many of her fellow immigrants probably felt:

> "I can't live with the old world, and I'm yet too green for the new. I don't belong to those who gave me birth or to those with whom I was educated."
>
> Was this to be the end of all her struggles to rise in America, she asked herself, this crushing daze of loneliness? Her driving thirst for an education, her desperate battle for a little cleanliness, for a breath of beauty, the tearing away from her own flesh and blood to free herself from the yoke of her parents—what was it all worth now? Where did it lead to? Was loneliness to be the fruit of it all? . . .
>
> She only felt she must struggle against her loneliness and weariness as she had once struggled against dirt, against the squalor and ugliness of her Ghetto home.
>
> . . . "But am I really alone in my seeking? I'm one of the millions of immigrant children, children of loneliness, wandering between worlds that are at once too old and too new to live in."

The struggles of those millions of "immigrant children, children of loneliness" to make a place for themselves in America gave rise to some of the country's most powerful and compelling poetry and fiction.

EMMA LAZARUS
AND THE STATUE OF LIBERTY

STATUE OF LIBERTY, LIBERTY ISLAND, NEW YORK HARBOR

… Give me your tired, your poor,
Your huddled masses yearning to be free,
The wretched refuse of your teeming shore.
Send these, the homeless, tempest-tost to me,
I lift my lamp beside the golden door!

A bronze plaque inscribed with the poem containing these famous lines
was mounted inside the lower level of the Statue of Liberty in New York
Harbor in 1903, where it remains today, an emblem of the idea of the United
States as beacon of hope and freedom to the oppressed and downtrodden
around the world. But the statue itself was not created with this message
in mind. It was the brainchild of a French jurist, historian, and antislavery
activist, Édouard René Lefèbvre de Laboulaye, who became president of a
French organization that aided former slaves in the United States after the
end of the Civil War. In 1865, at the war's end, Laboulaye began to discuss the
idea of some sort of monument France might present to the United States,
to commemorate and cement the friendship between the two countries that
dated back to the American Revolution. He and his friend the noted French
sculptor Frédéric Auguste Bartholdi found appealing the idea of a statue
to remind people of both nations of their shared commitment to ideas of
liberty associated with both the American and the French revolutions—ideas
that they saw the Emperor Napoleon III suppressing. When the tyrannical
Napoleon III was defeated in the Franco-Prussian War in 1870, and a new
French Republic was born, the climate seemed right to embark on this
project. Bartholdi originally called the statue he created *Liberty Enlightening
the World*. The tablet she holds in her left hand contains, in roman numerals,
the date America declared independence from England: July 4, 1776.

As Barry Moreno puts it, the statue was built "to pay tribute to the United
States of America, the Declaration of Independence, American democracy,
and democracy throughout the world. It honored the end of slavery, honored the end of all sorts of tyranny and also friendship between France and
America." It was also a gift to promote good commercial and political relations between the two countries in the future and to help dislodge the image

many had of France at the time as an oppressive, royalist monarchy. Neither the man who conceived it, nor the man who executed the statue, associated it with immigrants.

Gustave Eiffel, who would later design the Eiffel Tower, engineered the structure's internal iron framework. Begun in 1875 and completed in 1884, the statue was taken apart in 1885 to be shipped to the United States in 350 individual pieces and 214 packing crates. France paid the $400,000 it cost to construct the 151-foot statue, and the United States mounted the fundraising drive that paid for the 89-foot pedestal designed by architect Richard M. Hunt. The celebrated lines of poetry now so intimately connected with the statue come from a sonnet titled "The New Colossus" that Emma Lazarus wrote in 1883 as part of that fundraising effort.

When asked to contribute a piece to the benefit auction, Lazarus initially expressed doubts about being able to write something of any worth "to order." But, as her biographer Esther Schor has observed, one of the benefit's organizers, Constance Cary Harrison, claims to have then reminded Lazarus of how her "attempts to raise money to benefit the Russian-Jewish refugees of 1881–82 had largely fallen on deaf ears." Harrison wrote that she said to Lazarus, "Think of that Goddess standing on her pedestal down yonder in the bay, and holding her torch out to those Russian refugees of yours you are so fond of visiting on Ward's Island." As Schor notes, Lazarus was soon inspired to craft a sonnet that envisioned the statue as welcoming to America's shores not just Jewish refugees from Russian pogroms, but all "homeless" and "tempest-tost" refugees "yearning to breathe free."

Lazarus was born in New York City in 1849 into one of the oldest and most prominent Sephardic Jewish families in the city. She mastered German and French at an early age and showed a talent for poetry in her early teens. Her father, Moses Lazarus, a prosperous businessman who socialized with Vanderbilts, Astors, and other members of New York's Christian elite, recognized her talent and encouraged her work. In 1867, he privately published her first book, *Poems and Translations Written between the Ages of Fourteen and Seventeen*. The review of that book that appeared in the *New York Times* noted that in the "300 well-filled pages" are "quite passable translations" from writers such as Heinrich Heine, Alexandre Dumas, and Victor Hugo.

Lazarus sent a copy of the book to Ralph Waldo Emerson, who praised it, and became a friend and mentor, offering her helpful suggestions about her writing and inviting her on several occasions to be a guest in his home in Concord, Massachusetts. Lazarus, the first Jewish American poet and writer widely admired by the country's mainstream literary elite, dedicated her next book of poems to Emerson (*Admetus and Other Poems*, published in 1871). She was disappointed when she realized that Emerson had not seen fit to include any of her poems in his 1874 anthology, *Parnassus*, and told him so. She wrote to him, "Your favorable opinion having been confirmed by some of the best critics of England and America, I felt as if I had won for myself by my own efforts a place in any collection of American poets, and I find myself treated with absolute contempt in the very quarter where I had been encouraged to build my fondest hopes." His response is unknown, but their friendship seems to have continued.

Like Walt Whitman, a poet she admired, Lazarus urged American poets to forge new forms suited to the New World and not imitate Old World literary traditions. Using what in Yiddish (and now English) would be recognized as *chutzpah*, Lazarus was unafraid to challenge influential arbiters of literary taste when she disagreed with them. She criticized the influential poet and critic E. C. Stedman, for example, who had argued that American culture did not have themes required for poetic genius to emerge. "I have never believed in the want of a theme," Lazarus wrote, "Wherever there is humanity, there is the theme for a great poem."

Despite her family's wealth and connections, and despite the admiration she won from some of the country's leading intellectuals, Lazarus sensed that she would always be viewed as an outsider in American society. Personally she encountered no direct anti-Semitism. But, she noted in a letter, she was "perfectly conscious" that underlying "the general tone of the community towards us" was "contempt and hatred." This intuition may have helped shape her ability to empathize with the masses around the world who battled more overt forms of "contempt and hatred" every day of their lives.

If she felt herself to be both an insider and an outsider in America, her relationship with Judaism was no less contradictory. Although she was proud of her Jewish heritage, Lazarus had little patience for organized religion as she knew it, preferring "monotheism, purity of morals, and brotherly love" to an emphasis on observance and ritual. This "doomed her to a paradoxical sense of her Jewish identity," as Esther Schor observes. Schor quotes a letter in which Lazarus claims that she was "both one of the Jewish 'race' and 'somewhat apart' from it." "To us, more than a century later," Schor writes, "Emma Lazarus's Jewish identity in the late 1870s is not such a riddle; she was a secular Jew, a cultural Jew, an emerging Jewish writer." However, "in her own eyes," Schor adds, "she was simply a conundrum."

The privilege and comfort that Emma Lazarus enjoyed did not prevent her from feeling a sense of connection to the pain suffered by the thousands of Jews who fled the pogroms in Russia during the 1880s. She protested their persecution in eloquent, impassioned essays and poems, and worked hard in behalf of the refugees who made it to America. The wealthy and aristocratic young woman "often visited the immigrants' camp on Ward's Island in the East River" (as the writer Abraham Cahan recalled), and also taught an English class to Russian refugees. On some level, however, she suspected that the most tradition-bound of those immigrants might not actually be able to assimilate to America, a place that was "utterly at variance with their time-honored customs and most sacred beliefs." She disliked the image of backwardness and ignorance some presented, fearing that those who resisted assimilation and chose to "bulwark themselves within a citadel of isolation and defiance," might spark greater anti-Semitism here. For that reason, she was an ardent advocate for a Jewish homeland in Palestine.

In a letter to the editor of the *American Hebrew* written shortly after her death at age thirty-eight in 1887, the poet John Greenleaf Whittier wrote that "with no lack of rhythmic sweetness," Lazarus "has often the rugged strength and verbal audacity" of British poet Robert Browning. Although Lazarus herself received a fair amount of recognition as a poet before she died, "The New Colossus" was largely forgotten during her short lifetime. Rediscovered in a New York bookstore years later, it was not placed inside the pedestal of the statue until 1903, two decades after it was written.

THE TRIANGLE
SHIRTWAIST FACTORY

23—29 WASHINGTON PLACE, NEW YORK CITY

On March 25, 1911, the Triangle Shirtwaist Factory was the site of a horrendous industrial disaster. The factory had about six hundred employees and was the largest factory of its kind in New York at the time. Most were Jewish and Italian immigrants, many of them teenagers, most of them young women struggling to help their families keep bread on the table. They were buttonhole makers, sewing-machine operators, and finishers, and they were paid by the piece: about $15.40 a week for a nine-and-a-half-hour day. The sewing machines, dripping oil, stood on wooden tables amid thick piles of cloth, spewing flammable lint into the air and making a deafening roar. There were no sprinklers (none were required by law).

The ten-story, neo-Renaissance-style building, designed by John Woosley, was built in 1901 by Joseph Asch. It is now owned by New York University. The Triangle Shirtwaist Factory occupied the eighth, ninth, and tenth floors of the building in 1902. Retail stores were on the building's lowest floors.

Two years before, in 1909, the Triangle Factory's decision to fire 150 workers who were sympathetic to unions helped galvanize the Cooper Union rally, where the two thousand garment workers in attendance decided to strike. (The garment industry was then the largest industry in New York City.) The walkout that followed—called the "Uprising of the Twenty Thousand"—was the first large-scale strike by women workers in the United States. By the time the strike ended, the strikers had won their demand for a small wage increase, but not for working fire escapes and doors that would remain unlocked.

On March 25, 1911, the doors in the Triangle Factory were locked. Factory owners feared union organizers would come in if the doors were open. A man who lit a cigarette on the way to the toilet dropped a match, and some clippings caught fire. The fire hose they tried to use to douse the flames disintegrated when they reached for it, and the valve that controlled the water was stuck. A table saturated with highly flammable cleaning fluids caught on fire, and soon the whole front of the factory was a sheet of fire. The firemen's nets were not strong enough to hold the people who jumped from the building's eighth or ninth floors. Some impaled themselves on the iron fence below. One hundred and forty-six workers met their deaths that afternoon. Most were between ages fifteen and thirty. Eleven engagement rings were found in the ashes. At a mass funeral held for the victims on April 15, 1911, 120,000 working people marched in the procession while 400,000 lined the streets to watch. The Triangle Shirtwaist Factory disaster provided the impetus for new factory safety legislation, changing laws not just in New York but throughout the nation.

The tragedy inspired a number of poems by Yiddish poets. For example, "Cain's Curse (On the Victims of the Triangle Fire)" by Solomon Bloomgarten, who wrote under the pen name Yehoash, charges the "high priests at the altars of Mammon" who offer "one brief, stingy tear / for a hundred coffins" to accept responsibility for the fruits of their greed. And "Der Royte Beholle" (The Fiery Panic) by Morris Rosenfeld (translated by Aaron Kramer) probed the irony of the fact that

Not a war, nor demoniacal pogrom
choked this greatest city with laments.
No cannons raked the air,
no tremors shook the earth,
no thunder rocked,
no bolt of lightning struck,
no clouds grew black.
No! A frightful redness glowed
a slave-nest violently blazed.
The god of Gold, with mocking flames,
devoured our sons and daughters,
licked their lives away with flaming tongues . . .

Haunting images of the Triangle Shirtwaist Fire presented in the stream of consciousness of an eyewitness to it also appear in Hilton Obenzinger's 1989 poem "Triangle Shirtwaist Company, March 25, 1911."

· · · ·· · ·   ·

Out the windows cotton bundles fall with tails of smoke.
I think they must be tossing out the burning cuttings.
Then a bundle unfurls like a flag.
It's a black skirt with a girl
and she hits the sidewalk with such a force
she smashes through the deadlights into the cellar vault.

They are jumping, the girls are jumping from the ninth floor!
Oh God, how high up they are!
I grab my throat and don't let go.

"Put up the ladders!" the people cry out.
But the fire horses can't pull up to the building.
The bodies litter the sidewalk, quivering.
The horses panic at the pelting bodies.
Oh God, they are falling, so many falling

. . . .

The firemen bring out their nets
and they yell for them to jump.
They hold hands and jump and the firemen are somersaulted
down into the nets
and the girls die and the horses scream and kick.
Finally they throw up their ladders.
But they go only to the sixth floor—not to the ninth or the tenth.
They cannot reach
all the way up to the girls on the ledges
who fall in twos and threes holding hands.

. . . .

Then Anna Dougherty stumbles against us screaming
"Don't let them hurt me! Don't let them hurt me!"
until a policeman grabs her to calm her down
the same cop who broke up the picket line only months ago.

Back then Jake Kline stood by his machine and cried out
"People! Workers! Look at what they are doing to us!
Get up from your machines" and when Goldfarb lumbered over to him
we all stood up yelling *"Strike! Strike!"*
We picket and they break our heads and everyone in America learns
what a sweatshop is and they hear all about the union
but at the end the Triangle is the same
the bosses are the same

and even though the professor across the street at NYU
says he sees unsafe conditions from his window
every day they lock the doors
the cuttings pile up
and the sewing machines drip oil. . . .

The Triangle Shirtwaist Fire was the worst workplace disaster in the United States until September 11, 2001. The haunting image in Obenzinger's poem
of the "bundle" that "unfurls like a flag" that in reality is "a black skirt with
a girl" jumping to her death eerily prefigures the shocking image of people
jumping to their death from the World Trade Center to escape the twenty-
first-century fiery inferno that raged about three miles from the site of the
1911 disaster.

RELATED SITES

⚯ Lower East Side Historic District
*Roughly bounded by East Broadway and Allen, East Houston, Essex, Canal,
Eldridge, and Grand Streets, New York City*

Designated as a Historic District in 2000, this area encompasses much of the
world that Jewish, Irish, and Italian immigrants encountered when they came to
the United States in the nineteenth and early twentieth centuries. The Lower East
Side Tenement Museum is in the district, as is the Eldridge Street Synagogue, the
Bialystoker Synagogue, the Henry Street Settlement, and the Forward Building, as
well as historic commercial establishments, including Yonah Shimmel Knishes (137
East Houston Street), Katz's Delicatessen (205 East Houston Street), and Russ
and Daughters Appetizing (179 East Houston Street). In 2012, the district was expanded into the East Village / Lower East Side Historic District.

⚯ Eldridge Street Synagogue
12–16 Eldridge Street, New York City

This opulent structure, built by Jewish immigrants from eastern Europe in 1887,
was the Lower East Side's first major Orthodox synagogue built specifically as a

synagogue and was the first great house of worship that eastern European Jews built in the United States. Designed by Peter and Francis Herter (German immigrant brothers who also designed several Lower East Side tenement buildings in the late 1880s), the building is a blend of Gothic, Romanesque, and Moorish styles. It was one of the busiest synagogues on the Lower East Side at the turn of the century, with as many as one thousand people attending holiday services here. Weekly Sabbath and holiday services have been held here continuously from 1887 to the present. The building functions as both a synagogue and a museum.

●◆ Ellis Island, Part of the Statue of Liberty National Monument
Upper New York Bay, south of Lower Manhattan

Between January 1892 and November 1954, the more than twelve million steamship passengers who entered the United States through the port of New York after long ocean voyages in steerage or third class came through Ellis Island, where they were examined by medical personnel and immigration officials and told whether they would be allowed into the United States or deported. The Main Building has been restored and is now an immigration museum that is open to the public, featuring objects, photographs, prints, videos, oral histories, and interactive exhibits.

FOR FURTHER READING

The Writers: Works and Words

Antler, Joyce, ed. *America and I: Short Stories by American Jewish Women Writers.* Boston: Beacon Press, 1990.

Cahan, Abraham. *The Education of Abraham Cahan.* Translated by Leon Stein, Abraham P. Conan, and Lynn Davison from the Yiddish autobiography *Bleter fun mein leben.* Introduction by Leon Stein. Philadelphia: Jewish Publication Society, 1969.

———. *The Imported Bridegroom and Other Stories of the New York Ghetto.* Introduction by Gordon Hutner. New York: Signet, 1996.

———. *The Rise of David Levinsky.* 1917. Introduction by John Higham. New York: Harper, 1966.

Chametzky, Jules, John Felstiner, Hilene Flanzbaum, and Kathryn Hellerstein, eds. *Jewish American Literature: A Norton Anthology.* New York: W. W. Norton, 2000.

Crane, Stephen. *Prose and Poetry.* Edited by J. C. Levenson. New York: Library of America, 1984.

di Donato, Pietro. *Christ in Concrete.* Indianapolis, IN: Bobbs-Merrill, 1939.

Gold, Michael. *Jews without Money.* 1930. Afterword by Michael Harrington. New York: Avon Books, 1972.

Goldberg, Isaac, ed. and trans. *Six Plays of the Yiddish Theatre, by David Pinski, Sholom Ash, Perez Hirschbein, Solomon J. Rabinowitsch.* Boston: J. W. Luce, 1916.

Klepfisz, Irena. *A Few Words in the Mother Tongue: Poems Selected and New, 1971–1990.* Portland, OR: Eighth Mountain Press, 1991.

Kramer, Aaron, ed. and trans. *A Century of Yiddish Poetry.* New York: Cornwall Books, 1989.

Lazarus, Emma. *Admetus.* 1871. Upper Saddle River, NJ: Literature House, 1970.

———. *Emma Lazarus: Selected Poems and Other Writings.* Edited by Gregory Eiselein. Tonawanda, NY: Broadview Press, 2002.

Metzker, Isaac, ed. *The Bintel Brief: Sixty Years of Letters from the Lower East Side to the "Jewish Daily Forward."* New York: Schocken, 1990.

Mir Trogn a Gezang! Favorite Yiddish Songs of Our Generation. Introduction by Theodore Bikel. New York: Workman's Circle Education Department, 1982.

Obenzinger, Hilton. "Triangle Shirtwaist Company, March 25, 1911." In *New York on Fire* by Hilton Obenzinger, 70–75. Seattle: Real Comet Press, 1989.

Rosenfeld, Morris. *Poet of the Ghetto: Morris Rosenfeld.* Edited by Edgar J. Goldenthal. Hoboken, NJ: Ktav Publishing House, 1998.

Roth, Henry. *Call It Sleep.* 1934. Introduction by Alfred Kazin and afterword by Hana Wirth-Nesher. New York: Farrar, Straus and Giroux, 1991.

Schwartz, Israel Jacob. *Kentoki [Kentucky].* Translated by Gertrude W. Dubrovsky. Tuscaloosa: University of Alabama Press, 1990.

Singer, Isaac Bashevis. *The Collected Stories of Isaac Bashevis Singer.* New York: Farrar, Straus, Giroux, 1982.

———. *Yoshe Kalb.* Introduction by Isaac Bashevis Singer. Translated by Maurice Samuel. New York: Harper and Row, 1965.

Yezierska, Anzia. *Bread Givers.* 1925. Introduction by Alice Kessler Harris. New York: Persea Books, 1975.

———. *How I Found America: Collected Stories of Anzia Yezierska.* Introduction by Vivian Gornick. New York: Persea Books, 1991.

———. *The Open Cage: An Anzia Yezierska Collection.* Edited by Alice Kessler-Harris. New York: Persea Books, 1994.

———. *A Red Ribbon on a White Horse* 1950. Introduction by W. H. Aude. New York: Persea Books, 1981.

Backgrounds and Contexts

Berkowitz, Joel. *Shakespeare on the American Yiddish Stage.* Iowa City: University of Iowa Press, 2002.

Chametzky, Jules. *From the Ghetto: The Fiction of Abraham Cahan.* Amherst: University of Massachusetts Press, 1977.

Collins, Glen. "Cracks Found in the Myths around Statue." *New York Times*, October 28, 2000. http://www.nytimes.com/2000/10/28/nyregion/cracks-found-myths-around-statue-park-service-librarian-writes-book-clarify-lady.html.

Diner, Hasia R. *Lower East Side Memories: A Jewish Place in America*. Princeton, NJ: Princeton University Press, 2000.

Diner, Hasia R., Jeffrey Shandler, and Beth S. Wenger, eds. *Remembering the Lower East Side: American Jewish Reflections*. Bloomington: Indiana University Press, 2000.

Glenn, Susan A. *Daughters of the Shtetl: Life and Labor in the Immigrant Generation*. Ithaca, NY: Cornell University Press, 1990.

Hapke, Laura. *Labor's Text: The Worker in American Fiction*. New Brunswick, NJ: Rutgers University Press, 2000.

Henrikson, Louise Levitas, with Jo Ann Boydston. *Anzia Yezierska: A Writer's Life*. New Brunswick, NJ: Rutgers University Press, 1988.

Howe, Irving, with Kenneth Libo. *World of Our Fathers*. New York: Harcourt Brace Jovanovich, 1976.

Jones, Gavin. *American Hungers: The Problem of Poverty in U.S. Literature, 1840–1945*. Princeton, NJ: Princeton University Press, 2008.

Lawrence, Greg. *Dance with Demons: The Life of Jerome Robbins*. New York: Berkley, 2002.

Levinson, Julian. *Exiles on Main Street: Jewish American Writers and American Literary Culture*. Bloomington: Indiana University Press, 2008.

Marovitz, Sanford E. *Abraham Cahan*. New York: Twayne, 1996.

Moreno, Barry. *The Statue of Liberty Encyclopedia*. New York: Simon and Schuster, 2000.

Schor, Esther. *Emma Lazarus*. New York: Schocken Books, 2006.

Sollors, Werner. *Beyond Ethnicity: Consent and Descent in American Culture*. New York: Oxford University Press, 1986.

Tutela, Joelle Jennifer. "Becoming American: A Case Study of the Lower East Side Tenement Museum." Ph.D. diss., City University of New York. ProQuest/UMI, 2008 (Publication No. 3325429).

Wirth-Nesher, Hana. *Call It English: The Languages of Jewish American Literature*. Princeton, NJ: Princeton University Press, 2006.

———. *New Essays on "Call It Sleep."* Cambridge: Cambridge University Press, 1996.

Young, Bette Roth. *Emma Lazarus in the World: Life and Letters*. Foreword by Francine Klagsbrun. Philadelphia: Jewish Publication Society, 1997.

Main Street, Sauk Centre, Minnesota, around 1910. The town of Gopher Prairie in Sinclair Lewis's novel *Main Street*, published in 1920, was modeled on his hometown of Sauk Centre. *Main Street*, *Babbitt*, and the other novels that followed helped encourage Americans to be more self-aware and critical about their society, less complacent and naively self-congratulatory.

9

The Revolt from the Village

ORIGINAL MAIN STREET HISTORIC DISTRICT
SAUK CENTRE, MINNESOTA

When Sinclair Lewis's novel *Main Street* came out in 1920, it was an immediate best seller, widely reviewed and widely praised by newspapers across the country—everywhere, it seemed, but in Sauk Centre, Lewis's hometown, where the local paper ignored it for five months. Lewis admitted that he had modeled "Gopher Prairie" (the fictional town whose Main Street gave the book its title) on Sauk Centre, and the portrait was anything but flattering. The novel satirized more effectively than any book before it the narrow-minded dullness and the deadening pressures to conform in middle-brow, middle-class, middle America. In the prologue that opened the book, Lewis writes:

> The town is, in our tale, called "Gopher Prairie, Minnesota." But its Main Street is the continuation of Main Streets everywhere. The story would be the same in Ohio or Montana, in Kansas or Kentucky or Illinois. . . . Main Street is the climax of civilization. That this Ford car might stand in front of the Bon Ton Store, Hannibal invaded Rome and Erasmus wrote in Oxford cloisters. What Ole Jenson the grocer says to Ezra Stowbody the banker is the new law for London, Prague, and the unprofitable isles of the sea; whatsoever Ezra does not know and sanction that thing is heresy, worthless for knowing and wicked to consider. Our railway station is the final aspiration of architecture. Sam Clark's annual hardware turnover is the envy of the four counties which constitute God's Country. . . .

"Main Street" quickly became a symbol of the smug provincialism and the juvenile boosterism of America's small towns—and, indeed, some have said, of America itself.

Main Street made publishing history, reaching unprecedented numbers of readers with unprecedented speed. More than 180,000 copies sold during the first six months alone. Printers could hardly keep up with the orders. (More than three hundred thousand additional copies would be sold by the end of the decade, making it the best-selling novel of the 1920s.) Richmond, Virginia, and Buffalo, New York, thought about changing the name of their Main Streets to distance themselves from the negative image associated with Lewis's novel, as Amy Campion and Gary Alan Fine have noted. Sauk Centre's residents, silently seething at being the butt of jokes around the country, didn't have that option: even if they called it something else, everyone would still know that it was Sauk Centre's "Main Street" that gave the novel its name, and that it was Lewis's memories of small-town life during his childhood there that gave the novel its satirical bite. The final insult came when the book won a Pulitzer Prize in 1921.

But then a funny thing happened: as Lewis's reputation grew, instead of being an embarrassment to his hometown, Lewis became a source of pride. When Sauk Centre did end up changing the name of "Main Street," the change was designed not to mask the connection to Lewis's novel, but to cement it. Within three years of the book's publication, the *Sauk Centre Herald* began to print the slogan, "Sauk Centre—The Original Main Street" on its front page. Four years later, the Sauk Centre City Council erected a thirty-four-by-ten-foot sheet metal sign on the outskirts of the city that proudly proclaimed, "This is the Original Main St. (Sinclair Lewis) Sauk Centre." In 1960, the City Council would make the name change official with a formal vote. Fame was fame, and pride was pride, and every town needed something to be known for; Sauk Centre had Lewis, and meant to make the most of it. This did not mean that Sauk Centre residents read his books, or taught them in the local high school (where five years after *Main Street* appeared, the athletic teams began to refer to themselves as the "Main Streeters"). It was much easier to be proud of Lewis if one didn't read what he said. How else can one explain the lack of irony with which local organizations in the 1920s happily named themselves the "Gopher Prairie Shriners' Club" and the "Gopher Prairie 4-H Club"? Or the tourist brochure that described Sauk Centre as "a living museum of an American institution: the small town"?

The Original Main Street Historic District, ten blocks long, consists of a collection of commercial enterprises flanked on either side by residential neighborhoods. Most of the one- or two-story brick buildings date from the late nineteenth and early twentieth century; they are largely simple and unornamented, reflecting the utilitarian values of early-twentieth-century small-town commercial construction, with occasional Beaux Arts decoration. Built in 1880, for example, the drugstore on the corner of Main Street and Sinclair Lewis Avenue, has a distinctive decorative iron cornice that was added to the building in 1904, when Lewis's father still practiced medicine on its second floor. Although several ground-floor storefronts were altered after World War II, the upper stories of the buildings for the most part retain the design, materials, workmanship and feel of the late nineteenth and early twentieth centuries. The residential blocks in the historic district contain primarily early-twentieth-century, wood-frame, one-and-a-half-story single-family homes in the popular styles of the 1910s and 1920s: gabled Craftsman-style bungalows, with occasional examples of Italianate, Queen Anne, and Gothic Revival.

"Main Street" in the novel has a small motion-picture theater called the "Rosebud Movie Palace" and on a corner plot, Dyer's Drug Store. There's still a movie theater—Main Street Theatre—and across the street (at the intersection of The Original Main Street and Sinclair Lewis Avenue) the building that housed the drug store is still there (although it is currently vacant). Several of the establishments Lewis enumerates in the book still line the town's central artery. A couple of banks, a clothing store, a garage, a feed store, and a bakery, for example, are still there, but there are also some enterprises Lewis could not have imagined in 1920: a yoga studio and a copy shop. One can eat at the Main Street Café, feed the ducks in Sinclair Lewis Park, or stay at the Gopher Prairie Motel. Once a year, in an unabashed blast of the sort of small-town boosterism Lewis was so good at satirizing, there is a local celebration called "Sinclair Lewis Days." (When "Sinclair Lewis Days" began in 1968, it replaced an annual community festival called "Butter Days." The crowning of the "Butter Queen" became the crowning of a "Miss Sinclair Lewis." But shortly thereafter the monarch's name was changed to "Miss Sauk Centre," which is the name under which a crown is bestowed today.)

The Original Main Street today is immensely ordinary. It looks like the principal thoroughfare in any of a thousand American towns, as it did when Lewis was growing up there. About 4,300 people live in the town—up from around 3,000 during Lewis's childhood. Many of the unpretentious, comfortable homes that were there when he was young still stand on the town's tree-lined streets. When he lived here, any sidewalks in town were made of wood, and most streets were unpaved, becoming seas of mud whenever it rained. Main Street was first paved in 1924, four years after the novel appeared.

About a hundred miles northwest of the Twin Cities, Sauk Centre is surrounded by flat fields as far as the eye can see. Carol Kennicott, the central character in *Main Street*, describes her first view of the town like this: "The fields swept up to it, past it. It was unprotected and unprotecting; there was no dignity in it nor any hope of greatness." Her new husband takes her to "a prosaic frame house in a small parched lawn" that is to be her new home. The flatness, the drabness, the monotony, the endlessness of the prairie echoes in the flatness and the drabness of the lives of the book's characters, and in their aspirations. "It's one of our favorite American myths that broad plains necessarily make broad minds," Carol observes. "I thought that myself, when I first came to the prairie. 'Big—new.' Oh, I don't want to deny the prairie future. It will be magnificent. But equally I'm hanged if I want to be bullied by it, go to war on behalf of Main Street, be bullied and *bullied* by the faith that the future is already here in the present, and that all of us must stay and worship wheat-stacks and insist that this is 'God's Country'—and never, of course, do anything original or gay-colored that would help to make that future!"

"In scores of magazines every month," Carol tells us, one reads "that the American village remains the one sure abode of friendship, honesty, and clean sweet marriageable girls. Therefore all men who succeed in painting in Paris or in finance in New York at last become weary of smart women, return to their native towns, assert that cities are vicious, marry their childhood sweethearts, and, presumably, joyously abide in those towns until death." (Or, as Lewis would later put it in his Nobel Prize acceptance speech, "Our fictional tradition, you see, was that all of us in midwestern villages were altogether noble and happy; that not one of us would exchange the neighborly bliss of living on Main Street for the heathen gaudiness of New York or Paris or Stockholm.") But the reality, according to Carol Kennicott, is "an unimaginatively standardized background, a sluggishness of speech and manners, a rigid ruling of the spirit by the desire to appear respectable. . . . It is the prohibition of happiness. . . . It is dullness made God." Main Street, in Carol's view, features "a savorless people, gulping tasteless food, and sitting afterward, coatless and thoughtless, in rocking-chairs prickly with inane decorations, listening to mechanical music, saying mechanical things, about the excellence of Ford automobiles, and viewing themselves as the greatest race in the world." The target of Carol's diatribe and of Lewis's satiric jabs is really a Main Street of the mind where provincialism triumphs unchallenged, conversation does not exist, conformity exerts relentless pressure, innovation is suspect, and custom is king.

College-educated Carol Kennicott comes to Gopher Prairie bursting with ideas on how to help the boring, colorless town learn to value beauty, spontaneity, and originality only to bump up against a self-satisfied conventionality and mediocrity that stymies her at every point. She is no artist or genius, and the qualities she seeks in the town and tries to imbue the town with are themselves fairly commonplace, tame, and unexceptional; but this allows the book to convey all the more dramatically both how generally spirit-deadening small-town life can be, and particularly how oppressive "its vacuousness and bad manners and spiteful gossip" can be for "a woman with a working brain and no work." Lewis also provides sensitive and moving portraits of the hard-working and sometimes free-thinking Scandinavian immigrants in the area, whom the ethnocentric white Anglo-Saxon Protestant residents of Gopher Prairie employ, exploit, and feel superior to.

In his later years, Lewis occasionally softened his recollections of what it had been like growing up in Sauk Centre. In a nostalgic 1931 essay called "The Long Arm of the Small Town," written for the fiftieth anniversary of his high school yearbook, he wrote, "If I seem to have criticized prairie villages, I have certainly criticized them no more than I have New York, or Paris, or the great universities." Recalling many happy days spent "swimming and fishing in Sauk Lake, or cruising its perilous depths on a raft" or picnicking or hunting during his childhood, he concluded by saying, "It was a good time, a good place, and a good preparation for life." This essay is more widely quoted in Sauk Centre than any of Lewis's other writings.

But elsewhere Lewis's view of his childhood is less idyllic and rosy, and it is this latter, less airbrushed picture, that is ultimately more convincing, more corroborated, and more compelling. Gangly and unattractive in his youth, Lewis later described himself as "tall, awkward, rusty of hair, long-nosed, dressed neither handsomely nor with picturesque disarray." A bookish child who was a dismal athlete, he was bullied and ridiculed mercilessly by his peers, who played cruel pranks on him whenever the opportunity presented itself. He had one friend. Meanwhile his brother Claude, athletically and socially gifted, constantly overshadowed him and shamed him by excelling at all those things at which he failed. The local paper duly recorded some of Lewis's failures—such as the time he went swimming with Claude and some of Claude's friends, nearly drowned, and had to be rescued by his brother; or the time he tried to run away and enlist as a drummer boy in the Spanish-American War, only to be intercepted and fetched home by his father as he waited for an eastbound train in the town of Melrose, ten miles away. "The only people I ever wanted to impress," Lewis wrote later in life, "were my father and brother Claude. I never succeeded." His father, he wrote, "has never forgiven me for *Main Street*. . . . *Main Street* condemned me in his eyes as a traitor to my heritage—whereas the truth is, I shall never shed the little, indelible 'Sauk-centricities' that enabled me to write it."

Lewis's mother died when he was six years old. He got along well, however, with his stepmother, who read to him more than most parents read to their children at the time, and helped ignite the love of books that helped him survive the loneliness of his adolescence. Books were his constant companions, even when he was doing his assigned chores: he set up a reading stand next to the sawhorse and chopping block behind the house, and when he went out to mow the lawn, he'd mow for a few minutes and then read under a shade tree for half an hour. A high school classmate recalled that "he was easily the brightest scholar in all subjects. . . . But some of the teachers didn't like him; he was too odd and had ideas of his own."

Lewis must have suspected at the time that whatever destiny had in store for him, it surely involved leaving Sauk Centre. On that point he was correct. He left the town after high school to attend Oberlin Preparatory School, and then Yale, and, save for the occasional summer vacation, never lived in Sauk Centre for an extended period again. But he probably never suspected that his first truly memorable success in the career he eventually chose would come when he returned to Main Street—in his imagination.

Although *Babbitt*, the novel Lewis published two years after *Main Street*, was set in the fictional city of Zenith, a larger and more bustling place than Gopher Prairie, the two communities had much in common. Indeed, at the end of *Main Street*, Gopher Prairie launches a "campaign of boosting" directed by a go-getter whose speech at a local businessmen's banquet sounds a lot like the speech George Babbitt will give to the Zenith Real Estate Board in *Babbitt*. British writer H. G. Wells wrote to Lewis in a fan letter that George Babbitt "is the common American prosperous businessman got. You have got him. . . . He moves about. His baseness, his vile gregariousness, his vulgarity &—what is the hope of America—his suffering & struggling intimations of beauty, are all wonderfully done. . . . I wish I could have written *Babbitt*."

Lewis's Babbitt was so vividly drawn that his name has come into American English as an emblem of the hail-fellow-well-met booster and salesman-as-model-citizen, of modern man as consumer and conformist. Babbitt, Lewis tells us, "made nothing in particular, neither butter nor shoes nor poetry, but he was nimble in the calling of selling houses for more than people could afford to pay." For Babbitt and others like him, Lewis tells us, "the Romantic Hero was no longer the knight, the wandering poet, the cowpuncher, the aviator, nor the brave young district attorney, but the great sales manager, who had an Analysis of Merchandizing Problems on his glass-topped desk, whose title of nobility was 'Go-getter' and who devoted himself and all his young samurai to the cosmic purpose of Selling—not of selling anything in particular, for or to anybody in particular, but pure Selling."

BOOSTERS AND "BABBITRY"

Lewis's 1922 novel, *Babbitt*, continues the critique of self-satisfied provincial boosterism that helped make *Main Street* a best seller. George F. Babbitt, the middle-aged real estate salesman in the novel that bears his name, is happiest when braying contentedly about the superiority of Zenith, his hometown. The following passage is part of a speech he gives at a gathering of real estate salesmen:

> I tell you, Zenith and her sister-cities are producing a new type of civilization. There are many resemblances between Zenith and these other burgs, and I'm darn glad of it! The extraordinary, growing, and sane standardization of stores, offices, streets, hotels, clothes, and newspapers throughout the United States shows how strong and enduring a type is ours. . . .
>
> Yes, sir, these other burgs are our true partners in the great game of vital living. But let's not have any mistake about this. I claim that Zenith is the best partner and the fastest-growing partner of the whole caboodle. I trust I may be pardoned if I give a few statistics to back up my claims. If they are old stuff to any of you, yet the tidings of prosperity, like the good news of the Bible, never become tedious to the ears of a real hustler, no matter how oft the sweet story is told! Every intelligent person knows that Zenith manufactures more condensed milk and evaporated cream, more paper boxes, and more lighting-fixtures, than any other city in the United States, if not in the world. But it is not so universally known that we also stand second in the manufacture of package-butter, sixth in the giant realm of motors and automobiles, and somewhere about third in cheese, leather findings, tar roofing, breakfast food, and overalls!
>
> Our greatness, however, lies not alone in punchful prosperity but equally in that public spirit, that forward-looking idealism and brotherhood, which has marked Zenith ever since its foundation by the Fathers. We have a right, indeed we have a duty toward our fair city, to announce broadcast the facts about our high schools, characterized by their complete plants and the finest school-ventilating systems in the country, bar none; our magnificent new hotels and banks and the paintings and carved marble in their lobbies; and the Second National Tower, the second highest business building in any inland city in the

entire country. When I add that we have an unparalleled number of miles of paved streets, bathrooms, vacuum cleaners, and all the other signs of civilization; that our library and art museum are well supported and housed in convenient and roomy buildings; that our park-system is more than up to par, with its handsome driveways adorned with grass, shrubs, and statuary, then I give but a hint of the all round unlimited greatness of Zenith!

I believe, however, in keeping the best to the last. When I remind you that we have one motor car for every five and seven-eighths persons in the city, then I give a rock-ribbed practical indication of the kind of progress and braininess which is synonymous with the name Zenith!

But the way of the righteous is not all roses. Before I close I must call your attention to a problem we have to face, this coming year. The worst menace to sound government is not the avowed socialists but a lot of cowards who work under cover—the long-haired gentry who call themselves "liberals" and "radicals" and "non-partisan" and "intelligent-sia" and God only knows how many other trick names! Irresponsible teachers and professors constitute the worst of this whole gang, and I am ashamed to say that several of them are on the faculty of our great State University! The U. is my own Alma Mater, and I am proud to be known as an alumni, but there are certain instructors there who seem to think we ought to turn the conduct of the nation over to hoboes and roustabouts.

Those profs are the snakes to be scotched—they and all their milk-and-water ilk! The American business man is generous to a fault, but one thing he does demand of all teachers and lecturers and journalists: if we're going to pay them our good money, they've got to help us by selling efficiency and whooping it up for rational prosperity! And when it comes to these blab-mouth, fault-finding, pessimistic, cynical University teachers, let me tell you that during this golden coming year it's just as much our duty to bring influence to have those cusses fired as it is to sell all the real estate and gather in all the good shekels.

Not till that is done will our sons and daughters see that the ideal of American manhood and culture isn't a lot of cranks sitting around chewing the rag about their Rights and their Wrongs, but a God-fearing, hustling, successful, two-fisted Regular Guy, who belongs to some church with pep and piety to it, who belongs to the Boosters or the Rotarians or the Kiwanis, to the Elks or Moose or Red Men or Knights of Columbus or any one of a score of organizations of good, jolly, kidding, laughing, sweating, upstanding, lend-a-handing Royal Good Fellows, who plays hard and works hard, and whose answer to his critics is a square-toed boot that'll teach the grouches and smart alecks to respect the He-man and get out and root for Uncle Samuel, U.S.A.!

George Babbitt wakes up each day to "the best of nationally advertised and quantitatively produced alarm-clocks, with all modern attachments, including cathedral chime, intermittent alarm, and a phosphorescent dial. Babbitt was proud of being awakened by such a rich device." "Just as he was an Elk, a Booster, and a member of the Chamber of Commerce," Lewis writes, "just as the priests of the Presbyterian Church determined his every religious belief and the senators who controlled the Republican Party decided in little smoky rooms in Washington what he should think about disarmament, tariff, and Germany, so did the large national advertisers fix the surface of his life, fix what he believed to be his individuality. These standard advertised wares—toothpastes, socks, tires, cameras, instantaneous hot-water heaters—were his symbols and proofs of excellence; at first the signs, then the substitutes, for joy and passion and wisdom."

Indeed, it is Lewis's deft and meticulous social detail that makes Babbitt's physical world come alive, much as his sharp ear allows the reader to hear Babbitt's voice championing the Booster Club slogan, "Boosters-Pep!" in timbres that are distinctive yet familiar; it is a voice filled with self-satisfied arrogance, ignorance, and pride, with cocky illogic and unselfconscious bigotry. Listen to Babbitt on his fellow citizens' failure to grasp what is truly great about America: "Trouble with a lot of folks is: they're so blame material; they don't see the spiritual and mental side of American supremacy; they think that inventions like the telephone and the aeroplane . . . they think these mechanical improvements are all that we stand for; whereas to a real thinker, he sees that spiritual and, uh, dominating movements like Efficiency, and Rotarianism, and Prohibition, and Democracy are what compose our deepest and truest wealth."

Main Street challenged head-on the empty pieties that animated so much of American life. Lewis continued what he began here not only in *Babbitt*, but also in later works including *Elmer Gantry* and *Arrowsmith*, winning admirers around the world. In 1930, he became the first American to win the Nobel Prize in Literature. He titled his acceptance speech, delivered on December 12, 1930, in the great hall of Swedish Stock Exchange in Stockholm before members of Swedish Literary Academy and their guests, "The American Fear of Literature." "In America," Lewis told the gathering, "most of us . . . are still afraid of any literature which is not a glorification of everything American." *Main Street*, *Babbitt*, and the other novels that followed helped encourage Americans to be more self-aware and critical about their society, less complacent and naively self-congratulatory.

Sinclair Lewis (1885–1951), the first American to win the Nobel Prize in Literature, had his first major success as a writer with a novel about his hometown, Sauk Centre, Minnesota. His biographer, Mark Schorer, called *Main Street*'s success "the most sensational event in twentieth-century American publishing history."
PHOTO CREDIT: PHOTO BY ARNOLD GENTHE; COURTESY OF THE LIBRARY OF CONGRESS, PRINTS AND PHOTOGRAPHS DIVISION, WASHINGTON, DC.

Lewis was not the first American author to challenge the sentimental, idealized view of small towns as havens of goodness and innocence far removed from the evils and complexities of the big city. Some of the small towns in Mark Twain's fiction—such as St. Petersburg in *Huckleberry Finn*, Dawson's Landing in *Pudd'nhead Wilson*, and Hadleyburg, in "The Man That Corrupted Hadleyburg"—are far from idyllic. Charlotte Perkins Gilman's 1911 story, "The Unnatural Mother," published in the magazine the *Forerunner*, painted a town in which village housewives were deeply threatened by altruism, independence, and public-spiritedness. Edgar Lee Masters's 1915 collection of poetry, *Spoon River Anthology*, had the inhabitants of Spoon River, Illinois, unmask the hypocrisies of small-town life in soliloquies delivered from beyond the grave. And Sherwood Anderson's 1919 book, *Winesburg, Ohio*, also helped chip away at the myth that small towns were inhabited by folks who were invariably contented and fulfilled. But if Sinclair Lewis did not invent what has come to be called "the revolt from the village," he brought it to new heights and allowed it to have a deeper impact on the popular consciousness. He served as a liberating influence on later writers, including Richard Wright, for whom the American small town was far from placid, safe, and happy. In "The Ethics of Living Jim Crow, an Autobiographical Sketch," for example, Wright recalls that "the green trees, the trimmed hedges, the cropped lawns, grew very meaningful, became a symbol. Even today when I think of white folks, the hard, sharp outlines of white houses surrounded by trees, lawns, and hedges are present somewhere in the background of my mind. Through the years they grew into an overreaching symbol of fear." Lewis showed his own awareness of the racism that could lurk along pleasant, orderly, tree-lined streets in his 1947 novel, *Kingsblood Royal*, which ends with the world of Main Street, in effect, erupting into an apocalyptic race war.

It was twenty-two degrees below zero on January 28, 1951, the day that Lewis's ashes were to be buried in Sauk Centre after being shipped there in an urn from Italy, where he had died and been cremated. On Main Street, a department store window shattered from the cold. Charlotte Hedin, a young teacher who taught Lewis's work in the high school, went to Greenwood Cemetery to witness the event. The plan was to sprinkle Lewis's ashes in a grave between those of his parents, since the town wanted to keep the urn on display in the local library. But as his brother Claude began to pour the ashes into the opening of the grave, a terrible wind suddenly came up. The ashes "blew back on us," Hedin recalled when I interviewed her in 1998; "They blew back on the town," she said. How he managed it remains a mystery, but even in death, Lewis was still in their face.

RELATED SITES

•◦ Sinclair Lewis Boyhood Home
812 Sinclair Lewis Avenue, Sauk Centre, Minnesota

Harry Sinclair Lewis, who was born in 1885, moved into this three-bedroom, two-story, white-frame home with his parents and two brothers when he was four years old and lived here until he finished high school. The house, which was built in 1889, has been restored to look much as it did when Lewis lived here, complete with many of the family's original furnishings and household items.

It was in the formal family parlor that Isabel Lewis, his stepmother, hosted meetings of the "Gradatim Club," a group of women who met to discuss literature and public affairs (and also share the latest gossip); young Harry (as Lewis was called by his family) would often lurk in the next room and eavesdrop on their meetings. The club (which Isabel Lewis founded) served as the model for the "Thanatopsis Club" in *Main Street.*

The sitting room, which adjoins the parlor, was where the Lewis boys entertained themselves reading and playing chess. When Harry was fifteen, his father invented a steam-heating system for his home,

Sinclair Lewis Boyhood Home, Sauk Centre, Minnesota, where the author was born and raised.

PHOTO CREDIT: COURTESY OF THE HISTORIC AMERICAN BUILDINGS SURVEY, HABS MINN,73-SAUCE,1–2, LIBRARY OF CONGRESS, PRINTS AND PHOTOGRAPHS DIVISION, WASHINGTON, DC.

installing rows of large radiator pipes (which are still there today) in the front hall and in the master bedroom to protect his family from the chill of Minnesota winters; as Harry noted proudly in his diary, his home was one of the first to have this modern type of heating system. Modern bathrooms, however, were not installed in the house until after Harry left for college. Harry shared the upstairs bedroom overlooking the backyard with his two older brothers. The small wooden bed by the window is the one he used as a young boy. The picture above the bed is Harry as a baby, four months old.

His father, Dr. Edwin J. Lewis, saw patients in a downstairs office in his home even after he opened another office on Main Street. (On the library table in the doctor's office is the Western Electric RCA early vacuum tube radio that Lewis presented to his father in 1920, the year *Main Street* was published.)

In the china closet in the dining room is a large, white sugar bowl that came over on the *Mayflower* with Lewis's forebears on his father's side. It is fitting somehow that the leading satirist of small-town WASP America was a direct descendant of Peregrine White, who entered the world in 1620, the first white child born in the Plymouth Colony. The world of *Main Street* and *Babbitt* is a homogeneous place ruled by citizens of Anglo-Saxon descent and kept running by hard-working Scandinavian immigrants. In a later book—*Kingsblood Royal*—Lewis would paint a more diverse community that included African Americans, as well. But the world of *Main Street* was a world as white as the sugar bowl that still gleams through the glass of the china cupboard in Lewis's boyhood home.

☙ Palmer House Hotel

500 Sinclair Lewis Avenue, corner of The Original Main Street and Sinclair Lewis Avenue, Sauk Centre, Minnesota

The Palmer House Hotel, called the Minnimashie House in *Main Street*, was the finest hotel in the state outside Minneapolis when it was built in 1901. The three-story, rectangular-plan brick building with architectural detailing inspired by the Queen Anne style boasted such modern conveniences as running water and toilets, and it was the first building in town to have electricity. (The owner complained that the people played with the switches so much he had to replace them all after six months.) The hotel—which is still in operation—was a favorite stopping place for traveling salesmen, who took orders from local retailers in the lobby or basement. Although modern plumbing and air conditioning have been installed, the Palmer House retains its turn-of-the-century look and feel. During one of his high school summer vacations, Sinclair Lewis worked there as a substitute night clerk for two weeks from 6:00 P.M. to 6:00 A.M., for five dollars a week plus room and board. His take-home pay was often less than that, owing to his clumsiness and incompetence. He wrote in his journal, "Broke a show case last night by leaning on it. Cost me $2. Made a mistake in giving change to amt. of $1.50. Can't afford working at this rate!" But while he was a dismal failure as a night clerk, he was a bright success when it came to telling long, improvised stories to the Palmer children, who adored him.

☙ Edgar Lee Masters House

528 Monroe Street, Petersburg Historic District, Petersburg, Illinois

Edgar Lee Masters (1869–1950), author of the influential *Spoon River Anthology* (1915), a key book in the "Revolt from the Village," spent his childhood and early youth in this Petersburg house before moving with his family to Lewistown in 1882. The profile of small-town America that emerges in his most famous book was rooted, in part, in life as he knew it here. (He also drew on his adolescence in Lewistown.) *Spoon River Anthology* captured with eloquence and grace some of the repressed aridity of life in a small town for a single woman like the fictional "Mabel Osborne," who sighs,

> . . . I, who had happiness to share
> And longed to share your happiness;
> I who loved you, Spoon River,
> And craved your love,
> Withered before your eyes, Spoon River—
> Thirsting, thirsting,
> Voiceless from chasteness of soul to ask you for love,
> You who knew and saw me perish before you,
> Like this geranium which someone has planted over me,
> And left to die.

But it also evokes some of the joyful contentment of "Lucinda Matlock," who tells us that

> At ninety-six I had lived enough, that is all,
> And passed to a sweet repose.
> What is this I hear of sorrow and weariness,

Anger, discontent and drooping hopes?
Degenerate sons and daughters,
Life is too strong for you—
It takes life to love Life.

This modest white cottage, which contains many Masters family furnishings, is now a municipally owned memorial to Masters.

❧ Oakland Cemetery

Petersburg Historic District, south of city limits on County Route 9, Petersburg, Illinois

Edgar Lee Masters is buried here, along with other leading citizens in the town, some of whom have monologues in Masters's famous free-verse collection of monologues-from-the-grave, *Spoon River Anthology*. Buried here, for example, is Ann Rutledge, Abraham Lincoln's legendary first love. "Anne Rutledge" in *Spoon River Anthology*, rises from the grave to say,

Out of me unworthy and unknown
The vibrations of deathless music;
"With malice toward none, with charity for all."
Out of me the forgiveness of millions toward millions,
And the beneficent face of a nation
Shining with justice and truth.
I am Anne Rutledge who sleep beneath these weeds,
Beloved in life of Abraham Lincoln,
Wedded to him, not through union,
But through separation.
Bloom forever, O Republic,
From the dust of my bosom!

Also buried here is Hannah Armstrong, who, as "Hannah Armstrong" in *Spoon River Anthology*, pays a visit to the White House in an effort to get Lincoln to discharge her sick son, only to be turned away until she tells the guard, "Please say it's old Aunt Hannah Armstrong / From Illinois, come to see him about her sick boy / In the army." Then they let her right in. Lincoln " . . . dropped his business as president, / And wrote in his own hand Doug's discharge, / Talking the while of the early days, / And telling stories." *Spoon River Anthology* is credited with having helped inspire Thornton Wilder's play *Our Town* and Sherwood Anderson's collection of stories *Winesburg, Ohio.*

FOR FURTHER READING

The Writers: Works and Words

Anderson, Sherwood. *Winesburg, Ohio.* 1919. Edited by Glen A. Love. New York: Oxford University Press, 1997.

Gilman, Charlotte Perkins. *The Charlotte Perkins Gilman Reader.* Edited by Ann J. Lane. Charlottesville: University Press of Virginia, 1999.

Lewis, Sinclair. *Arrowsmith.* 1925. New York: New American Library, 1964.

———. *Dodsworth.* New York: Harcourt, Brace, Jovanovich, 1929.

———. *Elmer Gantry.* New York: Harcourt, Brace, Jovanovich, 1927.

———. *Kingsblood Royal.* New York: Random House, 1947.

———. *Main Street & Babbitt.* 1920 and 1922. Edited by John Hersey. New York: Library of America, 1992.

Masters, Edgar Lee. *Spoon River Anthology.* 1915. Edited by John E. Hallwas. Annotated. Urbana: University of Illinois Press, 1992.

Wright, Richard. "The Ethics of Living Jim Crow." In *Richard Wright: Early Works: Lawd Today! / Uncle Tom's Children / Native Son.* Edited by Arnold Rampersad. New York: Library of America, 1991.

Backgrounds and Contexts

Bucco, Martin, ed. *Critical Essays on Sinclair Lewis.* Boston: G. K. Hall, 1986.

Campion, Amy, and Gary Alan Fine. "*Main Street* on Main Street: Community Identity and the Reputation of Sinclair Lewis." *Sociological Quarterly* 39, no. 1 (Winter 1998): 79–99.

Fine, Gary Alan. *Difficult Reputations: Collective Memories of the Evil, Inept, and Controversial.* Chicago: University of Chicago Press, 2001.

Fleming, Robert E., and Esther Fleming. *Sinclair Lewis: A Reference Guide.* Boston: G. K. Hall, 1980.

Hilfer, Anthony Channel. *The Revolt from the Village, 1915–1930.* Chapel Hill: University of North Carolina Press, 1969.

Lingeman, Richard. *Sinclair Lewis: Rebel from Main Street.* New York: Random House, 2002.

Lundquist, James. *Sinclair Lewis.* New York: Ungar, 1973.

Schorer, Mark. *Sinclair Lewis: An American Life.* New York: McGraw-Hill, 1961.

———. *Sinclair Lewis: A Collection of Critical Essays.* Englewood Cliffs, NJ: Prentice-Hall, 1962.

Dust Storm at This War Relocation Authority Center [Manzanar] Where Evacuees of Japanese Ancestry Are Spending the Duration. July 3, 1942. The experience of being confined at Manzanar, Topaz, Minidoka, Poston, and other camps figures prominently in fiction, poetry, memoir, and drama by Jeanne Wakatsuki Houston, Lawson Fusao Inada, Miné Okubo, Monica Sone, Yoshiko Uchida, Mitsuye Yamada, Hisaye Yamamoto, and Wakako Yamauchi, all of whom were themselves internees.
PHOTO CREDIT: PHOTO BY DOROTHEA LANGE; COURTESY OF THE NATIONAL ARCHIVES, PHOTO NO. 210-GC-839.

10

Asian American Writers
and Creativity in Confinement

ANGEL ISLAND IMMIGRATION STATION
ANGEL ISLAND STATE PARK,
SAN FRANCISCO BAY, CALIFORNIA

MANZANAR NATIONAL HISTORIC SITE
U.S. ROUTE 395 BETWEEN LONE PINE AND
INDEPENDENCE, CALIFORNIA

ANGEL ISLAND IMMIGRATION STATION

Sometime between 1910 and 1940, a young laborer named Xu from the Pearl River Delta region of Guangdong Province in southern China decided to follow his dreams to "the land of the Flowery Flag," a name his fellow Cantonese villagers had given to the United States. He had worked hard to gather the thousand pieces of gold required for the journey. He choked up when it was time to say farewell to his parents. When it was time to part from his young wife, he couldn't hold back the tears. The ocean journey to *Gam Saan*, or "Gold Mountain," as his countrymen called America, seemed endless. But at last the day arrived! He glowed with anticipation as San Francisco loomed in the distance. At last, the ship docked! But instead of going ashore, he was put on a ferry that carried him back out into the San Francisco Bay to the immigration station at China Cove on Angel Island.

Here, others from his country who had been waiting days, weeks, months, sometimes more than a year, explained that one set of immigration laws applied if you were white, and another if you were Chinese. The Chinese Exclusion Act, passed in 1882 (and extended in the decades that followed) made it extremely difficult for Chinese workers to enter the United States. The 1882 act, the only racially based immigration law in the country at the time, was revised and tightened in 1892 and made "permanent" in 1902. Economic fears combined with raw racial prejudice to push

Panoramic view of the water and the docks leading to the barracks at Angel Island in the San Francisco Bay, one mile south of Tiburon, where the Angel Island Immigration Station operated between 1910 and 1940. In addition to being central to the poetry written and carved on the barracks walls, Angel Island figures prominently in books by Maxine Hong Kingston, Genny Lim, Shawn Wong, and other Asian American writers.

PHOTO CREDIT: PHOTO BY HART HYATT NORTH, COURTESY OF THE BANCROFT LIBRARY, UNIVERSITY OF CALIFORNIA, BERKELEY.

through a set of laws designed make it especially hard for young Chinese men like Xu to enter the country and prohibited him from becoming a citizen if he did, somehow, manage to get in.

The Angel Island Immigration Station occupies about fifteen acres at the north end of the largest island in San Francisco Bay. The miles of well-maintained hiking and biking trails edged by tall Monterey pine, big-leaf maple, and coast live oak trees, and the spectacular views of the Golden Gate Bridge that one encounters there today make this 740-acre state park (accessible by ferry from San Francisco or Tiburon) a favorite destination for pleasure trips. But it held more pain than pleasure for the hundreds of thousands of immigrants from China detained here between 1910 and 1940, when the immigration station was closed. The Chinese Exclusion Act was finally repealed in 1943 out of deference to China's status as America's ally during World War II. More than six decades later, the U.S. Senate and U.S. House of Representatives expressed their "deep regret" for decades of anti-Chinese legislation. On June 19, 2012, Congresswoman Judy Chu of California released a statement celebrating the fact that on that date, "both chambers of Congress officially and formally acknowledged the ugly and un-American nature of laws that targeted Chinese immigrants." "The Chinese Exclusion Act enshrined injustice into our legal code," Chu said. "It stopped the Chinese, and the Chinese alone, from immigrating, from ever becoming naturalized citizens and ever having the right to vote. The last generation of people personally affected by these laws is leaving us, and finally

Congress has expressed the sincere regret that Chinese Americans deserve and reaffirmed our commitment to the civil rights of all people."

The Chinese were not the only immigrants processed at Angel Island. Between 1910 and 1920, more than nineteen thousand Japanese "picture brides," for example, were processed there as well (along with immigrants from some eighty countries, including India, Korea, the Philippines, Russia, Spain, Mexico, Australia, and New Zealand, as Erika Lee and Judy Yung have noted.) The majority of detainees, however, were, as Maxine Hong Kingston called them, "China men." Other parts of the island, used by Coastal Miwok Indians for thousands of years as a fishing and hunting site, housed a range of military installations during the Civil War, the Spanish-American War, World War I, World War II, and the Cold War, several of which may be visited today. Military activities on the island ceased in 1962, when a Nike antiaircraft missile battery on the island was abandoned and the missiles were removed.

The roads now paved for cars were dirt paths for horse-drawn vehicles when the Immigration Station first opened. The administration building, which had contained a registration room, a general office, a doctor's office, a detention room, a kitchen, an Asian dining room, and a Caucasian dining room, burned down in 1940. But the barracks—the building in which the immigrants spent most of their time—still stands, looking much as it did when the detainees lived there. The two-story, long wooden dormitory covered in redwood shingles, was built to accommodate 82 detainees, 56 in the men's section, and 26 in the women's section. But six months after the immigration station opened, the barracks was home to 396 men and 120 women. Overcrowding and lack of privacy, however, were only two of the many problems the immigrants encountered.

The food was unfamiliar and repulsive. The interrogations were nerve-wracking. The detainees could sometimes exercise in a small yard, but most of the time they were confined with hundreds of others to a few rooms. They were, in effect, in prison, innocent men and women detained against their will, because of racist laws designed to keep them and other working people who looked like them from entering the country. As the weeks of his unexpected imprisonment dragged on, Xu's frustration mounted. One day he took out a small knife, grasped it firmly in his hand and . . . carved a poem in the soft redwood of the barracks wall.

It mimicked classical Chinese poetry in style and structure, with its metaphors and literary allusions. (The musical rhymes and cadences of some of the poems in the original Chinese may be heard by visitors today in a tape recording on the premises.) Xu's poem took its place on the walls alongside hundreds—some say thousands—of other poems, some pencil or ink, some carved in the wood—all expressing frustration, rage, uncertainty, longing, fear, ambition, insecurity and desire. As Xu observed in another poem he carved,

壁上題詩過百篇，Over a hundred poems are on the walls.
看來皆是嘆迍邅。Looking at them, they are all pining at the delayed
                                    progress
愁人曷向愁人訴，What can one sad person say to another?

Although more than 135 have survived, as Yunte Huang has observed in *Transpacific Imaginations*, it is impossible to tell the exact number of the calligraphic poems, partly because many of them "are barely legible and have thus not been transcribed, and partly because the transcribers do not always agree as to where one poem ends and another begins on the wall." Most of these poems were forgotten until they were rediscovered by a California State Park Ranger named Alexander Weiss in 1970. Connie Young Yu, a community historian and activist who would play a central role in getting the Angel Island Immigration Station designated a National Historic Landmark, said, "In 1970 all that remained on the site were the deteriorating barracks." The California State Parks administration had plans to demolish the entire site. Yu describes the arduous process by which that destruction was averted: Weiss told San Francisco State University professor George Araki about what he saw. Araki, whose grandmother, a picture bride from Japan, had entered America through Angel Island, went with photographer Mak Takahashi to document the calligraphy on the walls. Yu writes:

Takahashi's photographs were shared with students and community groups and jolted memories of older Chinese who had been interrogated and detained. Angel Island was never the symbol of liberty that Ellis Island was. The Exclusion Law made all Chinese suspects and disputed cases were taken from arriving steamships to the Island for questioning. Coming to America was a test of courage and determination, and those who struggled didn't want to talk about it, much less remember.

A young journalist and filmmaker, Christopher Chow, set out to reclaim this history. He said all Asian families had some connection to [Angel Island]. I knew of my maternal grandmother's long detention and her court case. Chris asked me to join him in researching more evidence of the human toll of Exclusion so dramatically set on Angel Island. Our findings would uncover a significant chapter of America's immigrant past and better inform our future policies on immigration.

Community interest in the barracks was mobilized to prevent their demolition. Yu notes that an Angel Island Immigration Station Historical Advisory Committee was created to develop plans for interpreting and preserving the site. On January 1, 1976, Christopher Chow, Paul Chow, Connie Young Yu, Philip Choy, Him Mark Lai, and others presented a report to the Department of Parks and Recreation. In July of that year, the state legislature appropriated $250,000 to restore and preserve the site as a state monument. During the decade that followed, the group built community support for the site's preservation. The Angel Island Immigration Station Foundation was established in 1983, the year the barracks were opened to the public, to partner with California State Parks and the National Park Service to help ensure the preservation of site and to foster the ways in which it could educate visitors about the role Pacific Rim immigration has played in the nation's history. In 1997, the National Park Service designated it as a National Historic Landmark. Support from the National Trust for Historic Preservation, the White House Millennial Council, and California voters have helped restore other buildings that were central to the operations of the Immigration Station and also develop exhibits that highlight the poetry on the barracks walls and connect it with what happened here. As Connie Yu observes, "Activism did indeed save this legacy. Long before our committee spoke out, before Ranger Weiss saw the writing on the wall, there was activism at work: when the first detainee carved a poem of grief and protest, when another organized the Liberty Association" [to pressure the administration to meet key needs of the detainees], and when the widow of an American citizen about to be deported appealed in court. They were the true activists who set the course and showed us the way."

According to Xiao-huang Yin, a few of the poems had appeared in print around the time they were written "in various Chinese newspapers, journals, and books in the United States and China. Perhaps the earliest was printed in the *World Journal*, a Chinese-language newspaper in San Francisco, on March 16, 1910, only three months after the immigration station opened officially." But the general public was largely unaware of the poems until 1980, when Him Mark Lai, Genny Lim, and Judy Yung transcribed, annotated, and published scores of them in both the original Chinese and English translation in their book, *Island: Poetry and History of Chinese Immigrants on Angel Island, 1910–1940*, bringing to light this previously hidden chapter of America's literary heritage. It is their translations that are used in this chapter.

The difficult journey had seemed interminable. "I ate wind and tasted waves for more than twenty days," one poet wrote. But the long wait on Angel Island was usually much longer. "The months and years are wasted and still it has not ended. / . . .

I am still trapped on a lonely island," wrote another. The progress of the seasons seemed to mock the lack of progress of the immigrant: "Today is the last day of winter, / Tomorrow morning is the vernal equinox. / One year's prospects have changed to another. / Sadness kills the person in the wooden building." The freedom of the crickets outside their windows inspired envy on the part of the increasingly lonely and despairing detainees: "The insects chirp outside the four walls. / The inmates often sigh. / Thinking of affairs back home, / Unconscious tears wet my lapel."

The Old World lay behind them; the New World lay ahead. On Angel Island, they were in neither, yet in both. What kind of a land was this that held out such promise to immigrants, yet treated them so badly when they came from China? "The harsh laws pile layer upon layer," one poet wrote, "how can I dissipate my hatred?" "America has power, but not justice," another wrote. The Chinese had been the victims of unjust laws for more than half a century before Angel Island was opened. An 1852 California state law aimed primarily at the Chinese required "foreign" miners to pay special taxes. An 1854 California Supreme Court decision (*People v. Hall*) prohibited the Chinese from testifying in court against white people. Chinese immigrants subjected to violence by young white hoodlums were unlikely to find any policeman coming to their aid. As a newspaper reporter in San Francisco in the mid-1860s, Mark Twain was appalled to witness one such incident; he wrote it up for his paper—only to find that his editor had no plans to run it, caring more for the sensibilities of subscribers, who shared the police's prejudices, than for the truth. Smarting from being censored, and outraged by the injustice the Chinese faced in a land they had come to with such faith in its commitment to democracy and equality, Mark Twain conveyed the shameful persecution of the Chinese in America in sardonic satires like "Disgraceful Persecution of a Boy," "What Have the Police Been Doing?," and "Goldsmith's Friend Abroad Again."

Throughout the nineteenth century, the California legislature continued to pass laws designed to discourage further Chinese immigration by creating a hostile climate for the Chinese who were already here. Laws penalized the Chinese for the way they lived, the way they wore their hair, the way they pursued their business, and the way they treated their dead. A statement that five Chinese men asked a local Methodist minister to read to San Francisco's Board of Supervisors in 1873 protested that laws were "designed not to punish guilt and crime, nor yet to protect the lives and property of the innocent" but simply to discriminate against the Chinese; they found them "most unjust, most oppressive, and most barbarous enactments." Their protests went unanswered.

The justice the sojourners encountered on Angel Island was no more just than that which awaited them on the mainland. "In prison, we were victimized as if we were guilty. / Given no opportunity to explain, it was really brutal," one anonymous Angel Island poet wrote. Another commented, "I thoroughly hate the barbarians because they do not respect justice. / They continually promulgate harsh laws to show off their prowess."

One poet wrote,

It is actually racial barriers which cause difficulties
    on Angel Island.
Even while they are tyrannical, they still
    claim to be humanitarian.

Another confided to the wall, "I cannot bear to describe the harsh treatment by the doctors." Yet another wrote, "My chest is filled with a sadness and anger I cannot bear to explain." The only "gold" that many detainees saw of the "Gold Mountain" were the hills of Oakland, across the bay, glinting in the evening sun.

One Angel Island detainee dreamed three times "of returning to the native village." Despite the fact that he was "uselessly depressed" by the "hard times" he had unexpectedly encountered, he vowed, "If at a later time I am allowed to land on the American shore, / I will toss all the miseries of this jail to the flowing current." Another channeled his anger into a dream of vengeance: "The dragon out of water is humiliated by ants; / The fierce tiger who is caged is baited by a child. / As long as I am imprisoned, how can I dare strive for supremacy? / An advantageous position for revenge will surely come one day." Another wove allusions to well-known figures from Chinese history into his poem to make his dream of ultimate revenge more convincing ("Goujian endured humiliation and ultimately avenged his wrong. / King Wen was imprisoned at Youli and yet destroyed King Zhou. . . . With extreme misfortune comes the composure to await an opportunity for revenge."). Yunte Huang has observed that as these writers wove allusions to historical figures and events into their poems, they were operating within a long tradition that used travel writing as a vehicle for commenting on history obliquely, in a context that carried none of the punishment that unauthorized writers who chose to write history often incurred. "Angel Island poems demonstrate the tenacity with which the powerless take advantage of the power of writing and inscribe themselves into the fabric of history," Huang writes. They were also continuing an ancient subgenre of Chinese travel writing known as *tibishi*: Huang adds that

literally "poetry inscribed on the wall," *tibishi* has been an important form of composing and disseminating poems in Chinese literary history. The space for inscription is actually not limited to "walls": poems written on cliffs, rocks, doors, windows, rafters, and even snow fields also belong to the genre. At inns and roadside pavilions, where travelers usually stop for a rest, special kinds of "poetry boards" were even set up for the convenience of the poetically inspired.

The poems inscribed on the walls of Angel Island Immigration Center reprise in a twentieth-century New World context the ancient tradition of *tibishi*.

Was the United States a country where those detained at Angel Island could ever feel "at home"? Would they always feel like aliens, interlopers in the world of the white "barbarians"? Should they forget the whole thing and go back to China? Few made that choice themselves; some had it made for them, deported for reasons of health, or for having failed their "exam."

By preparing for their trip with dedicated studiousness, many immigrants managed to slip through a loophole in the various laws passed to prevent them from entering the country. Foremost of these loopholes was one that allowed you to come in if your father was an American citizen. Since the San Francisco earthquake of 1906 destroyed many of the records of the local Chinese population, many would-be immigrants took on the role of "paper son" or "paper daughter," presenting themselves as the child of an American citizen on the basis of forged papers they purchased in China. To weed out the "paper" children from the real ones, immigration officials grilled each immigrant to make sure his or her version of things matched that provided by his or her supposed "parent." "Paper sons" and "paper daughters" often memorized crib sheets containing facts about their "families," so that they could answer correctly such questions as, "What was the floor made of in your house?" or "How many chickens did you keep?" or "What direction did the fireplace face?" Trick questions lurked menacingly around the edges of each interrogation, and answers that seemed to satisfy the "white demons" one week failed to satisfy them the next. It was a treacherous business, filled with hidden land mines, as Maxine Hong Kingston conveys in this scene from *China Men*:

The men spent long days rehearsing what they would say to the Immigration Demon. The forgetful men fingered their risky notes. Those who came back after being examined told what questions they had been asked. "I had to describe all the streets in my village." "They'll ask, 'Do you have any money?' and "Do you have a job?'" "They've been asking those questions all this week," the cooks and janitors confirmed, "What's the right answer?" asked the legal fathers. "Well, last week they liked 'No job' because it proves you were an aristocrat. And they liked 'No money' because you showed a willingness to work. But this week, they like 'Yes job' and 'Yes money' because you wouldn't be taking jobs away from white workers." The men groaned. "Some help."

Xu was not the only Angel Island poet to sign his poem. A "Yu of Taishan" signed a poem he called, "Random Thoughts Deep at Night": "In the quiet of night, I heard, faintly, the whistling of wind. / The forms and shadows saddened me; upon seeing the landscape I composed a poem. / The floating clouds, the fog, darken the sky. / The moon shines faintly as the insects chirp. / Grief and bitterness entwined are heaven sent. / The sad person sits alone, leaning by a window." But most of the poems carved on the walls of Angel Island are anonymous—perhaps because of the im-

Maxine Hong Kingston (1940–). Kingston's *China Men*, which won the National Book Award for Nonfiction in 1981, introduced many Americans to what Chinese immigrants experienced at Angel Island. A celebrated author of fiction, nonfiction, and poetry, Kingston has received many honors, including a 2008 Medal for Distinguished Contribution to American Letters from the National Book Foundation, and a 2013 National Medal of Arts.
PHOTO CREDIT: © MICHAEL LIONSTAR; COURTESY OF VINTAGE BOOKS.

migrants' fear that any records of their sojourn in the "Wooden House" might somehow be used to jeopardize their entry into the country or the entry of one of their countrymen. Kingston writes in *China Men* that even poems signed with the poet's last name were "still disguised" as "there were many of that name from that village."

In Frank Chin's play *The Chickencoop Chinaman*, one character observes "all our men here . . . burned all their diaries, their letters, everything with their names on it." Indeed, the Angel Island detainees were so reticent to leave any traceable records of this unpleasant chapter of their past, that forty years after the immigration station was closed, those former detainees who agreed to be interviewed by Him Mark Lai, Genny Lim, and Judy Yung for their book, *Island*, agreed to be interviewed only with the promise of anonymity. Even then, drawing them out was a challenge. As one of the anonymous Angel Island poets had carved on the wall, "It is unbearable to relate the stories accumulated on the Island slopes." But if the participants were loath to tell their own stories, their descendants have proven adept at imagining them. It is in the novels, poems, and plays by late-twentieth-century writers—often themselves the children of Chinese immigrants—that scenes of Angel Island during that painful chapter in its past come alive in three-dimensional detail.

In *China Men*, Kingston imagines what her father (whom she calls "the legal father" here) might have encountered when he found himself detained at the Immigration Station on Angel Island, almost within swimming distance of San Francisco.

In a wooden house, a white demon physically examined him, poked him in the ass and genitals, looked in his mouth, pulled his eyelids with a hook. This was not the way a father ought to have been greeted. A cough tickled his chest and throat, but he held it down. The doctor demon pointed to a door, which he entered to find men and boys crowded together from floor to ceiling in bunkbeds and on benches; they stood against the walls and at the windows. These must be the hundred China Men who could enter America, he thought. But the quota was one hundred a year, not one hundred per day, and here were packed more than one hundred, nearer two hundred or three. A few people made room for him to set down his suitcases. "A newcomer. Another newcomer," they called out. A welcome party made its way to him. "I'm the president of the Self-Governing Association," one of them was telling him in a dialect almost like his. "The most important rule we have here is that we guard one another's chances for immigration." He also asked for dues; the father gave him a few dimes toward buying newspapers and phonograph records, an invention that he had never heard before.

An educated man, "the legal father" wrote letters home for many of his fellow detainees, who gave their families a rather different version of how they were treated:

They told their wives and mothers how wonderful they found the Gold Mountain. "The first place I came to was The Island of Immortals," they told him to write. "The foreigners clapped at our civilized magnificence when we walked off the ship in our brocades. A fine welcome. They call us 'Celestials.'" They were eating well; soon they would be sending money. Yes, a magical country. They were happy, not at all frightened. The Beautiful Nation was glorious, exactly the way they had heard it would be. "I'll be seeing you in no time." "Today we ate duck with buns and plum sauce," which was true on days when the China Men in San Francisco sent gifts.

But most days, it was another story. Instead of receiving "a fine welcome," most immigrants endured what one Angel Island poet called "a hundred humiliations." The detainees' captors, supremely ignorant about Chinese culture and traditions, seem to have been oblivious to the many gratuitous offenses they inflicted. The

Western tradition of dressing doctors and medical personnel all in white, for example, horrified many of the Chinese, since in China the color white was associated with death. Putting the women's dormitory on the floor immediately above the men's forced the men to daily incur the bad fortune that accompanied the Chinese superstition about men "climbed over by women." And the Western food the dining hall served mystified and infuriated the detainees so much that food riots were not uncommon (they happened so frequently that a sign in Chinese warned diners of the penalties for throwing food). A merchant's wife detained at Angel Island in 1922 recalled the meals that were served there: "the melon was chopped in pieces and thrown together like pig slop. The pork was in big, big chunks. Everything was thrown into a big bowl that resembled a washtub and left there for you to eat or not. They just steamed the food till it was like a soupy stew. . . . After looking at it you'd lose your appetite!" We catch a glimpse of what might have gone on in the dining hall in Kingston's novel, *Tripmaster Monkey: His Fake Book*, when an elderly Chinese woman who had been detained on Angel Island remembers her reactions to the strange food: "'We didn't know how to eat Jell-O. We spread it on the white bread. Jell-O sandwiches.' She laughed at the greenhorns they used to be. There was too much we didn't know," the woman recalls.

Jell-O was not the only thing that was strange, new, and confusing; the ground itself deceived: "The ground on Angel Island is covered with jade," the woman thought, when she first arrived. "We walked on dark green jade clink-clinking underfoot from the boat to the Wooden House. When the soldiers turned their backs, I picked up a piece. We thought, the island is made of jade; the mainland must be made of gold." But, she adds, "Now I know, it's just mock jade. Monterey jade." The false jade, like the false gold mountain that glimmered across the bay at sunrise and sunset, mocked the would-be immigrants' dreams.

But that didn't mean they abandoned them. Genny Lim's play *Paper Angels*, set at the Angel Island Immigration Station in 1915, conveys the nature of two of those dreams by imagining a conversation one might have overheard in the men's barracks:

FONG: I've been here a year this coming January sixth.

LUM: (*whistles*): I would rather kill myself than be stuck here that long!

LEE (*to himself*): I want to get Mei Lai a western style house with a toilet that flushes and a stove that turns fire on and off. I'll take our son up the highest hill on Gold Mountain and we'll fly the biggest dragon kite you ever saw to heaven!

LUM: When I get to the Big City, you know what I'll get? A wide-brimmed hat. The kind the rich white men wear. I'll walk down Chinese Street like some rich

Mandarin and all the ladies will turn their pretty heads and whisper, "Who is that handsome fella." "Why, don't you know? That's brother Lum, a big-shot—made a killing in Gold Mountain. Yessir, big brother Lum—even the white folks call him 'Mis-tah Lum!'"

FONG (*opens a newspaper*): Ask me, I think you're all dreaming! Hmph, you'll be lucky if you can wash a basket of dirty laundry and earn twenty-five cents!

Just as Fong punctures the dream bubbles of Lee and Lum, the limited economic opportunities open to the Chinese after they actually made it across the bay often deflated even the most modest aspirations for material success.

The character Lee in *Paper Angels* is presented as the author of one of the best-known poems carved on the wall: "There are tens of thousands of poems composed on these walls. / They are all cries of complaint and sadness. / The day I am rid of this prison and attain success, / I must remember that this chapter once existed." One day, Lee asks a former railroad worker who has been to "Gold Mountain," Chin Gung, to tell him what America is like. "Are the streets really paved with gold?" he asks.

CHIN GUNG (*laughs uproariously*): Paved with gold!

LEE (*hurt*): If I am disrespectful, I apologize.

CHIN GUNG (*wipes the tears of laughter from his eyes*): No, no, my son, I can't help laughing. For one moment, I thought I was looking into a mirror. Your smooth face, the fire in your eyes—yes, the fire. Look at these hands! I've shoveled enough tons of sand and turned enough pans of mud in my time. I've blasted through enough granite hills to know that this mountain is no mountain of gold. And I say all of you on this Island (*Gesturing*) will taste fool's gold. You know how I know? Because America is just (*Pointing to his head*) a faraway place in the mind—a piece of dream that scatters like gold dust in the wind.

LEE: Then why are you going back?

CHIN GUNG: Why? Because, my son,

Scene depicting the interrogation of a detainee at Angel Island in Genny Lim's play *Paper Angels*, from a performance at the New Federal Theatre, New York City, in 1982.

PHOTO CREDIT: PHOTO BY JAMES DONG.

as you will learn some day, once a Gold Mountain boy, always a Gold Mountain boy. One foot in America, one foot in China.

As the would-be immigrants weigh what they've gained and what they've lost by claiming "paper identities" in order to enter the country, their "real" identities turn out to be undergoing profound changes. Lee may not really be "Moy Fook Sing or whatever his name is," a name he has tried to memorize from his coaching book, but he has, in some ways, ceased to be "Lee," as well—at least the Lee who left China for America. In the way station of Angel Island, "China Men" trying to become "Americans" become something else—people with "one foot in America, one foot in China," divided souls not quite in and not quite out of either their native land or the land they seek to make their new home.

If the immigrant generation would prefer to forget the Angel Island chapter of their lives, for some of their children and grandchildren—such as American-born writers Fae Myenne Ng in her novel *Bone,* or Shawn Wong, in his novel *Homebase*—the Angel Island experience provides a bridge between the present and the past, between China and the United States, that inspires them as writers. Both Ng and Wong write Angel Island interrogation scenes in efforts to understand the meaning of their ancestors' move from China to this country. For Wong, the ghosts of Angel Island help connect him to a past he can touch only in imagination, as he conjures up images of what his grandfather might have encountered when he arrived there. "There is a movement about the place that gives off sound like sleeping gives off dreams, like a haunted house moves people to realize that life still exists within." Projecting himself into his grandfather's experience, the narrator writes:

I am my grandfather come back to America after having been raised in China. My father is dead so I've had to assume someone else's name and family in order to legally enter the country. All this information about my new family has been memorized. . . . If you ran your fingers across the walls at night in the dark, your fingers would be filled with the splinters of poems carved into the walls. Maybe there is a dim light to help see what your fingers feel. But you can only read, "Staying on this island, my sorrow increases with the days. / My face is growing sallow and body is getting thin," before your fingers give out following the grooves and gouges of the characters. Sometimes the morning will show you someone has hanged himself in the night, someone who could no longer bear the waiting, or the interrogation, or failing the interrogation—someone waiting to be sent back to China.

The narrator of *Homebase* draws strength from entering imaginatively into the world his grandfather would have encountered on Angel Island, a site of cultural memory, a place of voices and spirits, of pain and hope.

Segregated not only from Caucasians but also from women, even the married men on Angel Island inhabited a bachelor society during their detainment and for much of the rest of their lives as well, given the difficulties the law threw in the path of women who were would-be immigrants. A Chinese American writer and filmmaker named Tam in Frank Chin's play *The Chickencoop Chinaman*, for example, notes the irony of the long-standing image in America of "the strong Chinese family": "The reason there was no juvenile delinquency was because there was no kids! The laws didn't let our women in . . . and our women born here lost their citizenship if they married a man from China." As late as 1940, the ratio of Chinese men to women in the United States was nearly three to one. One can see glimpses of that first generation's bachelor society in Louis Chu's novel *Eat a Bowl of Tea*, in which the wives of the characters Wah Gay and Lee Gong are unable to join their husbands in America.

Like the Angel Island poet who encouraged himself by recalling figures in Chinese history who had been humiliated as he had, but who lived to take revenge, Maxine Hong Kingston in *The Woman Warrior* finds in the story of the legendary swordswoman Fa Mu Lan a tale of empowerment that helps her cut through some of the gendered norms that threaten to constrain her coming into her own as an adult and as a woman. The Chinese women at Angel Island wrote no poems, probably owing to their lack of education, as well as their lack of self-esteem—their sense that their views, and their words, didn't matter. Kingston's *Woman Warrior* gives voice to the voiceless women in China's past—like "no name aunt"—restoring to them forms of expression they could not craft themselves. Oakland-born writer Amy Tan also gives voice to the immigrant women who could not write their stories themselves: one of the four Chinese immigrant women in the Joy Luck mahjong club, Ying-Ying, began her life in America at Angel Island. In books like *The Joy Luck Club* and *The Kitchen God's Wife*, Tan conveys the strength, courage, and ingenuity that allowed that first generation of Chinese women in America to survive and raise their American daughters. Kingston and Tan draw these Chinese women out of their silence and let their voices speak to us.

Speaking is certainly the strong suit of the word-drunk, nonstop talker who is the protagonist of Kingston's novel *Tripmaster Monkey: His Fake Book*. His very name—Wittman Ah Sing—playfully links both America's most famous poet and his most famous poem with a familiar Chinese surname. In his obsession to cast all of his friends and relations in 1960s Berkeley in a wild, anarchic, and audaciously original performance of a classic Cantonese opera, based on *Journey to the West*,

Wittman gloriously bridges the old world and the new, and stakes out new possibilities of letting the Chinese past suffuse the American present with an ebullience and vitality neither the old world or the new could capture on its own.

Wittman invokes the memory of Angel Island interrogations in the uninhibited, caffeinated monologue that caps his theatrical extravaganza. "Unemployed and looking," he announces, "my task is to spook out prejudice. They'll say any kind of thing to the unemployed. In Angel tradition, let me pass on to you the trick question they're asking: 'What would you say your weak point is?' They ask in a terribly understanding manner, but you don't confide dick. You tell them you have no weak point. Zip. 'None that I can think of,' you say. 'Weak point?' you say, 'What do you mean weak point? I only have strong points.' They get you to inform on yourself, then write you up, 'Hates business,' 'Can't add,' 'Shy with customers.'"

Wittman is American through-and-through like his namesake, Walt Whitman. Yet he still keeps bumping up against prejudice that assumes that, given the way he looks, he must be a "foreigner." Whitman riffs in his closing monologue:

> The one that drives me craziest is "Do you speak English?" Particularly after I've been talking for hours, don't ask, "Do you speak English?" The voice doesn't go with the face, they don't hear it. On the phone I sound like anybody, I get the interview, but I get downtown, they see my face, they ask, "Do you speak English?" Watch, as I leave this stage tonight after my filibuster, somebody's going to ask me, "You speak the language?" In the tradition of stand-up comics—I'm a stand-up tragic—I want to pass on to you a true story that Wellington Koo told doctor Ng, who told it to me. Wellington Koo was at a state dinner in Washington, D.C. The leaders of the free world were meeting to figure out how to win World War II. Koo was talking to his dinner partners, the ladies on his left and right, when the diplomat across from him says, "Likee soupee?" Wellington nods, slubs his soup, gets up, and delivers the keynote address. The leaders of the free world and their wives give him a standing ovation. He says to the diplomat, "Likee speechee?" After a putdown like that, wouldn't you think Mr. and Mrs. Potato Head would stop saying, "You speakee English?"

Perhaps the poet Mitsuye Yamada expresses it best in her poem, "Mirror, Mirror":

> People keep asking me where I come from
> says my son.
> Trouble is   I'm american on the inside
>   and oriental on the outside

No Kai
Turn that outside in
THIS is what American looks like.

While their forebears carved poems of sadness and frustration on the walls of the immigration station at Angel Island, contemporary Asian American writers are carving a place for themselves on America's cultural landscape that is rich with humor, confidence, and élan—but informed, as well, by an awareness of struggles that embittered those who came before them and the challenges that may face those who come after.

MANZANAR NATIONAL HISTORIC SITE

In Yoshiko Uchida's novel *Picture Bride*, Hana Omiya starts her life in the United States on Angel Island—as did thousands of other "picture brides." But decades later, starting in 1942, after President Franklin D. Roosevelt signs Executive Order 9066 as a wartime security measure designed to prevent sabotage and espionage, Hana Omiya and her husband—along with some 120,000 other Americans of Japanese descent living in California, Washington, Oregon, and Alaska—are forced to move from their homes to an isolated, inaccessible, hastily constructed "relocation center."

Everyone of Japanese descent was a "potential enemy" according to Lt. Gen. John DeWitt, the man charged with carrying out Executive Order 9066. Despite the fact that these "potential enemies" (a group that included nearly seventy thousand American citizens) were accused of no crime, they were taken under military guard to seventeen temporary assembly centers, from which they were sent to ten barbed-wire-enclosed relocation camps in California, Arizona, Idaho, Utah, Colorado, Wyoming, and Arkansas, where they were forced to undergo severe deprivations and were stripped of their constitutional rights. They had only days (sometimes only one day) to leave their homes and businesses, and they were allowed to bring only what they could carry. Families had to part with heirlooms (some broke them rather than sell them for the insulting prices potential buyers offered for them). Many burned or buried personal letters from family in Japan, because, as Gary Okihiro notes, "Any connection, any link with Japan, any expression, any thoughts indicative of Japanese culture and ethnicity, invited others' suspicion."

Greg Robinson, in *A Tragedy of Democracy: Japanese Confinement in North America*, suggests that "confinement" rather than the more familiar term "internment" more accurately describes their condition, given that "'internment' properly refers to the detention of enemy nationals by a government during wartime," whereas the majority of "those of Japanese ancestry who were summarily uprooted, moved, and held by the United States government during World War II were American citizens. The fact that there is no commonly understood term to describe such an action with precision hints at how unprecedented the government's policy was." Unprecedented as the government's policy was, it was not unique in our hemisphere: Robinson sets the U.S. experience in the context of Canada's confinement of twenty-two thousand citizens and residents of Japanese descent from British Columbia, the expulsion of some five thousand Japanese from Mexico's Pacific coast, and the kidnapping and confinement of people of Japanese descent from Latin America during the war.

A Family of Japanese Ancestry [the Mochida family] *Waits to Be Transported to a War Relocation Center,* 1942.

PHOTO CREDIT: PHOTO BY DOROTHEA LANGE; COURTESY OF THE NATIONAL ARCHIVES, PHOTO NO. 210-G-C153.

About 70 percent of those sent to the camps in the United States were *nisei*, second-generation American citizens born in the United States, while about 30 percent were *issei*, first-generation born in Japan. The internees also included a number of *sansei*, third-generation Japanese Americans, including the writers Janice Mirikitani and Lawson Fusao Inada. The experience prompted many to reexamine their sense of personal and national identity. Four decades later, the government would apologize to Japanese Americans who had been confined in these camps, conceding that racial bias had more to do with the massive relocation effort than any real threat to national security. In 1988, the passage of the Civil Liberties Act provided for cash payments to each survivor. Eventually, each one would receive $20,000—along with an official apology.

Manzanar, located in an arid desert valley in California near the eastern base of Mount Whitney, was the first of these camps. It was in operation from March 1942 to November 1946. Some ten thousand people—nearly two-thirds of whom were American-born citizens—lived in rows of tarpaper-covered barracks made of cheap pine wood with virtually no privacy. As many as eight people might be housed in a room that was twenty feet by twenty-five feet. The barracks were furnished with rudimentary cots and an oil stove. A single hanging light bulb provided all the light.

Manzanar's five-hundred-acre housing area was originally surrounded by a barbed-wire fence and eight watchtowers. A row of fence posts at the western side of the former camp is all that is left of the original fence, and some concrete foundation posts are all that remains of the watchtowers. But other structures are intact, many of which show the prisoners' efforts to maintain their ethnic heritage to the extent they could. The internee-built sentry houses have a hint of Japanese architecture about them—as does the Judo house, the Japanese inscriptions on the cemetery monuments, and what remains of landscaped rock gardens and ponds. Archeological digs here have turned up fragments of saki bottles, Japanese bowls and teacups, and discarded "Goh" game pieces. Under extraordinarily adverse circumstances, the evacuees did their best to create a semblance of "normal" life for their families. Scores of baseball teams in multiple leagues competed fiercely before thousands of spectators. Basketball and volleyball were popular, as was golf, played in a nine-hole "golf course" made of oiled sand. There were art clubs, sewing clubs, and lessons in Japanese calligraphy. But temperatures in this desolate location reached 110 degrees in the summer and often plunged below freezing in the winter. Frequent dust storms added to the trials of housekeeping. Primitive living conditions and a humiliating lack of privacy were also unavoidable parts of the prisoners' new "normal" life.

Jeanne Wakatsuki, the youngest of ten children, was seven when her family arrived at Manzanar in February 1942. Some thirty years later, she would chronicle her experiences in a memoir for young adults that would become one of the best-known books about the camps, *Farewell to Manzanar*. A film version of *Farewell to Manzanar*, the first Hollywood movie with an all–Japanese American cast, was seen by more than twenty million Americans when it was released in 1976. Today, a commemorative marker reminds visitors of the significance of the place: "May the injustices and humiliation suffered here as a result of hysteria, racism, and economic exploitation never emerge again." Manzanar National Historic Site is a powerful reminder of how easily the constitutional rights of Americans may be abrogated in times of crisis.

In addition to tearing apart neighborhoods and communities and forcing Japanese Americans to lose homes and businesses, the internment experience disrupted young people's education and derailed many of their parents' careers. An even greater loss, however, may have been the sense of betrayal so many felt: they were proud to be American citizens—but would they ever fully enjoy the constitutional rights other citizens took for granted? When the army decided to establish a combat team of Japanese Americans, a number of men from Manzanar volunteered, and the all-*nisei* 442nd Regimental Combat Team fought its way to victory in Italy and France. All told, some thirty thousand Japanese Americans would earn the gratitude of the U.S. military for their service during the war, mainly in intelligence work—in segregated units. Only ten people in the United States were convicted of spying for Japan during the entire war. All of them were Caucasian.

The experience of being confined at Manzanar, Topaz, Minidoka, Poston, and other camps figures prominently in fiction, poetry, and drama by Jeanne Wakatsuki Houston, Lawson Fusao Inada, John Okada, Monica Sone, Yoshiko Uchida, Mitsuye Yamada, and Hisaye Yamamoto, all of whom were themselves internees. Poet Mitsuye Yamada's *Camp Notes and Other Poems* follows her evacuation as a teenager from her home in Seattle to Minidoka and beyond, exploring the context of racism and discrimination that informed so many dimensions of American life, as well as the challenges of living in the desert and the efforts of internees to create a semblance of normality. In "Desert Storm," for example, she recalls that no amount of newspapers and rags stuffed between the cracks in the walls could stop the Idaho dust from seeping through. In "Minidoka, Idaho," she describes swaggering in a pair of white majorette boots she had ordered from Montgomery Ward, ankle deep in dust, while the boys caught snakes in mayonnaise jars. In "Inside News," a small group of people huddle around a contraband radio. In "The Trick Was," she describes writing letters, while at Minidoka, to all 133 colleges listed in the back of her Webster's dictionary. All of them turned her down: "THEY were afraid of ME," she writes.

Also interned at Minidoka was Seattle-born Monica Sone, who describes the experience in her autobiography, *Nisei Daughter*. Before being taken to Minidoka, Sone's family was removed to the temporary detention camp set up at the Puyallup Fairgrounds in Puyallup, Washington, for several months. *Nisei Daughter* conveys the "quiet hysteria" that filled her family's first weeks there.

> We peered nervously at the guards in the high towers sitting behind Tommy guns and they silently looked down at us. We were all jittery. One rainy night the guards suddenly became aware of unusual activity in the camp. It was after "lights out" and rain was pouring down in sheets. They turned on the spotlights, but all they could see were doors flashing open and small dark figures rushing out into the shadows. It must have looked like a mass attempt to break out of camp.
>
> We ourselves were awakened by the noise. Henry whispered hoarsely, "What's going on out there anyway?"
>
> Then mother almost shrieked, "Chotto! Listen, airplanes, right up overhead, too."
>
> "I wonder if by accident, a few bombs are going to fall on our camp," Father said, slowly.

I felt a sickening chill race up and down my spine. The buzzing and dron-
ing continued louder and louder. . . . Suddenly the plane went away and the
commotion gradually died down.

Early the next morning when we rushed to the mess hall to get the news,
we learned that the camp had suffered from food poisoning. The commotion
had been sick people rushing to the latrines. The guards must have thought
they had an uprising on hand, and had ordered a plane out to investigate.

Henry said, "It was a good thing those soldiers weren't trigger-happy or it
could've been very tragic."

Hisaye Yamamoto, born in Redondo Beach, California, was interned for three
years in the relocation camp at Poston, Arizona, where she published her first fiction in the camp newspaper. Her artfully crafted story "The Legend of Miss Sasaga-
wara," in her collection *Seventeen Syllables and Other Stories*, explores, against the
backdrop of life in a relocation camp, questions about freedom and confinement,
sanity and insanity, and how we read and interpret the people around us.

The author of one of the most acclaimed novels about the internment experience (a book also viewed as the first Japanese American novel) was not an internee
himself. Seattle-born writer John Okada enlisted in the U.S. Army Air Forces during World War II, where he served as a Japanese translator and rose to the rank of
sergeant. But Ichiro, the main character in his celebrated novel *No-No Boy*, makes
a different choice. To questions 27 and 28 on Selective Service Form 304A, which
ask whether he would be willing to serve in the United States armed forces, and
whether he would forswear allegiance to the Japanese emperor, U.S.-born Ichiro,
whose government treats him like an enemy, and who never had any allegiance to
Japan in the first place and therefore could not have any to forswear, answers "NO."
The two "No's" lead to his being sent to prison for two years. When he is released,
his awareness of the ways in which the internment experience has shattered lives
leaves him confused and bitter. Okada based much of the book on the experience
of an acquaintance of his, Hajime "Jim" Akutsu, who was interned in the Minidoka
Relocation Camp.

Artist and writer Miné Okubo, who was born in Riverside, California, was evac-
uated to the Tanforan Racetrack for six months, and then Topaz, Utah. She vividly
captures those experiences in pictures and words in her pioneering graphic novel,
Citizen 13660. Published by Columbia University Press in 1946, it was the first book
published in the United States on the subject of the internment experience by a
Japanese American internee. Since cameras were not allowed in the camp, the visual
record of life there that Okubo gives in 206 detailed and compelling pen-and-ink

sketches in the book provide a unique window on the world in which she and so many others struggled to survive and remain whole.

Between the ages of four and seven, poet Lawson Fusao Inada, who was born in Fresno, was sent with his American-born parents and grandparents to an assembly center in Fresno, California, and to Jerome War Relocation Camp in Arkansas and later to Granada War Relocation Camp in Colorado. Inada has explored the meaning of

Drawing by Miné Okubo. View of the camp, Tanforan Assembly Center, San Bruno, California, 1942, in Okubo's pioneering graphic novel, *Citizen 13660*, the first book published in the United States on the subject of the internment experience by a Japanese American internee.

PHOTO CREDIT: COURTESY THE JAPANESE AMERICAN NATIONAL MUSEUM (GIFT OF MINÉ OKUBO ESTATE, 2007.62.49).

that chapter in American history in two noteworthy collections of poems, *Legends from Camp* (winner of an American Book Award) and *Drawing the Line*, as well as in an edited volume, *Only What We Could Carry: The Japanese Internment Experience*. In "Concentration Constellation" in *Legends from Camp*, he marks the location of each of the ten internment camps on a map of the United States and then connects the dots. The result is

> . . . a jagged scar,
> massive, on the massive landscape.
> It lies there like a rusted wire
> of a twisted and remembered fence.

In luminous poetry, compelling fiction, and poignant memoirs, Japanese Americans have helped their fellow Americans come to terms with that shameful "jagged scar" on the landscape.

THE COST OF HATRED AND FEAR

AN EXCERPT FROM YOSHIKO UCHIDA'S *PICTURE BRIDE*

Yoshiko Uchida, a native Californian, was relocated with her family first to a horse stall at Tanforan Racetrack and then to the barracks of Topaz War Relocation Center. Although she may be best known for her novels for young adults that focus on the internment experience, such as *Journey to Topaz* and *Journey Home*, it is in her less-known novel *Picture Bride* that Uchida indelibly brings to life what she has called the "hatred and fear of the enemy . . . increasingly focused on the Japanese American presence along the West Coast" after Executive Order 9066. In this excerpt from *Picture Bride*, Henry Toda, a Japanese American farmer, sits down in his farmhouse kitchen in Livingston, California, rereads a letter from a friend interned in a relocation camp, thoughtfully puts together a "care package" of food for his friend, and makes himself a midnight snack—never dreaming that these ordinary acts might be his last:

It was long past midnight. Kiku and the boys had gone to bed, but Henry Toda was in no mood to sleep. . . . Henry paced about the room, finally sitting down to read again the letter from his friend, Sojiro Kaneda, interned in Montana.

"It is ten below zero here," he wrote, "and from the window I can see thick icicles reaching from the barrack roof to the ground. Until they issued us some army winter clothing, we feared we would all perish from pneumonia. One eighty-three-year old man has already died, and another has gone insane. There are over . . . men here from . . ." The censor had neatly clipped out names and numbers that he did not want revealed. Exasperated, Henry tossed the letter aside.

He sat in the stillness of the country night, remembering how he and Sojiro Kaneda had come to America in a ship so small, they feared it would founder in the Pacific, sending them to a watery grave. Until Kaneda earned enough to continue at medical school, they had worked together picking fruit in the orchards of the Sacramento Valley or washing dishes in greasy cafes. Henry knew that the only reason Kaneda was locked up in that frigid prisoner of war camp and he was still free in Livingston was because Kaneda liked to join organizations; because he wanted to help the Japanese farmers and teach the young Nisei the language of their parents; because he could not but help be a leader of men.

Engulfed for a moment in the pleasant network of the past, Henry longed to do something for his old friend. Deciding that a package of food might bring Kaneda some cheer, he went to the kitchen and took from the shelves a pound of coffee, three cans of condensed milk, a package of peanut brittle, some canned peaches and some tins of sardines in tomato sauce.

"That ought to give you a nice snack, old friend," he said, packing everything into a carton he found under the sink. Just before he wrapped it up, he put in some old Japanese magazines and two packages of cigarettes. He addressed the package, set it on the table to mail the next morning and felt better than he had all day.

The activity not only pleased him, it gave him an appetite as well, and he brewed a pot of coffee to go with the last piece of chocolate cake in the bread box. . . .

Henry put down his cup. Was that a footstep on the gravel walk outside? He listened quietly, but heard only the ticking of the clock. Who could be wandering around their house at two o'clock in the morning? He turned out the living room light and looked out into the frosty darkness. The night was quiet and there was no moon. Old Rick was dead, but somewhere on another farm, a dog was howling into the night. Henry felt a chill go down his back as he listened. This time he was sure of it, there was someone prowling about his yard. Henry found a flashlight, opened the door quietly and stepped outside. As he did, a dark figure darted into the shadow of the walnut tree.

"Who is it? Who's there?"

The man did not answer.

"What do you want?"

Henry's flashlight caught the shape of a man whose face was shadowed by a wide-brimmed hat. He held a gun in his hand.

"What do you want?" Henry demanded again.

"Filthy stinking Jap!" the man shouted in a quivering voice.

"Put down your gun. You're drunk." Henry waited, watching for a chance to disarm the man. "Put down your gun. You don't know what you're doing."

Henry took a slight step forward, and in that instant a shot rang out. The man uttered a cry of rage and desperation and ran off into the night.

Henry Toda slumped to the ground, as blood rushed from the bullet hole in his chest. . . .

RELATED SITES

⚭ Minidoka War National Historic Site
Between Twin Falls and Jerome, Idaho

This relocation center operated from August 1942 until October 1945. Although few of the original structures remain, a six-acre portion of the relocation center is listed on the National Register of Historic Places. This area includes the walls of the former guardhouse and waiting room, and historical markers, interpretive signs, and maps. Minidoka is central to two books of poems by Mitsuye Yamada, *Camp Notes and Other Poems* and *Desert Run* (both of which were reissued together in Yamada's *Camp Notes and Other Writings*). It is also central to Monica Sone's autobiography, *Nisei Daughter* and to John Okada's novel *No-No Boy*.

⚭ Topaz War Relocation Center/Central Utah Relocation Center
Near Delta, Utah (140 miles southwest of Salt Lake City)

Topaz operated from September 1942 to October 1945. None of the original World War II buildings remain, but portions of the perimeter security fence may be seen, as well as foundations of the watchtowers and some other structures. There is a monument with interpretive materials and photographs. Additional photographs and artifacts from Topaz are on display in the Great Basin Museum in Delta. A commemorative marker notes that the eight thousand Americans of Japanese ancestry "who for no justifiable reason, were uprooted from their homes and interned" here by "their own government" were "the victims of wartime hysteria, racial animosity, and a serious aberration of American jurisprudence." Although the physical remains of Topaz are scant, one can find a detailed record of what life was like there in Miné Okubo's moving graphic novel, *Citizen 13660*, and in the stories Yoshiko Uchida tells in her books *Journey to Topaz*, *Journey Home*, and *Desert Exile*.

⚭ Tule Lake War Relocation Center/Tule Lake Segregation Center
Newell, California

Although it began as a relocation center, operated from May 1942 to March 1946, in 1943 the Tule Lake site was converted into a maximum-security facility for individuals from all of the other relocation centers who had been designated as "disloyal" by the War Relocation Authority. Much of the original barbed-wire fence that surrounded the camp still remains, as do large portions of many of the original structures, including a stockade jail and buildings that housed the military police. On the walls of the jail one can see graffiti written by evacuees who were imprisoned there. One of the internees at Tule Lake was the poet Violet Kazue de Cristoforo, who shaped the melancholy and heartache of the camp experience into free-form haiku or kaiko, written on any scraps of paper she could find. She published them years later in books including *Poetic Reflections of the Tule Lake Internment Camp, 1944*. She also collected works by fellow internees in a volume she edited, *May Sky: There Is Always Tomorrow; An Anthology of Japanese American Concentration Camp Kaiko Haiku*. The Tule Lake Relocation Center has been designated a National Historic Landmark.

❖ Jerome War Relocation Center
Near McGehee, Arkansas (120 miles southeast of Little Rock)

Jerome was in operation from July 1942 through June 1944. It was one of the camps in which Lawson Fusao Inada was interned.

❖ Heart Mountain War Relocation Center
1539 Wyoming Route 19, Powell, Wyoming

This relocation center was in operation from August 1942 until November 1945. The thirty-acre portion of the original Relocation Center that is on the National Register of Historic Places includes portions of what was the administration hospital complex, a warehouse, and a high school, most of which is now on private land. Estelle Ishigo, a Caucasian artist and writer who married an American-born actor of Japanese descent, described and illustrated her years at Heart Mountain in her book, *Lone Heart Mountain*.

❖ Granada Relocation War Center
Southeastern Colorado, near the Kansas border (140 miles east of Pueblo)

This Relocation Center was in operation from August 1942 until October 1945. The major buildings are gone, but the roads and the foundations of many buildings remain intact. This relocation center, which was the third-largest city in Colorado during World War II, is a National Historic Landmark. Lawson Fusao Inada was interned here as a child.

✦ Poston War Relocation Center
Near Parker, Arizona

Poston operated from May 1942 through November 1945. Little remains of the three linked camps that made up the Poston Relocation Center, whose population, at its peak, reached seventeen thousand. One of the Japanese Americans interned at Poston was Hisaye Yamamoto, whose acclaimed fiction engages some of the most troubling issues surrounding this dark chapter in America's past. Japanese American playwright Wakako Yamauchi, who was also interned here, portrays the challenges of life here in her play, *12–1-A*, whose title is the address in the Poston camp where her protagonists, members of the Tanaka family, live.

✦ Rohwer War Relocation Center
Arkansas Route 1, Desha County, Arkansas (110 miles southeast of Little Rock)

Built during late summer and early fall of 1942 in response to Executive Order 9066, this camp was the temporary home of more than ten thousand evacuees of Japanese descent, more than two-thirds of whom were American citizens. The monuments in the camp's cemetery provide a poignant record of this period. Poet Janice Mirikitani, a *sansei*, or third-generation Japanese American, who was born in Stockton, California, was interned here during the war.

✦ Gila River War Relocation Center
Indian Route 24, Sacaton, Arizona

The camp, which operated between July 1942 and September 1945, at one point included more than one thousand buildings. The huge agricultural and livestock operation that developed here on thousands of acres that the War Relocation Authority leased from the Bureau of Indian Affairs produced 20 percent of the food used at all of the other relocation camps across the country. One of the internees here was the writer Michiko Nishiura Weglyn, who was born in Stockton, California, would later write *Years of Infamy: The Untold Story of America's Concentration Camps*, an award-winning a book that helped fuel the movement for reparations.

FOR FURTHER READING

The Writers: Works and Words

Chin, Frank, Jeffery Paul Chan, Lawson Fusao Inada, and Shawn Wong, eds. *Aiiieeeee! An Anthology of Asian American Writers*. 1974. New York: Plume Contemporary Fiction/Penguin Books, 1991.

Chu, Louis. *Eat a Bowl of Tea*. 1961. New York: Lyle Stuart, 2002.

de Cristoforo, Violet Kazue. *Poetic Reflections of the Tule Lake Internment Camp, 1944*. Santa Clara, CA: Communicart, 1987.

———, ed. *May Sky: There Is Always Tomorrow; An Anthology of Japanese American Concentration Camp Kaiko Haiku*. Los Angeles: Sun and Moon Press, 1997.

Fishkin, Shelley Fisher. "Interview with Maxine Hong Kingston." *American Literary History* 3, no. 4 (Winter 1991): 782–791.

Houston, Jeanne Wakatsuki, and James D. Houston. *Farewell to Manzanar*. Boston: Houghton Mifflin, 1973.

Inada, Lawson Fusao. *Legends from Camp: Poems by Lawson Fusao Inada* Minneapolis: Coffee House Press, 1992.

———, ed. *Only What We Could Carry: The Japanese American Internment Experience*. Berkeley, CA: Heydey Books; San Francisco: California Historical Society, 2000.

Ishigo, Estelle. *Lone Heart Mountain*. Los Angeles: Anderson, Ritchie and Simon, 1972.

Kingston, Maxine Hong. *China Men*. New York: Alfred A. Knopf, 1980.

———. *Tripmaster Monkey: His Fake Book*. New York: Alfred A. Knopf, 1989.

———. *The Woman Warrior: Memoir of a Girlhood among Ghosts*. New York: Alfred A. Knopf, 1976.

Lai, Him Mark, Genny Lim, and Judy Yung, eds. *Island: Poetry and History of Chinese Immigrants on Angel Island, 1910–1940*. [1980]. Seattle: University of Washington Press, 1991.

Lim, Genny. "Paper Angels" and "Bitter Cane": Two Plays. Honolulu: Kalamaku Press, 1991.

Lim, Shirley Geok-lin, Mayumi Tsutakawa, and Margarita Donnelly, eds. *The Forbidden Stitch: An Asian American Women's Anthology*. Corvallis, OR: Calyx Books, 1989.

Mirikitani, Janice. *Love Works*. San Francisco Poet Laureate Series. San Francisco: City Lights Foundation Books, 2003.

———. *Shedding Silence*. Berkeley, CA: Celestial Arts / Ten Speed Press, 1994.

———. *We, the Dangerous: New and Selected Poems*. Berkeley, CA: Ten Speed Press, 1995.

Ng, Fae Myenne. *Bone*. New York: Hyperion, 1993.

Okada, John. *No-No Boy*. 1957. Seattle: University of Washington Press, 1979.

Okubo, Miné. *Citizen 13660*. 1946. New York: Columbia University Press, 1983.

———. *Miné Okubo: Following Her Own Road*. Edited by Greg Robinson and Elena Tajima Creef. Seattle: University of Washington Press, 2008.

Sone, Monica. *Nisei Daughter*. Boston: Little, Brown, 1953.

Tan, Amy. *The Joy Luck Club*. New York: Putnam's, 1989.

———. *The Kitchen God's Wife*. New York: Putnam's, 1991.

Uchida, Yoshiko. *Desert Exile: The Uprooting of a Japanese American Family*. Seattle: University of Washington Press, 1982.

———. *Journey Home*. New York: Atheneum, 1978.

———. *Journey to Topaz*. Berkeley, CA: Creative Arts, 1985.

———. *Picture Bride*. Flagstaff, AZ: Northland Press, 1987.

Weglyn, Michi Nishiura. *Years of Infamy: The Untold Story of America's Concentration Camps*. New York: Morrow, 1976.

Wong, Shawn. *Homebase*. New York: Penguin Books, 1991.

Yamada, Mitsuye. *Camp Notes and Other Poems*. 1976. Latham, NY: Kitchen Table / Women of Color Press, 1992.

———. *Camp Notes and Other Writings*. New Brunswick, NJ: Rutgers University Press, 1998.

———. *Desert Run*. Latham, NY: Kitchen Table / Women of Color Press, 1988.

Yamamoto, Hisaye. *Seventeen Syllables and Other Stories*. Introduction by King-Kok Cheung. San Francisco: Women of Color Press, 1988.

Yamauchi, Wakako. *12-1-A*. In *West Coast Plays*. Los Angeles: California Theatre Council, 1982.

Background and Contexts

Cheung, King-Kok. *Articulate Silences: Hisaye Yamamoto, Maxine Hong Kingston, Joy Kogawa*. Ithaca, NY: Cornell University Press, 1993.

———, ed. *An Interethnic Companion to Asian American Literature*. Cambridge: Cambridge University Press, 1997.

Cheung, King-Kok, and Stan Yogi. *Asian American Literature: An Annotated Bibliography*. New York: Modern Language Association, 1988.

Creef, Elena Tajima. *Imaging Japanese America: The Visual Construction of Citizenship, Nation, and the Body*. New York: New York University Press, 2004.

Daniels, Roger. *Asian America: Chinese and Japanese in the United States since 1850*. Seattle: University of Washington Press, 1988.

Dempster, Brian Komei, ed. *From Our Side of the Fence: Growing Up in America's Concentration Camps*. San Francisco: Japanese Cultural and Community Center of Northern California/ Kearny Street Workshop, 2001.

Dubel, Janice L. "Remembering a Japanese-American Concentration Camp at Manzanar National Historic Site." In *Myth, Memory, and the Making of the American Landscape*, edited by Paul A. Shackel, 85–102. Gainesville: University Press of Florida, 2001.

Dupré, Judith. *Monuments: America's History in Art and Memory*. New York: Random House, 2007.

Foote, Kenneth E. *Shadowed Ground: America's Landscapes of Violence and Tragedy*. Austin: University of Texas Press, 1997.

Gordon, Linda, and Gary Okihiro, eds. *Impounded: Dorothea Lange and the Censored Images of Japanese American Internment*. New York: W. W. Norton, 2008.

Huang, Yunte. *Transpacific Imaginations: History, Literature, Counterpoetics*. Cambridge, MA: Harvard University Press, 2008.

Lee, Erika, and Judy Yung. *Angel Island: Immigrant Gateway to America*. New York: Oxford University Press, 2012.

Lim, Shirley Geok-lin, and Amy Ling, eds. *Reading the Literatures of Asian America*. Philadelphia: Temple University Press, 1992.

Lindquist, Heather C. *Children of Manzanar*. Berkeley, CA: Heyday Books, 2012.

Ling, Amy. *Between Worlds: Women Writers of Chinese Ancestry*. New York: Pergamon Press, 1990.

McClain, Charles J. *In Search of Equality: The Chinese Struggle against Discrimination in Nineteenth-Century America*. Berkeley: University of California Press, 1994.

Okihiro, Gary Y. *Whispered Silences: Japanese Americans and World War II*. Seattle: University of Washington Press, 1996.

Robinson, Greg. *By Order of the President: FDR and the Internment of Japanese Americans*. Cambridge, MA: Harvard University Press, 2001.

————. *A Tragedy of Democracy: Japanese Confinement in North America*. New York: Columbia University Press, 2010.

Robinson, Greg, and Elena Tajima Creef, eds. *Miné Okubo: Following Her Own Road*. Seattle: University of Washington Press, 2008.

Takaki, Ronald. *Strangers from a Different Shore: A History of Asian Americans*. Boston: Little Brown, 1989.

Tateishi, John, ed. *And Justice for All: An Oral History of the Japanese American Detention Camps*. New York: Random House, 1984.

Wong, Sau-ling Cynthia, and Stephen H. Sumida, eds. *A Resource Guide to Asian American Literature*. New York: Modern Language Association of America, 2001.

Yin, Xiao-huang. *Chinese American Literature since the 1850s*. Urbana: University of Illinois Press, 2000.

Yu, Connie Young. "Saving Our Legacy of Angel Island." February 12, 2010. Angel Island Immigration Foundation website. http://aiisf.org/about/articles/262-saving-our-legacy-of-angel-island.

Yung, Judy, Gordon H. Chang, and Him Mark Lai, eds. *Chinese American Voices from the Gold Rush to the Present*. Berkeley: University of California Press, 2006.

Reading room at the 135th Street Branch of the New York Public Library.

11

Harlem and the Flowering
of African American Letters

THE 135TH STREET BRANCH OF
THE NEW YORK PUBLIC LIBRARY

THE SCHOMBURG CENTER FOR
RESEARCH ON BLACK CULTURE
103 WEST 135TH STREET, NEW YORK CITY

On May 19, 1926, more than a hundred packing crates were delivered to the central building of the New York Public Library to be prepared for shipment to their final destination: the 135th Street branch of the library, where thousands of books, manuscripts, etchings, portraits, and pamphlets would be made available to the public the following January. That summer the man who had assembled the contents of those cartons—Arthur Alfonso Schomburg—toured Europe and came back with 185 additional books he had acquired during this trip, which he donated to the library on his return. As Elinor Des Verney Sinnette notes in her biography of Schomburg, the extraordinary collection was an overwhelming rejoinder to the assertion, made by Schomburg's fifth-grade teacher in Puerto Rico: "Black people have no history, no heroes, no great moments."

In the literary club to which Schomburg belonged as schoolboy in Puerto Rico, history was a favorite topic, and his white classmates took pride in recounting the heroic deeds of their forebears and discussing the books that documented those deeds. But what had people of African descent like himself ever written or done or achieved? Here young Arturo encountered a vast blankness that troubled him. Was his teacher right? Did black people have no past? Convinced that his teacher must be wrong, he embarked on a lifelong mission to gather materials that documented black history and black achievement in the arts and letters.

Schomburg came to New York in 1891 at age seventeen after a childhood in

Puerto Rico and the Virgin Islands. The following year, there were a record number of racially motivated lynchings in the United States, and a few years later, a bloody race riot took place less than two miles from his home. His growing awareness of the impact racism had on African Americans only increased his sense of urgency about filling in the gaps in the historical record. Library shelves at the time bulged with pseudoscientific treatises on the alleged inferiority of blacks. Schomburg was so infuriated by one such book, *Retrospection*, by white American historian Hubert Howe Bancroft, that, as Sinnette tells us, he typed out "onto two foolscap sheets" sections that "he found particularly objectionable." These included the comment, "The [Negro] is too incompetent and unreliable . . . as a citizen . . . he is an unmitigated nuisance and judging from the past he will remain so." Schomburg was mainly accurate in his transcription. When the words that Schomburg (or Sinnette) omitted with ellipses (and those that precede these sentences) are restored, Bancroft's comments are even more offensive: "Further, we do not need the negro for any purpose, and never shall. We did not need The Indian and so eliminated him. We cannot so dispose of the negro. He is too incompetent and unreliable for any use. As a citizen of the commonwealth, he is an unmitigated nuisance, and judging from the past he will so remain." Sinnette tells us, "On the second typewritten page, Schomburg copied more of Bancroft's invective: 'However learned he may become, however lofty his ideals or how high his aspirations, he must wear the badge of ignorance and servitude, he and his children forever. God hath made him so. . . . The freed African in America is a failure. . . . We do not need the Negro for any purpose and never shall.'"

Once again, what Schomburg (or Sinnette) skipped in the ellipses is particularly insulting. One of Bancroft's sentences omitted by the first ellipsis in the above passage is: "It was a cruel kindness to enslave him; it was cruelty pure and simple to enfranchise him." One of the many sentences omitted by the second ellipsis is: "As an American citizen he is a monstrosity." The full remark Bancroft made (that Schomburg quotes in part) is this: "Were it not better frankly to admit that the freed African in America is a failure, and that when made free he should have been sent away?" Bancroft may have been the child of two ardent abolitionists, but that did not mean that he entertained progressive ideas about the possibility of a multiracial society in America. On the contrary, like a number of prominent abolitionists of his parents' generation (including Harriet Beecher Stowe), he believed that there was ultimately no place for black people in America.

Sinnette notes that at the bottom of the page on which he copied the second extract Schomburg expressed his outrage at what he called Bancroft's "dastardly crime against the Negro race." That outrage helped make him more determined than ever to spend each lunch hour and weekend combing through dusty bins and shelves in New York's secondhand book stores, storage warehouses, and auction galleries unearthing books and pamphlets that told a very different story.

University-trained contemporaries such as W.E.B. Du Bois and Carter G. Woodson (both members, with Schomburg, of the American Negro Academy founded by Alexander Crummell in 1897) may have been more sophisticated at analyzing and interpreting the kinds of materials Schomburg was collecting than the self-taught Schomburg was. But no one was more indefatigable than Schomburg when it came to tracking those materials down. His visceral response to racist propaganda like the passages he encountered in Bancroft's work fueled his resolve to locate things that would help set record straight. Sinnette records some of the ways in which his contemporaries characterized his sense of determination and his mysterious gift: Claude McKay averred that he "possessed a bloodhound's nose" that led him to be able to "delve deep and bring up nuggets" which previously "had baffled discovery." Meanwhile, Arthur Spingarn recalled having seen "him approach an immense pile of apparently worthless material and unerringly find in its huge mass one or two treasures which would have been lost to a less inspired collector; how he found them I never could discover unless he smelled them out."

Arthur Alfonso Schomburg (1874–1938), whose indefatigable efforts to recover a black literary past resulted in the collection at the core of the library that now bears his name.

Schomburg was not a wealthy man. After working as printer, porter, elevator operator, and bellhop when he first came to New York, he found a job as a clerk-messenger in a law firm, and later a bank. But while his budget may have been small, his vision was large: black people *had* a past, and he meant to document it as fully as he possibly could. With money that he managed to set aside from the modest salary he earned typing and delivering law briefs and bank correspondence, he managed to acquire one of the world's most impressive collections of materials on black history and letters. By the time his collection (most of it having been purchased for the library by the Carnegie Foundation), arrived at the 135th Street branch, the New York Public Library had already become a center of African American literary activity. The three-story, Neoclassical, limestone building, designed by the distinguished architectural firm of McKim, Mead and White, had been built by the city of New York in what was then a predominantly Jewish neighborhood in 1905. But by 1920, the twenty-block part of central Harlem was half-black, its black population having doubled since the library was built. By 1924, as a result of the migrations of the preceding decade—from the Caribbean and Africa, as well as the American South—Harlem had become (as James Weldon Johnson put it) "the greatest Negro city in the world."

Rudolph Fisher's 1925 story "City of Refuge" gave the predominantly white readers of the *Atlantic Monthly* a glimpse of the magnetic pull Harlem exerted over African Americans by viewing it through the eyes of a recent arrival from the South:

> Ever since a traveling preacher had first told him of the place, King Solomon Gillis had longed to come to Harlem. The Uggams were always talking about it; one of their boys had gone to France in the draft and, returning, had never got any nearer home than Harlem. And there were occasional "colored" newspapers from New York: newspapers that mentioned Negroes without comment, but always spoke of a white person as "So-and-so, white." That was the point. In Harlem, black was white. You had rights that could not be denied you; you had privileges, protected by law. And you had money. Everybody in Harlem had money. It was a land of plenty. Why, had not Mouse Uggam sent back as much as fifty dollars at a time to his people in Waxhaw?

Harlem, as Rafia Zafar notes, was "a literal space of resistance to a dominant and dominating white America," a place that "figured as well as psychological and political fortress."

Langston Hughes recalled in "My Early Days in Harlem" in 1963, "I was in love with Harlem long before I got there, and I am still in love with it." This multicultural, international community abuzz with a sense of promise and possibility was home to dynamic jazz, blues, and dance clubs, to the headquarters of key African American organizations, and to the publishing offices of the some of the nation's leading black newspapers and periodicals, including the *New York Age*; the NAACP's journal *Crisis*; the National Urban League's *Opportunity*; the *Messenger*, the trade unionist journal with socialist sympathies; and the black nationalist *Negro World*.

The 135th Street Library was a central gathering place for the "New Negro," as Alain Locke and others came to dub the young men and women charting new ways of being black and American who came of age in Harlem in the 1920s. "The New Negro" had fought for democracy abroad during World War I only to come home to a country in which he was treated as second-class citizen, disenfranchised, disrespected, and victimized by discrimination and lynch law. Emboldened by having served his country with bravery and distinction, the "New Negro" refused to be dismissed, ignored, intimidated, or confined in the demeaning stereotypes of the past. The black soldiers who paraded up Lenox Avenue to a jazz step when they returned from the war helped set the tone. As the editor of the *Crisis* put it in 1919, "We return from fighting. We return fighting. Make way for Democracy! We saved it in France, and by the Great Jehovah, we will save it in the U.S.A., or know the reason why." But the fight could be grimly demoralizing: in 1919 alone, ten black veterans were lynched, several while wearing their uniforms. "In such a violent climate," Zafar notes, "many blacks came to believe that cultural achievement, manifested by race-proud publications, could serve as an alternate route to social and political progress."

Harlem was a site where many of the "race-proud" publications of the decade were produced—texts that were unafraid to address the problem of racism head-on, unafraid to express pride in being black, and unafraid to explore boldly experimental aesthetics. Much of this heady new self-confidence got channeled into the cultivation of a lush landscape of poetry, fiction, drama, music, and art. Decades later, the body of work produced by African Americans in the 1920s came to be known as products of the "Harlem Renaissance." Black communities in Chicago and Washington, DC, were sites of creative energy and achievement as well, during this period. Nonetheless, Harlem would come to symbolize the efflorescence of the arts among African Americans in the 1920s. As Steve Watson observes, "The Harlem Renaissance participants did not promote a consistent aesthetic or write in a recognizably 'Renaissance' style. Their work ranged from the most conservatively crafted sonnet to modernist verse to jazz aesthetics to documentary folklore. Their agenda was contradictory and dualistic: their mission was both race propaganda and 'pure' art; they incorporated the high culture of literature with the low culture of cabaret and the blues; they forged identities as 'writers' and as 'Negro writers.'"

But by whatever forms they chose to express themselves, Watson tells us, "defining their selfhood—psychological, racial and aesthetic—proved pivotal" to the key Harlem writers and artists of this era. The collection of research materials Schomburg had gathered patiently over many years—materials housed in the building in which much of this ferment centered—affirmed the notion that whatever was being born in Harlem in the 1920s had roots that were much deeper and richer than Hubert Howe Bancroft could ever have imaged. The 135th Street branch of the library inspired, nurtured, and celebrated some of the most accomplished poets and fiction writers of this era, providing a place where they could meet each other, read, write, offer one another encouragement and support, and try out their work in front of an audience.

It was Langston Hughes's first stop after finding a fourth-floor room for seven dollars a week at the Y.M.C.A., down the street. "On a bright September morning in 1921," he recalled in "My Early Days in Harlem."

> I came up out of the subway at 135th and Lenox into the beginnings of the Negro Renaissance. I headed for the Harlem Y.M.C.A. down the block, where so many new, young, dark, male arrivals in Harlem have spent early days. The next place I headed to that afternoon was the Harlem Branch Library just up the street. There a warm and wonderful librarian, Miss Ernestine Rose, white, made newcomers feel welcome, as did her assistant in charge of the Schomburg collection, Catherine Latimer, a luscious café au lait.

Before she was put in charge in 1920, Ernestine Rose, from Bridgehampton, Long Island, had worked in several different library branches across the city. In a largely Chinese neighborhood on the Lower East Side, Rose had added books to the library's collection in Chinese, as well as English. Ann Sandford notes that she was one of the first public librarians in the country to promote the idea that a library should "serve as the vehicle for implementing what we today would call a multicultural vision." When she worked in a branch in New York's Czech and Slovak immigrant community, as George Hutchinson tells us, she collected publications in these immigrants' mother tongues as well as English, held exhibits of work by local artists, and made the library a place of refuge "for those who needed help negotiating the bewildering rules of an alien society"—particularly people who, "because of past experience, associated state and civic institutions with repressive force." As librarian in a branch in a neighborhood of mainly Russian Jewish immigrants, Hutchinson notes, Rose and her fellow gentile assistants learned to become familiar with Jewish holidays and customs, "studied Yiddish and Russian literature under Jewish colleagues and visitors," and organized lectures and book discussions of particular interest to the community. (Hutchinson observes that "All of this 'sensitivity training'" as we might call it today, "screened out assistants harboring ethnic or religious prejudices and targeted behavior that might inadvertently have aroused resentment or distrust.") During World War I, working with the Library War Service of the American Library Association, Rose distributed books to African American soldiers in Paris and Germany. Her experience with a range of immigrant communities, her work with blacks during and after the war, and her track record when it came to making libraries dynamic cultural spaces integral to the neighborhoods that surrounded them made her an ideal choice as head librarian of the 135th Street branch. As she put it in an article she wrote in *Library Journal* the year after she was hired, she saw her mandate there as serving New York's "black city." To this end, she surrounded herself with a superb, integrated staff and offered a model of how an interracial group of dedicated librarians could help the library play a vital role in the community. The same year that Rose signed on as chief librarian, Catherine Latimer joined the staff, the first African American librarian to be hired by the New York Public Library. Others soon followed, including Regina Anderson, who set aside a small work area in the library for writers (a group that would include Langston Hughes, Eric Walrond, and Claude McKay), and Countee Cullen's cousin Roberta Bosely, who took charge of services for children.

The 135th Street Branch of the New York Public Library, which would become the Schomburg Center for Research on Black Culture. The 1905 building was designed by the famous architectural firm of McKim, Mead, and White.
PHOTO CREDIT: COURTESY OF THE PHOTOGRAPHS AND PRINTS DIVISION, SCHOMBURG CENTER FOR RESEARCH IN BLACK CULTURE, NEW YORK PUBLIC LIBRARY, ASTOR, LENOX, AND TILDEN FOUNDATIONS.

At the 135th Street branch, as she had in the other branches where she had worked, Ernestine Rose endeavored to make the library a hub of cultural vitality for the surrounding community. She decided to put an art exhibit on the agenda in 1921. This exhibit, which ran from August to September, and included work by Henry Ossawa Tanner, Meta Fuller, and Laura Wheeler Waring, would mark, as George Hutchinson notes, "the beginning of the Harlem Renaissance in the visual arts." A young volunteer who, with other members of the community, worked nights and weekends to organize the exhibit with Rose, had been working as a public health nurse. Her name was

Langston Hughes (1902–1967). "I was in love with Harlem long before I got there, and I am still in love with it," Hughes wrote in 1963. The 135th Street Library was an important part of what made Harlem so special for him. Hughes met a number of fellow poets there and sometimes wrote in a small work area that was set aside for writers.

PHOTO CREDIT: PHOTO BY CARL VAN VECHTEN; COURTESY OF THE LIBRARY OF CONGRESS, PRINTS AND PHOTOGRAPHS DIVISION, WASHINGTON, DC.

Nella Larsen (then Nella Larsen Imes). Rose, impressed by her intelligence, articulateness, charm, and diplomacy (as Hutchinson notes), soon began encouraging her to consider going to library school: "Larsen was the first black woman ever to graduate from library school, hand picked by Rose to break the barrier." Surrounded by books all day, paid to read them and talk about them and think about them, Larsen found herself propelled toward a career as a writer herself. When her first novel, *Quicksand*, appeared in 1928, W.E.B. Du Bois called it "the best piece of fiction that Negro America has produced" in several decades. A second novel, *Passing*, was published the following year. Both novels explored the complex challenges black women faced as they tried to carve out a place for themselves in modern America.

Jessie Fauset was already literary editor of the *Crisis*, the journal of the National Association for the Advancement of Colored People (NAACP) (a position she held from 1919 to 1926), when she began volunteering at the library. In addition to encouraging writers including Nella Larsen, Claude McKay, and Langston Hughes, she was a prolific novelist herself, publishing four novels between 1924 and 1933 (*There Is Confusion*, *Plum Bun*, *The Chinaberry Tree*, and *Comedy, American Style*). A central theme in fiction by both Larsen and Fauset was the ways in which race is socially constructed rather than biologically determined. The exceptional staff of evening volunteers who assisted Rose at the library also included Gwendolyn Bennett, another young woman who would leave her mark on American letters as a poet and fiction writer.

The readings and lectures organized at the library brought writers from diverse backgrounds together. Langston Hughes met Countee Cullen there in 1922 when both were twenty years old. Cullen, the adopted son of a Harlem pastor, had won a citywide poetry competition sponsored by the white Federation of Women's Clubs for the best poem by a high school student. Hughes, who had published well-received poems in his high school literary magazine in Cleveland, had written his first poem shaped by jazz rhythms, "When Sue Wears Red" while still in high school, and a month after graduation, had written what would be later considered one of his greatest poems, "The Negro Speaks of Rivers," which the *Crisis* published in 1921. Cullen and Hughes admired each other and became friends, sharing each other's work and occasionally dedicating poems to one another. Hughes was at work as a seaman on a ship docked at Jones Point, New York, when Ernestine Rose organized a poetry reading at the library at which Cullen was to be featured. Cullen offered to perform some of Hughes's poems for him. As Arnold Rampersad notes, Hughes took him up on it, sending along "Syllabic Poem," a poem with no words in it that poked fun at the pretentiousness of most poetry readings. Hughes may have been shy about reading his work at the library in 1922, but he increasingly took his writing very seriously. By the end of the following year, he would have written some of his best-loved poems, including "Mother to Son," "Jazzonia," and "The Weary Blues." ("The Negro Speaks of Rivers" inspired *Rivers*, an art installation designed by sculptor Houston Conwill in honor of Langston Hughes and Arthur Schomburg that dominates the floor of the lobby entrance to the library's auditorium. Beneath the brass floor medallion, which was completed in 1991 and features quotations from the poem, Langston Hughes's ashes are permanently interred.)

At a time when writing poetry may have struck many Americans as a rather insignificant line of work, there was an implicit political edge and importance to even the most seemingly apolitical poetry coming out of Harlem. In 1922, James Weldon Johnson, then head of the NAACP, wrote in his preface to *The Book of American Negro Poetry*:

> A people may become great through many means, but there is only one measure by which its greatness is recognized and acknowledged. The final measure of the greatness of all peoples is the amount and standard of the literature and art they have produced. . . . No people that has produced great literature and art has ever been looked upon by the world as distinctly inferior. The status of the Negro in the United States is more a question of national mental attitude toward race than of actual conditions. And nothing will do more to change that mental attitude and raise his status than a demonstration of intellectual parity by the Negro through the production of literature and art.

Johnson's showcase volume was just the beginning.

During the next eight years alone Harlem would witness an amazing outpouring of creativity. In 1922, the year Johnson's preface appeared, Claude McKay published his most important book of poems, *Harlem Shadows*, a book widely viewed as having inaugurated the Harlem Renaissance. The volume grew out of McKay's desire to put "inside of a book" the militant sonnet, "If We Must Die," inspired by the bloody antiblack violence that raged in the country during the "red summer" of 1919. Poems in this volume like "Enslaved," "The White House," and "America" addressed issues of racism and oppression with a strength and controlled passion that was new to American letters. In 1923, Jean Toomer came out with *Cane*, an intense, complex, lyrical, and self-consciously avant-garde collection of thematically intertwined free verse, prose poems, stories, dialogues, and vignettes that explored rural settings and contemporary urban scenes, the slave past and the modernist present—an innovative experiment that immediately garnered critical acclaim.

Jessie Redmon Fauset's *There Is Confusion* came out in 1924, along with Walter White's *The Fire in the Flint* and W.E.B. Du Bois's *The Gifts of Black Folk: The Negroes in the Making of America*. In 1925, Alain Locke edited a special "Harlem" issue of the journal *Survey Graphic*, which he later that year expanded into the anthology, *The New Negro: An Interpretation*, a volume that included poetry by Cullen, Hughes, Toomer, McKay, Arna Bontemps, Georgia Johnson, and Anne Spencer; fiction by Zora Neale Hurston, Rudolph Fisher, Bruce Nugent, and Eric Walrond; a play by Jessie Fauset; and essays by Locke, Johnson, Kelly Miller, Walter White, and Du Bois—a book that would come to be viewed as the definitive text of the Harlem Renaissance. Also in 1925, Countee Cullen published his first collection of poems, *Color*, the first book of poems by an African American to be published by a major American publisher in two decades. James Weldon Johnson published *The Book of American Negro Spirituals* that year, as well.

Walter White's novel *Flight* appeared the following year, in 1926, as did Alain Locke's *Four Negro Poets* and Langston Hughes's *The Weary Blues*, whose title poem represented the first use of the blues form by a black poet. The year 1927 brought two collections of poems from Cullen, Locke's coedited anthology of plays, Hughes's second poetry collection, and James Weldon Johnson's *God's Trombones: Seven Negro Sermons in Verse*. In 1928, Nella Larsen published *Quicksand*, Jessie Redmon Fauset published *Plum Bun*, Claude McKay published *Home to Harlem*, W.E.B. Du Bois published *Dark Princess*, and Zora Neale Hurston published "How It Feels to Be Colored Me" in the May issue of *World Tomorrow*.

HARLEM JAZZ
IN BLACK AND WHITE

EXCERPT FROM ZORA NEALE HURSTON'S
"HOW IT FEELS TO BE COLORED ME"

The energy and buzz of Harlem in the 1920s intrigued and titillated many white Americans whose faith in European civilization had been shaken by the Great War, and whose growing interest in alternative aesthetics—romantic, primitive, sensuous, vaguely resonant of Africa—helped make them appreciate the some of the fresh artistic achievements coming out of Harlem in that decade. As Langston Hughes writes in *The Big Sea*, "white people began to come to Harlem in droves." The neighborhood's ordinary black residents, according to Hughes, did not like "the growing influx of whites toward Harlem after sundown, flooding the little cabarets and bars where formerly only colored people laughed and sang, and where now the strangers were given the best ringside tables to sit and stare at the Negro customers—like amusing animals in a zoo." The following excerpt from Zora Neale Hurston's 1928 sketch "How It Feels to Be Colored Me" reflects both her efforts to translate into print the emotional impact a jazz performance in a Harlem club has on her (if not on her white companion), while also playfully signifying on the primitivist lens through which white tourists often viewed Harlem's black residents:

> We enter chatting about any little nothing that we have in common, and are seated by the jazz waiters. In the abrupt way that jazz orchestras have, this one plunges into a number. It loses no time in circumlocutions, but gets right down to business. It constricts the thorax and splits the heart with its tempo and narcotic harmonies. This orchestra grows rambunctious, rears on its hind legs and attacks the tonal veil with primitive fury, rending it, clawing it, until it breaks through to the jungle beyond. I follow those heathen—follow them exultingly. I dance wildly inside myself, I yell within. I whoop, I shake my assegai above my head, I hurl it true to the mark yeeeeooww! I am in the jungle and living in the jungle way. My face is painted red and yellow and my body is painted blue. My pulse is throbbing like a war drum. I want to slaughter something—give pain, give death to what, I do not know. But the piece ends. The men of the orchestra wipe their lips and rest their fingers. I creep back slowly to the veneer we call civilization with the last tone

and find the white friend sitting motionless in his seat, smoking calmly.

"Good music they have here," he remarks, drumming the table with his fingertips.

Music. The great blobs of purple and red emotion have not touched him. He has only heard what I felt. He is far away and I see him but dimly across the ocean and the continent that have fallen between us. He is so pale with his whiteness then and I am *so* colored.

In 1929, Larsen's *Passing* appeared, as did Wallace Thurman's *The Blacker the Berry*, Claude McKay's *Banjo*, and Walter White's *Rope and Faggot: A Biography of Judge Lynch*. In 1930, Langston Hughes's first novel, *Not without Laughter*, was published, along with Charles Johnson's *The Negro in American Civilization* and James Weldon Johnson's *Black Manhattan*—a very incomplete and cursory sampling of the range of works that appeared during the remarkable first decade of the period that would be known as the Harlem Renaissance.

The 135th Street Library came to play a key role in both preserving the literature of the past and encouraging emerging young writers of the present. The library offered these young poets and novelists a place to work as well as books and articles that were crucial to their research and that ignited their imaginations; most important, perhaps, it gave them the chance to share their work with each other. As Arnold Rampersad has observed, "the library hosted an increasing number of readings, lectures, and soirees that brought Harlem book lovers together." For writers, the opportunity to read their work before a knowledgeable—and candid—audience was enormously significant. The audiences who responded to their work at the 135th Street Library told Jean Toomer, Countee Cullen, Jessie Fauset, and others whether they had succeeded or failed.

Starting in the 1920s and continuing into the 1930s and beyond, in addition to readings of poetry and prose, the library sponsored discussions led by writers including James Weldon Johnson, W.E.B. Du Bois, Jessie Fauset, Arna Bontemps, Nella Larsen, Gwendolyn Bennett, Rudolph Fisher, Wallace Thurman, Alain Locke, Countee Cullen, and Zora Neale Hurston on topics ranging from "The Outrages in Haiti" committed by U.S. Marines then occupying the country to "Recent Negro Poetry" and "Negro Literature." The library sponsored a public forum in 1923 at which Columbia University anthropologist Franz Boas spoke about the widespread myth of racial superiority to a "large and appreciative audience" (according to the *Amsterdam News*). Work by earlier writers would come alive at events like the "Dunbar Evenings" that took place in 1924. Schomburg himself came and spoke about his passion for uncovering and collecting texts by black writers. In 1930, the "Harlem Experimental Theater" met at the library on Wednesdays and Saturdays, January through May, while the "Negro Players" rehearsed there Fridays in November and December; there was an evening of "Readings by Gwendolyn Bennett, Mrs. Jessie Fauset Harris, [and] Dr. Rudolph Fisher," a reception featuring talks by Langston Hughes and George Schuyler, and a series of rotating art exhibits throughout the year.

The library engaged in extensive outreach to the community, as well. It advertised its services in churches, schools, and theaters, even employing a popular and eloquent local soapbox orator to urge people to borrow books and to attend library-sponsored events. Librarians visited schoolchildren's homes and Sunday schools and organized a rich series of discussion groups, readings, and lectures at the library on literary, social, and political topics. A "Book-Lovers' Club" met there every first and third Tuesday evenings for years. Regina Anderson would often devour seven or eight books a night in order to present brief reviews of them at the library the following day. For years the library sponsored a weekly "Reader's Advisor" column, "What to Read," that ran on Thursdays in the *New York Age* and the *Negro World* of New York City, as well as out-of-town black newspapers, including the *Atlanta Daily World*, the *Pittsburgh Courier*, and the *Norfolk Journal and Guide*. One author of "Reader's Advisor" columns recalled that many people from small southern towns without library facilities wrote to the "Reader's Advisor" asking not for advice about books, but for the books themselves, particularly for books by black writers. In response to these poignant requests, the library organized a small "Traveling Collection" of duplicate volumes, which it made available to out-of-town readers.

Some of the library's rarest materials were removed from circulation in 1924 to become the core of a reference collection called the Division of Negro History, Literature, and Prints; these materials were supplemented by donations from private libraries of individual collectors. With the purchase in 1926 of what Schomburg had been painstakingly gathering for decades, the library became the Northeast's leading research institution on African American life. Although over the years the reference collection experienced tremendous growth, the extraordinary materials that Schomburg himself had collected—and continued to collect—shaped its scope in profound ways.

In 1932, after a two-year stint as curator at the library of Fisk University, Schomburg himself was asked to develop his collection of materials at the 135th Street branch. He would occupy this position until his death in 1938. Two years later, the Division of Negro History, Literature, and Prints was renamed the Schomburg Collection of Negro Literature, History, and Prints in his honor. During his first four years as curator, as he noted in a report to Ernestine Rose, he did his best to make the collection widely available to the public, and reported that it was used by increasingly greater numbers of people every year. He wrote that a number of significant books had been written by scholars using the resources of the library. These included James Weldon Johnson's *Black Manhattan* and Nancy Cunard's *Negro Anthology*. As Schomburg had written in his famous essay, "The Negro Digs Up His Past," which appeared in the Harlem number of *Survey Graphic* 1925,

> The American Negro must remake his past in order to make his future. Though it is orthodox to think of America as the one country where it is unnecessary to have a past, what is a luxury for the nation as a whole becomes a prime social necessity for the Negro. For him, a group tradition must supply compensation for persecution, and pride of race the antidote for prejudice. History must restore what slavery took away, for it is the social damage of slavery that the present generations must repair and offset. So among the rising democratic millions we find the Negro thinking more collectively, more retrospectively than the rest, and apt out of the very pressure of the present to become the most enthusiastic antiquarian of them all.

Even a cursory glance at Schomburg's papers—preserved on twelve rolls of microfilm—suggests the astonishing breadth and depth of his interests, and his generosity as a scholar. What is particularly striking, however, is how attuned he was to what scholars care about in the academy in the *twenty-first century*. His sense of the future of the past helped construct the past of the future not only because of the role his collection played in shaping his culture's vision of what mattered, but also because of his remarkable prescience. The fields of African American studies, American studies, American literature, and American history are today struggling to reach the place where Schomburg lived, intellectually, during the first decades of the twentieth century—a place in which writers, artists, intellectuals, and ordinary people attend to the transnational dimensions of culture and culture formation; a place where diasporic imaginations are valued for the dazzlingly hybrid syntheses they produce; a place where the term "American" is understood in its broadest hemispheric sense; a place where it is recognized that there is an important body of American literature written in languages other than English; a place where the act of scholarship is inseparable from the act of sharing one's insights with a broad, public audience, and where that public is integral to shaping the scholar's agenda to begin with; a place where the walls between disciplines and media evaporate, and the walls between the academy and the street crumble to insignificance as well.

Perhaps it was overdetermined that Schomburg would understand culture and history as the complex webs of influences that we understand them as today. Schomburg, as Jesse Hoffnung-Garskof has observed, was "a product of multiple migrations as well as colonial displacement" who "negotiated a dizzying array of ethnic and national identities—West Indian, Spanish, Puerto Rican, Cuban, Antillano, North American, African, Negro, and (even on one trip to Europe) German—never fitting exactly into any of them." Key bits of history and culture might surface, Schomburg, knew, just about anywhere—in any tongue. And the dispersion of that record was itself a part of the record that interested him. He collected a Swedish translation of a work by Frederick Douglass, a German edition of the *Narrative of Olaudah Equiano*, a Portuguese translation of *Réflexions sur l'esclavage des nègres* by Condorcet, and a Danish edition of *Uncle Tom's Cabin*. His papers include letters to him in Spanish, French, English, and German, from correspondents in Paris, Rome, Port-au-Prince, London, Trinidad, Seville, St. Kitts, and Guatemala City, all confident of receiving answers in their own tongues.

Three-quarters of a century before the Longfellow Institute and New York University Press recognized the existence of American literature in languages other than English with the publication of *The Multilingual Anthology of American Literature*, Schomburg was making that literature integral to his collection, tracking down obscure work by the now-famous nineteenth-century New Orleans born African American playwright, poet, and fiction writer who wrote American literature in French, Victor Séjour. Séjour is now recognized as the author of the earliest known work of fiction by an African American (the story "Le Mulâtre," or "The Mulatto," which was published in *Revue des Colonies* in March 1837). Indeed, Schomburg was widely known as the one person who could be counted on to come up with Séjour's work—a fact not lost on the librarian at Dillard University who wrote asking whether Schomburg might lend him Séjour's *Les volontaires* for a member of his university's French department. Although Dillard University was in Séjour's hometown of New Orleans, no copy of the play was available to this French professor there; he had to send to Harlem for a copy. If politics makes strange bedfellows, book collecting may make even stranger ones. Schomburg maintained a cordial correspondence with a New Orleans bookseller who specialized in books on the South and the Confederacy; he was Schomburg's source for a volume by Rodolphe Lucien Desdunes, a historian of Creoles of color. One can only imagine Schomburg's delight when, as an aside, this bookseller also told Schomburg about a black composer named Justin Holland who had published a number of popular songs; in a Holland scrapbook, this correspondent mentioned casually, was pasted a manuscript poem by Frederick Douglass.

At a time when even the most forward-looking research libraries commonly collected little more than books and manuscripts, Schomburg was buying sheet music, theatrical programs, magazines, newspapers, games, paintings, sculptures, and everyday objects. Through all his collecting, Schomburg stalked serendipity with a determination—and a joy—that was unequalled among his peers. His papers include invoices for nineteenth-century sheet music—for songs like "Coal Black Rose" and "Sambo to His Brethren," and for "Good Evening," a song written by Paul Laurence Dunbar. One undated record tells us that he bought, on this occasion, "8 musical numbers by Negro composers, 46 Negro magazines . . . and 3 Negro theatrical programs" as well as Lancela's "Game of Africa," and *Dick's Ethiopian Scenes*, the latter being an obscure 1873 collection of dramatic pieces from a London publisher. Schomburg's efforts, as he put it, to "recapture my lost heritage," led him to mine the past for riches whose value we are just beginning to recognize. His transnational, multilingual, hemispheric, democratic, diasporic vision has become ours. His work as a collector and his generosity as a scholar helped make Harlem the vital international center of research it continues to be today, where the Schomburg Center for Research on Black Culture is living proof of its namesake's conviction that the past, indeed, has a future.

There was good synergy between the library's engagement with the visual arts and Schomburg's interest in them throughout his career as a collector. The art exhibit the library mounted in 1921 became an annual event, supplemented by solo shows by some of the more prominent contemporary artists, and exhibits of African sculpture organized by Alain Locke. The more than five hundred prints and etchings by black artists that Schomburg had collected were also often on display. One of the artists who most dramatically shaped our visual memory of the era, who was brilliant at melding text and image himself, would leave his mark not only in books the library would collect but on the walls of the library itself. Aaron Douglas moved to Harlem from Kansas City, Missouri, in 1925 when he received a scholarship to study in New York at the art school run by German émigré artist Winold Reiss, who encouraged him to combine designs drawn from African traditions with designs of European origin. The distinctive style Douglas developed has sometimes been referred to as Afro-cubist. Soon after he arrived, he began to draw illustrations for the *Crisis* and *Opportunity*. He collaborated with Langston Hughes and other writers and artists on projects that brought out dramatic resonances between image and text (these included work on the short-lived 1926 journal, *FIRE!!*). Douglas's gift for crafting images that illuminated the texts with which they were paired led to commissions to design dust jackets for books by Langston Hughes, Claude McKay, Wallace Thurman, and James Weldon Johnson.

In 1934, the Public Works of Art Project, a relief agency that was part of the WPA, commissioned Douglas to paint four murals that are collectively known as *Aspects of Negro Life* for the auditorium at the 135th Street Library. The epic mural cycle moves from scenes of Africa to scenes of slavery, Reconstruction, the Great Migration, and the Great Depression. As Stephanie Fox Knappe has observed, "It is in this mural cycle that Douglas integrated into the stylized vocabulary he employed to express his customary message of hope some of his most distinctly political messages and overt social criticism. The murals include ghostly images of mounted Ku Klux Klan members, an aftermath of a lynching, as well as traces of Marxist theory that Douglas and many others in Harlem were studying in the mid-1930s." The murals are on permanent display today in the reading room of the Schomburg Center for Research on Black Culture.

As Harlem's population grew, so did demands on the library, which continued to do much more than circulate books and provide reference resources for scholars and educators. An enormous amount of activity was packed into the three-story building, which often led all the libraries in the system when it came to the number of clubs, classes, readings, story hours, discussion groups, and community meetings that took place there. A 1936 report concluded that "The library is increasingly used as an intellectual and cultural center in Harlem. Its opportunities for growth are great, but its physical capacity is not only completely inadequate at present, but admits of no

Artist Aaron Douglas and Arthur A. Schomburg in front of one of Douglas's murals in the *Aspects of Negro Life* series in 1934. The murals are on permanent display in the reading room of the Schomburg Center for Research on Black Culture.

PHOTO CREDIT: COURTESY OF THE PHOTOGRAPHS AND PRINTS DIVISION, SCHOMBURG CENTER FOR RESEARCH IN BLACK CULTURE, NEW YORK PUBLIC LIBRARY, ASTOR, LENOX, AND TILDEN FOUNDATIONS.

expansion whatever for the future." Over the next sixty years, new buildings were built adjacent to the original structure as the library struggled to keep pace with increasing demands on its services. In the early 1940s, the circulating collection was relocated to a new building next door, designated as the Countee Cullen Branch of the New York Public Library. In 1982 and 1991, other new buildings were added to the complex, which now included archives of film as well as print and photography. The original 1905 building was remodeled inside to make space for offices, a gallery featuring rotating exhibits, and the American Negro Theater.

The optimism and exuberance of the Harlem Renaissance was partially deflated by the stock market crash of 1929 and the ensuing nationwide depression. Even at Harlem's height as a center of literary achievement in the 1920s, the living conditions for the majority of Harlem's residents were difficult. In the late 1920s, infants born in Harlem were twice as likely to die as infants born in the rest of the city, and the death rate among adults was substantially higher too. Harlem residents were four times more likely to die of tuberculosis than residents of other parts of the city. The unemployment rate was 40 percent.

In the1920s, the stately, turn-of-the-century buildings that lined Harlem's streets represented sturdier and more elegant housing than recent arrivals from the South had ever known, as James Weldon Johnson had observed. But as those buildings took in more and more tenants and fell into greater and greater disrepair, overcrowding and physical deterioration threatened their residents' health and well-being and exacerbated the frustrations of the unemployment and the discrimination they still had to endure.

By the time Ann Petry published her novel *The Street* in 1943, the Harlem streets that had exhilarated a young Langston Hughes or Gillis, in Rudolph Fisher's "City of Refuge," now were simply the place that seduced you and abandoned you, depriving you, in the process, of your dreams. Lutie, a single, black, working mother who is the main character in *The Street*, is sure it won't happen to her:

> As for the street, she thought, getting up at the approaching station signs, she wasn't afraid of its influence, for she would fight against it. Streets like 116th Street or being colored, or a combination of both with all it implied, had turned Pop into a sly old man who drank too much; had killed Mom off when she was in her prime . . . and the superintendent of the building—well, the street had pushed him into basements away from light and air until he was being eaten up by some horrible obsession; and still other streets had turned Min, the woman who lived with him, into a drab drudge so spineless and so limp she was like a soggy dishrag. None of those things would happen to her, Lutie decided, because she would fight back and never stop fighting back.

Lutie is shocked when her young son Bub surprises her by turning up with a shoeshine box on the street in front of their apartment house: "'You get in the house,' she ordered and yanked him to his feet. . . . Her voice grew thick with rage. 'I'm working to look after you and you out here in the street shining shoes just like the rest of these little niggers.'" She explained her anger to herself as she pulled him inside ". . . you're afraid that this street will keep him from finishing high school; that it may do worse than that and get him into some kind of trouble that will land him in reform school because you can't be home to look out for him because you have to work." Sadly, Lutie's fears come true; Harlem, now an emblem not of artistic liberation but of racism and poverty, defeats her. Petry's painfully honest tale of how circumstances crush ideals and aspirations was inspired by the scenes she witnessed when she worked at an after-school program in Harlem—by the lonely children she saw making their way past men with bottles of liquor in brown paper bags, coming home to empty apartments, their working parents too poor to afford child care. Petry recalled that the children "wouldn't stay in the house after school because they were afraid in the empty, silent, dark rooms. And they should have been playing in wide stretches of green park and instead they were in the street. And the street reached out and sucked them up."

As the poverty and racism that had never been adequately addressed took an increasingly grim toll on African Americans during the decades that followed, brilliant poets like Langston Hughes were there to chronicle the sense of hopelessness, frustration, anger, and despair that he saw settling over the landscape. His poem "Harlem," for example, first published in 1951, chillingly prefigures the urban riots of the 1960s:

Harlem
What happens to a dream deferred?
    Does it dry up
    like a raisin in the sun?
    Or fester like a sore—
    And then run?
    Does it stink like rotten meat?
    Or crust and sugar over—
    like a syrupy sweet?

    Maybe it just sags
    like a heavy load.
    Or does it explode?

Hughes's "Harlem" captures perhaps more succinctly and more memorably than any other American poem the tragedy of the nation's color-coded "American dream," in which equality and opportunity are real "for whites only" (as the Jim Crow signs proclaimed).

Harlem continued to figure prominently in fiction by black writers in the second half of the twentieth century and the start of the first decade of the twenty-first. It is the setting of key scenes in Ralph Ellison's magnum opus, *Invisible Man* (1952), which won the National Book Award in 1953. Between 1957 and 1969, Chester Himes wrote a series of detective novels set in Harlem featuring two New York City police detectives; these include *A Rage in Harlem, The Real Cool Killers, The Crazy Kill, All Shot Up, The Big Gold Dream, The Heat's On, Cotton Comes to Harlem,* and *Blind Man with a Pistol* (several of his books inspired feature films from 1970s to the 1990s). Harlem is the setting for much of Claude Brown's autobiographical coming-of-age novel, *Manchild in the Promised Land,* which appeared in 1965, as well as Louise Meriwether's female coming-of-age novel, *Daddy Was a Numbers Runner,* set during the Depression and published in 1970. It is the setting of Rosa Guy's wrenching 1966 novel *Bird at My Window,* and is central to later fiction by Guy, including *A Measure of Time* (1983), in which, as Lynda Koolish puts it, "Harlem itself is a protagonist" that is "observed and eulogized, its 'warped and twisted soul' exposed and lamented." Memorable scenes of Harlem figure prominently in John Oliver Killens's satirical novel, *The Cotillion; or, One Good Bull Is Half the Herd* (1971), which was nominated for a Pulitzer Prize. Harlem is also the setting of Grace F. Edwards's novel, *In the Shadow of the Peacock* (1988), as well as host of other novels by Edwards including her Mali Anderson mysteries—*If I Should Die* (1997), *A Toast before Dying* (1998), *No Time to Die* (1999), and *Do or Die* (2000). It is the setting for Toni Morrison's novel *Jazz* (1992); for Brian Keith Jackson's novel *The Queen of Harlem* (2002); and for many young adult novels by Walter Dean Myers including *Monster* (2001), *Harlem Summer* (2007), *Street Love* (2007), and *Slam!* (2008)—as well as Myers's young-adult memoir of coming of age in Harlem in the 1940s (2001), and his Caldecott Medal–winning children's book, *Harlem* (1997).

Surrounded by a community that is at once a center of dazzling creative vitality and daunting economic and social challenges, the Schomburg Center has preserved and collected literature, history and the arts of the African diaspora for nearly a century and has made its collections more readily available to the public through series such as the Schomburg Library of Nineteenth-Century Black Women Writers, edited by Henry Louis Gates Jr., which restored to readers around the world forty volumes of obscure and often forgotten works by black women writers that are well worth rediscovering, and the digital collection that builds on and expands it, African American Women Writers of the 19th Century, which recovers fifty-two published works by nineteenth century black women writers. A vital international center of research that continues to nurture scholarship and the arts in the twenty-first century, it is a living testimony to the wisdom of Arthur Alfonso Schomburg's vision, and a worthy heir to what he called his lifelong "mission of love to recapture my lost heritage."

RELATED SITES

◦◦ The Harlem YMCA
180 West 135th Street, New York City

"I can never put on paper the thrill of that underground ride to Harlem," Langston Hughes writes in *The Big Sea*. "I had never been in a subway before and it fascinated me—the noise, the speed, the green lights ahead. At every station I kept watching for the sign: 135TH STREET. When I saw it, I held my breath. I came out onto the platform with two heavy bags and looked around. It was still early morning and people were going to work. Hundreds of colored people! I wanted to shake hands with them, speak to them. I hadn't seen any colored people for so long—that is, any Negro colored people. I went up the steps and out into the bright September sunlight. Harlem! I stood there, dropped my bags, took a deep breath and felt happy again. I registered at the Y."

Arnold Rampersad has called the Harlem YMCA "the single most important address for an unconnected young black man arriving in New York after the war." The Y's history dates back to Reconstruction, when a lobbying effort by a group of prominent black ministers in the city resulted in the formation of an unofficial "Colored Young Men's Association" as an auxiliary to the established, all-white YMCA in 1866. The present building—an eleven-story, Neo-Georgian, red brick structure with a pyramid-shaped tower—opened in 1933. For many years it was the tallest building in Harlem, and it has served as a key cultural, religious, and educational center in the community.

The YMCA has been a haven for many of Harlem's writers when they were getting their start, a place for a room, a rest, a swim, a meal, a literary discussion, a political meeting, a "history club" gathering, a lecture, an art exhibit, a play, a vocational class or a literacy class, a stimulating conversation, some quiet reading, or even a job. (In 1936, at the height of the Great Depression, a young Ralph Ellison worked as a server behind the food bar here.) When he was a boy, Paul Robeson, who would soon become one of the most famous actors of his era, had his stage debut in the play *Simon the Cyrenian* at the Harlem Y's Little Theater. At age twenty-one, Jacob Lawrence, who would become world-renowned for his series of paintings titled *The Migration of the Negro*, had his first exhibition here. A mural by Aaron Douglas titled *Evolution of the Negro Dance*, which he created for the Y in 1933, may be seen inside the Y's former billiards room, now a hair salon. In addition to Langston Hughes, other prominent writers who made this building their home for a time included Ralph Ellison and Claude McKay. Jamaica-born McKay, whose many memorable contributions to literature include the sonnet "If We Must Die" (1919); the poetry collection *Harlem Shadows* (1922); *Home to Harlem* (1928), the first novel by an African American to make the best-seller list; the autobiography *A Long Way from Home* (1937); and the nonfiction portrait of Harlem, *Harlem: Negro Metropolis* (1940), was a resident from 1942 to 1946. Today, the Harlem YMCA is still a fully-functioning YMCA.

❧ Langston Hughes House
20 East 127th Street, New York City

A virtuoso writer whose poetry, fiction, drama, lyrics, and nonfiction helped define his era, Missouri-born Hughes lived in this Harlem townhouse with his adopted uncle and aunt, Emerson and Ethel (Toy) Harper, during the last twenty years of his life, from 1947 to 1967; it is the only house in which he lived for any period of time, and is emblematic of his close ties to Harlem, the place where his literary career took off.

❧ James Weldon Johnson House
187 West 135th Street, New York City

While he was living in this house, Johnson published the *Book of American Negro Spirituals* (1925), the *Second Book of American Negro Spirituals* (1926), and the free-verse *God's Trombones: Seven Sermons in Verse* (1927). His many extraordinary contributions to literature also include his novel *The Autobiography of an Ex-Colored Man* (1912), the nonfiction book *Black Manhattan* (1930), and the autobiography

Along This Way (1933); two editions (1922 and 1931) of *The Book of American Negro Poetry*; and hundreds of song lyrics, including "Lift Ev'ry Voice and Sing," the song adopted by the NAACP as the black national anthem. Johnson also served as editorial page editor of the *New York Age* and as the first African American head of the NAACP. This was his home from 1925 through his death in 1938.

Edward Kennedy "Duke" Ellington House
935 St. Nicholas Avenue, Apartment 4A, New York City

The great jazz composer and musician "Duke" Ellington, creator of such jazz classics as "Satin Doll," "Mood Indigo," and "It Don't Mean a Thing (If It Ain't Got That Swing)," lived here from 1931 to 1961. Ellington significntly shaped the art form that helped inspire much of African American literature in the twentieth century.

Apollo Theater
253 West 125th Street, New York City

Built as a burlesque house in 1914, the Apollo Theater became the leading Harlem venue for African American entertainers, and a place that helped inspire many African American writers, including Ralph Ellison. Prominent musicians and comics who performed here or who were discovered at the Apollo's Amateur Night programs include Bessie Smith, Louis Armstrong, Billie Holiday, Ella Fitzgerald, Sarah Vaughn, Aretha Franklin, and Moms Mabley.

Minton's Playhouse
206 West 118th Street, New York City

Located on the ground floor of the Cecil Hotel, built in 1895, Minton's Playhouse became a key Harlem meeting place for jazz musicians in the 1940s. The jam sessions that took place here, involving such musicians as Kenny Clarke, Thelonius Monk, Dizzy Gillespie, and Charlie Christian, helped give rise to the form of jazz that came to be known as "be-bop," a complex, improvisational style that left its mark on a number of writers. In one of Langston Hughes's stories centering on a comic Harlem-based character named Jesse B. Semple (nicknamed "Simple") that features a discussion of the music made by Dizzy Gillespie, Thelonius Monk, and others, Simple suggests that term "be-bop" comes from the sound of a policeman hitting a black man with a billy club ("That's where Be-Bop came from, beaten right out of some Negro's head into them horns and saxophones and piano keys that plays it"). Simple's definition may be fanciful, but few would argue with his hypothesis that pain played a role in forging the distinctive blend of sounds born in Minton's Playhouse.

FOR FURTHER READING

The Writers: Works and Words

Brown, Claude. *Manchild in the Promised Land*. 1965. Introduction by Nathan McCall. Reprint, New York: Touchstone, 2011.

Cullen, Countee. *My Soul's High Song: The Collected Writings of Countee Cullen, Voice of the Harlem Renaissance*. New York: Doubleday, 1991.

Cunard, Nancy. *The Negro Anthology*. 1934. Introduction by Hugh Ford. New York: Frederick Ungar Publishing, 1984.

Digital Schomburg. African American Women Writers of the 19th Century. http://digital.nypl.org/schomburg/writers_aa19/toc.html.

Du Bois, W.E.B. *Writings*. Edited by Nathan Huggins. New York: Library of America, 1986.

Edwards, Grace F. *Do or Die*. 2000. New York: Crimeline Books, 2001.

———. *If I Should Die*. 1997. New York: Bantam Books, 1998.

———. *In the Shadow of the Peacock*. 1988. New York: Harlem Writers Guild Press, 2000.

———. *No Time to Die*. 1999. New York: Bantam Books, 2000.

———. *A Toast before Dying*. 1998. New York: Bantam Books, 1999.

Ellison, Ralph. *Invisible Man*. 1952. New York: Random House, 1982.

Fauset, Jessie Redmon. *The Chinaberry Tree: A Novel of American Life*. [1936]. New York: G. K. Hall, 1995.

———. *Comedy: American Style*. 1933. Introduction by Thadious Davis. New York: G. K. Hall, 1995.

———. *There Is Confusion*. New York: Boni and Liveright, 1924.

Gates, Henry Louis, Jr., ser. ed. The Schomburg Library of Nineteenth-Century Black Women Writers. 40 volumes. New York: Oxford University Press, 1988–2002.

Gates, Henry Louis, Jr., and Nellie Y. McKay, gen. eds. *The Norton Anthology of African American Literature*. New York: W. W. Norton, 1997.

Guy, Rosa. *Bird at My Window*. 1966. Introduction by Sandra Adell. Minneapolis: Coffee House Press, 2001.

———. *A Measure of Time*. 1983. London: Virago Press, 1984.

Himes, Chester. *All Shot Up*. 1960. New York: New American Library, 1975.

———. *The Big Gold Dream*. 1960. New York: New American Library, 1975.

———. *Blind Man with a Pistol*. 1969. New York: Vintage, 1989.

———. *Cotton Comes to Harlem*. 1965. New York: Vintage, 1988.

———. *The Crazy Kill*. 1959. New York: Vintage, 1989.

———. *The Heat's On.* 1959. New York: Vintage, 1988.

———. *A Rage in Harlem.* 1957. New York: Vintage, 1989.

———. *The Real Cool Killers.* 1959. New York: Vintage, 1988.

Honey, Maureen, ed. *Shadowed Dreams: Women's Poetry of the Harlem Renaissance.* New Brunswick, NJ: Rutgers University Press, 1989.

Huggins, Nathan Irvin, ed. *Voices from the Harlem Renaissance.* New York: Oxford University Press, 1995.

Hughes, Langston, *The Best of Simple.* New York: Hill and Wang, 1961.

———. *The Big Sea.* 1940. New York: Hill and Wang, 1963.

———. *The Collected Poems of Langston Hughes.* Edited by Arnold Rampersad and David Roessel. New York: Alfred A. Knopf, 1994.

———. "My Early Days in Harlem." *Freedomways* 3 (Summer 1963): 12–14. Reprinted in *The Collected Works of Langston Hughes: Essays on Art, Race, Politics and World Affairs.* Edited, with an introduction, by Christopher C. De Santis, 9:395–398. Columbia: University of Missouri Press, 2002.

Hurston, Zora Neale. *Folklore, Memoirs & Other Writings.* Edited by Cheryl Wall. New York: Library of America, 1995.

———. *Novels and Stories.* Edited by Cheryl Wall. New York: Library of America, 1995.

Jackson, Brian Keith. 2002. *The Queen of Harlem.* New York: Broadway Books, 2003.

Johnson, James Weldon. *Along This Way.* 1933. New York: Viking, 1968.

———. *Autobiography of an Ex-Colored Man.* 1912. New York: Vintage, 1989.

———. *Black Manhattan.* 1930. New York: Arno Press, 1968.

———, ed. *The Book of American Negro Poetry.* New York: Harcourt Brace, 1922.

———, ed. *The Book of American Negro Spirituals.* New York: Viking Press, 1925.

Johnson-Feelings, Diane, ed. *The Best of the Brownies' Book.* New York: Oxford University Press, 1996.

Killens, John Oliver. *The Cotillion; or, One Good Bull Is Half the Herd.* 1971. Introduction by Alexs D. Pate. Minneapolis: Coffee House Press, 2002.

Knopf, Marcy, ed. *The Sleeper Wakes: Harlem Renaissance Stories by Women.* New Brunswick, NJ: Rutgers University Press, 1993.

Larsen, Nella. *The Complete Fiction of Nella Larsen.* Edited by Charles R. Larson and Marita Golden. New York: Anchor Books, 2001.

Lewis, David Levering, ed. *The Portable Harlem Renaissance Reader.* New York: Viking, 1994.

Locke, Alain, ed. *Four Negro Poets.* New York: Simon and Schuster, 1927.

———. *The New Negro.* 1925. Introduction by Arnold Rampersad. New York: Atheneum, 1992.

Locke, Alain, and Montgomery Gregory, eds. *Plays of Negro Life.* New York: Harper, 1927.

McKay, Claude. *Harlem Shadows.* New York: Harcourt, Brace, 1922.

———. *Home to Harlem.* (*See* Zafar, below.)

Meriwether, Louise. *Daddy Was a Numbers Runner.* 1970. Foreword by James Baldwin. New York: Feminist Press at CUNY, 2002.

Morrison, Toni. *Jazz.* New York: Knopf/Random House, 1992.

Myers, Walter Dean. *Bad Boy.* 2001. New York: Amistad, 2002.

———. *Harlem.* New York: Scholastic Press, 1997.

————. *Harlem Summer*. 2007. New York: Scholastic Press, 2012.

————. *Monster*. 2001. New York: Amistad, 2004.

————. *Slam!* New York: Scholastic Press, 2008.

————. *Street Love*. 2006. New York: Amistad, 2007.

Petry, Ann. *The Street*. [1946]. New York: Houghton Mifflin, 1974.

Reed, Ishmael. *Mumbo Jumbo*. Garden City, NY: Doubleday, 1972.

Schomburg, Arthur Alfonso. *Arthur Alfonso Schomburg Papers, 1874–1938*. 12 reels of microfilm. Schomburg Center for Research in Black Culture.

Smith, Lillian. *Strange Fruit*. New York: Reynal and Hitchcock, 1944.

Thurman, Wallace. *The Blacker the Berry*. (*See* Zafar, below.)

Toomer, Jean. *Cane*. (*See* Zafar, below.)

White, Walter. *The Fire in the Flint*. New York: Alfred A. Knopf, 1924.

————. *Flight*. New York: Alfred A. Knopf, 1926.

Wilson, Sondra Kathryn, ed. *The Crisis Reader: Stories, Poetry, and Essays from the N.A.A.C.P.'s "Crisis" Magazine*. New York: Modern Library, 1999.

Zafar, Rafia, ed. *Harlem Renaissance Novels: The Library of America Collection*. New York: Library of America, 2011. Includes *Cane*, Jean Toomer (1923); *Home to Harlem*, Claude McKay (1928); *Quicksand*, Nella Larsen (1928); *Plum Bun*, Jessie Redmon Fauset (1928); *The Blacker the Berry*, Wallace Thurman (1929); *Not without Laughter*, Langston Hughes (1930); *Black No More*, George Schuyler (1931); *The Conjure-Man Dies*, Rudolph Fisher (1932); and *Black Thunder*, Arna Bontemps (1936).

Background and Contexts

Anderson, Sarah A. "'The Place to Go': The 135th Street Branch Library and the Harlem Renaissance," *Library Quarterly* 73, no. 4 (October 2003): 383–421.

Bancroft, Hubert Howe. *Retrospection: Personal and Political*. New York: Bancroft Co., 1912.

Banks, William H., Jr., ed. *Beloved Harlem: A Literary Tribute to Black America's Most Famous Neighborhood, from the Classics to the Contemporary*. New York: Broadway, 2005.

Blue, Thomas. "A Successful Library Experiment." *Opportunity* 2 (August 1924): 244–246.

Carpio, Glenda R., and Werner Sollors, eds. Special issue, *African American Literary Studies: New Texts, New Approaches, New Challenges*. *Amerikastudien/American Studies* 55, no. 4 (2010).

Davis, Thadious M. *Nella Larsen, Novelist of the Harlem Renaissance: A Woman's Life Unveiled*. Baton Rouge: Louisiana State University Press, 1994.

Hoffnung-Garskof, Jesse. "The Migrations of Arturo Schomburg: On Being Antillano, Negro, and Puerto Rican in New York, 1891–1938." *Journal of American Ethnic History* 21, no. 1 (November 2001): 3–49.

Huggins, Nathan Irvin. *Harlem Renaissance*. New York: Oxford University Press, 1971.

Hutchinson, George. *The Harlem Renaissance in Black and White*. Cambridge, MA: Harvard University Press, 1995.

Jenkins, Betty L. "A White Librarian in Black Harlem." *Library Quarterly* 60, no. 3 (July 1990): 216–231.

Knappe, Stephanie Fox. "Aaron Douglas: African American Modernist; The Exhibition, the Artist, and His Legacy." *American Studies* 49, nos. 1/2 (Spring/Summer 2008): 121–130.

Koolish, Lynda. *African American Writers: Portraits and Visions*. Jackson: University Press of Mississippi, 2001.

Lewis, David Levering. *When Harlem Was in Vogue*. [1982]. New York: Oxford University Press, 1989.

New York Public Library. *Dictionary Catalog of the Schomburg Collection of Negro Literature and History*. 9 vols. Boston: G. K. Hall, 1962.

Rampersad, Arnold. *The Life of Langston Hughes*. 2 vols. New York: Oxford University Press, 1986–1988.

Rose, Ernestine. "Books and the Negro." *Library Journal* 52 (November 1, 1927): 1012–1014.

———. "A Librarian in Harlem." *Opportunity* 1 (July 1923): 206–207, 220.

———. "Serving New York's Black City." *Library Journal* 46 (March 15, 1921): 255–258.

Sandford, Ann. "Rescuing Ernestine Rose (1860–1961): Harlem Librarian and Social Activist." *Long Island History Journal* 22, no. 2 (2011): https://lihj.cc.stonybrook.edu/2011/articles/rescuing-ernestine-rose-1880-1961-harlem-librarian-and-social-activist.

Shuler, Marjorie. "New York Public Library Shows Exhibit of Negro Achievements." *Christian Science Monitor*, August 30, 1925.

Sinnette, Elinor Des Verney. *Arthur Alfonso Schomburg: Black Bibliophile and Collector; A Biography*. Detroit: New York Public Library and Wayne State University Press, 1989.

Watson, Steven. *Harlem Renaissance: Hub of African-American Culture, 1920–1930*. New York: Pantheon, 1996.

Whitmire, Ethelene. *Regina Anderson Andrews, Harlem Renaissance Librarian*. Champaign: University of Illinois Press, 2014.

Behind the pink Portscheller facade of the Manuel Guerra House and Store in the Plaza of the Roma Historic District, Roma, Texas, Manuel Guerra mobilized the region's Mexican American working-class majority to consolidate the power of his mentor, political boss Jim Wells. Wells was the model for Judge Norris, the character who sets the plot in motion in Américo Paredes's novel *George Washington Gómez*.

PHOTO CREDIT: PHOTO BY SHELLEY FISHER FISHKIN.

12

Mexican American Writers
in the Borderlands of Culture

LA LOMITA HISTORIC DISTRICT
ROMA HISTORIC DISTRICT
SAN YGNACIO HISTORIC DISTRICT
SAN AGUSTIN DE LAREDO HISTORIC DISTRICT
LOWER RIO GRANDE VALLEY, TEXAS

Around 1830, when Jesús Treviño built a stone compound for himself and his family in the ranching outpost of San Ygnacio on the northern bank of the Rio Grande (in what is now the San Ygnacio Historic District), his home and the land around it was part of Mexico (according to Mexico, that is—but not in the eyes of the Native American tribes in the area). By 1836, it was claimed by the Republic of Texas—although Mexico did not recognize that claim. For a brief period in 1840, it was claimed by the Republic of the Rio Grande, a breakaway Mexican state that included parts of Texas and northern Mexico. With the signing of the Treaty of Guadalupe Hidalgo, which ended the Mexican War in 1848 and established the Rio Grande as a southern border between the United States and Mexico, Jesús Treviño's fortified residence was recognized by Mexico as being in the United States. But what may have appeared to the United States as a "natural" boundary between the two countries was highly unnatural for the many families who lived on both sides of the river, who went back and forth frequently, and who, in time, would have trouble adjusting to the complex regulations governing a passage that for many had become as routine as crossing from one side of the Mississippi River to the other was for many citizens of, say, Missouri and Illinois. What did it mean, many must have wondered, to all of a sudden be living in a new and different country—without ever having left home? Unlike the immigrants who came to this country from abroad, the Mexicans of the Lower Rio Grande Valley had not chosen to come to the United States at all: they were Mexicans living in Mexico, who were conquered by military force and who now found themselves a minority in a nation run by people who did not even speak their language.

From the 1750s (when the first Europeans settled here) to the present, the Lower Rio Grande Valley has been a place where Indian, Spanish, and Anglo cultures rub against each other, sometimes setting off sparks of violent physical conflict, other times sparking boldly original creativity. In the four National Register Historic Districts of this region—San Ygnacio, La Lomita, Roma, and San Agustin—one can see and touch the physical remains of the complex cultural heritage that shaped this area in such distinctive ways. These places evoke the past with architecture and artifact. But if we want that past to live and breathe and if we want to understand the ways in which it continues to suffuse the present, we must read it through the powerful and luminous poetry and prose of imaginative writers from the Valley such as Gloria Anzaldúa, Américo Paredes, Tomás Rivera, Jovita González, and Rolando Hinojosa.

The two-hundred-mile border area between Laredo and Brownsville on U.S. Routes 83 and 281 includes scores of sites on the National Register, ranging from rural chapels to town plazas, from houses and stores to ranch buildings, agricultural fields, forts, and an irrigation pumping station—as well as many other historic sites not yet on the register (the National Trust for Historic Preservation has named the Lower Rio Grande Heritage Corridor one of America's Most Endangered Historic Places). The San Augustin, San Ygnacio, Roma, and La Lomita Historic Districts, in Webb, Zapata, Starr, and Hidalgo Counties, respectively, on the banks of the Rio Grande include a rich sampling of many of these sites, and together evoke much of the history that infuses the work of twentieth-century Chicano writers from this region. Poet and essayist Gloria Anzaldúa, author, editor, or coeditor of books including the groundbreaking *Borderlands/La Frontera; This Bridge Called My Back: Writing by Radical Women of Color*; and *Haciendo Caras: Making Face, Making Soul*, was born and raised in Hidalgo County, not far from La Lomita Historic District, as was the prolific fiction writer Rolando Hinojosa, author of *Estampas del valle y otras obras*, recast in English as *The Valley*, as well as more than half a dozen other novels. Jovita González de Mireles, author of *Caballero, Dew on the Thorn*, and other fiction, was born and raised on her family's ranch in Roma. Américo Paredes, the pioneering novelist and folklorist of the border, whose books include the remarkable novel *George Washington Gómez* and *With His Pistol in His Hand: A Border Ballad and Its Hero*, was born and raised in Brownsville in nearby Cameron County. And Tomás Rivera, author of the original and compelling coming-of-age novel about a young migrant farmworker, . . . *Y no se lo tragó la tierra* [. . . *And the Earth Did Not Devour Him*], worked as a child in fields in this region. The Lower Rio Grande has nourished creativity in its valley with both mortar and metaphor: the sites we can still visit today along its banks were constructed out of stones, mud, clay, and other building materials drawn from the river; and the literature that has given this part of the country a special place in the American imaginary has been drawn from the river, as well, as writers reared on its banks have wrought from the cultures that clash and mingle in its flow works of the imagination of rare and lasting power.

Before the Spaniards colonized this region, the land now occupied by these historic districts was inhabited by Coahuiltecan Indians, and later by Lipan Apaches, Comanches, and other Native American tribes. The first European settlements in the areas that would become the San Augustin, San Ygnacio, Roma, and La Lomita Historic Districts were organized in the mid-eighteenth century by José de Escandón, a Spaniard charged by the governor of New Spain with establishing Spanish colonial settlements in northern Mexico. All of the districts occupy land that was divided by Spanish royal commissioners in the mid-eighteenth century into *porciones*, or land grants, each of which included about two-thirds of a mile of river frontage and extended back from there for eleven to sixteen miles. San Ygnacio was settled in 1830 by Jesús Treviño and other former residents of the Escandón-founded settlement of Revilla on a corner of a land grant that Escandón had made to José Vázquez Borrego in 1750. San Agustin Historic District in Laredo was a colonial city of New Spain (San Agustin de Laredo), founded under the authority of Escandón in 1755. Roma-Los Saenz was founded in the mid-1760s by local ranchers who were his followers. And La Lomita sits on two *porciones* originally awarded in 1767. The region became officially a part of the United States in 1848 with the Treaty of Guadalupe-Hidalgo—but to this day, many residents conduct their lives in Spanish rather than English, in communities suffused by Mexican culture, Mexican architecture, and Mexican traditions. The "natural" border between the two nations turns out to be a highly *un*natural border for many who grew up there, like Anzaldúa, who sees the border as a

1,950 mile-long open wound
    dividing a *pueblo*, a culture,   staking fence rods in my flesh,
        running down the length   splits me   splits me
           of my body,   me raja   me raja

"This is my home," she continues, "this thin edge of / barbwire." "The U.S.-Mexican border," Anzaldúa writes, "*es una herida abierta* where the Third World grates against the first and bleeds. And before a scab forms it hemorrhages again, the lifeblood of two worlds merging to form a third country—a border culture."

The Jesús Treviño fort and residence in the San Ygnacio Historic District—a compound composed of several one-story buildings made of local river sandstone, with hand-hewn doors made of local mesquite—was surrounded by a high stone wall with *troneras*, or gun ports, to defend against attacks by Comanches and Lipan Apaches. In 1851, an unusual sundial was constructed above the fort's main entrance. It has two faces, one facing north (for summer) and one facing south (for winter). It serves as a daily reminder that in this region of contested identities and allegiance, one must look both north toward the United States and south toward Mexico to get one's bearings.

Getting one's bearings in this turbulent part of world has never been easy. The late-eighteenth- and early-nineteenth-century Spanish-Mexican *hacienda* society gave way to an Anglo-Mexican ranch society in the mid-nineteenth century, which was transformed into a segregated farm society by an agricultural revolution at the turn of the century, which gave way—only in part—to an urban-industrial society as the twentieth century neared its close. What we see today at the San Ygnacio, La Lomita, Roma, and San Agustin historic districts reflect all of these historical moments, superimposed on one another over time. The Chicano writers from the Valley whose lives were shaped by this history help us see in vividly concrete terms those complex layers of human experience.

For the residents of hundreds of scattered ranches that dotted the Valley in the middle of the nineteenth century, the black-robed *padre* on horseback was a familiar sight. The Missionary Oblates of Mary Immaculate—a Catholic order founded in France in 1816—dispatched its first five missionary priests to Texas in 1849, one year after the Mexican War, headquartered them in Brownsville, and sent additional priests each year to minister to the spiritual needs of the ranching families and everyone who worked the land in the area. A convenient way station between Brownsville and the second headquarters they set up in Roma was the ranch of a devout French Catholic named René Guyard, where the *padres* built an adobe chapel in 1865 and named it La Lomita Chapel, after the "little hill" on which it sat. Guyard willed his land to two Oblate priests "for the propagation of the faith among the barbarians." When a flood destroyed the small chapel in 1899, a new one was built that can still be seen today. The intimate little twelve-by-twenty-five-foot white stuccoed building with its original pews and railings, surrounded by scores of acres of farmland, reflects the austere and simple life of circuit-riding missionary priests in rural South Texas. It is the centerpiece of La Lomita Historic District (five miles south of Mission, Texas, on Texas route FM 1016, in Hidalgo County).

In her novel *Dew on the Thorn*, a loosely autobiographical blend of folklore and fiction whose story begins in 1904, Roma native Jovita González conveys the excitement that a visit from an Oblate priest provokes in a rural ranch in this area. The children "fell upon him as an avalanche."

He laughed and talked with them pretending not to know the foremost thought in their minds. And when he saw their wide-opened eyes and the longing glances they cast upon his bulging saddlebags, he opened them with ceremonious precision. For these saddlebags, contained the mysterious wonders and riches of Aladdin's cave. He brought bright-colored pictures which satisfied their love for the bizarre: Daniel in the lions' den; .... the adoration of the Magi; pictures of Saint Francis, gaunt and ethereal, a skull, at which the children shuddered, hanging from the rosary at his belt; Saint Cecilia, at the organ, a shower of roses falling on her hands; a guardian angel in blue, watching over two children dressed in purple and pink.

"See this medal," he said, holding it up beyond their reach. "I'd give it to the one who can say the Our Father best." They hesitated timidly at first, but encouraged by his friendly nods and smiles, he got the results he wanted.

Known as the "cowboy priest" by his flock, "this black-robed Oblate was a quaint figure as he rode through the country on his white horse, wearing deerskin leggings, a big cloak

La Lomita Chapel, in La Lomita Historic District, five miles south of Mission, Texas, built by the Oblate Fathers, was a base from which "*vaquero priests*" like those described by Jovita González in her novel *Dew on the Thorn* could serve the rural ranching communities between Brownsville and Roma.

PHOTO CREDIT: PHOTO BY SHELLEY FISHER FISHKIN.

and a broad-brimmed hat tied under the chin. Many were the stories that were told about him and his fortitude and nothing pleased his friends more than to tell the exploits of this, their *vaquero* priest. For Father José María was an expert horseman and could ride any beast that walked on four legs." In the twentieth century, the Oblate fathers and brothers would continue to serve the people who worked the land in South Texas, positioning themselves at the forefront of the fight to give farmworkers wages on which they could live. In 1930, an Oblate father organized the first farmworkers' union in Texas, and in 1966, another led a march of ten thousand farmworkers from Rio Grande City to Austin to demand a minimum wage. Two days later, Congress voted to extend the minimum wage to farmworkers.

In Gloria Anzaldúa's memorable poetry, in the lyrical prose-poems of Tomás Rivera, and in the colloquial sketches of Rolando Hinojosa-Smith, we encounter in vivid, concrete detail the lives of those who worked the fields of this region and whose plight the Oblate fathers championed. Anzaldúa grew up on a small ranch settlement called Jesús Maria in Hidalgo County where she worked in the fields and tended cows and chickens. She labored as a migrant worker when she was seven or eight and then moved to the Hidalgo County town of Hargill—but continued working in the fields of her home valley until she earned her B.A. from Pan American University. The seventh generation in her family to live in the Valley, Anzaldúa was the first to leave (to do graduate work at the University of Texas at Austin). But, as she tells us in *Borderlands/La Frontera*, her firsthand knowledge of "the hardships of working in the fields and of being a migrant laborer" herself formed her, and imbued her with "a very deep respect for all the migrant laborers, the so-called *campesinos*," a respect that prompted her to teach migrant children after she finished college and to write the poems that capture some of the texture of that life. She wrote the poem "Sus plumas el viento" for her mother, Amalia Anzaldúa:

Swollen feet
tripping on vines in the heat,
palms thick and green-knuckled,
sweat drying on top of old sweat,

. . . .

She husks corn, hefts watermelons.
Bends all the way, digs out strawberries

half buried in the dirt.
Twelve hours later
roped knots cord her back

. . . .

Burlap sack wet around her waist,
stained green from leaves and the smears of worms.
White heat no water no place to pee
the men staring at her ass.
Como una mula,
she shifts 150 pounds of cotton onto her back.

. . . .

cutting   washing   weighing   packaging
broccoli spears carrots cabbages in 12 hours   15
double shift the roar of machines inside her head.

. . . .

She folds wounded birds, her hands
into the nest, her armpits
looks up at the Texas sky.
Si el viento le diera sus plumas.

She vows to get out
of the numbing chill, the 110 degree heat.

. . . .

[*Si el viento le diera sus plumas*—if the wind would give her its feathers]

Hidalgo County produced more cabbages (and more onions, cantaloupes, carrots, and watermelons) than any other county in Texas in the 1980s, when Anzaldúa published *Borderlands/La Frontera*. She dedicated one of the poems in that book, "*Un mar de repollos*" or "A Sea of Cabbages" (written in Spanish and translated by

Anzaldúa into English), to *"la gente que siempre ha trabajado en las labores"*—which she translates as "those who have worked in the fields." The farmworker in this poem is

> On his knees, hands swollen
> sweat flowering on his face
> his gaze on the high paths
>
> . . . .
>
> Century after century swimming
> with arthritic arms, back and forth
> circling, going around and around
> like a worm in a green sea
>
> . . . .
>
> At noon on the edge
> of the hives of cabbage
> in the fields of a *ranchito* in *Tejas*
> he takes out his chile wrapped in tortillas
> drinks water made hot soup by the sun.
> Sometimes he curses
>
> his luck, the land, the sun.
>
> . . . .
>
> His hands tore cabbages from their nests,
> ripping the ribbed leaves covering tenderer leaves
> encasing leaves yet more pale
>
> . . . .
>
> Century after century flailing,
> unleafing himself in a sea of cabbages. . . .

The average life span of a Mexican farm laborer, according to Anzaldúa, is fifty-six. But, she writes, her own father, who worked as a sharecropper and a migrant worker, lived to be only thirty-eight—"having worked himself to death."

Gloria Anzaldúa's family had farmed their own land in the Valley for generations. But after her maternal grandfather's death, her widowed grandmother lost the land when she fell behind on her taxes after two years of crushing drought. "'A smart *gabacho* lawyer took the land. *No hablaba inglés*, she didn't know how to ask for time to raise the money.' My father's mother, Mama Locha, also lost her *terreno*," Anzaldúa writes. "For a while we got $12.50 a year for the 'mineral rights' of six acres of cemetery, all that was left of the ancestral lands." As David Montejano notes in *Anglos and Mexicans in the Making of Texas,*

Gloria Anzaldúa (1942–2004), the Lower Rio Grande Valley's uncrowned poet laureate, has helped ensure the Valley's survival in American literature—as a site of paradox and ambivalence, of conflict, crossfire, and creativity.

PHOTO CREDIT: PHOTO BY ANNIE VALVA; COURTESY OF THE PHOTOGRAPHER AND RARE BOOKS AND MANUSCRIPTS, BENSON LATIN AMERICAN COLLECTION, UNIVERSITY OF TEXAS LIBRARIES, AUSTIN, TX.

1836–1986, "By 1920, the Texas Mexican people had generally been reduced, except in a few border counties, to the status of landless and dependent wage laborers." In an extraordinary and chilling poem, "We Call Them Greasers," Anzaldúa impersonates the voice of an Anglo who coolly describes what for him is a typical, run-of-the-mill land grab (less "typical," perhaps, but nonetheless not unknown, alas, are the rape, murder, and lynching that he casually perpetrates while taking the land):

We Call Them Greasers

I found them here when I came.
They were growing corn in their small *ranchos*
raising cattle, horses
smelling of woodsmoke and sweat.
They knew their betters:
took off their hats
placed them over their hearts,
lowered their eyes in my presence.

Weren't interested in bettering themselves,
why they didn't even own the land but shared it.
Wasn't hard to drive them off,
cowards, they were, no backbone.
I showed 'em a piece of paper with some writing
tole 'em they owed taxes
had to pay right away or be gone by *mañana*.
By the time me and my men had waved
that same piece of paper to all the families
it was all frayed at the ends.

Some loaded their chickens children wives and pigs
into rickety wagons, pans and tools dangling
clanging from all sides.
Couldn't take their cattle—
During the night my boys had frightened them off.
Oh, there were a few troublemakers
who claimed we were the intruders.
Some even had land grants
and appealed to the courts.
It was a laughing stock
them not even knowing English.
Still some refused to budge,
even after we burned them out.
And the women—well I remember one in particular.

She lay under me whimpering.
I plowed into her hard
kept thrusting and thrusting
felt him watching from the mesquite tree
heard him keening like a wild animal
in that instant I felt such contempt for her
round face and beady black eyes like an Indian's.
Afterwards I sat on her face until
her arms stopped flailing,
didn't want to waste a bullet on her.
The boys wouldn't look me in the eyes.
I walked up to where I had tied her man to the tree
and spat in his face. Lynch him, I told the boys.

Unfortunately, the racism that Anzaldúa captures in this poem is not one poet's nightmare fantasy: it is echoed in fiction and journalism by virtually every Tejano writer from the Valley and is widely documented by historians, as well. Even Jovita González, famed for her stories of intermarriage and acculturation, writes in *Caballero* (a book she coauthored with Margaret Elmer, who wrote under the name Eve Raleigh) that "Mexicans were killed for a cow or horse, for no reason at all." Legal recourse was a myth for many Tejano victims of Anglo violence along the Lower Rio Grande. As Rolando Hinojosa writes in his novel *The Valley*, "Van Meers shot young Ambrosio Mora on a bright, cloudless afternoon, and in front of no less than fifteen witnesses. It took the People of the State of Texas some five years to prepare the case against him, and when it did, the State witnesses spoke on behalf of Van Meers and against the victim."

Lynchings of both Mexican Americans and African American men by Anglos reached such terrifying proportions that Anglo women like Jessie Daniel Ames and Chicana writer Jovita Idár launched major campaigns to shame their fellow Texans into stopping the violence. (Greater silence has surrounded the kind of brutality against women that Anzaldúa's poem depicts, but that does not mean that such scenes are solely the fruit of a poet's imagination; Anzaldúa was responding to a context of violence against women that she saw both Mexican and Anglo patriarchal culture in South Texas tolerating to varying degrees.)

Not all Mexican Texans were defrauded of their land. The family of Manuel Guerra in Roma, for example, managed to retain land around the Roma plaza that had been in the family since the original Spanish land grant. In *The Valley*, Rolando Hinojosa gives us a glimpse of how some Valley families fought to keep what was theirs:

The Vilches, Garrido, and Malacara families formed an unshakeable alliance in the defense of their lands (all original grants from the Crown). The first run-in against the Rangers—*los rinches*—was at the old Toluca Ranch, a Vilches family holding, hard by Relámpago, but closer to the old burned church. The second engagement took place at the Carmen Ranch held by don Jesús Buenrostro, who was also called *El quieto.* The fighting started on a Palm Sunday and ended the following Easter Sunday. *Los rinches* stopped their harassment at that end of the Valley when the mexicano ranch hands started firing back at them.

At other times, and other places, however, the mexicano property owners lost both lands and friends, legally at times, and as a result of backstabbing at others. Those who died in these affrays died facing North and with their backs to the Río Grande; as they said, "We were born here, we may as well die and be buried here, too. Come on, you *rinche* bastards!"

(Part of the old Toluca Ranch to which Hinojosa refers is now a historic site located near Route 281 in Hidalgo County in the vicinity of Progreso.) The story of how Mexican families who had owned lands in the Valley for generations lost their land to Anglo newcomers is no less troubling for being slightly different in each case. Whether by law or by force, by persuasion or intimidation, by honest businessmen, or by swindling opportunists, the end result was the same: old landowning Tejano families like Anzaldúa's were reduced to working on other people's land.

In *Borderlands/La Frontera*, Anzaldúa writes:

In the 1930s, after Anglo agribusiness corporations cheated the small Chicano landowners of their land, the corporations hired gangs of *mexicanos* to pull out the brush, chaparral and cactus and to irrigate the desert. The land they toiled over had once belonged to many of them, or had been used communally by them. Later, the Anglos brought in huge machines and root plows and had the Mexicans scrape the land clean of natural vegetation. In my childhood I saw the end of dryland farming. I witnessed the land cleared; saw the huge pipes connected to underwater sources sticking up in the air. As children, we'd go fishing in some of those canals when they were full and hunt for snakes in them when they were dry. In the 1950s, I saw the land cut up into thousands of neat rectangles and squares, constantly being irrigated. In the 340-day growth season, the seeds of any kind of fruit or vegetable had only to be stuck in the ground in order to grow.

While the ancients had offered blood sacrifices for rain, Anzaldúa writes, "Now for rain (irrigation) one offers not a sacrifice of blood, but of money."

During the first wave of irrigation in this region, the Old Irrigation Pumphouse at Hidalgo (part of the Louisiana–Rio Grande Canal Company Irrigation System) pumped water to fields in Hidalgo County. The industrial complex (the housing, the pumps, boilers, motors, and other equipment needed to irrigate the fields) was built between 1910 and 1912. The pumping station used boilers heated with mesquite wood fires to power irrigation pumps that were 20 feet in diameter. The pumps could push up to 250,000 gallons of water per minute from the Rio Grande into irrigation canals that supplied forty thousand acres of land in Hidalgo County with water. Citrus, cotton, and sugar cane, along with cabbage, onions, carrots, green beans, melons, lettuce, and corn were among the crops that

The pumps of the Old Irrigation Pumphouse at Hidalgo (part of the Louisiana–Rio Grande Canal Company Irrigation System) pushed up to a quarter-million gallons of water per minute from the Rio Grande into irrigation canals that supplied forty thousand acres of land in Hidalgo County with water, making possible a year-round growing season. As a child, Gloria Anzaldúa picked fruits and vegetables in the fields it irrigated, alongside other members of her family. She evokes the exploitation and hardship endured by farmworkers like her parents in moving poetry and searing prose in *Borderlands/La Frontera*. The complex is now home to a branch of the World Birding Center, run by Texas Parks and Wildlife.

PHOTO CREDIT: PHOTOS BY SHELLEY FISHER FISHKIN.

the irrigation made possible or facilitated. The railroad, which had come to the Valley in 1904, allowed crops to reach a national market. Opened to the public in 1999, the pumphouse is the last extant example of a steam-powered irrigation pump in the nation.

The water may have made the year-round growing season possible; but it was the workers—like Gloria Anzaldúa and her parents—who turned that possibility into wealth that passed by the people who produced it. She recalled that during her childhood, "sometimes we earned less than we owed, but always the corporations fared well." Hidalgo County may have been one of the most prosperous agricultural regions in the country in terms of the vegetables and fruits its labor force produced, but those workers themselves were some of the poorest in the nation. In 1987, the year that *Borderlands/La Frontera* was published, the county's largest metropolitan area had the lowest per capita income in the United States.

*E*n 1521 nació una nueva raza, el mestizo, el mexicano (people of mixed Indian and Spanish blood), a race that never existed before," Anzaldúa tells us. "Chicanos, Mexican-Americans, are the offspring of those first matings." Three hundred years later, Anglos and other Europeans were added to the cultural mix of the Lower Rio Grande Valley—through conquest, but also through intermarriage. The fifteen-block Roma Historic District in Starr County (also known as Roma-Los Saenz, since two adjoining settlements have incorporated) embodies the distinctive cultural blend of the region in an area that looks much the way it did in 1900. Located on U.S. Route 83 and the Rio Grande, directly across from Ciudad Miguel Alemán in the Mexican state of Tamaulipas, Roma, with more than a dozen historic homes, stores, and other buildings around the main plaza, chronicles in river sandstone, *caliche* limestone, and molded brick the mingling of families, nations, and traditions that Roma-born novelist Jovita González chronicles in fiction in her novel *Caballero: A Historical Novel*. The site of the last surviving international suspension bridge on the Rio Grande (the Roma–San Pedro Steel Suspension Bridge, still standing but no longer in use), the Roma Historic District is itself a bridge—between two countries, and between the present and the past. The houses and stores in the Historic District, which date from the 1850s through 1880s, blend Spanish, Mexican, American, and German building techniques and architectural tastes—as a direct result of a marriage between a German immigrant who became the master-builder of the region and the daughter of an old Mexican family.

The idea of intermarriage was highly threatening to many of the old *hidalgo* or *ranchero* class. It was to this class that Jovita González traced her own eighteenth-century Spanish settlement roots (although she herself was financially strapped throughout her life). In *Caballero*, she depicts some of the ignorance and prejudice that made intermarriage so dreaded for many old families in this region.

Susanita, daughter of a prominent Mexican *ranchero* near Roma, is shocked when an itinerant Mexican trader from whom she has just purchased elegant satin, wool, and lace casually mentions that his daughter is "married to a man from the north whose ancestors came from England." "Susanita said timidly, 'Papa says none of them are gentlemen. Is he—good to her?' The trader laughed at the thought of his very correct Bostonian son-in-law not being a gentleman. 'Either your *papa* has not known any of them or views them with the eyes of prejudice. If pampering and deferring can be called good, then he is very good indeed to her.'" For a time Susanita refuses to believe that "men of an inferior race, as the Americans were viewed, could treat a girl with greater courtesy and gentleness than a Mexican *caballero*." But ultimately she succumbs to the charms of a dashing *americano* army officer, and, to the dismay of her father, decides to marry him.

It is quite possible that the family of Leonarda Campos in Mier, a Mexican town across the river from Roma, may have had some of the same doubts about the suitability of a man named Heinrich Portscheller as a husband for their daughter, for he came from another culture—Germany—a place about which they probably knew as little as Susanita knew of Boston. Born in Germany in 1840, Portscheller had fled the Russian army for Mexico only to be impressed in Vera Cruz in 1865 into the Imperial Army of Maximilian—which he later deserted to fight for the opposing side. In 1879, Portscheller proposed to Leonarda Campos, and his proposal was accepted. The couple lived in Mier for a few years after their marriage; by 1883 they had moved across the river to Roma. Over the next eleven years, Roma's architectural landscape would be changed forever by his enterprise and craft.

Portscheller became the preeminent master-builder and designer of the city. In partnership with a Mr. Margo and a Mr. Perez, he established a brickyard that manufactured large, salmon/buff-colored molded bricks (2¾ inches by 4⅛ inches by 8¾ inches). Portscheller's attractive, sophisticated, decorative molded brick was used to construct numerous buildings in Roma, Rio Grande City, and Laredo, as well as in Mier, across the border. The local building techniques before Portscheller built his brick factory consisted principally of technologies that came directly from eighteenth-century traditions in northern Mexico. One can see the earlier model in the 1850 Garcia House, on the Roma plaza, constructed out of river sandstone, featuring the typi-

Roma-born novelist and folklorist Jovita González (1904–1983), author of *Dew on the Thorn* and *Caballero* (coauthored with Eve Raleigh). The architecture of her hometown reflects the blend of Mexican and Anglo-European culture she delineates in her novels.

PHOTO CREDIT: COURTESY OF THE
E. E. MIRELES AND JOVITA GONZÁLEZ
MIRELES PAPERS, SPECIAL COLLECTIONS
AND ARCHIVES, TEXAS A&M
UNIVERSITY–CORPUS CHRISTI, MARY
AND JEFF BELL LIBRARY.

cally Mexican enclosed walled courtyards with interior patios; the remnants of the enclosing walls of the Garcia House can still be seen at the rear of the house, sloping toward the river. When Portscheller designed the nearby Antonia Sáenz House in 1884, he kept the enclosed courtyard design, but used molded brick from his brick factory instead of river sandstone, allowing him to fashion elaborate classical detailing around the house's doors and windows, as well as on its cornice. He may have learned some of his brickmaking techniques (such as the technology of flat brick roofing) in Monterrey, Mexico, where he lived before moving to Mier, and then Roma; indeed, the decorative, second-story, wrought iron balconies that his buildings often featured were characteristic of buildings in Monterrey (as well as New Orleans, where Portscheller's wrought iron railings came from). But some of the decorative details that made his buildings so different and pleasing were probably informed by brickwork he recalled from his native Germany.

While the majority of houses in Roma when Portscheller arrived followed the typical northern Mexico interior-courtyard design, the two-story, stucco-covered, stone Noah Cox House built in 1850 by a Swedish immigrant named John Vale sticks out as being distinctly different, looking more like houses one might find in New England. The difference between the two approaches to home design comes across clearly in a conversation in *Caballero* that takes place the late 1840s between Dona Maria Petronilla, who lives in a traditional *hacienda* outside Roma, and American soldier Robert Warrener, would-be suitor of her daughter Susanita. This is the first conversation Dona Petronilla and Robert Warrener have ever had. "It is like heaven," Warrener says, "coming from the heat of the plains into this delightful *patio*." Dona Petronilla agrees, adding, "I have heard that among your people the houses are not built with a patio. How then have you comfort and a friendly place to meet your visitors?" She is thinking "(What sort of home would you take my baby to, if you took her away from here? Love is not enough when the family is alien and living is ugly. . . .)" Warrener says, "My father's home, as are all the large houses, is high, *señora*, with bedrooms and the ladies' *salas* on the second floor. A wide and open stairway leads to them from the *sala* downstairs, so that . . . the ladies can look like beautiful queens as they come down the steps. . . . Our houses have many windows of glass, *señora*, and are not dark inside as yours are, for we have many days without sun and winter is too cold to sit outdoors." Dona Petronilla is shocked at the idea of days so dark and cold that one lives inside all the time. The houses Portscheller built in Roma were set near the street (behind raised sidewalks, or *banquetas*) in the Mexican style, with interior courtyards, rather than set back behind lawns like the American homes Warrener described to Dona Maria Petronilla. Big lawns were fancifully improbable in this sun-drenched, arid land.

Portscheller-designed buildings in Roma that display his distinctive ornamental brickwork include the Manuel Guerra House and Store, the Nestor Sáenz Store, and the Raphael García Ramírez House. His designs and construction were favored by the prosperous merchant class in this vibrant hub of commerce and trade. (Other Portscheller-designed buildings in Starr County from the 1880s that are on the National Register of Historic Places include the beautiful, classically proportioned Silverio de la Peña Post Office and Drugstore, now a private residence, in Rio Grande City.)

The union of Mexican and American in this region, imagined in the marriage of Susanita de Mendoza and Robert Warrener in *Caballero*, and reflected in the blending of Mexican and American architectural styles in Portscheller's buildings, existed against a backdrop of violence, corruption, and racial and political tensions. Behind the pleasing pink facade of the Manuel Guerra House and Store in Roma, for example, Democratic political boss Manuel Guerra worked to mobilize the region's Mexican American working-class majority and consolidate his political power in the face of challenges from Anglo farmers and businessmen in northern Starr County. Guerra, whose reign in Starr County was characterized by widespread corruption, controlled its politics until his death in 1915; his family continued to rule the county until after World War II.

The Manuel Guerra House and Store recalls an important dimension of the blending of Anglo and Mexican culture along the Lower Rio Grande. Behind Portscheller's ornate brick cornices, in the building's traditional enclosed courtyard and in the ground-floor store and upstairs residence, political deals were cut between Mexican and Anglo politicians that sealed the political fate of the residents of Starr County for more than a generation. The first member of the Guerra family came to the Roma area in 1767 and received *porciones* 80 and 81 from the Spanish Crown. Manuel Guerra was born in Mexico in 1856 at the family home in Mier and came to Roma in 1877, where he opened a business and married Miss Virginia Cox, the daughter of a Kentuckian father and a Mexican mother. He was the leading Mexican businessman, banker, rancher, and politician on the border. His political ambitions led him to become an American citizen, and shortly thereafter he became the recognized leader of Starr County's Democratic Party, a political boss who was the right-hand man of Jim Wells, the Cameron County–based Anglo political boss whose powerful influence stretched across the Valley. Guerra accumulated political power through loans and favors, as well as through the aid of his large extended family. At his store on the Roma plaza, for example, he gave credit to area ranchers and bartered other favors for votes. The political campaigns and elections were bloody and deeply corrupt.

Américo Paredes's brilliant epic novel, *George Washington Gómez: A Mexicotexan Novel*, provides a window on both the political battles and the modus operandi of Guerra's key mentor and ally, Jim Wells. Paredes, the dean of Chicano letters, wrote the novel in the 1930s but did not publish it until 1990. *George Washington Gómez* captures with drama and power the political and racial tensions of the Valley—as well as the manner in which Anglo politicians like Wells earned Mexican American

Américo Paredes (1915–1999), a folklorist and novelist born in Brownsville, Texas, was the author of *George Washington Gómez: A Mexicotexan Novel*, a brilliant work that captures the political, social, and psychological complexity of growing up Mexican American in the Lower Rio Grande Valley.
PHOTO CREDIT: PHOTO BY JESSE HERRERA.

allies. In testimony he gave in a legal case in 1919, Wells maintained that any influence he had on Mexican citizens of Texas was due to the fact that in his forty-one years in the Valley, he "tried to so conduct myself as to show them that I was their friend and that they could trust me." Wells is the model for Judge Norris (initially called "the Gringo"), a key figure who sets the plot in motion in Paredes's novel.

The story begins shortly after the 1915 effort by Mexican Americans and Mexican nationals to create an independent Spanish-speaking republic of the Southwest. (It was not the first time a plan of this general nature won supporters in the region, as the 1840 effort commemorated in the Museum of the Republic of the Rio Grande in the San Agustin de Laredo Historic District makes clear.) In the aftermath of the failed uprising, Texas Rangers gunned down hundreds of innocent Mexican American farmworkers if they suspected that the workers had even a shred of sympathy for the *sediciosos*, or seditionists, as they were called, who fomented the rebellion. Over the next four years, literally thousands more Mexican Americans would be killed by Texas Rangers, as a state investigation later revealed. *George Washington Gómez* begins with one such murder. The innocent victim is Gumersindo Gómez, a man who had just named his infant son "George Washington" because he believed that he was "going to be a great man among the Gringos" someday. (When he had been trying to choose a name, he asked his brother-in law, Feliciano, "'What great men have the Gringos had?' 'They are all great,' growled Feliciano, 'Great thieves, great liars, great sons-of-bitches.'")

After the Rangers kill Gumersindo, Feliciano leaves his home (the small town of

San Pedrito) with his sister and her children, and is en route to Jonesville-on-the-Grande (Brownsville) when he has his own terrifying encounter with six men he believes to be *rinches*, or Texas Rangers, who block his way. One of the men starts

> staring at Maria, appraising her as he would a horse. Feliciano felt real fear for the first time that afternoon. . . .
>
> "Let me pass," he said fiercely in Spanish. "*Dejame pasar, gringo sanavabiche!*"
>
> Abruptly the *rinche* stopped laughing. His face took on a nasty, deliberate expression. . . . Feliciano's eyes fixed on that freckled hand as it traveled slowly, slowly up the dirty leather chaps toward the pistol holster. . . . Naked, helpless he waited for the *rinche* to draw and fire. Finally the *rinche* drew and aimed at Feliciano, who stared at the end of the barrel.

At that point, however, "a massive Gringo sitting on a big and powerful horse" who "dressed like a city man except for his Stetson and boots" arrives, talking loudly and angrily, and "soon the *rinche* puts away his gun. . . . The *rinches* looked sullen and uncomfortable." The old Gringo orders the *rinches* to "*Vamoose!*" and to Feliciano's shock, that's what they do. After they've gone, Judge Norris learns that Feliciano is headed to Jonesville, and he asks him about his plans.

> "What are you going to do when you get to Jonesville?"
>
> "Look for a job. And a place for us to stay."
>
> "Can you read and write?"
>
> "Only in Spanish."
>
> "That's good enough."
>
> Again the old Gringo looked Feliciano over. "On Polk Street," he said, "right close to Fort Jones, there is a *cantina* called El Danubio Azul. . . . Go there and ask for the man who runs the place and tell him Judge Norris sent you. . . . Tell him I said for him to find you some place to stay, and that I've hired you as a bartender."
>
> "*Señor juez,* I don't know how to thank you."
>
> "No need to." The judge picked up his reins and pulled his horse's head to one side. "By the way," he said, "were you born in San Pedrito?"
>
> "Yes sir."
>
> "Have you ever voted?"
>
> Feliciano shook his head. "You'll learn," said the judge, and he trotted away ahead of them on his giant of a horse.

Judge Norris not only saves Feliciano's life, but sets him up with a job and a house—as well as a second job as a political operative charged with persuading Mexican Texans to let the Blues (the judge's political faction) pay their poll tax and control their vote. Although in most of Texas, Mexican American and African American men were denied the vote in the early twentieth century despite the fact that voting was their legal right, in Jonesville-on-the-Grande, "which was more than 90 percent Mexican," Paredes tells us, "everybody voted, including some gentlemen residing in the cemetery, not to mention a few of the living and breathing whose residence and place of birth was the sister city of Morelos across the river."

The Democratic Party "was always in power, but that did not preclude the free exercise of democracy," given the party's division into two factions, the Blues and the Reds. "The successful side," Paredes write, "always was the one that was able to convince the most voters to allow their campaign workers to buy their poll taxes and to school them in the voting process." Feliciano proved to be as effective at delivering the Mexican American vote in Jonesville-on-the-Grande for Judge Norris's Blues as Manuel Guerra was at delivering the Mexican American vote in Starr County for Jim Wells's Blues.

> Feliciano was outfitted with a buggy drawn by a fine-looking sorrel gelding. His job was to visit every house in the Second and Third Wards and talk the men into letting the Blues buy their poll taxes. If they were willing, he took down their names, addresses and their ages. Feliciano discovered he was very good at this kind of work. He was an earnest and fluent speaker. . . . He talked to people in their homes, convincing them of the benefits of voting for the Blues. . . .
>
> Once the canvassing for votes was over, it was time for the *carne asada* parties given the faithful, where barbecued beef and goat were abundant as were cold beer and mescal.

Paredes's novel focuses principally on Feliciano's nephew, Guálinto—what "Washington" sounded like in Spanish to his family when they named him—as he deals with the challenge of divided identity in the borderlands of culture that is the Lower Rio Grande Valley: "In the schoolroom he was an American; at home and on the playground he was a Mexican. Throughout his early childhood these two selves grew within him without much conflict, each an exponent of a different tongue and a different way of living," Paredes writes.

The boy nurtured these two selves within him, each radically different and antagonistic to the other, without realizing their separate existences. It would be several years before he fully realized that there was not one single Guálinto Gómez. That in fact there were many Guálinto Gómezes, each of them double like images reflected on two glass surfaces of a show window. The eternal conflict between two clashing forces within him produced a divided personality, made up of tight little cells independent and almost entirely ignorant of each other, spread out over his consciousness, mixed with one another like squares on the checkerboard.

The intriguing coming-of-age novel, which bears comparison to Abraham Cahan's book, *The Rise of David Levinsky*, follows Guálinto from birth, through his childhood, high school, college, and marriage to Ellen, an Anglo woman whom he meets he met at college, whose father—currently a resident of Boulder, Colorado—had briefly been a Texas Ranger in his hometown. "George Washington Go-maize," Ellen's father says when the two meet for the first time.

> "They sure screwed you up, didn't they, boy? . . . You look white but you're a goddam Meskin. And what does your mother do but give you a nigger name. George Washington Go-maize."
>
> "Now Daddy," Ellen said, as if chiding a naughty child. "There's nothing wrong with his name. It was George's father who gave it to him because he admired the father of our country."
>
> "Anyway," the old man said, "it don't sound right."
>
> It was then that he decided to legally change his name to George G. Gómez, the middle G. for Garcia, his mother's maiden name.

At the book's close, Gómez is secretive about the new job on which he is about to embark—in border security, as a spy who watches his people—an irony all the more rich given the complex personal and family history that has made him who he is.

If Paredes's George Washington Gómez chose to forget George Washington, one of the most "Mexican" cities in the United States did not: since 1898, the city of Laredo has sponsored a gigantic celebration of George Washington's birthday, which has become the largest annual festival in South Texas. The San Agustin Historic District (bounded by Iturbide Street on the north, Water Street on the south, Santa Ursula on the east and Convent on the west)—the center of the original city founded in 1755—has always been the site of some of the festivities. Although today Laredo proudly celebrates its bicultural heritage, the Capitol of the Republic of the Rio Grande Museum on the plaza in the Historic District is a reminder of the many times that the city insisted on its independence—from *both* the United States and Mexico. In 1836, during the Texas Revolution, Laredo served as a base for the forces commanded by Mexican general Antonio López de Santa Anna. After the war, residents of Laredo still thought of themselves as citizens of the northern Mexican state of Tamaulipas—and Texas made no serious effort to argue the point. While proudly Mexican, Laredans felt their needs had been ignored for years by the Mexican government. A revolt that had begun among area *rancheros* in 1838 became a full-blown insurrection by 1840 when insurgents announced Laredo to be the capital of a new independent state controlled by neither Mexico nor Texas: the Republic of the Rio Grande. The central government of Mexico responded with decisive force, ending the Republic after 283 days. (The Capitol of the Republic of the Rio Grande Museum—the actual building that served as the short-lived republic's Capitol—tells the story in detail.)

During the Civil War, Laredo took on importance to the Confederacy as a point of entry to Mexico from which Confederate cotton (diverted from the southern coast by Union blockades) could be shipped. In 1864, Union troops with orders to destroy all the bales of cotton stored around San Agustin Plaza advanced on Laredo but were repulsed by Colonel Santos Benavides and his Laredo Confederates. During the years leading up to the Mexican Revolution, Laredo was abuzz with Mexican activists who wanted to topple Mexican dictator Porfirio Díaz. And it was in Laredo that the legendary Gregorio Cortez of *corrido* fame (the subject of Paredes's book *With His Pistol in His Hand*) was forced to turn himself in. Whether they were fighting Texas for their right to be Mexicans, or battling Mexico for their right to be their own country, whether they were taking up arms to support the Confederacy or to support the Mexican people in their efforts to oust an evil dictator, whether they were helping Santa Anna or informing on Gregorio Cortez, citizens of Laredo of both American and Mexican descent have deep roots in the political and social history of both Mexico and the United States.

This distinctive history may help explain why, in the early twentieth century, Laredo writer Jovita Idár took the lead in advocating the respect for diversity necessary for a genuinely bicultural land to survive. In a 1911 article titled "For Our Race: Preservation of Nationalism" in *La Crónica*, a newspaper she edited with her father and brothers, Idár emphasized the importance of creating a place for both Spanish and English in the nation's schools, and of ensuring that Mexican American schoolchildren be taught the history and geography of Mexico, as well as that of the United States—that they be as familiar with the biography of Hidalgo (the father of Mexican independence) as with that of Washington—a cause that Jovita González would champion later in the century. In Spanish-language newspapers in Laredo, Jovita Idár, her father, Nicasio Idár, and her brothers, Eduardo and Clemente, documented the widespread exclusion of Tejano children from U.S. public schools, the discrimination those who made it to school were forced to endure, and the unequal treatment Tejanos received in the justice system. The Idárs were outspoken in documenting the effects of segregation, and in reporting lynchings. When the Texas Rangers tried to close down the newspaper *El Progreso*, angered by an editorial Jovita Idár had written, she heroically stood in the doorway of the newspaper office, preventing them from entering. Outspoken, too, on the issue of feminism and women's role in society, Jovita Idár organized and served as the first president of the League of Mexican Women, a feminist organization that championed education for poor children. The Spanish-language newspapers the Idár family edited in Laredo also played a key role in the cultural life of the city, publishing poets like Sara Estela Ramírez, who, like Jovita Idár, addressed the bicultural nature of life on the border.

Borderlands/La Frontera, Gloria Anzaldúa's hymn to "*mestiza* consciousness" is the late-twentieth-century heir to Jovita Idár's feminism and passion for social justice; to Tomás Rivera's sensitive empathy for the migrant child; to Rolando Hinojosa's dry irony; to Américo Paredes's assumption that "conflict—cultural, economic, and physical" has always "been a way of life along the border between Mexico and the United States"; and to Jovita González's conviction that the two cultures that have clashed from the start in this sunbaked, blood-drenched corner of the world are destined to mingle and coexist. Anzaldúa writes in her poem "*Una lucha de fronteras*/A Struggle of Borders":

> Because I, a *mestiza*,
> continually walk out of one culture
> and into another,
> because I am in all cultures at the same time,
> *alma entre dos mundos, tres, cuatro,*
> *me zumba la cabeza con lo contradictorio.*
> ["Soul between two worlds, three, four,
> My head buzzes with contradictions"].

Anzaldúa is Anglo in a Mexican world, Mexican in an Anglo world, and Indian in neither yet both; female in a male world, lesbian in a heterosexual world—and unwilling to reject any part of herself to stop the contradictory voices that buzz through her head.

But the miracle of *Borderlands/La Frontera* is that she transmutes the buzzing into a wellspring of creativity. In perceiving conflicting information and points of view, she tells us, "the new *mestiza* copes by developing a tolerance for contradictions, a tolerance for ambiguity. She learns to be an Indian in Mexican culture, to be Mexican from an Anglo point of view. She learns to juggle cultures. She has a plural personality. She operates in a pluralistic mode—nothing is thrust out, the good, the bad, and the ugly, nothing is rejected, nothing abandoned. Not only does she sustain contradictions, she turns the ambivalence into something else." "*En unas pocas centurias*," Anzaldúa writes, "the future will belong to the *mestiza*. Because the future depends on the breaking down of paradigms; it depends on the straddling of two or more cultures."

The "new *mestiza*," she tells us, is willing "to make herself vulnerable to foreign ways of seeing and thinking. She surrenders all notions of safety, of the familiar." "Indigenous like corn, like corn, the *mestiza* is a product of crossbreeding, designed for preservation under a variety of conditions. Like an ear of corn—a female seed-bearing organ—the *mestiza* is tenacious, tightly wrapped in the husks of her culture. Like kernels she clings to the cob; with thick stalks and strong brace roots, she holds tight to the earth—she will survive the crossroads."

"*Tierra natal.* This is home, the small towns of the Valley," Anzaldúa writes:

> *los pueblitos* with chicken pens and goats picketed to mesquite shrubs. *En las colonias* on the other side of the tracks, junk cars line the front yards of hot pink and lavender-trimmed houses—Chicano architecture, we call it, self-consciously. I have missed the TV shows where hosts speak in half and half, and where awards are given in the category of Tex-Mex music. I have missed the Mexican cemeteries blooming with artificial flowers, the fields of aloe vera and red pepper, rows of sugar cane, of corn hanging on the stalks, the cloud of *polvareda* in the dirt roads behind a speeding pickup truck, *el sabor de tamales de rez y venado.* . . .
>
> I still feel the old despair when I look at the unpainted, dilapidated, scrap lumber houses consisting mostly of corrugated aluminum. Some of the poorest people in the U.S. live in the Lower Rio Grande Valley, an arid and semi-arid land of irrigated farming, intense sunlight and heat, citrus groves next to chaparral and cactus. I walk through the elementary school I attended so

long ago, that remained segregated until recently. I remember how the white teachers used to punish us for being Mexican.

How I love this tragic valley of South Texas, as Ricardo Sánchez calls it; this borderland between the Nueces and the Rio Grande. This land has survived dispossession and ill-use by five countries: Spain, Mexico, the Republic of Texas, the U.S., the Confederacy, and the U.S. again. It has survived Anglo-Mexican blood feuds, lynchings, burnings, rapes, pillage.

Today I see the Valley still struggling to survive.

Gloria Anzaldúa, the Lower Rio Grande Valley's uncrowned poet laureate, has helped ensure the Valley's survival in American literature—as a site of paradox and ambivalence, of conflict, crossfire, and creativity. Her landmark poem, "To live in the Borderlands means you," eloquently captures the contradictions and challenges of living on the border:

To live in the Borderlands means you
    are neither *hispana india negra española*
    ni gabacha, eres mestiza, mulata, half-breed
    caught in the crossfire between camps
    while carrying all five races on your back
    not knowing which side to turn to, run from;

To live in the Borderlands means knowing
    that the *india* in you, betrayed for 500 years,
    is no longer speaking to you,
    that *mexicanas* call you *rajetas,*
    that denying the Anglo inside you
    is as bad as having denied the Indian or Black;

Cuando vives en la frontera
    people walk through you, the wind steals your voice,
    you're a *burra, buey,* scapegoat,
    forerunner of a new race,
    half and half—both woman and man, neither—
    a new gender.

To live in the Borderlands means to
    put *chile* in the borsht,

eat whole wheat *tortillas,*
speak Tex-Mex with a Brooklyn accent;
be stopped by *la migra* at the border checkpoints;

. . . .

To survive the Borderlands
you must live *sin fronteras*
be a crossroads

gabacha—a Chicano term for a white woman
rajetas—literally, "split," that is, having betrayed your word
burra—donkey
buey—oxen
sin fronteras—without borders

TOMÁS RIVERA'S PROSE POEMS OF THE VALLEY'S MIGRANT FARMWORKER

. . . Y NO SE LO TRAGÓ LA TIERRA
[*. . . AND THE EARTH DID NOT DEVOUR HIM*]

If Gloria Anzaldúa is the poet laureate of the Valley's migrant farmworker, Tomás Rivera is the migrant farmworker's leading delineator in prose. His award-winning 1971 coming-of-age novel, *. . . Y no se lo tragó la tierra* [*. . . And the Earth Did Not Devour Him*], captures the world of the migrant child in lyrical prose-poems that are as haunting as they are disturbing—such as the section called "Los niños no se aguantaron" ["The Children Couldn't Wait"]. The English translation that appears in this bilingual book is by Evangelina Vigil-Piñon.

The Children Couldn't Wait

The heat had set in with severity. . . . It was so hot that the bucket of water the boss brought them was not enough. He would come only two times for the midday and sometimes they couldn't hold out. That was why they took to drinking water from a tank at the edge of the furrow. The boss had it there for the cattle and when he caught them drinking water there he got angry. He didn't much like the idea of their losing time going to drink water because they weren't on contract, but by the hour. He told them that if he caught them there again he was going to fire them and not pay them. The children were the ones who couldn't wait.

"I'm very thirsty, Dad. Is the boss gonna be here soon?"

"I think so. You can't wait any longer?"

"Well, I don't know. My throat already feels real dry. Do you think he's almost gonna be here? Should I go to the tank?"

"No, wait just a little longer. You already heard what he said."

"I know, that he'll fire us if he catches us there, but I can't wait. . . . Why doesn't this one let us bring water? Up north . . ."

"Because he's no good, that's why."

" . . . . [W]hat if I make like I'm gonna go relieve myself by the tank?"

And this was what they started doing that afternoon. They pretended they were going to relieve themselves and they would go on to the edge of the tank. The boss became aware of this almost right away. But he didn't let on. He wanted to catch a bunch of them and that way he could pay fewer of them and only after they had done more work. He noticed that one of the children kept going to drink water every little while and he became more and more furious. He thought then of giving him a scare and he crawled on the ground to get his rifle.

What he set out to do and what he did were two different things. He shot at him once to scare him but when he pulled the trigger he saw the boy with a hole in his head. And the child didn't even jump like a deer does. He just stayed in the water like a dirty rag and the water began to turn bloody.

Water was not the only liquid that irrigated the Valley's lush citrus groves and rolling fields of vegetables, but no National Landmark commemorates the sweat and tears and blood that also drenched this landscape. Only in the searing prose poems of a writer like Tomás Rivera can we touch the human thirst and human pain that coursed through the valley alongside the water pumped from the Rio Grande. Rivera, who drew on his own experiences as a migrant worker in his fiction, went on to become a university chancellor in California and a prominent figure nationally in higher education.

RELATED SITES

❧ The Alamo (San Antonio de Valero Mission)
300 Alamo Plaza, San Antonio, Texas

The cornerstone of the chapel of this mission founded to Christianize and educate the Indians was laid in 1744. In 1762, however, just five years after the church was completed, the symmetrical stone towers flanking its facade, its dome, and its nave vaultings all collapsed; they were never fully rebuilt. The buildings continued to deteriorate, and the church was abandoned as a mission in 1793; it later became a fortress. By 1836, the buildings were mainly roofless ruins. That year the Alamo was the site of a famous thirteen-day siege during the Texas Revolution, when approximately 5,000 men led by General Antonio López de Santa Anna killed approximately 187 men fighting with Colonel William B. Travis. (Travis's men included thirteen native-born Texans, eleven of whom were of Mexican descent; forty-one men born in Europe; and the remainder from states other than Texas in the United States. The group included two Jews and two African Americans.) Stephen Harrigan's epic novel, *The Gates of the Alamo*, published in 2000, explores the 1836 event through the eyes of multiple eyewitnesses, Texan and Mexican. One of the figures who was instrumental in getting the Alamo preserved as a historical shrine was also an author who wrote and collected literature related to it—Adina de Zavala, granddaughter of the first vice president of the Republic of Texas and one of the original founders of the Daughters of the Republic of Texas. At one point in the early 1900s, Adina de Zavala barricaded herself inside the Alamo to protect it from demolition. Zavala, who lived from 1861 to 1955, was the author of *History and Legends of the Alamo and Other Missions in and around San Antonio*. Zavala's own story, and the rivalry between her own faction of the DRT and that led by Clara Driscoll in the early-twentieth-century battle to preserve the Alamo is the subject of Scott Zesch's 1999 novel, *Alamo Heights*.

San Antonio Missions National Park
San Antonio, Texas

The four Spanish missions comprised by this 819-acre national park—Missions San José, San Juan, Espada, and Concepción—were built in the eighteenth century in an effort to convert the Native American tribes in the area (mainly the Coahuiltecans when the Spanish arrived) to Catholicism. They remain an emblem of Spain's efforts to make this region its own. As Maria Cotera has noted, the writer Jovita González (*Dew on the Thorn, Caballero*) voiced concern about Anglos' interest in preserving and celebrating these emblems of the Spanish heritage of the United States while continuing to deny equal rights to Americans of Spanish descent. In an essay in a book called *Our Racial and National Minorities*, González writes, "When one sees the great sums of money spent to reconstruct the Spanish missions . . . , one cannot help but wonder at the inconsistency of things in general. If Anglos accept their art and culture, why have they not also accepted the people?" Increasingly, González came to believe that restoring old Spanish missions and collecting the Valley's folklore (an enterprise in which she had been engaged for some time) ultimately failed to address (as Cotera put it) "the wretched circumstances in which many Mexicans [in the United States] found themselves during the Depression."

◆ Fort Brown

600 International Boulevard, Brownsville, Texas

The land on which the original earthwork fort here on the banks of the Rio Grande was built in 1846 was claimed by both the United States and Mexico. The very location of this fort, the first U.S. military installation in Texas, was a provocation that helped trigger the Mexican War. The fort, popularly known as "Fort Texas," was renamed for Major Jacob Brown, who died defending it against Mexican attacks in one of the earliest clashes between U.S. and Mexican forces. Although a small portion of the earthwork walls of the original fort remains, most of the buildings here date from the post–Civil War era. This Brownsville fort and the areas surrounding it are the setting of much of Américo Paredes's novel *George Washington Gómez*, as well as some of his short fiction, including the story "The Hammon and the Beans." Paredes calls it Fort Jones and calls the town Jonesville.

◆ Palo Alto Battlefield National Historic Site

Junction of Texas Routes FR 1847 and 511, near Brownsville, Texas

The first major engagement of the Mexican War was fought here on May 8, 1846, between American troops commanded by General Zachary Taylor and Mexican troops commanded by General Mariano Arista, following Mexico's declaration of a "defensive war" against the United States in response to the United States' annexation of Texas. (The United States and Texas claimed the Rio Grande as the border, while Mexico claimed that the border was the Nueces River, considerably farther north.) The armies fought to a draw. Taylor's "flying artillery" (guns mounted on light horse-drawn carriages) gave his forces an advantage, and resulted in more casualties on the Mexican side than on the American side. Interpretive exhibits here explore the origins and consequences of the Mexican War from both U.S. and Mexican perspectives, endeavoring to transform a site of conflict into a site of binational exchange and understanding. One of the notable participants at the Battle of Palo Alto was then Lt. Ulysses S. Grant. Both the Battle of Palo Alto and the Battle of Resaca de la Palma are described in volume 1, chapter 7 of his autobiography, *The Personal Memoirs of Ulysses. S. Grant*, a lucid and beautifully written book, published by Mark Twain's publishing company. The Guadalupe-Hidalgo Treaty that ended the war would indelibly shape the sense of personal and national identities that would inform American literature from this region for the next 150 years and beyond.

FOR FURTHER READING

The Writers: Works and Words

Anzaldúa, Gloria. *Borderlands/La Frontera: The New Mestiza*. 1987. 25th Anniversary 4th ed. Introduction by Norma Cantú and Aída Hurtado. San Francisco: Aunt Lute Books, 2012.

———. *The Gloria Anzaldúa Reader*. Edited by AnaLouise Keating. Durham, NC: Duke University
Press, 1999.

———, ed. *Making Face, Making Soul/Haciendo Caras: Creative and Critical Perspectives by Women of
Color*. San Francisco: Aunt Lute Foundation, 1990.

Anzaldúa Gloria, and AnaLouise Keating, eds. *This Bridge We Call Home: Radical Visions for Transformation*. New York: Routledge, 2002.

González, Jovita. *Dew on the Thorn*. Edited by José Limón. Houston: Arte Público Press, 1997.

———. "Latin Americans." In *Our Racial and National Minorities*, edited by Francis J. Brown and
Joseph S. Roucek. New York: Prentice-Hall, 1937.

———. *Life along the Border: A Landmark Tejana Thesis*. Edited by María Eugenia Cotera. Emma
Dill Russell Spencer Series in the West and Southwest. Annotated ed. College Station: Texas A
& M University Press, 2006.

González, Jovita, and Eve Raleigh. *Caballero: A Historical Novel*. Edited by José Limón and María
Cotera. College Station: Texas A & M Press, 1996.

Grant, Ulysses S. *Personal Memoirs of Ulysses S. Grant*. New York: Charles L. Webster and Co.,
1885–1886.

Harrigan, Stephen. *The Gates of the Alamo*. New York: Penguin Books, 2000.

Hinojosa, Rolando. *Estampas del valle*. Tempe, AZ: Bilingual Press/Editorial Bilingüe, 1994.

———. *The Rolando Hinojosa Reader*. Edited by José Saldívar. Houston: Arte Público Press, 1985.

———. *The Valley*. Ypsilanti, MI: Bilingual Press/Editorial Bilingüe, 1983.

Ikas, Karin Rosa. "Gloria Anzaldúa." In *Chicana Ways: Conversations with Ten Chicana Writers*.
Reno: University of Nevada Press, 2002.

Kanellos, Nicolás, ed. *Herencia: The Anthology of Hispanic Literature of the United States*. New York:
Oxford University Press, 2002.

Moraga, Cherríe, and Gloria Anzaldúa, eds. *This Bridge Called My Back: Writings by Radical Women
of Color*. Watertown, MA: Persephone, 1981.

Paredes, Américo. *Folklore and Culture on the Texas-Mexican Border*. Austin: CMAS Books, Center
for Mexican American Studies, 1993.

———. *George Washington Gómez: A Mexicotexan Novel*. Houston: Arte Público Press, 1990.

———. *The Hammon and the Beans and Other Stories*. Houston: Arte Público Press, 1994.

———. *With His Pistol in His Hand: A Border Ballad and Its Hero*. 1958. Austin: University of Texas
Press, 1990.

Rivera, Tomás. . . . *Y no se lo tragó la tierra* [. . . *And the Earth Did Not Devour Him*]. Translated by
Evangelina Vigil-Piñon. Houston: Arte Público Press, 1992.

Zavala, Adina de. *History and Legends of the Alamo and Other Missions in and around San Antonio*.
Edited by Richard Flores. Houston: Arte Público Press, 1996.

Zesch, Scott. *Alamo Heights*. Fort Worth: Texas Christian University Press, 1999.

Background and Contexts

Alonzo, Armando C. *Tejano Legacy: Rancheros and Settlers in South Texas, 1734–1900.* Albuquerque: University of New Mexico Press, 1998.

Camacho, Alicia Schmidt. *Migrant Imaginaries: Latino Cultural Politics in the U.S.-Mexico Borderlands.* New York: New York University Press, 2008.

Cantú, Norma E., ed. "Comparative Perspectives Symposium: Gloria E. Anzaldúa, an International Perspective." *Signs* 37, no. 1 (Autumn 2011), 1–52.

———. "Doing Work That Matters: Gloria E. Anzaldúa in the International Arena." *Signs* 37, no. 1 (Autumn 2011): 1–5.

Cantú, Norma E., Christina L. Gutiérrez, Norma Alarcón, and Rita E. Urquijo-Ruiz, eds. *El Mundo Zurdo: Selected Works from the Meetings of the Society for the Study of Gloria Anzaldúa, 2007 and 2009.* San Francisco: Aunt Lute Foundation, 2011.

Cotera, Maria. *Native Speakers: Ella Cara Deloria, Zora Neale Hurston, Jovita González and the Poetics of Culture.* Austin: University of Texas Press, 2008.

Fishkin, Shelley Fisher. "The Borderlands of Culture: Writing by W.E.B. Du Bois, James Agee, Tillie Olsen, and Gloria Anzaldúa." In *Literary Journalism in the Twentieth Century*, edited by Norman Sims. New York: Oxford University Press, 1990.

———. "Reflections on Gloria Anzaldúa." In *Bridging: How and Why Gloria Evangelina Anzaldúa's Life and Work Transformed Our Own*, edited by AnaLouise Keating and Gloria González-López. Austin: University of Texas Press, 2011.

Graham, Don, et al., eds. *The Texas Literary Tradition.* Austin: College of Liberal Arts, University of Texas at Austin and Texas State Historical Association, 1983.

Gutiérrez, Ramón, and Genaro Padilla, eds. *Recovering the U.S. Hispanic Literary Heritage.* Houston: Arte Público Press, 1993.

Henríquez-Betancor, María. "Gloria Anzaldúa in the Canary Islands." *Signs* 37, no. 1 (Autumn 2011): 41–46.

Joysmith, Claire. "Anzaldúa's Bordercrossing into Mexico." *Signs* 37, no. 1 (Autumn 2011): 46–52.

Keating, AnaLouise, ed. *Entre Mundos/Among Worlds: New Perspectives on Gloria Anzaldúa.* New York: Palgrave/Macmillan, 2005.

Keating, AnaLouise, and Gloria González-López, eds. *Bridging: How and Why Gloria Evangelina Anzaldúa's Life and Work Transformed Our Own.* Austin: University of Texas Press, 2011.

Koegeler-Abdi, Martina. "Shifting Subjectivities: Mestizas, Nepantleras, and Gloria Anzaldúa's Legacy." *MELUS* 38, no. 2 (2013): 71–88.

Kynčlová, Tereza. "Prospects of Anzaldúan Thought for a Czech Future." *Signs* 37, no. 1 (Autumn 2011): 23–29.

León, Arnaldo de. *The Tejano Community, 1836–1900.* Dallas: Southern Methodist University Press, 1997.

———. *They Called Them Greasers: Anglo Attitudes toward Mexicans in Texas, 1821–1900.* Austin: University of Texas Press, 1983.

Majewska, Ewa. "La Mestiza from Ukraine? Border Crossing with Gloria Anzaldúa." *Signs* 37, no. 1 (Autumn 2011): 34–41.

Montejano, David. *Anglos and Mexicans in the Making of Texas, 1836–1986.* Austin: University of Texas Press, 1987.

Montes, Amelia M. L. "'Doing the Work That Matters'—The Society for the Study of Gloria Anzaldúa." *La Bloga* 2 (2012): http://labloga.blogspot.com/2012/02/doing-work-that-matters-society-for.html.

Oliver-Rotger, Maria Antónia. "Gloria Anzaldúa's Borderless Theory in Spain." *Signs* 37, no. 1 (Autumn 2011): 5–10.

Radlwimmer, Romana. "Searching for Gloria Anzaldúa: A Fictional Dialogue on Realities Somewhere between Austria and Spain." *Signs* 37, no. 1 (Autumn 2011): 18–23.

Rivera, John-Michael. *The Emergence of Mexican America: Recovering the Stories of Mexican Peoplehood in U.S. Culture.* New York: New York University Press, 2006.

Ruíz, Vicki, and Virginia Sánchez Korrol. *Latina Legacies: Identity, Biography and Community.* New York: Oxford University Press, 2005.

Saldívar, José David. *Trans-Americanity: Subaltern Modernities, Global Coloniality, and the Cultures of Greater Mexico.* Durham, NC: Duke University Press, 2012.

Saldívar, Ramón. *The Borderlands of Culture: Américo Paredes and the Transnational Imaginary.* Durham, NC: Duke University Press, 2006.

———. *Chicano Narrative.* Madison: University of Wisconsin Press, 1990.

Sanchez, Mario L., ed. *A Shared Experience: The History, Architecture, and Historic Designations of the Lower Rio Grande Heritage Corridor.* Austin: Los Caminos del Rio Heritage Project and the Texas Historical Commission, 1991.

Tyler, Ron, ed. *The New Handbook of Texas.* 6 vols. Austin: Texas State Historical Society, 1996.

Zaccaria, Paola. "Medi-terranean Borderization." *Signs* 37, no. 1 (Autumn 2011): 10–18.

Zygadło, Grażyna. "'Where the Third World Grates against the First': Teaching Gloria Anzaldúa from a Polish Perspective." *Signs* 37, no. 1 (Autumn 2011): 29–34.

Grauman's Chinese Theatre, 6925 Hollywood Boulevard (now the TCL Chinese Theatre), a frequent site of movie premieres like those in Nathanael West's novel *Day of the Locust*, was inspired not by authentic Chinese temple architecture, but by popular, contemporary, Chinese-influenced Chippendale design featured in photos the architects clipped from *Connoisseur* magazine.

13

American Writers and
Dreams of the Silver Screen

HOLLYWOOD BOULEVARD COMMERCIAL
AND ENTERTAINMENT DISTRICT
LOS ANGELES, CALIFORNIA

The fierce-looking stone creatures—half-lion, half-dog—that flank the entrance were carved during the Ming Dynasty some three centuries ago to guard sacred royal tombs. Behind each dog stand massive coral columns topped by immense wrought-iron masks and burnished copper minarets that frame a jade-green pagoda ninety feet off the ground. Inside, in an ornate red and gold space vaguely suggestive of an ancient Chinese shrine, one can see . . . a movie. The most famous movie theater in the world, the outrageously gaudy Grauman's Chinese Theatre (now known as the TCL Chinese Theatre) that towers over the 6900 block of Hollywood Boulevard, was inspired as much by its designers' fantasies as by any shrine in China. But it is a shrine in its own right: a shrine to the dreams of the silver screen that built it and that Hollywood continues to produce.

Hollywood and American writers have had a love-hate relationship—sometimes symbiotic, sometimes antagonistic, always complex. American writers have made Hollywood—the careers and dreams it nurtures and destroys, the values it projects and fails to project—a central subject in their fiction. They have also joined with Hollywood, working as screenwriters or selling screen rights to their fiction for paychecks that help subsidize their less profitable literary ventures. From the start, Hollywood has mined American literature for its most memorable plots and characters, introducing millions of nonreaders and readers alike to the shadow-versions of hundreds of American novels. But Hollywood has also distorted many of those works beyond recognition, erasing subtlety, flattening depths, and gutting what matters most. The film industry has distorted history, as well, in ways that have enraged writers struggling with their own efforts to make sense of America's past. Sometimes that anger has been productive, prompting these writers to talk back in powerful new poetry and prose.

"Hollywood." The name connotes the movies and the moviemakers—the actors, producers, writers, directors, makeup artists, set designers, and extras who make films happen, and the values that shape the products they produce. But "Hollywood" is also a physical place, the part of Los Angeles where the movie industry was centered during that era when it first took the twentieth century by storm. The motion picture business in this country began on the East Coast in the early 1900s. But soon after director D. W. Griffith began shooting footage in Hollywood in 1910, the word was out: the temperate climate (which allowed shooting most days of the year), the proximity of virtually every kind of natural scenery (ocean, mountains, desert, forest, fields, tropics), and the vast supply of cheap, nonunion labor, soon attracted East Coast filmmakers to Southern California. By the early 1920s, Hollywood had become the center of American moviemaking. Despite the toll taken over the years by earthquakes, riots, physical decay, and commercial redevelopment, the Hollywood Boulevard Commercial and Entertainment District, a twelve-block stretch along Hollywood's main thoroughfare, still contains dozens of buildings that date from Hollywood's glory days in the 1920s and 1930s, when glitz and glamour joined with audacity and imagination to give birth to the industry that would generate one of the United States' prime cultural exports to the world.

The Hollywood Boulevard Commercial and Entertainment District, runs from 6200 to 7000 Hollywood Boulevard, and includes some adjacent stretches of North Vine Street, North Highland Avenue, and North Ivar Street. More than forty buildings in this twelve-block area show aspects of their original design, preserving the distinctive identity of one of the most famous streets in the world. The district, like the movies Hollywood made, is an eclectic hodge-podge of invention and appropriation, of creativity and cliché. A dizzying variety of architectural styles nestle next to each other, just as equally diverse facades might face each other on one of the fabled movie studio back lots. Unlike those structures, these buildings are more than facades. However, in a large sense they *are* stage sets—for the pageants Hollywood stages periodically to celebrate itself—the openings, the Academy Awards, the "footprint ceremonies" at the TCL Chinese Theatre. Walk down Hollywood Boulevard and time and space evaporate as fantasy Egyptian meets flamboyant Spanish Colonial and gaudy East Indian, as Gothic brushes up against 1930s commercial vernacular, Italian Renaissance, Neoclassical, Art Deco, and Streamline Moderne.

The most spectacular and extravagant structures on Hollywood Boulevard—appropriately enough—are the theaters. During the 1920s, cities across the country built lavish movie palaces filled with marble staircases, plush carpets, oil paintings, and crystal chandeliers. But few could rival those palaces of Hollywood Boulevard in sheer sumptuousness and lush exoticism. The first "fantasy" movie palace on the block was the Egyptian Theatre (6712 Hollywood Boulevard) designed by the architectural firm of Meyer and Holler and built by developer Charles Toberman for film exhibitor Sid Grauman in 1921 and 1922. Both the stage and the imposing palm-studded forecourt were surrounded by layer upon layer of brilliantly colored Egyptian-style hieroglyphs and mosaics; the ceiling was a dazzling maze of gold grillwork. Its design was inspired by the 1922 discovery of King Tut's tomb, and gestured, as well, to the temples of Ramses and Karnac along the Nile.

Five years after the Egyptian opened, the same team of architects and developers designed a second fantasy movie palace for Sid Grauman that soon surpassed the Egyptian in renown. Grauman's Chinese Theatre (6925 Hollywood Boulevard), was inspired not by authentic Chinese temple architecture—which would have given the building a heavier feeling—but by popular, contemporary, Chinese-influenced Chippendale design as featured in photos the architects clipped from recent copies of *Connoisseur* magazine. The carpets and rugs of the foyer were woven in China, and the colossal stone columns on each side of the auditorium gave the impression of entering an ancient shrine. On opening night, the carpets and columns were lined by ushers and usherettes decked out in elaborate gold-embroidered outfits copied from ancient Chinese theatrical costumes. The carpets and rugs have deteriorated over the years, and were replaced, along with most of the other original furnishings. The basic structure and the original architectural detail, however, survive.

The glitzy, glamorous Hollywood "premiere," born at these theaters in the 1920s, continues to this day, sparking scenes like those described in the climactic chapter of Nathanael West's great Hollywood novel, *The Day of the Locust*, where "a dozen great violet shafts of light" move "across the evening sky in wide crazy sweeps."

Whenever one of the fiery columns reached the lowest point of its arc, it lit for a moment the rose colored domes and delicate minarets of Kahn's Persian Palace Theatre. The purpose of this display was to signal the world premiere of a new picture. . . .

Although it was still several hours before the celebrities would arrive, thousands of people had already gathered. They stood facing the theatre with their backs toward the gutter in a thick line hundreds of feet long. A big squad of policemen was trying to keep a lane open between the front rank of the crowd and the façade of the theatre. . . .

The police force would have to be doubled when the stars started to arrive.

At the sight of their heroes and heroines, the crowd would turn demoniac. Some little gesture, either too pleasing or too offensive, would start it moving and then nothing but machine guns would stop it. . . .

A young man with a portable microphone was describing the scene. His rapid, hysterical voice was like that of a revivalist preacher whipping his congregation toward the ecstasy of fits.

"What a crowd, folks! What a crowd! There must be ten thousand excited, screaming fans outside Kahn's Persian tonight. The police can't hold them. Here, listen to them roar."

In West's novel, the violence beneath the surface soon explodes, and the adulatory mob transforms itself in moments into an angry mob, underlining the potentially out-of-control nature of mob energy and the mindlessness of mob mentality. The people in the novel who assemble to gawk at stars at the Hollywood opening and who patrol Hollywood Boulevard day in, day out, hoping to catch a glimpse of a celebrity, are people for whom movies and the world that surrounds them are more real than life itself. West originally had planned to call the book "The Cheated," focusing as it did not only on people who cheated each other, but who were all cheated out of their dreams by the illusions Hollywood held out to them. Hollywood's daydreams don't fill their needs: they just fuel them. Chasing their dreams of the silver screen—wanting to be in movies, or at least someplace where they could catch glimpses of people connected to them in some way—these people inhabit a world that promised vitality, wealth, beauty, and romance, but gave them dullness, poverty, loneliness, and a sordid emptiness that they refused to see or name. Everyone in the crowd—the extras and the aspiring stars, the hangers-on and the hopefuls, the hotel clerk from Iowa and the set designer from Yale—all looking for something Hollywood couldn't give them—find themselves reduced to a mob as swarming and mindless as a plague of locusts.

"Kahn's Persian Palace" in West's novel blends a real place—an exotic fantasy theater on Hollywood Boulevard—with an imagined one, an allusion to the famous poem "Kubla Khan" by Samuel Taylor Coleridge ("In Xanadu did Kubla Khan a stately pleasure dome decree . . ."). In some ways, however, the "real" theaters were as much a product of untrammeled fantasy and imagination as the Persian pleasure dome dreamed by the poet. They quickly became apt symbols of the celluloid dreams whose openings they trumpeted with such fanfare. While the Egyptian and the Chinese may be the best-known of Hollywood Boulevard's movie palaces, other theaters retain their original distinctive designs, as well, reflecting Hollywood's readiness to pillage motifs and mix and match designs from around the globe. The

Paramount Theatre, also known as El Capitan (6838 Hollywood Boulevard), built, like the Chinese and Egyptian, by Toberman, presents a lavish Spanish Revival facade to the street, but just behind the entrance is a lushly ornate, gloriously gilded homage to the fine arts of East India, designed by G. Albert Landsburgh. A legitimate theater when it opened in 1926, it was converted into a movie house in 1942. It was restored in 1990 and continues to operate as a movie theater today.

The Avalon Hollywood (1735 North Vine Street), built in 1927 when it was called the Hollywood Playhouse, is a fine example of Spanish Colonial Revival style; a bay window on the second floor is surrounded by incredibly flamboyant Churrigueresque decorations, giving it the much-of-a-muchness look of a faded leading lady decked out in diamonds-and-rubies-and-emeralds-and-sapphires *and* a floor-length mink coat (the style was a variant of Spanish Rococo developed by José de Churriguera, an eighteenth-century Spanish church architect and sculptor). The Hollywood Palace, as the Avalon Hollywood was known from the 1960s through 2002, was the scene of the Beatles' first West Coast appearance; it is now a nightclub and music venue.

When the Warner Pacific Theatre at 6433 Hollywood Boulevard opened in 1928, its seating capacity of 2,700 made it Hollywood's largest theater. (The massive Italian Renaissance–style structure is still there, but as of 2015 it was shuttered.) It was surpassed in size two years later when the Art Deco–style Pantages Theatre opened at 6233 Hollywood Boulevard: the last great movie palace built in Hollywood originally seated 2,800. Designed by theater architect B. Marcus Priteca (who designed more than one hundred theaters around the country), it has an ersatz-stone exterior decorated with Egyptian lotus patterns on the second story and sculptured goddesses on the roofline. The Academy Awards were held at the Pantages Theatre during the 1950s, and the Emmy Awards were held here during the 1970s. It was transformed into a legitimate house for Broadway musicals and comedy productions in the 1970s.

The oldest Hollywood movie house still standing today is the Hollywood Theatre (6764 Hollywood Boulevard), which opened in 1913. In the 1930s, as automobile traffic increased on Hollywood Boulevard, the Hollywood Theatre changed its movie marquee from flat to three-sided in order to be more easily seen by motorists. It was one of the first triangular movie marquees in the country. Today it houses the Guinness World Records Museum.

The films that opened in these theaters mixed and matched historical backdrops with the same eclectic abandon that the architects and designers of these theaters used to create wild mélanges of periods and styles, as the memorable back-lot scene in West's *The Day of the Locust* reminds us. Here a young set designer named Tod searches through a studio's back lot for a friend who is working as an extra in a picture called *Waterloo*. Tod seeks a bit of shade from the hot sun "under an ocean liner made of painted canvas with real lifeboats hanging from its davits." He then "went on toward a great forty-foot papier-mâché sphinx that loomed up in the distance. He had to cross a desert to reach it, a desert that was continually being made larger by a fleet of trucks dumping white sand." He then comes to "a Western street with a plank sidewalk" and sits down on a rocking chair "on the porch of the 'Last Chance Saloon.'" Off to one side he "could see a jungle compound with water buffalo," while on another side he spots "a truck with a load of snow and several malamute dogs." Soon after walking down "a Paris street that ends in a Romanesque courtyard," he follows "a little path that ended at a Greek temple dedicated to Eros." As he pushes his way "through a tangle of briars, old flats and iron junk," he needs to step around "the skeleton of a Zeppelin, a bamboo stockade, an adobe fort, the wooden horse of Troy, a flight of baroque palace stairs that started in a bed of weeds and ended against the branches of an oak, part of the Fourteenth Street elevated station, a Dutch windmill," and "a Mayan temple."

Hollywood's producers were adept at appropriating any culture, invoking any climate, commandeering any army from any era to storm any target at will: it was manifest destiny run amuck. No wonder some of the tycoons came to be thought of as omnipotent gods who could cause pleasant winds to blow or destructive hurricanes to rage, who could transform a frog of an extra into a prince of a star at whim, who commanded that history be writ with lightning and saw that it was good—or at least a success at the box office. F. Scott Fitzgerald gives us a portrait of one such figure in his novel *The Last Tycoon*, a character named Monroe Stahr, based on MGM's Irving Thalberg. Fitzgerald was intrigued by the autocratic autonomy of this brilliant boy-wonder of the movies, who, when told that he couldn't have a moonlit seaside scene in a film supposedly set in Paris, ended discussion with the ruling, "We can't cater to a handful of people who know Paris."

But sometimes the unexpected thwarted the most powerful directors as surely as the unexpected thwarted Napoleon at Waterloo. In *The Day of the Locust*, the young set designer finds resonances between what happens on the set and what happened to Napoleon. At Waterloo, Napoleon "had ordered the cuirassiers to charge Mont St. Jean not knowing that a deep ditch was hidden at its foot to trap his heavy cavalry. The result had been disaster for the French; the beginning of the end." This time, Tod realizes, "the same mistake had a different outcome." As Napoleon had before him, here a man in a checked cap ordered the cuirassiers to charge Mont St. Jean without knowing that "Mont St. Jean was unfinished. The paint was not yet dry and all the struts were not in place. Because of the thickness of the cannon smoke, he had failed to see that the hill was still being worked on by property men, grips and carpenters. It was the classic mistake, Tod realized, the same one Napoleon had made." Instead of the battle being lost, however, this time it had to be "fought over again the next day. Big losses, however were sustained by the insurance company in workmen's compensation. The man in the checked cap was sent to the dog house by Mr. Grotenstein just as Napoleon was sent to St. Helena."

Like the back lot, Hollywood Boulevard itself features grand gestures to ancient Greece, such as the Neoclassical colonnade of the El Capitan Entertainment Center at 6840 (formerly known as the Masonic Temple) and the mammoth Corinthian columns of the L. Ron Hubbard Theatre at 7051 (formerly known as the Security Trust Bank), alongside a building whose porthole windows and rounded corners—the two-story Streamline Moderne building at 6349—vaguely suggest a beached ocean liner.

The renovated Max Factor Building that now houses the Hollywood Museum (1666 North Highland Avenue), a sophisticated pink Art Deco/Regency Revival structure that epitomizes one kind of theatrical Hollywood "look," features an elaborate display of the cosmetics with which Max Factor transformed the movies—including the grease paint made for photographing in artificial light, and the pancake makeup he developed in the 1940s that made grease paint obsolete. (The original colors, cases, and architectural details have all been restored.) Max Factor bought the building in 1928 and moved his base of operations there from downtown Los Angeles. In 1935, after remodeling on a grand scale, he staged a headline-making "premiere" for his new makeup salon. More than eight thousand people attended. Max Factor's fame for turning ordinary-looking women into stunning beauties transformed the makeup and hair-styling habits of women everywhere that movies were seen and newspapers and magazines were read. It was in this building that Max Factor turned Marilyn Monroe into a blond and Lucille Ball into a redhead. It was also Max Factor who devised the makeup that allowed ostensibly Caucasian actors to play so-called ethnic roles. For Hollywood's unspoken rule was that you could play anything as long as you started out "white." If you started out clearly "ethnic," you were typecast in relatively minor roles. Frank Chin addresses this issue in his novel *Gunga Din Highway* (1994), in which fictional actor Longman Kwan dreams of being the first Chinese man to star as a Chinese man in a Hollywood movie. Tired of being cast as an "evil Jap baby-killer," Longman Kwan is thrilled, at last, by the news that he is to be cast as Genghis Khan in a film called *I Rode with Genghis Khan*. His wife, however, is skeptical, and insists that "a Chinese man will never star as a Chinese man in a Hollywood movie! Never! . . . They'll get a white woman to play the Chinese detective before they star a Chinese man." Longman protests, but his wife's "words were prophetic." He "was bumped for John Wayne." "Only a white known for playing heroes," he concludes, "—not a yellow known for comic relief—could play Genghis Khan." The racism that prevented actors like the fictional Longman Kwan from playing a heroic Asian leading man cast minority actors in limited stereotypical roles for much of the twentieth century.

Hollywood has long been, and continues to be, a setting hospitable to American detective fiction. This may well be, at least in part, because the granddaddy of so much of modern detective fiction placed his memorable leading man in an office on Hollywood Boulevard. Ever since Philip Marlowe set up shop at the corner of Cahuenga and Hollywood in the 1930s and 1940s (or at the various other locations Raymond Chandler places him at in the novels), literary murder and mayhem have woven through Hollywood's streets. For example, Ross Macdonald (the pseudonym of Kenneth Millar) published *Archer in Hollywood* in 1967, a collection of three novels featuring private eye Lew Archer. Macdonald writes in the book's foreword, "If California is a state of mind, Hollywood is where you take its temperature. There is a peculiar sense in which this city existing on film and tape is our national capital, alas, and not just the capital of California. It's the place where our children learn how and what to dream and where everything happens just before, or just after, it happens to us. American novelists have a lover's quarrel with Hollywood."

Only one novel by the inimitable Raymond Chandler, *The Little Sister*, deals with characters, plots, and themes directly related to the movie business (the novel paints the world of criminal intrigue and blackmail surrounding a Hollywood leading lady and her duplicitous family). But Chandler's Philip Marlowe remains one of the most vivid characters ever to set foot on Hollywood Boulevard, and Chandler's own role as a screenwriter and as a writer who held forth eloquently and at length on the art (or lack thereof) of screenwriting is unique. Although he worked on some extremely successful films, and although some of the films that have defined the genre of film noir murder mysteries were based on his fiction, no writer has had more cutting things to say about the place of the writer in Hollywood. In 1945, he wrote in the *Atlantic Monthly*:

> The basic art of motion pictures is the screenplay; it is fundamental, without it there is nothing.... But in Hollywood the screenplay is written by a salaried writer under the supervision of a producer—that is to say, by an employee

without power or decision over the uses of his own craft, without ownership of it, and, however extravagantly paid, almost without honor for it. It is the essence of this system that it seeks to exploit a talent without permitting it the right to be a talent. It cannot be done; you can only destroy the talent, which is exactly what happens—when there is any to destroy.

Erica Jong captures the nature of the difference between the novelist and the screenwriter in her satirical novel set in Hollywood, *How to Save Your Own Life.* Isadora, the book's narrator and a novelist herself, describes "a certain kind of grayish, stoop-shouldered beaten screenwriter one meets in Hollywood," who once (he says) could have written a novel, but who believes it is now too late. "He was rich, but he was not happy," Isadora says. "He had seen his lifework rewritten by illiterate producers, his best aphorisms mangled by arrogant actors, his philosophical nuggets crushed by directors, mushed by assistant directors, and trampled to dust by the Italian-leather soles of executive producers' shoes. He was a beaten man, an intellectual derelict, a Bowery bum of letters. They had taken away his words and given him money instead. And it was a lousy bargain."

Writers often made their way to Hollywood following the commercial failure of a novel. Nathanael West came after the commercial failure of *Miss Lonelyhearts*, and after his publisher went bankrupt. William Faulkner came when he found that the earnings from six novels, each of which sold about two thousand copies, was not enough for him and his extended family to live on. (He wrote to his publisher that he was "the sole, principal and partial support—food, shelter, heat, clothes, medicine, kotex, school fees, toilet paper and picture shows—of my mother, an inept brother, and his wife and two sons, another brother's widow and child, a wife of my own and two step children, my own child.")

Soon after his novel *The Great Gatsby* was a financial flop, Fitzgerald accepted an invitation from United Artists to write "a fine modern college story." But his tale of flappers and Princeton undergraduates included such unfilmable lines as the one in which the heroine is described as "so lonesome that she [tries] to look as if she hopes no one will speak to her." If Fitzgerald did not get a dependable new source of wages from Hollywood, however, he did get Monroe Stahr, the last great character of his career as a novelist.

Nathanael West was delighted to accept a "junior writer" salary from Columbia studios of $350 a week, renewable on a week-to-week basis, after his publisher went bankrupt. "This stuff about easy work is all wrong," West wrote (contradicting a writer like Ben Hecht, who had claimed that Hollywood offered "tremendous sums of money for work that required no more effort than a game of pinochle"). "My hours are from ten in the morning to six at night with a full day on Saturday. They gave me a job to do five minutes after I sat down in my office—a scenario about a beauty parlor—and I'm expected to turn out pages and pages a day. There's no fooling here. All the writers sit in cells and the minute a typewriter stops someone pokes his head in the door to see if you are thinking." A couple of B pictures were the result. At Warner Bros., Jack Warner insisted that writers keep a nine-to-five schedule, take no more than a half hour for lunch, and wear their pencils down to a certain length by the end of the day.

William Faulkner first arrived in Hollywood in 1932 and would work there on and off for a number of years, for MGM, Twentieth Century Fox, and Warner Bros., working on film adaptations of his own novels and on treatments of other writers' work (most of which were never produced). According to a widely recounted story (set in each of three studios in which Faulkner worked, depending on who's doing the telling), Faulkner complained about not being able to work in his studio office and asked whether it would be all right for him to work at home. Fine, said his employer, assuming that "home" was somewhere in Beverly Hills. But when the studio tried to find him, he turned up at Rowan Oak, his home in Oxford, Mississippi. When he *was* in Hollywood, Faulkner was infamous for showing up drunk and late for work and for claiming (probably correctly) that he knew nothing about writing movies. "I can't see things. . . . I can only hear," he once said. He also professed decidedly limited taste in films, announcing, "Newsreels and Mickey Mouse are the only movies I like." Despite his well-founded, misfit-in-Hollywood image, however, he was enormously admired by famed director Howard Hawks, who gave him work whenever he could. Faulkner seems to have had some success as a script-doctor for an adaptation of Ernest Hemingway's *To Have and Have Not*, and he played a key role in adapting Raymond Chandler's novel *The Big Sleep* to film. He viewed his time in Hollywood as an abysmal failure. "I have made a bust at moving picture writing," he wrote Jack Warner in 1945, asking to be released from his contract. In what may be an all-time low point in the relationship between Hollywood and a major American writer, Warner Bros.' legal department argued that Faulkner's contract made *all* of his work the studio's property, including the novel he was writing. Only the intervention of his publisher and New York agent got the studio to back off.

Even writers who complain about the film industry's disregard for authors can find themselves vulnerable to its seductions. As Michael Connelly, author of popular detective novels and crime fiction, said not long ago, "I know about the history of writers and Hollywood. The denial of the source and inspiration. Everything in the business, creative side or not, starts with the words. They launch everything. The writer is the only one in the chain that must make something out of nothing. Everybody else starts with his words. But everybody wants to feel important and creative. So they take those words and put their imprint on them. From location scout to actor to director, everyone is engaged in both the service and denial of the writer." He added, "I know all of that, and yet, like my legal attack dogs, I am melted by the prospect of a meeting with a movie star."

The writer's status in Hollywood irritated some, but didn't bother others. Fitzgerald said that he liked Sam Goldwyn because "you always knew where you stood with him: nowhere." Poor working conditions, low status, and the industry's demand for clear, unambiguous stories were offset for some writers by the exorbitant amounts of money they were paid. Some writers, like Dorothy Parker, used the Hollywood paychecks to reach new milestones of conspicuous consumption (she reputedly rang up $300 lingerie bills on a regular basis). Others of a less profligate nature banked the bonanza for a rainy day or lived in it: David Bradley's unproduced screenplays about Otis Redding and Malcolm X provided the down payment for his California home.

During Hollywood's golden decades, writers like Chandler, West, Faulkner, Fitzgerald, Hemingway, Parker, Dashiell Hammett, and Lillian Hellman could be found eating lunch or dinner and drinking at Musso and Frank Grill (6663–6667 Hollywood Boulevard). This dark, noisy, and clubby restaurant, favored by stars from Charlie Chaplin to Rudolph Valentino to Greta Garbo, has been a Hollywood mainstay since 1919 and is still going strong today (in the building it has occupied since 1937), with a number of menu items virtually unchanged. Characters in Raymond Chandler's novels occasionally dine here as well.

In addition to producing films based on books by writers mentioned in this book who worked in Hollywood themselves (such as Chandler, Fitzgerald, Faulkner, West, and Anzia Yezierska), Hollywood has mined the work of innumerable other American novelists and dramatists for its characters and plots—with decidedly mixed results Sometimes the writers viewed Hollywood's version of their books as an unmitigated disaster. Hemingway complained that Dudley Nichols, one of Hollywood's most respected screenwriters, "botched everything up" in the screen version of *For Whom the Bell Tolls*. Nichols agreed to take a number of suggestions Hemingway offered, but Paramount largely overruled him, thereby squeezing most of the politics and drama out of Hemingway's dramatic political novel. Dreiser used virtually the same language to characterize what Paramount did to *An American Tragedy* in its film version, *A Place in the Sun*: the screenwriters, Dreiser complained, "have botched my novel," reducing a complex work of art to a cheap murder story. Despite the fact that Hemingway and Dreiser were horrified by what Hollywood did to their work, Hollywood's own arbiters of excellence were well pleased: *For Whom the Bell Tolls* was nominated for a "Best Picture" Oscar in 1943, and *A Place in the Sun* was nominated for the same award in 1951. (Both Hemingway and Dreiser may have had the bad luck to end up with some of the real-life models for Pat Hobby, the hack screenwriter in Fitzgerald's story "A Man in the Way." He "was a writer but he had never written much, nor even read all the 'originals' he worked from, because it made his head bang to read much.")

Wary of Hollywood's track record with serious fiction, John Steinbeck put the money he was paid for the screen rights to *The Grapes of Wrath* in escrow just in case he decided to sue the studio for messing it up. Although Columbia Pictures deviated from the novel in a number of ways, Steinbeck was delighted with the result—"a hard, straight picture in which the actors are submerged so completely that it looks and feels like a documentary film and certainly it has a hard, truthful ring. No punches were pulled—in fact, with descriptive matter removed, it is a harsher thing than the book, by far. It seems unbelievable but it is true." The film was nominated for an Academy Award. (Steinbeck was so pleasantly surprised by the results that when Nunnally Johnson, the screenwriter who had done *Grapes of Wrath* and was then working on the script for another Steinbeck novel, *The Moon Is Down*, asked its author if he had any suggestions, Steinbeck responded: "Tamper with it.")

Hollywood's dramatization of a novel or memoir can give it a kind of immortality, exposing generations of viewers to a story long after the book on which it was based may have been forgotten. Films can go places that texts cannot, reaching people who might never have picked up the book in the first place. But a film can also do something else: so *enrage* a young viewer with no clear sense of his or her future vocation that he or she decides to *become* a writer in order to be able to "talk back" to that infuriating screen. Poet Tino Villanueva first saw the movie *Giant*, based on Edna Ferber's novel of that name, in the Holiday Theater in San Marcos, Texas, in 1956 when he was fourteen. Novelist David Bradley first caught a glimpse of part of the movie *The Birth of a Nation* in 1968 at a toga party at a fraternity house at the University of Pennsylvania when he was eighteen. In each case the film captured a painful truth about American culture that left Villanueva and Bradley feeling raw, violated, shocked, and scared. From that pain, Villanueva and Bradley each forged a determination to write. Their anger fueled an eloquence and intensity that allowed them to write dazzling works of poetry and fiction that would garner some of the nation's top literary prizes.

TINO VILLANUEVA AND SCENE FROM THE MOVIE "GIANT"

At the 1957 Academy Awards ceremony held in the ornate Pantages The-atre—the first Art Deco movie palace in the country—*Giant*, a spectacular, blockbuster movie released the previous year garnered frequent applause. Its director, George Stevens, won the Best Director award, and the film received nominations for Best Picture, Best Actor (Rock Hudson as Bick Benedict and James Dean as Jett Rink), and Best Supporting Actress (Mer-cedes McCambridge as Luz Benedict). But few in that audience might have predicted the effect that the movie would have on a teenage boy who saw it that year in another Art Deco–style movie theater thousands of miles away.

From a back-row seat in the darkened Holiday Theater at 118 East San Antonio Street in the Courthouse Square Historic District of San Marcos, Texas (a theater built in 1941 that is a live-music venue today), fourteen-year-old Tino Villanueva watched the three-and-a-half-hour saga of the lives of three generations of Texans. Edna Ferber, author of the novel on which the film was based, had experienced vicious anti-Semitism in the Midwest as a child—a fact that may have made her particularly sensitive to white Texans' racism toward Mexican Americans, a theme that both the novel and the film explore with blunt candor. The climax of the film is a scene set in a roadside diner owned by Sarge, a huge, beefy, arrogant white Texan who has no inten-tion of serving food to any Hispanic patron. As Villanueva would summarize the scene in *Tinta* in 1989, "The Yellow Rose of Texas" plays on the jukebox, "confirming the personal, regional, and national identity of the proprietor, Sarge." Fourteen-year-old Villanueva watches Sarge abuse and try to eject the Mexican family, and "a sickening sensation and an unspeakable feeling of powerlessness" overtakes him. Silent in the face of the torment inflicted on a family that could easily have been his own, he is paralyzed by the assault on his identity. The unsettling scene dramatized the precariousness of his own position in painful, visceral ways. When Villanueva sees *Giant* again in 1973, he finds a voice in which to meet the challenge that Sarge's racism posed to his adolescent sense of self. Excavating the meaning of the scene in fresh ways al-lows him to articulate resistance to it. He realizes that the anger and fear that this scene sparked had ignited his desire to write. In ink drenched with quiet fury, he revisits that seminal early encounter with evil in a highly acclaimed book titled *Scene from the Movie "Giant,"* a book that draws much of its style, as well as its content, from the world of film.

The poem called "The Existence of Sarge," for example, narrates both what is happening on the screen and what is happening in Villanueva's mind. He introduces Sarge, who is "well past six-feet, oppressive / Everywhere, in a white shirt, sleeves rolled / Up that declare the beefiness of his arms. . . ." He announces, "with the weight of / A dozen churches behind him" to an elderly man who has entered the café with two women, "You're in the / Wrong place amigo. Come on, and let's get out of / Here. Vamoose. *Ándale.*" The old man, whose / Skin is second-stage bronze from too much sun" begins to feebly search in his pocket, and takes out the sum he needs to pay for his food. But then the "tight-wound voice of Sarge"

Echoes through the café walls, out onto the
Street, and back inside the Holiday Theater
Where I sit alone in the drop-shadows of the
Back—: "Your money is no good here. Come on,
Let's go. You too," he says to the women,
Their torment half inside me. And with that:
He plops the old man's hat on his head and
Picks him up by the lapels. *Put the film*
In reverse (I think). *Tear out those frames*
From time-motion and color; run the words
Backward in Sarge's breath and sever the
Tendons of his thick arms in bold relief.

Villanueva remembers wondering, "If I yell, 'Nooooo!, nooooo!,' / Would the projectionist stop the last / Reel of the machine? Would the audience / Rise up with me to rip down the screen?"

Bick Benedict, the patrician Texas rancher at the center of the film, has also just arrived at Sarge's with his family, including his Mexican American daughter-in-law, Juana, and his one-year-old grandson, Jordy (in Villanueva's words), "her child, half Anglo, who in Juana's womb / Became all Mexican just the same" in Sarge's eyes. Benedict orders ice cream for his grandson, where-upon "Sarge, moved by deep familiar / Wrath, talks down: 'Ice-cream—thought that kid'd / Want a tamale. . . .'" Benedict rebukes Sarge for his abusive treatment of the old man and his family, saying, he "would sure appreciate it if Sarge "'Were a / Little more polite to these people.'" Whereupon, Sarge, "Who has something to defend, balks; asks / (In a long shot) if: 'that there papoose down / There, his name Benedict too?'" Benedict says "'Yeah, . . . Come to think of it, it is.'" And so acknowledges,

In his heart, his grandson, half-Anglo, half—
Brown. Sarge repents from the words, but no
Part of his real self succumbs: "All right—
Forget I asked you. Now you just go back
Over there and sit down and we ain't gonna
Have no trouble. But this bunch here is
Gonna eat somewhere's else." . . .

Still from the climax of the 1956 film *Giant* (which was based on a novel by Edna Ferber), in which the character Bick Benedict is shown punching Sarge, the racist owner of a roadside diner. This scene inspired Tino Villanueva's book-length poem *Scene from the Movie "Giant."*

An excruciatingly tense and dramatic fistfight follows. Sarge wins.

Villanueva writes, "What the screen had released through darkness was too / Much for a single afternoon. . . ." He felt himself transformed: "[W]hat I took in that afternoon took root and a / quiet vehemence arose. It arose in language— / . . . Now I am because I write. . . ." As he told Gary Susman, "Per-

Tino Villanueva (1941–). The racism against Mexican Americans that fourteen-year-old Villanueva saw depicted on the big screen when he saw the movie *Giant* in San Marcos, Texas, in 1956 angered him and inspired him to become an award-winning poet.

PHOTO CREDIT: PHOTO BY KALMAN ZABARSKY; COURTESY OF BOSTON UNIVERSITY PHOTOGRAPHY.

haps deep down, the reason I wrote the book is that the adult didn't want to see the little 14-year-old boy sitting in the movie house helpless. . . . Words have this saving power. Memory lets you go back in time and rescue yourself from this impotent situation that you couldn't articulate." His response to seeing *Giant* was to embark on a career as a writer, penning memorable and powerful poetry in both Spanish and English. In not only *Scene from the Movie "Giant"* but also in six other books of poetry, including *Chronicle of My Worst Years* [*Crónica de mis años peores*] and *Hay otra voz* [*There Is Another Voice*], Villanueva, who was born into a family of migrant workers, probes the dynamics of racism and marginalization, and explores the toll that discrimination and prejudice take on individual psyches. *Scene from the Movie "Giant"* won an American Book Award in 1994.

DAVID BRADLEY
AND *THE BIRTH OF A NATION*

In 1948, in the Neoclassical 1921 Masonic Temple at 6840 Hollywood Boulevard a memorial service was held for the director D. W. Griffith, whose 1915 film *The Birth of a Nation* was so central to the development of Hollywood and the modern motion picture. Griffith's film would help give birth not only to the modern film industry, but also to a brilliant late-twentieth-century novel.

In his essay "*The Birth of a Nation*" in *The Movie That Changed My Life*, David Bradley describes his first encounter, at age eighteen, with Griffith's most famous film. The year was 1968, and the University of Pennsylvania had just "launched a recruitment drive intended to make the undergraduate student body look less like vanilla and more like chocolate chip. I was a chip." The dean of men had been pressuring all-white fraternities to make a good-faith effort to integrate. The fraternities quickly learned that putting up a show of effort mattered more than results, and there developed between Bradley and several houses "a kind of gentleman's agreement" whereby "as evidence of their good-faith effort I would eat, drink, and make merry through the fall—and disappear come spring," when future members were actually tapped. But when an invitation to a toga party came from the legendary "Animal House," even Bradley was shocked. Members of the hard-drinking fraternity were rumored to harbor strong sympathy for the Confederacy and allegedly engaged in an initiation rite that "was indistinguishable in form and content from that of the Ku Klux Klan." Bradley "didn't believe the rumors," so he went.

When he arrived, the president of the fraternity showed him where to hang his clothes, draped him with a sheet, put a plastic garland on his head, handed him a bourbon, and introduced him to an attractive dateless blonde with whom he "proceeded to culturally diversify the dickens out of the Animal House dance floor." Shortly thereafter, to his surprise, the young woman led him to "The Den," "a dark, comfortably furnished room" where "a whirring film projector cast inhibiting illumination on couples petting on the floor along with bright images of Woody Woodpecker on the wall." Some time later Bradley realized that Woody Woodpecker had been replaced by the "washed-out pinkish-white" projected image of "a black man, his eyes wide, white, rolling, surrounded by figures wearing white robes and weird headdresses. He was pleading—and I knew atavistically for what, and why."

As he watched sheeted figures in the film drag the man away, Bradley "went crabbing across the mattress, scuttling for the door."

Still from a scene set during Reconstruction in D. W. Griffith's 1915 film *The Birth of a Nation*, in which the Ku Klux Klan lynches a freedman named Gus, played by Walter Lang in blackface.
PHOTO CREDIT: D. W. GRIFFITH CORPORATION.

The next day, back in his dorm, the following scene took place:

... [T]he President of Animal House came by my room to return my clothes and find out what prompted my impromptu exit—the brothers had a bet. I boasted of inebriation, and then, trying to learn what atrocity had been on the Animal House agenda, I added that I was sorry I'd missed the end of the film—the latest in-thing in porno, I supposed. The president was shocked. "Porno? That was *The Birth of a Nation*. Hollywood classic. Come by some night, we'll show you the rest." He left me holding my pants.

I was furious, because I'd run home at 2:00 A.M. wearing nothing but Jockey shorts and a Cannon sheet, with visions of excruciation, emasculation, and excoriation dancing in my head, and because even now, and even knowing that those visions were inspired by nothing more than shadows made for mass consumption, I remained afraid. I'd not been terrified; I'd been terrorized. And, if the president was to be believed, by something I should have recognized. I'd been terrorized by my own ignorance, far beyond the Animal House's power to add or detract. The only thing I knew that would set me free was to know the truth. So I'd hied myself to the library. . . .

The first thing I learned about *The Birth of a Nation* was that the Klan won. I couldn't believe it. Once I'd realized it was a Hollywood film, I'd assumed I'd seen the scene that frightened me out of context—in the next reel the cavalry would come to the rescue. It hadn't happened like that in history: the 1870s edition of the Klan had in fact waged a successful guerilla campaign against Reconstruction before being investigated by Congress and officially disbanded. But accuracy never bothered Hollywood; the good guys always won. Which meant that in 1915 Hollywood, the Klan was the good guys.

The excursion into history that he began that afternoon took Bradley into some dark corners of the past that his textbooks had ignored—the history of the Klan, of Thomas Dixon's extolling of it in his 1905 novel, *The Clansman: A Historical Romance of the Ku Klux Klan*, and of D. W. Griffith's glorification of it in the film; the positive reactions to the film from government officials, including the president of the United States and the chief justice of the Supreme Court; the scattered protests and riots that met the film when it opened; the fact that it ended up grossing $18 million; the role it played in stimulating the rebirth of the Klan and the Klan's later adoption of techniques of terror that it learned from the movie; and the full scope of the horrific violence against blacks that the film helped ignite.

Fair-minded scholar that he was, Bradley decided to see the film in its entirety when it was shown at a college film festival shortly thereafter. The lecture by a film scholar that preceded the film focused on "Griffith's cinematic innovations: the fade-in and the fade-out, the close-up, the montage, crosscutting, flashcuts, pre-shot rehearsals, masking, the use of a film stock called Peach Blossom, which gave the black-and-white an antiquated-looking tint. Griffith had not necessarily invented these techniques, the lecturer said, but he had brought them all together to their fullest advantage in

The Birth of a Nation. Then the film began. "Absent the realization that the 'blacks' were whites in blackface," Bradley writes, "I could not have watched it.

> . . . Take a bunch of ignorant immigrants, show them a black-faced beast chasing a girl—not a woman, but a child—until she leaps to her death; then show them the man being shot in the back and the bastard being strung up and then dumped on the lawn of a mulatto named Lynch. . . . How could the audience not think that nigger-bashing, not baseball, was the national pastime? How could they not riot? . . . .
>
> The lights came up. The audience applauded. The lecturer invited questions. Someone inquired about Griffith's symbolism. The lecturer responded with a sophomoric discussion of kittens, cooing doves, and bedposts rampant with references to Freud. That was it. . . . And so I rose—trembling, for reasons I did not then understand—and asked the lecturer quite politely if he was an idiot, or merely blind? . . . [D]idn't he know—didn't any of them know—that it wasn't just empty symbolism? . . . [D]idn't they know that *The Birth of a Nation* had been the rebirth of the Klan, a "High Class Order for Men of Intelligence and Character" with a taste for terrorism? Didn't they know how many black folk died at the Klan's fraternal hands, how many black women were raped by fraternal phalluses, how many families had fled in fear of a fraternal visitation? Didn't they understand what had been inspired by this misbegotten movie? Didn't they care?
>
> The audience was silent, made uneasy by my outburst, unsure of what further form it might take. . . .

Bradley writes that he had felt safe that night, "entering a lecture hall to confront the very images that had inspired [his] prior terror," because he had "believed that this audience would not countenance racist drivel. But they *had* countenanced it. They'd *applauded* it. They'd pronounced it wonderful. They'd pronounced it art. And now I knew that I had not been safe, that I was not safe, that I would never be safe." The lecturer he tells us, was angry, "although he seemed calm as he decried my objections as the very ones that had been used by those who'd tried to suppress Griffith's magnificent film. . . . But, perhaps because I'd stayed standing, or because he saw some danger in my face, he added, 'What you say happened, happened. But you have to get beyond history and deal with the aesthetics.' I have hated men before and since but I have never hated any man more."

The film sparked in Bradley not only a passionate interest in the history that shaped it and that it in turn helped shape, but an intense awareness of the impossibility of getting "beyond history" whether you were a filmmaker, writer, viewer, or reader. He came to realize that "while it is wrong to make war on shadows, it is just as wrong to forget that sometimes shadows lead to acts." Those flickering shadows on the wall of Animal House set off a process by which a college freshman would transform himself into one of America's most original writers, probing history both to understand its dynamics and to challenge, as an imaginative artist, its inevitability. In his novel *The Chaneysville Incident*, white-sheeted Klansmen do their best to do what they are best known for doing, but they fail, bested by the quick-witted *chutz-pah* of their intended victims. The novel won the Pen/Faulkner Prize in 1982 as well as an Academy Award from the American Academy and Institute of Arts and Letters. Talking back to *The Birth of a Nation* turned out to be a lifelong project for Bradley, who is currently completing a nonfiction work titled *The Bondage Hypothesis: Meditations on Race and American History.*

David Bradley (1950–). When David Bradley saw D. W. Griffith's 1915 film *The Birth of a Nation* during his freshman year in college, he could not believe that "the Klan was the good guys." It helped set in motion the process by which he became one of America's most original writers, probing history both to understand its dynamics and to challenge its inevitability.
PHOTO CREDIT: PHOTO BY LYNDA KOOLISH.

L iterature in which slavery features prominently inspired two of the most widely seen, record-setting films of the twentieth century. The first was *The Birth of a Nation* in 1915, based on Thomas Dixon's novel *The Clansman*; it was the most complex and costly motion picture ever made when it came out. The second was *Gone with the Wind* in 1939, based on Margaret Mitchell's novel by that name; it was the first blockbuster talkie, the first major color film, and the most successful film ever made when it appeared. But despite the centrality of slavery to the history of America, and despite the existence of literally hundreds (some say thousands) of autobiographical narratives published by former slaves themselves that could have served as the basis for a film, for the entire twentieth century Hollywood failed to make a major motion picture based on a slave narrative. Even Frederick Douglass's gripping autobiographies failed to inspire a feature film.

The closest thing to a feature film made from a slave narrative was a low-budget made-for-TV movie directed by Gordon Parks that aired on PBS in 1984. *Solomon Northup's Odyssey* was based on Solomon Northup's *Twelve Years a Slave: Narrative of Solomon Northup, a Citizen of New-York, Kidnapped in Washington City in 1841, and rescued in 1853, from a Cotton Plantation near the Red River, in Louisiana* (1853). The film came and went with relatively little notice taken of it—although reviewers praised the "nobility and humanity" of Avery Brooks's portrayal of Northup and lauded the film's portrait of slavery as "extraordinarily affective and moving."

While Northup's *Twelve Years a Slave* had not sunk into complete oblivion, it was certainly not well known among the general public before British director Steve McQueen's film adaptation appeared in 2013. A deft screenplay by John Ridley, a compelling performance by actor Chiwetel Ejiofor playing the role of Northup, and a stellar supporting cast that included Lupita Nyong'o, Benedict Cumberbatch, Michael Fassbender, Paul Giamatti, Alfre Woodard, and Brad Pitt combined to make *12 Years a Slave* both a critical and commercial success. It earned kudos as the best film of the year in competitions from Stockholm to San Francisco, from London to Las Vegas, and in the Golden Globe awards. On March 2, 2014, in the Dolby Theater on Hollywood Boulevard, *12 Years a Slave* made Hollywood history when it won the most coveted prize in the industry, the Academy Award for Best Picture. McQueen was the first black director—and the first black producer—to win Hollywood's top award. Ridley also won the award for the Best Adapted Screenplay, and Nyong'o for Best Supporting Actress.

Seventy-four years earlier in Hollywood a film with a very different take on slavery had won the Best Picture award at the Twelfth Academy Awards: *Gone with the Wind*. It was impossible for black Americans not to resent all the praise heaped on a film that portrayed the slave South as sympathetically as it did at a moment when Jim Crow was still the law of the land. History was made at the 1940 ceremony, to be sure, when black actor Hattie McDaniel won the Best Supporting Actress award, the first African American to be honored by the motion picture industry. But despite the dignified eloquence of her heartfelt acceptance speech, many were embarrassed by the fact that the first award of this sort to a black actor honored her performance as the quintessential slave mammy, a role that could be seen as reinforcing demeaning stereotypes. In addition, according to W. Burlette Carter, a close examination of a photo of the guests at the awards ceremony reveals that "on the very night in 1940 that she would become the first Negro to win an Oscar, McDaniel and her escort would be segregated because of their race; they were not allowed to sit with the rest of the *Gone* cast and not welcomed among the rest of McDaniel's white Hollywood colleagues." Instead, they were given a table to themselves near the kitchen.

The scene could not have been more different in 2014 when the man who directed and produced the year's Best Picture rose to accept the highest award Hollywood had to offer. As the assembled crowd warmly applauded the director-producer, screenwriter, and cast of *12 Years a Slave*, there was a sense in which they were also cheering for themselves and for the motion picture industry, as if celebrating the achievement of this impressive film might somehow cleanse Hollywood of its past sins when it came to the politics of representing race on screen. Amidst all the congratulatory festivities on the "black firsts" of the evening, nobody thought to ask why Solomon Northup had to wait 160 years for someone to turn his dramatic story to into a feature film. And why, after all those years, it had taken a British director to accomplish the feat.

Whether providing authors with settings, subjects, and themes; employing destitute writers; creating shadow-versions of popular American fiction; challenging authors to talk back to Hollywood's version of America's past or breathing new life into forgotten literary works, Hollywood and the motion picture industry have had—and will probably always have—a major impact on American literature and the writers who create it.

RELATED SITE

❧ Broadway Historic Theater District
South Broadway, Los Angeles, California

With twelve historic theaters (built between 1910 and 1931) packed into six blocks of South Broadway between 3rd and 9th Streets, the Broadway Historic Theater District in the heart of downtown Los Angeles boasts the greatest concentration of opulent movie palaces on the planet. Before Sid Grauman opened his theaters in Hollywood, the Million Dollar Theater (307 South Broadway), originally known as "Grauman's Theater," was often the site of film premieres. This elaborate theater in the Spanish Rococo (Churrigueresque) style—Los Angeles's first grand movie palace—opened in 1918; it was designed by Albert C. Martin (interior by William Lee Woollett). Sculptures by Joseph Mora on the facade include heroic figures of the arts and symbols of the American West—longhorn cattle skulls, bison heads, and eagles. The Million Dollar got its name reputedly because of the value of the land and the buildings on it. In the 1940s, it hosted performances by famous jazz bands and big bands, and from the 1950s through the 1980s, it also presented headlining acts from Mexico City and elsewhere in Latin America. It was the scene of Luis Valdez's acclaimed Teatro Campesino stage adaptation of *La Virgen del Tepeyac*. This was one of the first theaters in the country to use a reinforced concrete girder in the construction of its balcony, eliminating the need for supporting the balcony with columns that obstructed the view of those seated below it. The city would not certify this design—which soon became the standard in theater design—until its strength was tested with one and a half million pounds of sandbags.

The Los Angeles Theatre (612 South Broadway), completed in 1931, the most lavish of all the Broadway movie palaces, was finished in a record ninety days, using prefabricated steel walls. The structure was designed by the property owner's son, S. Tilden Norton, with decorative details added by the well-known architect S. Charles Lee. Lee believed that "the show starts on the sidewalk," and made sure that every aspect of the building would lure the potential moviegoer inside. Attendees at the theater's first big premiere—Charlie Chaplin's *City Lights*, which debuted the year the theater was built—included physicist Albert Einstein, who, along with other opening night patrons, was booed by the onlookers standing on breadlines across the street. The theater's grand French Baroque six-story lobby featured mosaics, wall and ceiling murals, crystal chandeliers, a three-tiered fountain, a hall of mirrors, a grand stairway, and gilded plaster ornaments that echo designs associated with Louis XIV, France's "Sun King." The Los Angeles Theatre also featured, in addition to a supervised children's playroom, a soundproof "crying room" for mothers to repair to when their babies cried. The building also had restaurants and ballrooms for events held after the show.

The district has benefited from a series of ongoing restoration efforts. But although one can still view the imposing facades of these once-sumptuous theaters from the street, most of the buildings have been repurposed for other uses—such as churches, flea markets, and stores selling wedding gowns, casual wear, jewelry, DJ equipment, and cell phones. The Orpheum and the Palace still function as theaters, mainly presenting live events.

FOR FURTHER READING

The Writers: Works and Words

Bradley, David. "*The Birth of a Nation.*" In *The Movie That Changed My Life*, edited by David Rosenberg. New York: Viking, 1991.

———. *The Chaneysville Incident*. 1981. New York: Harper Perennial, 1990.

Chandler, Raymond. *Later Novels and Other Writing*. Edited by Frank MacShane. New York: Library of America, 1995.

———. *Stories and Early Novels*. Edited by Frank MacShane. New York: Library of America, 1995.

———. "Writers in Hollywood." *Atlantic Monthly*, November 1945. http://www.theatlantic.com/magazine/archive/1945/11/writers-in-hollywood/306454.

Chin, Frank. *Gunga Din Highway: A Novel*. Minneapolis: Coffee House Press, 1994.

Connelly, Michael. "The Source: As *The Lincoln Lawyer* Opens, the Author Shares the Joy and Trepidation of Watching His Words Go from Book to Big Screen." *Los Angeles Times Magazine*, March 2011. http://www.latimesmagazine.com/2011/03/the-source-michael-connelly.html.

Dixon, Thomas. *The Clansman: An Historical Romance of the Ku Klux Klan*. New York: Doubleday, Page and Co., 1905.

Fitzgerald, F. Scott. *The Love of the Last Tycoon: A Western*. Edited by Matthew J. Bruccoli. Cambridge: Cambridge University Press, 1993.

———. *The Pat Hobby Stories*. Introduction by Arnold Gingrich. New York: Charles Scribner's Sons, 1962.

Jong, Erica. *How to Save Your Own Life*. New York: Holt, Rinehart and Winston, 1977.

Macdonald, Ross. *Archer in Hollywood*. New York: Alfred A. Knopf, 1967.

Mitchell, Margaret. *Gone with the Wind*. New York: Macmillan, 1936.

Northup, Solomon. *Twelve Years a Slave: Narrative of Solomon Northup, a Citizen of New-York, Kidnapped in Washington City in 1841, and Rescued in 1853, from a Cotton Plantation near the Red River, in Louisiana*. 1859. Chapel Hill: University of North Carolina Press, 2011.

Villanueva, Tino. *Chronicle of My Worst Years* [*Crónica de mis años peores*]. Chicago: Triquarterly, 1994.

———. "Fight Scene from Movie *Giant*." *Tinta: Revista de Letra Hispánicas y Luso-Brasileño* 2, no. 1 (Autumn 1989): 45–46.

———. *Hay otra voz* [*There Is Another Voice*]. New York: Editorial Mensaje, 1979.

———. *Scene from the Movie "Giant."* Willimantic, CT: Curbstone Press, 1993.

———. *So Spoke Penelope*. Cambridge, MA: Grolier Poetry Press, 2013.

West, Nathanael. *Novels and Other Writing*. Edited by Sacvan Bercovitch. New York: Library of America, 1997.

Background and Contexts

Basten, Fred E. *Max Factor's Hollywood*. Los Angeles: General Publishing Group, 1995.

Boller, Paul F., and Ronald L. Davis. *Hollywood Anecdotes*. New York: William Morrow, 1987.

Carter, W. Burlette. "Finding the Oscar." *Howard Law Journal* 55, no. 1 (2011). http://ssrn.com/abstract=1980721.

Dardis, Tom. *Some Time in the Sun: The Hollywood Years of Fitzgerald, Faulkner, Nathanael West, Aldous Huxley, and James Agee.* New York: Scribner's, 1976.

Hall, Ben M. *The Best Remaining Seats: The Story of the Golden Age of the Movie Palaces.* New York: Clarkson Potter, 1961.

Hamilton, Ian. *Writers in Hollywood, 1915–1951.* New York: Harper and Row, 1990.

Heimann, Jim. *Out with the Stars: Hollywood Nightlife in the Golden Era.* New York: Abbeville Press, 1985.

Martin, Jay. *Nathanael West: The Art of His Life.* New York: Farrar, Straus and Giroux, 1970.

———. ed. *Nathanael West: A Collection of Critical Essays.* Englewood Cliffs, NJ: Prentice-Hall, 1971.

Schatz, Thomas. *The Genius of the System: Hollywood Filmmaking in the Studio Era.* New York: Pantheon, 1988.

Schickel, Richard. *D. W. Griffith: An American Life.* New York: Simon and Schuster, 1984.

Siegel, Ben, ed. *Critical Essays on Nathanael West.* New York: G. K. Hall, 1994.

Slide, Anthony. *The Hollywood Novel: A Critical Guide to over 1200 Works.* Jefferson, NC: McFarland, 1995.

Stock, Ann. "Talking Back, Looking Ahead: The Revisionist Cine-Poetry of Tino Villanueva." *Bilingual Review/La Revista Bilingüe* 23, no. 3 (September-December 1998): 237–247.

Stokes, Melvyn. *D. W. Griffith's "The Birth of a Nation": A History of the Most Controversial Motion Picture of All Time.* New York: Oxford University Press, 2008.

Susman, Gary. "Screen Saga: The Film *Giant* Spawned a Big Slim Volume of Poems." Supplement to the *Boston Phoenix*, no. 75 (July 1994).

Torrence, Bruce T. *Hollywood, the First Hundred Years.* New York: New York Zoetrope, 1982.

Wells, Walter. *Tycoons and Locusts: A Regional Look at Hollywood Fiction of the 1930s.* Preface by Harry T. Moore. Carbondale: Southern Illinois University Press, 1973.

ACKNOWLEDGMENTS

This book is the distillation of many years of reading, writing, and exploring in the company of an extraordinary cast of colleagues, mentors, students, curators, archivists, activists, family members, friends, and others who have contributed more than they will ever know. The book's shortcomings, however, are my responsibility alone. My mother, the late Renée B. Fisher, and my grandmother, the late Yetta Breger, took me on childhood excursions to the Lower East Side to see where our family began its life in America and also exposed me to fiction and poetry set in that world, planting seeds that would sprout into *Writing America*. My father, the late Milton Fisher, shaped this book from the start with his sharp editorial eye, his impatience with cant, and his endearing and unshakeable faith in its author. I have fond memories of seeking out, with the late Lillian Robinson and the late W. Keats Sparrow the North Carolina house where Mary Ann Cord was reunited with the son from whom she had been separated on the auction block; of exploring Frederick Douglass's home in Anacostia with the late Ralph Wiley and our two families; of visiting the Tenement Museum with Betti-Sue Hertz; of exploring Harlem with Carla Peterson; of tracking down sites along the Texas-Mexico border with Jeanne Campbell Reesman; of hiking around Walden Pond in the rain with Kevin and Pegge Bochynski; of driving to Hannibal with Bob Lamb for the opening of the town's newest museum; of going to Paris, Illinois, with Michael Shelden to hunt for confirmation of the existence of William Evans; of sharing New Bedford, Ellis Island, Bryce Canyon, Yosemite, and other sites with my family.

This book stands on the shoulders of the many outstanding scholars whose books and articles are cited in the "Background and Contexts" sections at the end of each chapter. It would not have been possible without their important publications. In addition, personal contact with several authors in this book about locales that shaped their work and writers who influenced them deepened my awareness of contexts informing the literature they produced. I was privileged to create a course with the late Gloria Anzaldúa at the Universidad Nacional Autónoma de México and to have conversations with her over the years about mestiza consciousness, the culture of the border, and the locations in which she worked in the fields as a child. I had the pleasure of asking the late Tillie Olsen—and also Erica Jong—why they cared so much about Whitman; of corresponding with the late Arthur Miller about what Mark Twain meant to him in high school; and of exploring with Ursula Le Guin, Bobbie Ann Mason, and Russell Banks how Twain had influenced them as writers. Coediting two books with David Bradley gave me the opportunity to have extended conversations with him about Twain, Dunbar, Melville, Hollywood, race, racism, and a host of other topics. I interviewed Maxine Hong Kingston and the late Ralph Ellison, collaborated on two screenplays with the late Ralph Wiley, appeared on a panel in Hartford with Dick Gregory, and had conversations with Kenzaburō Ōe in Austin, and with Yusef Komunyakaa in Prague.

On several occasions, conversations with individuals who were present at historic events or played important roles in the revitalization of a historic site enriched my research. I value my interview with the late Charlotte Hedin, a retired English teacher at Sauk Centre Senior High who had witnessed the burial of Sinclair Lewis's ashes in Sauk Centre and described it to me. Conversations with Connie Young Yu about her efforts to preserve and restore the Angel Island Immigration Station were illuminating. I am greatly indebted to Faye Dant, founder of Jim's Journey: The Huck Finn Freedom Center in Hannibal, for conversations and correspondence about her efforts to recover the history of Hannibal's black community, and for welcoming me into her extended family—a family descended from Henry Dant, a slave born near Sam Clemens's birthplace the same year Clemens was born. I appreciate what I learned from conversations in Hannibal with Joel Dant, Donald Scott, Joe Miller, Larry McCarty, and Brenda Thompson.

I benefited from responses to my work when I presented portions of this book over the years in endowed lectures at the University of Texas–San Antonio, Indiana State University, Washington University, Purdue, Nicholls State, and East Carolina University; in invited talks at Yale, Stanford, University of Cambridge, University of California–Berkeley, University of Regensburg, Ritsumeikan University, University of Hyderabad, University of Southern Denmark, St. Petersburg University, Université du Québec à Montreal, the South Street Seaport Museum, and the Morgan Library; and at presentations at conferences of the American Studies Association, the Modern Language Association, and the American Literature Association.

I am indebted to Stanford University Librarian Michael Keller for having developed a collection of resources and people that has allowed my research to flourish. I am grateful to archivists and librarians at Stanford University, the Huntington Library, the University of Texas at Austin, Yale University, the Schomburg Center for Research on Black Culture, the Gannett-Tripp Library at Elmira College, and the Joyner Library at East Carolina University. I owe a special thanks to the editors of the Mark Twain Project at the Bancroft Library, UC-Berkeley—General Editor Robert H. Hirst, Victor Fischer, Benjamin Griffin, Lin Salamo, and Michael Frank (and staff member Neda Salem)—for producing vital publications and for sharing their vast knowledge of Twain as generously as they do. I am grateful for institutional support from Stanford that has helped me research and write this book. The research fund that President John Hennessy provides to humanities faculty at Stanford has been invaluable. Also helpful was a year as a fellow of the Clayman Institute for Research on Gender. I am grateful for the assistance I received from staff members Monica Moore and Rachel Meisels in American studies and Alyce Boster, Dagmar Logie, Laura Ma, Nelia Peralta, and Nicole Bridges in English.

My insight into global dimensions of American literature, history, and culture has been enriched by ongoing, lively conversations with my fellow editors of the *Journal of Transnational American Studies*—Tom Bender, Caroline Kyungah Hong, Alfred Hornung, Shirley Geok-lin Lim, Eric Martinsen, Nina Morgan, Greg Robinson, Chris Suh, and Takayuki Tatsumi. Former students have played an important role in shaping many aspects of this book. I am particularly grateful to Beth Piatote and Katie Jones for all they taught me about Native American literature (and I thank Katie for connecting me with her young pupils at the Rosebud Indian Reservation). I appreciate the opportunity that Brian Goodman gave me to share several chapters of this book with a graduate workshop in American studies at Harvard. Conversations with Nigel Hatton about human rights and literature helped me focus on some of the ways in which literature can engage key pressing moral concerns. Chiyuma Elliott was an extraordinary research assistant at the University of Texas at Austin, whose tireless digging turned up extremely useful material about the 135th Street Library and Wounded Knee.

I could not have reached the finish line without the Herculean efforts of three extremely bright Stanford graduate students who helped track down photos and collect permissions: first and foremost, Corey Johnson, an impressive photographer himself, whose painstaking efforts and initiative over several years led to many of the photos in this book; also Adrienne Johnson and Max Suechting, whose attention to detail and organizational skills were crucial. I am grateful to Selina Lai-Henderson and Ella Elbaz for their help in checking that quoted texts in Chinese and Yiddish, respectively, appeared in proper form on the page; to Alberta Hemsley for venturing out during one of Ohio's coldest winters to photograph the Parker house; to Lynda Koolish for the use of her luminous photo of David Bradley; and to Terrell Dempsey not only for stimulating e-mail conversations over the years and his groundbreaking book, but also for his recent photo of Jim's Journey.

It is impossible to adequately thank all the individuals whose generosity, intelligence, hospitality, and kindness have been essential to the process by which this book came into being over many years. Colleagues, friends, and family members who have offered important insights; suggested key references, leads, and contexts; sent me relevant books; helped solve technological problems; opened their homes to me during research trips; or provided stimulation, inspiration, assistance, and general encouragement include Elizabeth Alexander, Donald and Jody Atha, Russ and Margie Baris, Polina and Andrei Belitski, John Bird, Michael Blakemore, Kevin Bochynski, Bob Boyett, Joanne Braxton, the late Louis Budd, Gregg Camfield, Jocelyn Chadwick, Gordon Chang, Steve Courtney, the late Robert Morse Crunden, the late Charles T. Davis, Mark Dawidziak, Joel Dinerstein, Michele Elam, Pinchia Feng, William Ferris, Carol Plaine Fisher, David and Jill Fishkin, Barre Fong, Gwen Frankfeldt, Estelle Freedman, Michael Frisch, Henry Louis Gates Jr., John Grassie, Teri Hessel, Allyson Hobbs, Steve Hoelscher, Hal Holbrook, Anthony Hom, Bill Howarth, Hsinya Huang, Evelyn Hu-DeHart, Tsuyoshi Ishihara, Hillary Jenks, Adam Johnson, Calvin and Maria Johnson, Gavin Jones, Meta Jones, Annette Kolodny, Lynda Koolish, Nacny Kuziemski, Selina Lai-Henderson, Irene Langdon, Paul Lauter, Min Jin Lee, Steve Lee, the late J. R. LeMaster, Jim Leonard, Sandy and Cynthia Levinson, Amanda Licato, Jim Loewen, Cindy Lovell, Sharon Luk, Lynne Lumsden, Kevin MacDonnell, Elaine Tyler May, Sarah Meer, Christina Mesa, Pete Messent, Ana Minian, Linda Morris, Toni Morrison, Paula Moya, Masako Notoji, Hilton Obenzinger, Dennis O'Neil, Margaret Osborne, Kathy Parker, Patricia Parker, Bill Paul, Peggy Phelan, Eliza Pickering, Moss Plaine, Ron Powers, Arnold Rampersad, Vaughn Rasberry, Kent Rasmussen, Judy Richardson, John-Michael Rivera, Michael Robertson, Forrest Robinson, Max Rudin, La Vonne Brown Ruoff, Gabriella Safran, Ramón Saldívar, Richard Saller, Cintia Santana, Ray Sapirstein, Debra Satz, Jessica and John Schairer, Barbara Schmidt, Laverne Sci, Dongfang Shao, Gretchen Sharlow, Michael Shelden, David E. E. Sloane, Barbara Snedecor, Stephen Sohn, Werner Sollors, Eric Sundquist, Lynne and Howard Tag, Edward Test, Mina Tobin, Siva Vaidhyanathan, Greg and Marion Werkheiser, Mark Woodhouse, Richard Yarborough, Xiao-huang Yin, Rafia Zafar, Martin Zehr, and the late Jim Zwick.

It has been a true joy to work with Leslie Mitchner, editor in chief of Rutgers University Press, who is a superb editor and a kindred spirit whose insight, guidance, and wisdom have been invaluable. It has also been a pleasure to work with all of the other smart and sensible individuals Rutgers assigned to work on this book: Lisa Boyajian, Marilyn Campbell, Beth Gianfagna, Jeremy Grainger, Brice

Hammack, Anne Hegeman, and Sharon Sweeney. I indebted to Sam Stoloff, my agent at Frances Goldin Literary Agency, for all of his efforts in my behalf. I owe my greatest debt to Jim Fishkin, Joey Fishkin, Bobby Fishkin, Cary Franklin, and Maya Belitski, who took time out from writing their own books, plays, articles, syllabi, grant proposals, and dissertations to share the adventure and cheer me on—and to the newest member of our family, Anna, whose birth inspired me to try to write a book she will want to read when she grows up.

COPYRIGHTS AND PERMISSIONS

369

INDEX OF WRITERS

Page numbers in italics refer to illustrations.

INDEX OF HISTORIC SITES

Page numbers in italics refer to illustrations.

ABOUT THE AUTHOR

Shelley Fisher Fishkin is the Joseph S. Atha Professor of Humanities, a professor of English, and the director of the American Studies Program at Stanford University, where she has taught since 2003. She is the award-winning author, editor, or coeditor of more than forty books and more than one hundred articles, essays, columns, and reviews on literature and cultural history. She holds a Ph.D. in American Studies from Yale and is a past president of the American Studies Association.